World is Afri

World is Africa

Writings on Diaspora Art

Eddie Chambers

BLOOMSBURY VISUAL ARTS
LONDON • NEW YORK • OXFORD • NEW DELHI • SYDNEY

BLOOMSBURY VISUAL ARTS
Bloomsbury Publishing Plc
50 Bedford Square, London, WC1B 3DP, UK
1385 Broadway, New York, NY 10018, USA

BLOOMSBURY, BLOOMSBURY VISUAL ARTS and the Diana logo are trademarks of Bloomsbury Publishing Plc

First published in Great Britain 2021

Cover design: Charlotte Daniels
Cover image: Hurvin Anderson, *Hope Gardens*, 2005, detail, Oil on canvas, 130 x 173 cm, © Hurvin Anderson. All Rights Reserved, DACS/Artimage 2020.

A catalogue record for this book is available from the British Library.

A catalog record for this book is available from the Library of Congress.

ISBN: HB: 978-1-3501-4032-5
PB: 978-1-3501-7013-1
ePDF: 978-1-3501-4033-2
eBook: 978-1-3501-4034-9

Typeset by RefineCatch Limited, Bungay, Suffolk
Printed and bound in India

To find out more about our authors and books visit www.bloomsbury.com and sign up for our newsletters.

Black people can cope

Ini Kamoze, *How U Livin*

Contents

Illustrations

Chapter 5

Chapter 6

Chapter 7

Chapter 9

Chapter 10

Chapter 11

Chapter 12

Chapter 13

Chapter 16

Chapter 18

Chapter 19

Chapter 20

Chapter 21

Chapter 22

Chapter 23

Chapter 25

Chapter 27

Chapter 28

Chapter 29

Chapter 30

Chapter 42

Chapter 43

Foreword

Eddie Chambers' preface to *Roots & Culture: Cultural Politics in the Making of Black Britain* (2016) begins with a defiant dedication: 'Black: For Those Who Have Been for Generations in "The Lower Case"'.

Eddie's terms of engagement with the arts are unashamedly, thrillingly polemical, preferring bias to balance – unless, that is, it is in the cause of re-balancing dominant narratives to take account of the contributions of non-white individuals and communities to the art, culture and politics of this country which have largely been ignored or marginalised. In that regard Eddie has achieved so much through his work, his writing and teaching and through his advocacy.

Re-reading that preface reminded me of my first conversation with Eddie, in my capacity as editor of *Art Monthly* magazine. In the days before email and even before we had invested in a fax machine, all edits were discussed with the writer over the telephone – a time consuming, but in my conversations with Eddie in particular, an ultimately rewarding process. We had reached a sticking point over his use of an uppercase 'B' in all references to black artists and art. It will immediately be noticed that I have used lower case, a reflection of the amicable compromise that we reached following a long and intense discussion at the end of which we agreed that Eddie would continue to submit his copy using uppercase, but in the published version we would revert to the use of lower case.

Our discussion covered a huge amount of ground from the issue of positive discrimination, or affirmative action as it was then called in the US, concerns about the use of the descriptive 'black'/'Black' specifically to designate individuals and communities of Afro-Caribbean background, to the problematics of such collective descriptors in general, and with reference to black artists in particular. Eddie was gracious throughout, and, while he remained firm in his conviction, he was respectful of *Art Monthly*'s editorial position. In principle I was against such direct forms of intervention, whether with respect to, for example, artists from black and ethnic minority backgrounds, women artists or, in the usage of the period, gay and lesbian artists (this was before the repeal of the notorious section 28 of the Local Government Act 1988 which targeted LGBTQ+ people). I believed rightly or wrongly that, as a contextual and issues-based magazine, it would mean that we were failing structurally in our purpose such that no amount of affirmative action could redress the situation. This did not mean that there was any room for complacency. On the contrary, these issues were – and are – kept constantly under review, including the issue of the loaded deployment of upper- and lowercase. Eddie is right to police such usages and abuses; one instance is the habitual and unthinking use of uppercase for privileged adjectives like 'western', for which we at *Art Monthly* now deploy lower case – a small but important shift, if only at the level of language. Conversations such as the one Eddie and I had that day, and continue to have today, have helped to bring about change.

I found myself thinking of that conversation again in the light of broadcaster Jon Snow's 'unscripted' remark, at the end of his report on a rally in front of Parliament by Brexiters on 30 March 2019, that he'd never seen so many 'white people' in one place, a not unreasonable observation given that 40 per cent of London's population is of black and ethnic minority heritage. *Channel 4 News* reportedly received over 2,500 complaints. It seems that we white people are used to racializing the other, but are not ourselves used to being racialised. This is partly what Eddie means when he inveighs against 'white art history' from which all 'other' histories are hierarchically descended. Snow's implication was clear, particularly given that earlier that day the leader of a far-right extremist organisation intent on 'weaponizing whiteness' had addressed the rally. Cravenly, *Channel 4 News* issued a hasty public apology.

The recent fall-out from the Windrush scandal, a direct result of the 'hostile environment' for migrants created during Theresa May's tenure as Home Secretary which saw people deported, families divided and the lives – and livelihoods – of thousands of legal UK residents ruined, reminds us of how little things have really changed in the UK. In *Roots & Culture* Eddie writes poignantly of that generation of Caribbean migrants, many of them veterans of the Second World War, who were coming to a country whose society they thought they knew but which didn't want to know them. But, as he points out, Britain's decision to 'close the door' (p. 35) on further Afro-Caribbean immigration after 1962 'marked a decisive point in the beginning of a formulation of a distinct Black-British culture', which found its foremost political and cultural theorist in the Jamaican-born Stuart Hall. Inadvertently the Conservative government of the day helped to trigger that change.

Anyone concerned with colonial and post-colonial art and culture will be indebted to Frantz Fanon's seminal work first published in 1952, *Black Skin, White Masks*, which anatomized the ways that colonized people initially seek to adapt to white culture by masking, in Fanon's famous phrase, 'the fact of their blackness' behind a white mask. Eddie charts this same process in the UK, and its rejection by the descendants of the first wave of migrants to the UK. This generation fully understood that their identity as black 'was both an imposed and a self-created one' (p. 75). In the introduction to his 2014 book, *Black Artists in British Art: A History Since the 1950s*, Eddie discusses the problematics of his use of the conjunction of 'Black' and 'British' in scrupulous detail (he revisited the subject, from the perspective of the 1970s, for the special '1978 Missing Issue' online edition of *Art Monthly* on the occasion of our 40th anniversary in 2016). The introduction is a fascinating essay in itself, not least because many white readers can identify with his reasons for preferring '"Britain", as a national and a geographic entity (and as an attendant signifier of identity)', than 'England', 'the latter having arguably greater and more pronounced connotations of insularity and racism than the former' (p. 3).

Eddie singles out the 1970s as a crucial decade during which a new generation began to forge a distinct Black British identity, and in *Black Artists in British Art*, Eddie devotes a chapter to its significance and to the role played by black artists in articulating it. However, as he notes at the end of *Roots & Culture*, by the late 1980s and early 1990s (p. 228), as second and third generation Black Britons looked beyond their Afro-Caribbean roots, Black-British cultural identity ceased to be 'a self-referencing entity', and by the 21st century the situation had changed to the extent that the dominant white culture has 'absorbed aspects of Black culture, even as it continues to demonise those it deems immigrants, refugees or asylum seekers' (p. 229).

In *Black Artists in British Art* Eddie tackles the greater complexity of the issues surrounding black identity (and indeed identity as a construct) today, and the challenges to the dominant 'masculinist' (p. 138), white, hetero-normative discourse from both within and without black culture, that arises from feminist, class, sexual and gender politics in the work of more recent artists who have also found expression in a wider range of media. In his final chapter Eddie reflects on the 2012 Tate Britain exhibition, '*Migrations: Journeys into British Art*', which finally posed the question: 'What is British Art?' Covering some five centuries, it acknowledged how much Britain, and British art has, in Eddie's words, 'been shaped by successive waves of migration, from Europe, from the Caribbean, from Asia, and other parts of the world.' At the same time he notes that, just as artists from 'across the globe' have been attracted to the UK 'as an international destination of choice', so have artists from the UK successfully sought 'to establish themselves in other parts of the world' (p. 200), a somewhat positive note on which to end his account, but this was before the divisive 'Brexit' Referendum of 2016, which no one could have foreseen and which has enabled a rise in nationalism which, as always, poses the greatest threat to minorities.

At the beginning of *Black Artists in British Art*, Eddie points out that, while 'Certain histories are being excavated and reconsidered . . . the overwhelming body of material and knowledge on Black-British artists remains vulnerable to the same sorts of adverse pressures and conditions that have existed in this country for centuries, when it comes to the contribution of certain artists and people' (p. 2). Among those 'histories' being revisited, he cites the Blk Art Group of the early 1980s, of which Eddie himself was a co-founder, along with Keith Piper, Donald Rodney and Marlene Smith. These artists came together not only to share and to represent their own experiences, but they also organised several exhibitions of their work as well as The First National Black Art Convention in 1982. At various times, this group of artists included Dominic Dawes and Claudette Johnson, who joined while a student at the Polytechnic, Wolverhampton (and who was the subject of a – belated but welcome – solo exhibition at Modern Art Oxford, during the summer of 2019), Wenda Leslie, Ian Palmer, and Janet Vernon. Indeed, in 1983, while an MA student at the Royal College of Art, Lubaina Himid wrote to *Art Monthly* (AM 66) to express her excitement at seeing the exhibition *Pan-African Connection* at the Herbert Art Gallery and Museum in Coventry, featuring a number of artists including Johnson, Piper, Rodney and Eddie: 'I have never seen a more exciting body of work from young contemporaries' she wrote, 'They all are, or were until recently art students in the Midlands. They are all black'. The work, she added was 'very diverse', 'huge' and, but for some 'quiet' sculpture, 'angry, noisy and powerful'. She ended, significantly: 'The balance of this show was what made it work, and is the way that black art, or if you like Black Art, can work'. Her testimony bears witness to the importance of such initiatives as the Blk Art Group in empowering black artists in the UK, or as Eddie might say, 'putting in the upper case, those who have been for generations in the lower case'.

This new collection of essays and articles, *World is Africa*, which I am proud to say includes some texts written for *Art Monthly*, as well as several new texts, begins to some extent where he left off in his previous two books. However, the net is cast more widely embracing the 'outernational', a wonderfully expansive term associated with Jamaican musical usage, though its derivation is by no means certain, as well as, or in contradistinction to the narrower and somewhat debased concept of the 'international'. The title itself deliberately reverses the telescope, so to speak, so that it is Europe and the West that is reduced, receding into the far distance while Africa and its diaspora come into greater magnification. At the same time, in one of the longest articles, Eddie holds up a mirror to white society by analysing the critical responses to exhibitions of black artists in the UK which, as he puts it, offers a 'veritable treasure trove of reading race through art criticism'.

The articles selected for this collection, including the new ones, reveal Eddie to be as polemical as ever – indeed one of the texts included is titled 'Africa 05: Polemic', a critique of the festival of the same name – another article, 'Dead Artists Society', is a swingeing attack on the posthumous exhibition of black artists who were not deemed worthy of being shown in our museums and galleries in their lifetimes. Arguably one of the most polemical – and timely – article is the one dealing with the consequences of the introduction, *c.* 2001, of the term ‘postblack’ (‘The Harmful Consequences of Postblack’), and its conjoined relative ‘postrace’, defined as ‘the theory that the United States has transcended racial inequality’, which would be laughable were it not so serious. Neither term gained traction in the UK, nor, it is to be hoped will they ever do so, but Eddie’s text serves as a warning.

What this collection reveals above all is Eddie’s continued and unwavering commitment to his cause, because a cause it is: to redress the imbalance in white accounts of post-war art in the UK. This includes the teaching of ‘white art history’. While there are, I would argue, a few exceptions (Sussex University teaches art history within schools, one of which was the School of African and Asian Studies, affectionately referred to by its acronym AFRAS when I was a undergraduate there), and one could cite the work of the late Jean Fisher at Goldsmiths and of writer and art historian Virginia Whiles, Eddie is right in asserting that it is white art history, ‘with its consistent omissions and partial accounts’ that, by and large, is being ‘served up’ in university art history departments. Eddie’s powerful advocacy – his anger at times – as well as his critical engagement with his subject comes through all his writings. As an editor, I have always respected his anger because it is both legitimate and targeted. He is fearless and focused, unafraid of taking on the biggest institutions and power brokers and, even when our views have differed on occasion, I have always admired and been inspired by his conviction and the cogency of his arguments, whether expressed in upper or lower case.

Patricia Bickers

Acknowledgements

In undertaking *World is Africa*, I have incurred a number of debts of gratitude. I would, in the first instance, like to thank Lisa Goodrum, formerly of I.B. Tauris. I began the *World is Africa* project with her, several years ago, and she has consistently offered invaluable and greatly appreciated guidance for this book, whenever I have reached out to her. I owe her unbounded thanks, not only for responding with warmth and enthusiasm to my original proposal, but also for the enormous support she has given me, since we first worked together, several years ago. I would similarly like to thank Anna Coatman, again, formerly of I.B. Tauris, and latterly, of Bloomsbury, for keeping *World is Africa* on Bloomsbury's radar, particularly during a period of transition. This book would certainly not have been possible without the steadfast professionalism of Camilla Erskine. She has taken enormous care and attention in the ways in which she has guided this project. She took a pronounced interest in bringing *World is Africa* to fruition and I cannot thank her enough for her tenacity, her attention to detail and the warmth of her communications. A special note of thanks to Veidehi Hans, Editorial Assistant at Bloomsbury, for offering gratefully received guidance and assistance in the latter stages of preparing this book for publication and also to Sandra Creaser, for her diligent and thorough copy-editing of *World is Africa*.

I would like to thank everyone who has given me permission to reproduce the texts in *World is Africa*. The prompt, unrestricted and generous granting of permissions has made the project considerably easier and smoother, and I have been sustained by the warmth and enthusiasm with which permissions have been granted. I owe each of you, heartfelt thanks. Namely: Dr. Persephone Braham; Tom Eccles; Dr. Richard Hylton; Chuu Krydz Ikwuemesi; Jessica Litherland; Beverly Mason FRSA; Dr. Kimberly Robinson-Walcott and her colleagues at the *Jamaica Journal*/Institute of Jamaica; Dr. Vanessa Thaxton-Ward; and Jonathan Watkins.

I would similarly like to thank everyone who has facilitated my access to the images that appear in *World is Africa*. Over the several years during which *World is Africa* was in various stages of preparation, a number of people assisted me with image permissions and licenses. Likewise, a number of artists greatly helped by granting me permissions to reproduce images of their work. I'm grateful to all of you, namely the following: Hurvin Anderson; Alice Chubb, Hurvin Anderson Studio Manager; Alison Bevan Director, RWA; Rose Jones and Pat Saro, Frank Bowling Archive; Vanley Burke; Brenda L. Croft; Mary Evans; Ben Jones; Jonathan Jones; Tam Joseph; Indra Khanna; Errol Lloyd; David Lawson, Smoking Dogs Films, London; Tina McIntyre, Photo Sales Manager, the Herald and Times Group, Glasgow; Dr. Gene Sherman AM; Timothy Nicol-Ford, Fashion Programme Manager, Executive Assistant to Dr. Gene Sherman AM (Sherman Centre for Culture and Ideas); Daisy Tyszkiewicz, Production Manager and Events Booking Coordinator, Sherman Centre for Culture and Ideas; Simon Norfolk; Katty Pearce, Guildhall Art Gallery, City of London; Keith Piper; Erin Rice; Chloe Robinson, Coordinator, Synch Licensing, Concord, Independent Music group; Laura-Jade Vaughan, Nottingham Contemporary; Barbara Walker; Pat Ward Williams; Helen Wilson-Roe; and Pete Woronkowicz of DACS, the Design and Artists Copyright Society. The granting of permissions to reproduce texts, and the granting of access to images are reflective not only of much appreciated professionalism, but in many instances, is also reflective of strong working relationships with artists and others, built up over the course of several decades. My life is the better, for the strength and depth of these relationships and friendships.

A special note of thanks, gratitude and appreciation must go to Patricia Bickers, editor of *Art Monthly*, who has been particularly generous in not only granting permissions but also writing a foreword for this book. Our working relationship goes back many years and *Art Monthly* more than any other factor, has shaped my critical writing and assisted in making me the scholar I am. Patricia always responded positively to my suggestions for texts and it has always been an unrestrained pleasure to work, over a great number of years, with her and her *Art Monthly* team. I am enormously gratified by the ways in which my relationship with *Art Monthly* has evolved and been sustained over several decades, and I am particularly proud to now be, (together with Liam Gillick, Hans Haacke, Mona Hatoum, Alfredo Jaar, and Martha Rosler), an *Art Monthly* Foundation Honorary Patron.

Thanks, and appreciation to Professor Jeffrey C Smith of the Department of Art and Art History at the University of Texas at Austin, for facilitating my access to funds from the Houston Endowment to undertake research relating to this publication. The support was gratefully received.

A final note of profound thanks and appreciation to Merv Honeywood and his team at RefineCatch Limited, for extraordinary diligence and attention to detail.

If I have inadvertently overlooked anyone, please forgive me.

Eddie Chambers

June 2020

Introduction

At the time of the publication of my previous collection of texts – *Run Through the Jungle: Selected Writings by Eddie Chambers*, London: inIVA, the institute of International Visual Arts, 1999 – the term *African Diaspora* was perhaps in earlier stages of widespread use and recognition. One of my earliest recalled introductions to the language of *Diaspora* came in the mid-1990s, when I started reading Ronald Segal's *The Black Diaspora: Five Centuries of the Black Experience Outside Africa* (1985). Though it might not have been the first of its kind, Segal's book was a revelation to me, telling as it did, in deeply imaginative, yet scholarly terms, 'the enthralling story of African-descended people outside Africa, spanning more than five centuries and a dozen countries of settlement, from Britain, Canada, and the United States to Haiti, Guyana, and Brazil.'[1] Certainly, by 2003, when I began the first of three periods as a visiting professor of art history at Emory University, Atlanta, I was formally and consistently applying the term *African Diaspora* to my teaching. Indeed, I recall being hired to teach African Diaspora art history and by the time of my move to the University of Texas at Austin in 2010, the field of African Diaspora art history increasingly became synonymous with my areas of teaching, research, scholarship and aspects of my service, such as my time as a field editor for *caa.reviews*, the online review portal of the College Art Association.[2]

My proximity to African Diaspora art history means that I am, in the first instance, in my teaching, research and scholarship, dealing with particularly critical ideas and questions that very much have a contemporary, as much as a historical, resonance. It's useful, of course, to start with questions. What is 'Diaspora'? What is the 'African' Diaspora? Originally applied to the dispersion of the Jewish people, the term 'Diaspora' became – during the latter part of the twentieth century – a singular and compelling means by which the dispersal of African people during slavery and subsequent periods of movement and migration could be understood. So rather than existing as some sort of formulaic, predictable, humdrum, or run-of-the-mill approach to the compartmentalizing and structuring of learning and history, 'African Diaspora art history' has a requirement to locate critical thinking at the core of its associated teaching, research and scholarship.

Beyond art history itself, African Diaspora studies represents a wider area of learning in which new ideas, new ways of critical thinking, can germinate. Who would have thought that out of mid-nineteenth- to mid-twentieth-century strategizing and activism around 'Pan-Africanism' and the 'Back-to-Africa' movements would emerge the now-widely-used concept of the 'African Diaspora'? Or that in the late twentieth century, sociologist Professor Paul Gilroy could deliver the fascinating and nuanced theoretical Diaspora-related concept of the 'Black Atlantic'? That terms such as 'African Diaspora' and 'Black Atlantic' are now in relatively widespread use speaks volumes about profound cultural shifts that were centuries in the making. At the end of the nineteenth and beginning of the twentieth century, comparatively few Black people throughout the world (visionary figures such as Edward Wilmot Blyden and Marcus Garvey aside) regarded themselves as in any way connected to Black people in other parts of the globe. And although a number of remarkable figures before him had advanced ideas about the international dimensions of the Black experience, it was the towering personality of Garvey who popularised the revolutionary idea that important cultural connections existed between Black people, by way of their common African ancestry. With the word *diaspora* being particularly and fortuitously close to the word *dispersal*, the term African Diaspora has evolved into a compelling means of understanding and appreciating the global dimensions of the Black presence.

Time and again within my scholarship, I find myself adopting and utilising musical references, in the titling of some of my texts and other publications, and in the theoretical framing of some of my arguments. For example, I borrowed from the Notorious B.I.G's 'Things Done Changed' for the titling and theoretical framing of my book, *Things Done Change: The Cultural Politics of Recent Black Artists in Britain* (Amsterdam and New York: Rodopi Editions, 2012). I remain forever grateful to Jacqueline Francis for her review of the book, in which she drew close and important attention to what I was seeking to do, both within the book itself and within its title. Wrote Francis,

> In title, *Things Done Change* nods to a popular musical touchstone: it references 'Things Done Changed,' a track by African American rapper Notorious B.I.G. (a.k.a Biggie Smalls) on his debut album *Ready to Die* (1994) that sold more than a million copies. Smalls's rap sits somewhere between a nostalgic lament and a jeremiad, and by name-checking it, Chambers tips us off about his mood on the subject at hand: the fortunes of black British artists who gained a degree of critical notice in the 1980s and those who, since the 1990s, are much better known and have attracted more widespread praise from mainstream commentators.[3]

Previously, at the turn of the millennium, I reached for Roy Ayers Ubiquity's 1975 track '2000 Black' for '2000's Got to be Black', an essay in the catalogue for

Beyond the Pale 2000 Adelaide Biennial of Australian Art, (Art Gallery of South Australia, Adelaide, Australia). And now, for this collection of texts written over the course of the past two decades, I find myself reaching for, and utilizing, Black Uhuru's 'World is Africa', as a means of giving further form to the embrace of the African Diaspora that this book reflects.

There comes a time in a person's life – most often some point between their early teens to early twenties – when the brain is particularly susceptible to receiving favoured music, its rhythms and its messages in pure, almost concentrated forms. Forms which see the lyrics, sentiments and content of the music to which said person gravitates make particular impressions that remain intense, unrivalled and easily recalled during the rest of that person's life. For me personally, reggae music of the mid-1970s to mid-1980s, particularly that which insistently declared themes of *sufferation* and racial uplift, had a profound impact on my art practice, my sense of identity, and the ways in which I have approached pretty much all of my work, from art school to now. With its distinctive Sly and Robbie riddim, hearing Black Uhuru sing 'The whole world is Africa. . .', provided me with an original, remarkable and quite beautiful means of understanding and appreciating not only the existence of the African Diaspora, but equally as importantly, my own place within it.

My own art practice at the time – together with the art practices of other young Black artists and art students with whom I interacted and collaborated – had a particular embrace of the international at its core. My work/our work, reached out and found common cause with Black Africans buckling under, and also resisting, the tyranny of South Africa's apartheid system. My work/our work, reached out and found common cause with Black Americans, buckling under, and also resisting, the tyranny of the country of their birth waging ceaseless, centuries-long, war against them. I/we drew strength from regarding and visualizing myself/ourselves as having both an explicit and an implicit relationship to Black people of the world. We didn't use the term 'diaspora', but that's what we were performing. As an art student in my late teens and early twenties, reggae music seared itself into my consciousness and to this end, the lyrics, sentiments, and content of the music made profound and lasting impressions on me that remain key aspects of both my identity and my practices as first an art student, then an artist, then as a PhD student, and then through the subsequent stages of my work.

I was at pains, within *Roots & Culture: Cultural Politics in the Making of Black Britain,*[4] to stress the ways in which reggae music shaped Black Britain's sense of itself as a component of the African Diaspora. To this end, I utilized not only, or not so much, Jamaican reggae such as Black Uhuru, but also Black British reggae by groups such as Birmingham's Steel Pulse and London's Merger. Steel Pulse's first release had been a 45, titled *Kibudu – Mansatta – Abuku.*[5] It was a song that called for consciousness about African culture and Black history, just as much as it expressed solidarity with sufferers and reminded them of the healing embrace of Jah.[6] Wisdom was again evoked in the opening line of Steel Pulse's breakthrough album, and its title track, 'Handsworth Revolution', when a centuries old proverb was quoted – 'I say the people of Handsworth, knows that/ One hand wash the other, so they say.'[7] Rastafari was, at the time of my being an art student, offering itself as a particularly compelling counter-cultural expression that had more than a thing or two to say about the abuses of racist Britain, heaped on its Black citizens and residents.

Rastas designated the whole of the society around them, particularly the twin pillars of church and state, as *Babylon*, the biblical overtones giving the description a particularly forceful validity. In 'Handsworth Revolution', Steel Pulse evoked the parable of the wise and foolish men, who built their houses on rock and sand respectively.[8] Thus Handsworth, a famous/infamous Black district of Birmingham, was cast as the rock on which the wise man built his house, even as the wider society was cast as Babylon. 'Babylon is falling / Babylon is falling / It was foolish to build it on the sand / Handsworth shall stand, firm – like Jah rock / fighting back. . .' If ever there was a single song that contained a wide-ranging manifesto of Black British resistance and affirmation, this was it. There was even a reference to the place of armed struggle in the Black youth's attempts to confront their oppressors. 'Striving forward with ambition, And if it takes ammunition. . .' In its proclaimed Pan-Africanist orientation, the song declared 'One Black represents all, all over the world', and to this end, the anti-apartheid struggle in South Africa was evoked as being part and parcel of Handsworth's revolution.

Reggae was the principal means by which the detail of Rastafari spread from Jamaica to Britain and indeed across the world. And once Rastafari had crossed the Atlantic, reggae continued to be the principal and dominant means by which adherents availed themselves of no end of nuanced messages. Furthermore, such messages were simultaneously constructed so as to bring understanding to wider African diasporic peoples about their history and the true nature of their existence. In this regard, the average *roots and culture* reggae record was a veritable treasure trove of ideas and information. Scholars such as Paul Gilroy have provided expansive scholarship that chronicles the interplay between Rastafari, reggae music, and the theoretical and actual mutation of the African Diaspora. There is always, of course, more to be written on these subjects. Merger was a London reggae group whose first album, *Exiles Ina Babylon*, contained much in the way of clear, succinct and coherent summary on the conditions under which Black people, including Black Britons lived, as well as pointers to the appeal of Rastafari. Their track 'Understanding' told of the extent to which exiled Africans were a truly global presence, and in turn, how critically important it was for Black people to 'take a stand' and halt the disempowering, isolating feeling of having been scattered to the four winds. The song firmly located London as a space that linked with the African presence in the USA, as much as it linked with the African presence elsewhere in the Americas.

'We are scattered all over the world, from America to London to Jamaica/We are scattered all over the world, from Africa to Russia down to Asia/For 400 years we've been on the run, on the run, on the run/Now it's time for us to stop and take a stand.'[9] Black Uhuru, Steel Pulse, Merger, et al. were all, in their own respective songs, poets and prophets of the African Diaspora.

My contact with Aboriginal and Torres Strait Islander Australian artists and curators such as Brenda L. Croft and Hetti Perkins afforded me important opportunities to further and deepen my international framings that went beyond the African Diaspora. As part of my *satellite* curatorial work relating to the then-emerging institute of International Visual Arts (inIVA) I worked with Croft and Perkins to present *True Colours: Aboriginal and Torres Strait Islander Artists Raise the Flag*. Curated by Australian arts activist Hetti Perkins, *True Colours* was shown at Bluecoat Gallery, Liverpool, from 7 May to 11 June 1994, before touring.[10] Perkins' exhibition could in many respects be bracketed with my own curated group exhibition of a year earlier, *Black People and the British Flag*, which had shown at Cornerhouse, Manchester, from 8 May–13 June 1993.[11] I had, for a decade or more, got used to the idea, the manifestation, of the African Diaspora. But working with Perkins and Croft required me to think in decidedly different international terms – creating a synonymy between the colonial legacies manifest in Black Britain, and the colonial legacies manifest in Aboriginal Australia. Being made aware of, and fashioning overlapping histories of colonialism that affected Black Britons and Aboriginal Australians, led me, in due course, to more explicitly fashion an interplay between the experiences of Black artists in Britain and the experiences of Black artists in Australia. Both broader groupings of artists were, in their respective ways, subject to *raced* stresses and strains reflective of white supremacist art worlds, in Britain and in Australia, that seemed to me to have much in common. I was, consequently, grateful for the opportunity afforded me by Brenda L. Croft, to contribute the previously-mentioned essay, '2000's Got to be Black', to the catalogue for *Beyond the Pale*, a group exhibition she curated for the 2000 Adelaide Biennial of Australian Art, which was shown at the Art Gallery of South Australia.

An altogether different, but no less gratifying opportunity to provide another Australia-contexted essay was afforded me in 2008, when I was asked to contribute an essay on the work of Jonathan Jones, a dynamic Sydney based Indigenous artist (born in 1978) whose visually powerful sculptures made him a particularly important presence in not only the contemporary Aboriginal art scene in Australia, but also, equally as importantly, the contemporary Australian art scene. Jones' distinctive work could be read as a commentary on histories of modernism, even as he created wonderful, immersive sculptural installations that were truly wondrous. My essay on Jonathan Jones – 'Jonathan Jones: untitled (the tyranny of distance)'[12] – represented what was for me an important opportunity to go beyond a framing of the African Diaspora and engage with a singular artist utilizing a different set of references.

In 2020 we can perhaps regard African Diaspora art history as the most recent addition to the discipline of art history. Year on year, it may well be the case that African Diaspora art history is becoming more embedded in academia, even though those of us as professors whose primary areas of research and teaching are African Diaspora-related are relatively few, certainly in comparison to the comparatively greater number of professors whose areas of research and teaching relate to the more dominant branch of art history – that of African American art. In some respects, we might regard African American art history as part of a bigger African diasporic whole, but surprisingly perhaps, African Diaspora and African American art histories within US academia tend to be regarded, taught, and offered as separate rather than overlapping entities.

Within my own scholarship and teaching, I have always resisted the African Diaspora/African American art history schism and have insisted on relating to African American art history as a component – albeit a hugely significant one – of the broader framework of African Diaspora history and culture. It is for reasons such as this that *World is Africa* includes texts on American artists such as 'Pat Ward Williams: Isolated Incidents' and 'Charles White's 10- and 12-Inch Vinyl Messages.'

Within my work as a curator I always sought to undertake what I regard as strategic interventions. From the mid to late 1980s onwards, I worked, for the most part, with emerging artists, or artists whose careers I believed I could materially assist. I reasoned that artists who were doing well (and being supported with substantial exhibitions and decent amounts of press coverage) had no great need of curatorial attention from me. I gravitated toward working with lesser known practitioners; an approach that was in many respects the inverse of an art world that tended and tends to pamper already over-exposed artists, while ignoring those in far greater need of gallery attention. I brought this strategic intervention to my work as a writer, and *World is Africa* includes several such texts, including two early considerations on the work of Barbara Walker, an artist who now, year on year, becomes ever more recognized, and rightly so; but an artist who for many years caught precious few breaks and, were it not for the resolute ways in which she stayed true to her own vision, could easily have disappeared from wider view. The first of these two texts was 'Barbara Walker, Private Face' written for the catalogue accompanying her exhibition of the same name at mac (Midlands Arts Centre), Birmingham, in May/June of 2002. The second text was 'It's a Bit Much', an essay for the brochure accompanying *Barbara Walker: Louder Than Words*, at Unit 2 Gallery, London Metropolitan University, (November/December 2006). In the same ways that art historians can make a difference, by producing scholarship that challenges that which is over-attended to, my strategy as a writer of art criticism was to draw attention to those artists who have been, and in some instances continue to be, systemically set to one side by an art world disinclined to recognise more than the favoured few.

World is Africa is an opportunity to present a range of texts that reflect my concerns and interests as regards modern and contemporary art practices, relating for the most part to practitioners of the African Diaspora. None of the texts assembled here are available online and there are six new texts in this publication – 'Black Artists and the Fetishization of the 1980s', 'Frank Bowling and the Enigma of Guyana', 'Charles White's 10- and 12- Inch Vinyl Messages', 'Independence and Cultural Nationalism in Caribbean Art', 'Black Artists and the Greater London Council', and 'Criticize: Press Responses to *Black Art an' done* and *The Pan-Afrikan Connection* Exhibitions.' The reader will find, at the bottom of each of the book's previously published texts, details of where and when the text was first published. The earliest text dates from the turn of the millennium and the most recent republished text first appeared in print in 2020. It is my hope that *World is Africa* will function as a substantial contribution to scholarship on African Diaspora art history.

Note: A number of texts in *World is Africa* appear as they were first published, with 'black', the racial signifier, in lower case.

Notes

1 New York: Farrar, Straus and Giroux, 1996.

2 For a text by me, reflecting on the challenges of the field editor position, vis-a-vis framings of African Diaspora art history, see http://www.caareviews.org/reviews/2969#.V3p44o5FCZA.

3 Jacqueline Francis, *Journal of American Studies*, Volume 48, Issue 4, November 2014.

4 I. B. Tauris & Co Ltd, London and New York, Series: International Library of Visual Culture, 2017.

5 Steel Pulse, *Kibudu – Mansatta – Abuku,* written by R. McQueen, Concrete Jungle label, 1976.

6 Jah is the word for God, the Creator, the Giver of life, the Redeemer, the Almighty. As a declaration of faith, or a greeting, or an utterance at the point of departure, the word Jah is often spoken or chanted as 'Jah Rastafari!'

7 The proverb had previously shown up in reggae records such as 'One Hand Washes the Other', Prince Buster, (written by Cecil Campbell, Blue Beat Melodisc Records, 1962) and 'Blazing Fire', by Derrick Morgan (written by Derrick Morgan, Island Records, 1963).

8 Matthew 7.24–27, King James Version. 'Therefore whosoever heareth these sayings of mine, and doeth them, I will liken him unto a wise man, which built his house upon a rock:/And the rain descended, and the floods came, and the winds blew, and beat upon that house; and it fell not: for it was founded upon a rock./And every one that heareth these sayings of mine, and doeth them not, shall be likened unto a foolish man, which built his house upon the sand:/And the rain descended, and the floods came, and the winds blew, and beat upon that house; and it fell: and great was the fall of it.'

9 'Understanding', written by Barry Ford, from Merger, *Exiles in a Babylon*, Sun-star Muzik Co., 1977.

10 South London Gallery, 6 July to 7 August 1994, and City Gallery, Leicester, 10 September to 8 October 1994.

11 The exhibition then toured to City Gallery, Leicester, 6 October to 13 November 1993.

12 Jonathan Jones: *untitled (the tyranny of distance)*, Sherman Galleries, Sydney, Australia, 14 August to 11 October 2008.

SECTION ONE

On Art History, Institutions, and Academia

Chapter 1
Section One Introduction

Before entering the academic world (for me, a twice-renewed visiting professor position at Emory University, Atlanta, beginning in 2003) much of my writing took the form of art criticism, reviews, catalogue introductions, and so on. My first conscious foray into art criticism had come in 1989, when my text, 'Makonde African sculpture', a review of what I regarded as a troubling and hugely problematic exhibition at Oxford Museum of Modern Art, appeared in *Art Monthly*, London, Number 129, September 1989. The text afforded me an opportunity to reflect on what I regarded as exclusionary practices of supposedly leading gallery spaces, such apparent ignoring of Black British artists made all the more vexatious by a simultaneous, self-regarding, though piecemeal embrace of African art, bringing with it no end of problematic framings. My association with *Art Monthly* has continued for over three decades, and has afforded me the opportunity to publish a significant number of texts, including a critique of the then upcoming 'Africa 05' festival, following on the heels of africa 95 (sic), and 'Dead Artists' Society', a critique of posthumous exhibitions of Black artists' work, typified, it seemed to me, by the Whitechapel's 1998 belated showing of Aubrey Williams' work, years after the artist's death and years after he had had (despite some successes) art world doors slammed in his face. It seems to me that as much as art historians have the right to undertake whatever research they are inclined to, or the right to avail themselves of whatever catalogue essay opportunities might come their way, there is also a pressing need to critically consider the antics of an art world frequently disinclined to substantially recognize certain artists until they are dead. In various ways, art history, institutions, and academia are all, or certainly should be, in the dock.

Chapter 2
The Harmful Consequences of Postblack

Time flies. It has now been well over a decade since the Studio Museum opened its *Freestyle* exhibition in 2001, ushering in the term *postblack*. The term encompasses art that seeks to undermine the role of race within black artists' practices and yet also explore the black experience – an idea as intriguing as it is confusing.

In some respects, it feels like postblack has been around for a lot longer. It's now pretty much the only game in town for a new generation of black artists in the United States who wish to achieve any sort of visibility within a gallery system still not particularly minded to treat black artists as individual practitioners – each distinct in his or her own right. There is now a postblack authoritarianism that dictates what sort of black artists, and which practitioners in particular, get exposure. If an artist's work can be deemed postblack, this affords them greater chances of passage into the firmament of an art establishment torn between gestures of liberalism and pathologies of prejudice (not that those two patterns of behavior are mutually exclusive of course).

It might well be easier to dismiss – or indeed, embrace – postblack were it not for its fiendish entanglement with *postrace* (the theory that the United States has transcended racial inequity). Postblack might ultimately mean a thousand different things to a thousand different artists, curators, gallerists, and critics; postrace might similarly mean a thousand different things to people in different strands of public life. But these enigmatic terms, notwithstanding their structural manifestations, now dominate in ways that speak loudly about this country's continued discomfort around matters of race.

There are a large number of white people in the art world who view certain types of black artists as being too strident, too accusatory, too finger-pointing. Postblack art is considered more playful, less hung up about race, and viewed as a blessed relief by some gallerists. Time and again, we have seen the ways in which certain black artists win approval 'for not making an issue out of race' or the 'lightness of touch' they apply to the perceived racial dimensions of their practice. Such sentiments are coded references to *good* black artists and serve as lessons, or warnings, for those not yet regarded as good black artists, or, even worse, those regarded as *bad* black artists.

It was perhaps fitting that postblack should emerge out of a Studio Museum exhibition. The gallery is self-defined as a 'black space.' As the Studio Museum has demonstrated from its earliest exhibitions, this 'black space' dynamic has given it distinct latitude in its approach to exhibition curating. From its championing of the work of non-figurative painters and sculptors, to its appraisals of art coming out of the era of the black arts movement, to its posing of the postblack proposition, the museum has done singular work in its mission of showcasing the work of African American (and to a lesser extent) African Diaspora artists.

Problems tend to arise when other galleries start bandying around their own versions of postblack without treating the wider body of black artists with respect. It is in this context that postblack assumes decidedly problematic and sorrowful consequences.

In this respect, an exhibition such as the Studio Museum's recent *Fore,* which examines art's relationship to US and global communities, is appropriately located. *Fore* is the latest of the museum's series of *F* word shows, following *Freestyle*, 2001; *Frequency*, 2005–2006; and *Flow*, 2008. The museum has developed the critically-necessary curatorial mindset and operational framework that is able to put all manner of black artists' work into wider artistic contexts.

Bluntly put, not every exhibition that the Studio Museum shows is in the vein of its epoch-making *Freestyle* exhibition. In contrast, there are white-run galleries, beyond number, that have declared themselves wedded to only exhibiting those African American artists that it can regard as postblack. This situation turns the fluidity, the nuance, and the boldness, of the postblack proposition from an intriguing idea emanating from a distinct cultural space, into a nationwide out-and-out tyranny embraced by galleries and museums whose senior staffs are as hung up on race as they have ever been.

A discrete but nevertheless important aspect of *Fore* and its predecessors is the extent to which it disrupts dominant definitions of the contemporary African American artist. The dominant definition used to be a decidedly insular one. There were African American artists, and there were immigrant artists, and curatorially, *never the twain shall meet*. The curators of exhibitions such as *Fore* are now starting to be cognisant of particularly fluid aspects of African diasporic existence within the United States.

Fore reveals the extent to which the very notion of African American art has been disrupted by a new generation of artists for whom old-fashioned borders no longer neatly apply. Of the nearly thirty artists in the exhibition, one was born in Santiago, Dominican Republic, and lives in New York; one was born in Prince George's County, Maryland, and lives in New York and Amsterdam; one was born in Ife, Nigeria, and lives in San Francisco, California; and one was born in Kigali, Rwanda, and now lives in New York.

We should perhaps thank the Studio Museum for its nuanced approach to curating African American and African Diaspora artists. But as things currently stand, postblack has created a mandate by an army of curators with neither the wit nor the imagination to treat the full range of black artists with proper respect.

'The Harmful Consequences of Postblack' was an Op-Ed piece that first appeared in an issue of *International Review of African American Art*, titled, *Triple Consciousness: Diasporic Art in the American Context*, Vol. 24, No 3A, 2013: 6–8.

Chapter 3
Africa 05: Polemic

Museums, galleries, concert halls and cinemas will this year 'be reverberating with the sights, sounds, colours, stories, art, images, textures, fashion, sculpture, photography, film, debate and discourse that will create one of the most significant events in London and the UK in years.' 'Africa 05' has described itself as 'a series of major cultural events taking place in London that celebrates contemporary and past cultures from across the continent and the diaspora.'

The last time that London saw anything like this was of course 'africa 95', on which this latest initiative appears to have been modelled. 'Africa 05' provides a useful barometer of the commitment (or lack thereof) of major London galleries towards the art of Africa. With the dubious exception of exhibitions such as the Serpentine's showing of South Africa's William Kentridge, 'Africa 05' reminds us that it has been a full decade since many of London's major galleries exhibited any art from Africa. If London's biggest galleries are only prepared to take art from Africa seriously once every ten years, and if the 'africa 95'/'Africa 05' model is to be the one with which we are saddled, then there can presumably be little genuine hope of African art gaining lasting acceptance and prominence. Several months of feast followed by a decade of famine doesn't make no sense. Furthermore, once-a-decade festivals are guaranteed to ensure the continued marginalisation of art from Africa, assuming that we accept as a certainty the debatable premise that contemporary African art has indeed yet to take up a prominent place in the so-called mainstream.

The 'Africa 05' programme director makes the claim that this is 'not just a series of exhibitions and events, it's a watershed moment in the development and promotion of African arts and culture in the UK. We are confident that the year will challenge many people's preconceptions about Africa and will place many African artists firmly within the UK and international arts scene.' However, this approach is a denial of the altogether more serious and credible work that has been done by writers, art historians, curators, artists and others, over the course of the past several decades. The message of Africa's well established links with modernity might indeed not be getting through to the certain types of people, but quick-fix solutions like 'Africa 05' won't help.

One also has to wonder at the motives of those who continue to suggest that African artists are not yet 'firmly within the UK and international arts scene' and that there are caricatures of Africa that perpetually need dispelling. Contemporary African art has had a vigorous if patchy presence within the international art world for decades now. We can go back as far as we'd like to, for evidence of this. For example, when I was still in short trousers, Camden Arts Centre held an important exhibition of Contemporary African Art in the Summer of 1969. More than two decades later, Chéri Samba – regarded at the time as being the most contemporary of Africa's contemporary artists – had a major exhibition at the ICA in 1991. A decade on from that particular exhibition, in the early 21st Century, and no biennale, no Documenta, no mega-exhibition held anywhere in the world, is now deemed complete without at least a smattering of African artists. Many exhibitions of contemporary or modern African art, too numerous to mention, have been held over the past three or four decades. So where does the idea of an absence of contemporary African art come from?

From another perspective, it is probable that 'Africa 05' will, at best, do comparatively little or, at worst, nothing to facilitate or engender much in the way of debate and exhibition activity within the continent itself. Africa consistently finds itself being plundered for the gratification of those living and consuming art in the West. There are of course one or two biennales in countries such as Senegal, but these, compared to the blow-out that is 'Africa 05', are patchy, low budget undertakings. Contemporary African art has become an exported commodity no less than its traditional counterpart. We have grown used to seeing many of the finest pieces of traditional or historical African art in museums in Europe and the United States. Likewise, over the past ten or 15 years we have grown accustomed to seeing much of what constitutes contemporary African art in the leading art galleries of Europe and the United States. Furthermore, in a relatively short space of time we have come to expect ongoing debates about the nature of contemporary African art to originate and to take place in centres of the art world such as London and New York, rather than anywhere within the continent itself. 'Africa 05' might exist for our gratification, but London doesn't really need this festival of African art. But cities such as Lagos, Accra, Lusaka and Johannesburg surely could benefit from a regular flow of exhibitions by the continent's most important expatriate(d) artists.

It is of course perfectly reasonable that contemporary African artists would want their work to be exhibited widely. Likewise, there can be little doubt that many contemporary African artists have now made their homes in some of the major cities of Europe and the United States. Nevertheless, blowouts such as 'Africa 05' are tantamount to, or representative of, an ongoing plundering of African art for consumption elsewhere. That is, consumption outside of the continent of Africa itself. The export of this new commodity to the West is in many ways the most conspicuous feature of the globalisation of the art market. The inclusion of contemporary African wares in international mega-exhibitions is now taken as evidence of institutional liberal posturing and of a comprehensive and rigorous searching for curatorial excellence and inclusion. And if African curators can be brought in to stage-manage or front this stuff, so much the better.

WOMAD has been presenting African music since the early 80s. Publishers such as Heinemann have been issuing anthologies of contemporary African literature for years. Africa does not need presenting, or explaining. The impulse to homogenise the continent, and to put it on display periodically as, in the words of the Hayward Gallery, an ‘eye-popping’ spectacle, must be resisted. For those who care to observe, compelling evidence of Africa’s links with modernity and post modernity are apparent, almost to the point of being mundane, if it’s possible to use that word in a non-pejorative sense. Africa has had too many discoverers crawling over it for far too long for any of the continent to remain in need of discovering or of presenting.

The whole ‘Africa 05’ enterprise has very uncomfortable overtones of those liberal abolitionists who took the view that, if only the world – or more specifically, the slave-trading powers – could see how civilised and cultured Africans could become, then scales would fall from ignorant eyes and the iniquities of slavery would instantly become apparent, swiftly leading to the demise of the institution. In contemporary terms, this translates into the idea that if only the West, or, more specifically, the art world could see how modern and contemporary Africans and their art have become, then caricatures would inevitably be dispelled and African art could be shown all over the place and commodified accordingly. But the art world has already taken contemporary African art to its bosom, and any lingering pejorative attitudes towards Africa will never be dislodged, not even by a spectacular blowout such as ‘Africa 05’. ‘Africa 15’ anyone?

‘Africa 05: Polemic’ was previously published in *Art Monthly*, London, Number 284, March 2005: 44.

Chapter 4
Dead Artists' Society

During the course of the relatively long period of time during which Rasheed Araeen's 1989 Hayward Gallery exhibition, *The Other Story* was in preparation, no fewer than four of the 24 artists included in the eventual exhibition died. A fifth, Aubrey Williams, lived just about long enough to witness the realisation of the exhibition, dying in April 1990, a few months after it opened. Had the Hayward Gallery taken up the exhibition when it had first been proposed by Rasheed Araeen, then Ronald Moody, Ahmed Parvez, Ivan Peries and A J Shemza would all have lived to see their work in the show. As it turned out, their inclusion was posthumous. People die all the time. Artists die all the time. But somehow, what happened to Moody and company, set against the time line of The Other Story, provides a sobering and salutary lesson about the art establishment's prevarication and unease at dealing with black artists as living and fully functioning practitioners.

We know of course that the art world in many ways prefers to deal with dead artists rather than live ones. The work of a dead artist is a finite (and, therefore, a potentially lucrative) commodity; the work of a living artist, frequently less so. A dead artist can be canonised; he or she can be reborn as a tragic martyr or heroic precursor. Jean-Michel Basquiat, Ana Mendieta and Bob Thompson remain preeminent examples of this. Basquiat, Mendieta and Thompson received extensive recognition and attention during their respective lifetimes as artists. Frequently though, an artist's death can be the best thing to happen to that particular artist's career – it can kindle art world interest in someone who, for as long as they lived, would have been just another has-been, could-have-been or might-have-been artist.

In such a way, over the years, black artists have frequently been doubly wronged by the art establishment. On the one hand they are, above all others, most consistently ignored and pushed to one side when it comes to the dishing out of exhibition opportunities. And on the other hand, this discrimination is echoed by the posthumous attention they occasionally receive. Donald Rodney's work was not considered good or interesting enough for any of his exhibitions to be reviewed by the *Guardian* during his lifetime. Yet the *Guardian* was able to run what by anybody's standards was a generously sized obituary. Likewise, the organisers/selectors of *The British Art Show* never thought his work good enough to be included in the exhibition while he was alive. In death however, his inclusion in 'The British Art Show' was as inevitable as it was assured.

Over the past few years we have witnessed several instances in which inIVA, (the institute of International Visual Arts) has aided and abetted in the promotion of dead artists' work at high profile London venues, when inIVA ought really, in my view, to be concentrating on promoting the work of those artists who live and breathe. After all, considered attention in the form of large exhibitions and big fat monographs have been traditionally withheld from black artists during their lifetimes.

Hammad Butt was, I believe, the first artist to receive this posthumous treatment. This 'brilliant young artist' had graduated from Goldsmiths College in 1990, dying just a few short years later. The very stylish publication *Familiars* was produced by inIVA in association with the John Hansard Gallery subsequent to the artist's death. But Hammad Butt had not spent several decades knocking on the art establishment's doors and getting precisely nowhere. In that sense he represents a much less troubling example of a dead artist's career being resurrected, compared to the likes of first, Aubrey Williams and now, Li Yuan-chia.

Williams was never considered good enough to exhibit in the Whitechapel during his long and prolific career. He couldn't even get his work into that gallery for their 1986 'come one, come all' black artists' exhibition, *From Two Worlds*. Williams' exclusion from spaces like the Whitechapel bore eloquent testimony to the concerted and consistent exclusion of black artists from major and important London galleries. And yet inIVA were still able to willingly involve itself in the 1998 Aubrey Williams exhibition at the Whitechapel. The preface to the accompanying catalogue opened with a reference to Williams being 'one of the key figures in painting in post-war Britain'. It is to the eternal shame of the Whitechapel that none of its directors felt able to express this view of Williams during his lifetime or their tenure. The Whitechapel's belated embracing of a dead black artist does nothing to diminish or reduce the discriminatory nature of that exclusion. Why should Williams have to wait for the best part of a decade after his death to be accorded the respect, status and acknowledgement that should, from the 1950s onwards, have been his by right?

Such posthumous exhibitions do nothing to lessen the discrimination faced by black artists and do much to give that discrimination a cynical veneer of inclusion. Williams' most comprehensive catalogue to date is the one accompanying his 1998 Whitechapel exhibition. But dead black artists don't need flashy catalogues. Dead black artists don't need major exhibitions or any sort of posthumous attention from gallery curators. Posthumous exhibitions might be to the benefit of curators, collectors, academics and researchers, but they are of no earthly use to dead artists themselves. The best tribute that galleries can pay to dead black artists is to show proper attention to the living ones.

InIVA of course undertakes many exhibition projects with many different living artists. But the impression exists that inIVA's most high profile exhibitions continue to feature the work of dead artists. This is a troubling development. When inIVA was first researched, developed and established, it was quite reasonably envisaged that its principal beneficiaries would be living artists from here and elsewhere in the world. Curiously, inIVA involved itself in the 1997 Hayward Gallery 'Rhapsodies in Black' exhibition of art from the Harlem Renaissance – a movement that occurred way back in the early part of last century. InIVA's next high profile exhibition was the Williams show, already mentioned. And now Camden Arts Centre is hosting a posthumous exhibition of work by Li Yuan-chia, who died in 1994. One of the most remarkable aspects of his fascinating career was that hardly anyone within the art establishment took any notice of him during his lifetime. But in death, he gets the major exhibition, the doorstop catalogue and fulsome praise ('He was an artist of great sensibility and a strikingly original mind'). All too late.

There is perhaps little we can do about art world discrimination, though we can at least not compound it. We should reject the idea that it is only in death that the most prolific and talented black artists deserve attention. We are after all in a bizarre situation in which grieving relatives of dead black artists must think that a telephone call from inIVA is as essential a part of the mourning process as a trip to the undertaker.

Whilst deserving black artists live and breathe (and continue to be discriminated against), posthumous exhibitions of their work have no place whatsoever in the scheme of things. Dealing with dead black artists is just another way for the art establishment to avoid having to deal with living black artists. InIVA should draw a line under these dead black artists' exhibitions.

'Dead Artists' Society' (a critique of posthumous exhibitions of Black artists' work), was previously published in *Art Monthly*, London, Number 244, March 2001: 52.

Chapter 5
Black Artists and the Fetishization of the 1980s

Month on month, year on year, we have witnessed a pronounced escalation of what might be regarded as the fetishization of the 1980s, as regards the fortunes and profiles of Black British artists. Rather than their wider and respective individual practices being engaged with and keeping step with the onward march of time, it is work from the best part of four decades ago that has come to represent the current profile of Black artists. More than that, certain practitioners associated with the Black artists' visual arts activity of the 1980s have come to be a conduit for this fetishization. Whilst it might possibly now be on the wane, it is perhaps difficult to say for certain when the excessive and irrational commitment to, or obsession with, Black artists of the 1980s, began. Certainly, David A. Bailey, Ian Baucom, and Sonia Boyce had it right when, in their introduction to *Shades of Black: Assembling Black Arts in 1980s Britain*, they cited the persuasive view that beginnings are unstable things.[1] But whilst identifying the starting point for the fetishization of Black British artists of the 1980s might be a matter of conjecture and speculation, the publication of the aforementioned book, and the related conference, might well have been the moment the fetishization of the 1980s was set in train. The conference from which the 2005 book drew its title had taken place four years earlier at Duke University, Durham NC, 19–22 April 2001. Baucom et al. had though, cited a conversation that had taken place some four years before the conference, in 1997, as a possible starting point for what started out as a perhaps not unreasonable interest in certain Black artists' practices. Baucom had, apparently, asked Boyce, Sutapa Biswas and Keith Piper (the three set to exhibit together in a show called *The Unmapped body: 3 Black British artists*, at Yale University Art Gallery, 13 October 1998–January 1999), 'What do you think of doing a book about the black British art movement of the 1980s?'[2]

This conversation reportedly took place in the autumn of 1997, which is as significant a period as any in the history of Black British artists. Firstly, the British art world had begun to reiterate its ambivalence to what it perceived as the overly strident, out-of-step-with-the-times practices of certain artists who emerged into visibility in the 1980s.[3] Secondly, a consideration of immense proportion was the ways in which the 1990s gave rise to a *new* type of Black British artist. Steve McQueen, Chris Ofili, and Yinka Shonibare distinguished themselves, and were recognized, for the ways in which they made *new* types of work, and both critiqued and utilized the Black image in ways that the art world regarded as setting these practitioners apart from the *mass* of Black artists who emerged during the 1980s.[4] At precisely the moment in which McQueen et al. were, in terms of exposure, adulation, and critique, starting to run rings around Black artists of the 1980s, certain people were choosing to disregard truly fascinating developments and begin instead to fix their gaze on a decade that had either slipped into history, or been superseded by cataclysmic 1990s changes in the *zeitgeist*.

Perhaps the quest to identify just where the fixation with Black artists of the 1980s began, and started to gather steam, is something of a fruitless task. After all, Baucom, in posing his question to Boyce, Biswas, and Piper, was apparently motivated by a consideration of the *Ten.8* publication, *Critical Decade: Black British Photography in the 80s (Ten.8* magazine, Birmingham, Volume 2 No. 3, Spring 1992). Thus, we move backwards in time, from 2005, to 2001, to 1997, to 1992. The attention paid to Black British artists of the 1980s was, in any event, short-lived and by the late 1980s much of the mainstream art world declared itself to be either bored with what it took to be the totality of their practices, or declared itself outraged that this practice had garnered any sort of attention or exposure in the first place. A selection of Black British artists of the 1980s were included in Rasheed Araeen's landmark exhibition of 1989, *The Other Story*. Most of these artists found themselves swept up in vociferous reactions to the exhibition, perhaps typified by *Evening Standard* art critic Brian Sewell, whose review of the show was titled 'Black Pride and Prejudice'. Underneath the title in enlarged type was the following quote: 'They argue that they are rejected and ignored, when they are nothing of the kind.' Within the review Sewell was described as 'critic of the year', and in the language which would come to see him excel as a pantomime villain of choice during the following decade, he opined,

> Apart from [Sonia] Boyce and [Donald] Locke, we have seen it all before. Having either no traditions of their own, or traditions so exhausted that no nourishment is to be drawn from them, these artists parrot Western visual idioms that they do not understand and that have been exposed as silly and pretentious. That they should demand serious attention for their third-rate imitations of the white man's cliché must seem outrageous to all who care to judge by quality. Talent in the white west is an extremely rare phenomenon

> and most Western art is indifferent at best. I see no reason to distort the judgement that damns it so as to praise the work of artists just as bad, or worse, because they make a noisy business of being black.[5]

The year 1992 notwithstanding, it was, beyond question, the *Shades of Black* book that gave a fillip to partial, revisionist, nostalgic and decidedly curious reading of the 1980s with which the British art world is currently fixated. The book gave the 1980s a certain convenient and opportunistic elasticity, in effect creating a bandwagon that all manner of people with little to nothing in the way of pronounced associations with Black British artists of the 1980s could jump on. Somewhat as a matter of routine, Black artists found themselves being studied, reviewed, even curated by those with a calculated interest in using said artists as some sort of career stepping stone. This piecemeal and short-term attention created particularly unstable foundations. The contents of *Shades of Black* threw into sharp relief an arguably accentuated role for certain artists who emerged into visibility in the 1980s, but equally worryingly and problematically, the book demonstrated a comprehensive setting to one side of many artists – Sokari Douglas-Camp, Denzil Forrester et al. – for whom the 1980s was an important decade in the launching or establishing of their careers. It is this double deficiency on which the current fetishization of Black artists of the 1980s rests.[6]

Not surprisingly perhaps, the resurgence of interest in Black artists' work of the 1980s is taken, in certain circles, to be of a part and parcel of a celebratory moment, of the unstoppable progress of Black artists within British art. Caroline Roux, writing in the *Financial Times*, began her review of *The Place is Here* (a key exhibition in these fetishization of the 1980s narratives, discussed presently, in this text) with

> Last week the artist John Akomfrah received the prestigious £40,000 Artes Mundi prize for Auto da Fé, a film delving into the reality of persecution through the lens of luscious period drama. Sonia Boyce (a Royal Academician since 2016) opened a solo show at the ICA in London, in which stills of filmed dancers are abstracted into a (nearly) domestic wallpaper. Zarina Bhimji was just back from a research trip to her place of birth, Uganda – preparation for a show at Tate Britain next year. And Lubaina Himid was celebrating the positive reviews of simultaneous solo exhibitions, one in Oxford and one in Bristol.[7]

Notwithstanding such blinkered and partial adulation, institutional support of Black artists has always been skewed and dysfunctional and, the favoured few aside, the vast majority of Black artists find that success or status is generally accorded them only retrospectively. What I mean by this is that we have a pronounced history of acclaim being assigned to Black artists upon their passing, or years after their passing. It was a number of years following his death in 1990 that Aubrey Williams was recognized by increased attention from Tate Britain; likewise, Ronald Moody, having died in 1984, was eventually (and of course posthumously) hailed as 'one of Britain's most remarkable Modernist sculptors'[8] nearly two decades after his death. Donald Rodney, who passed away in 1998 has subsequently been the subject of much scholarly and institutional attention, including the acquisition of his work by Tate Britain. His work had not been considered good enough for inclusion in 1990 and 1995 iterations of the *British Art Show*, though in death, his work was promptly included in the manifestation of the exhibition that took place in 2000. Such institutional antics are nothing new for Black artists, but the fetishization of the 1980s opened up a new front in that certain artists found themselves being recognized thirty or so years after they had made a variety of contributions:

> In retrospect, these young black artists were pioneers, making bold, brave work fit to be shown in tough and sometimes ad hoc spaces. Its strong physical presence has stood the test of time. And if collage and image and text prevail, it is perhaps because these practitioners, as well as being influenced by movements like Dada and artists such as Rauschenberg that education had brought to them, were quite literally finding a way to piece together alternative dialogues.[9]

Probably the most celebrated of Lubaina Himid's curated exhibitions centred on the practices of Black women artists was the *Thin Black Line*, which took place in a concourse/passageway area of London's ICA in the autumn of 1985.[10] In 2011, however, Himid (and Paul Goodwin) worked with Tate Britain to stage *Thin Black Line(s)*, a revisiting of her three women artists' exhibitions of the 1980s, which brought together a number of pieces and related documentation. The display took place in a spacious, roomy gallery in Tate Britain and its installation was in marked contrast to the environment in which its namesake was located some quarter of a century earlier.[11] The year before *Thin Black Line(s)*, Aicon Gallery, London presented an appraisal, of sorts, of *The Other Story* exhibition.[12] Put together by Niru Ratnam and titled *A Missing History: The Other Story Re-visited*, it featured a number of artists included in the original exhibition, plus two (Chila Kumari Burman and Sutapa Biswas) who were not.[13] The press release for *A Missing History: The Other Story Re-visited* likened *The Other Story* to several previous, historically significant, exhibitions:

> Along with 'Magiciens de la Terre', the 1993 edition of the Whitney Biennial and Documenta XI, 'The Other Story' is one of the key exhibitions that over the last twenty years have impacted on the ways in which a previously closed art world was opened up to issues around post-colonialism, migration, exile, diaspora

> and globalization. Unsurprisingly each of these exhibitions generated controversy, with heated discussions taking place at the time of each one. 'A Missing History: "The Other Story" re-visited' is an opportunity to look back on these debates at the twenty-year anniversary mark as well as to exhibit the works of 11 of the 24 artists in the original show and two artists who were not in the show . . .

It is perhaps in the nature of curating, art criticism and art scholarship to revisit exhibitions, artists and art movements from the recent past, the more distant past, and points in between, but the relative proliferation of displays and exhibitions such as these, in London and elsewhere in the country, tended to be the means by which certain artists achieved any sort of return to visibility. Having been somewhat short-changed in terms of their original Warholian fifteen minutes, certain artists found that it was only through looks back to 1980s' moments that their work was temporarily restored to the public visibility.

Another undertaking that benefitted from, as well as contributed to, an enhanced remembering of the 1980s was the conference *Reframing the Moment: Legacies of the BLK Art Group*, held on Saturday 27 October 2012. In 1982, a group of Black art students and young artists had organized an event they titled *The First National Black Art Convention*, which took place at the Polytechnic, Wolverhampton, in October of that year. This had in many respects been an unprecedented coming together of Black artists of different ages, from different parts of the country. The Blk Art Group itself was a short-lived affair, being formed in 1983 and existing for about a year. By the middle of the first decade of the twenty-first century, however, the Blk Art Group name was being retrospectively and indiscriminately applied to the exhibitions and symposia organized between the early and mid-1980s and involving artists and art students such as Claudette Johnson, Keith Piper, Donald Rodney, Marlene Smith, Janet Vernon, and others. One of the most irksome and tiresome consequences of the conflation of multiple iterations of the loose group (which at different times during its existence was variously known as Wolverhampton Young Black Artists, the Pan African/Afrikan Connection, Art for Uhuru, and, in its final stages, The Blk Art Group) is the problem of omission. The Blk Art Group has become increasingly identified with only a very limited number of artists, primarily Piper, Rodney, Smith and Johnson. Conspicuous by their absence from pretty much all 1980s-related attention are the likes of Vernon, Dominic Dawes, Ian Palmer, Andrew Hazel, and Wenda Leslie, all of whom have as much right to be recalled and cited as anyone else. The partiality of citations of The Blk Art Group exist as a pointer to the sorts of erasure discussed in the next text in *World is Africa*, 'Black-British Artists and Problems of Systemic Invisibility and Eradication: Creating Exhibition Histories of That Which Is Not There.'

Sonya Dyer, in reviewing an exhibition by Claudette Johnson, to be referenced subsequently in this text, began,

> 2017 has turned out to be a rather momentous year for many artists associated with the Blk Art Group. Formed in Wolverhampton in 1979, initially by four young black British artists [Dyer then cites several names, including Keith Piper, Marlene Smith, and Donald Rodney], the group became synonymous with work that articulated concerns around institutional racism and the UK's imperial past in conversation with the contentious history of European art.[14]

With a number of half-truths and inaccuracies crammed into a couple of sentences, one wonders about the extent to which other branches of art history are peppered with such misremembering and falsehoods. Art critics might balk at the idea that what they offer is equivalent to journalism, but where sloppy art criticism and sloppy journalism meet is in the realm of the wilful or uninformed peddling of untruths. Partial, incomplete and decidedly fragmentary scholarship is part and parcel of the fetishization of the 1980s.

Returning briefly to the *Reframing the Moment: Legacies of the BLK Art Group* conference, there may well have been a compelling thirty-year symmetry that led to a conference of October 1982 being revisited and reframed in October 2012, even as far as it being held in the same venue. But the timing of certain anniversaries and commemorations throw up a tranche of questions over and above the sorts of questions raised within the respective Black artists' conferences and symposia themselves.

We know that culturally, this society has a preference for and attraction to, anniversaries in five, ten, twenty-five, fifty, one-hundred-year increments. Outside such increments, other odd or even numerical increments just don't cut it, in the public imagination. Let's apply the ten-year increment to a recognition of the 1982 *First National Black Art Convention*, which took place in Wolverhampton. Why was the conference not remembered in 1992, which surely would have been an apt moment to reflect on what was supposedly a decade of significant advances for Black British artists? The year 1997 would have marked fifteen years since the 1982 gathering, but no commemoration or event of remembrance took place. A twenty-year reflection might also have been apt, given that 2002 could possibly still be counted as being the start of the new millennium. Twenty-five-year 'silver' celebrations are also culturally popular, but the confluence of factors that might lead to a major reflection on the 1982 Convention were clearly still not in sufficient alignment. A twenty-nine-year reflection might not have made the cut; neither would a thirty-one-year consideration. The thirty-year reflection on *The First National Black Art Convention* in 2012 can be read as according with the cultural preference for certain blocks of time being used to aid or facilitate *memory*, but *Reframing the Moment: Legacies of the BLK Art Group* can also be read as contributing to the fetishization of the 1980s that was beginning to take shape. We can be assured that whatever factors led to the 2012 gathering will not be in favourable alignment come 2022, the fortieth anniversary; and like so much of what happens in Black British art history, by 2032, the fiftieth anniversary of *The First National Black Art Convention,* the gathering will likely be an obscure and largely forgotten historical footnote.[15]

Perhaps one of the most substantial manifestations of the fetishization of the 1980s was *The Place Is Here,* a large-scale exhibition that took place at Nottingham Contemporary, from 4 February to 1 May 2017.[16] Though other, smaller reflections of the period had taken place previously (such as *Blk Art Group 1983–1984*, Graves Art Gallery, Sheffield, the exhibition's Launch Event being held on Wednesday 7 September 2011, with the show itself running through to 24 March 2012). *The Place Is Here* proved to be the largest curatorial undertaking that had the Black 1980s as its focus.

> The starting-point for this exhibition is a pivotal decade for British culture and politics: the 1980s. Spanning painting, sculpture, photography, film and archives, *The Place Is Here* brings together a wide range of works by more than 30 artists and collectives. The questions they ask – about identity, representation and what culture is for – remain vital today.
>
> In 1982, a group of artists and thinkers met in Wolverhampton at the First National Black Art Convention, to discuss the 'form, future and function of Black Art'. Two years later, the second 'working convention' took place here in Nottingham. What constitutes 'black art', or the 'Black Arts Movement' was, and continues to be, heavily contested.
>
> This exhibition traces some of the urgent conversations that were taking place between black artists, writers and thinkers during the 80s. Against a backdrop of civil unrest and divisive national politics, they were exploring their relationship to Britain's colonial past as well as to art history. Many artists were looking to the Civil Rights movement in America, Black feminism, Pan-Africanism, the struggle over apartheid, and the emergent fields of postcolonial and cultural studies.
>
> *The Place Is Here* does not present a chronological survey. Instead, it is conceived as a kind of montage. For many of these artists, montage allowed for identities, histories and narratives to be dismantled and reconfigured according to new terms. The exhibition assembles different positions, voices and media to present a shifting portrait of a decade while refusing to pin it down. The presentation is structured around four overlapping groupings, each of which is titled after a work on display: Signs of Empire; We Will Be; The People's Account; and Convenience Not Love.[17]

This was truly an everything-but-the-kitchen-sink revisiting of the 1980s, which even found room, or made room, for an early to mid-1970s work by Rasheed Araeen.[18] Alongside work from the 1980s, *The Place is Here* made room for film, video, archival and contextual material. Curiously perhaps, this

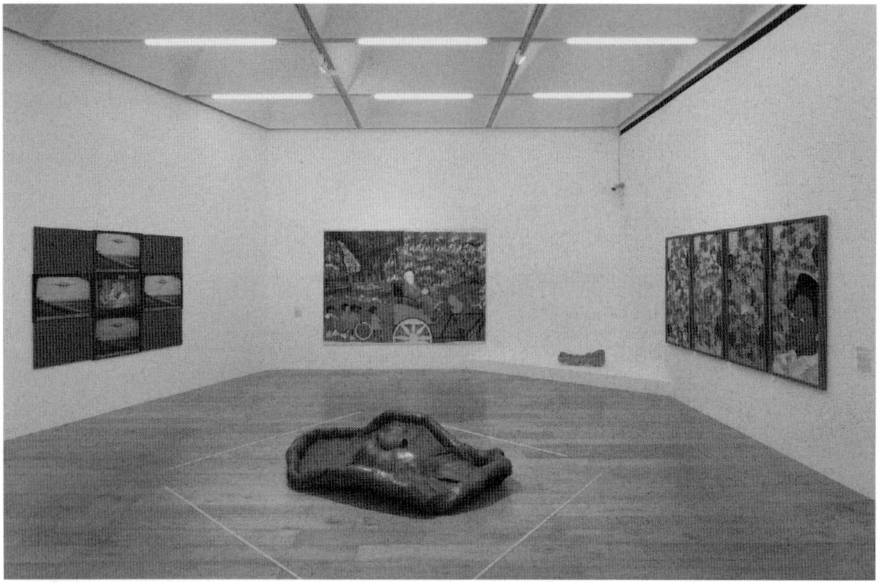

Figure 5.1 Installation view of work by Rasheed Araeen, Sutapa Biswas, Veronica Ryan and Sonia Boyce, *The Place Is Here*, Nottingham Contemporary, 4 February–1 May 2017. Photograph © Andy Keate, courtesy of Nottingham Contemporary.

concerted attempt to fashion and present a tangible history of the 1980s had no room, within its constructions, for a catalogue, a somewhat counterintuitive omission, given the self-evident need for, and importance of, substantial published materials relating to the period.[19] Given the pretensions of *The Place is Here* for breadth and depth, the exhibition had the unmistakable appearance of giving itself over to a disproportionately large body of work by Himid. Her work appeared in several of the exhibition's sections (indeed, the title of the exhibition was borrowed from her work and the second of the previously referenced overlapping groupings was named *We Will Be*, another explicit reference to one of her works) and in addition to this, the display included a sizeable installation by Himid. With her work appearing on the poster/brochure, and becoming synonymous with *The Place is Here*, Himid very much became the female equivalent of the exhibition's poster boy.[20] Indeed, so ubiquitous was Himid's presence within the exhibition that together with concurrent displays of her work at Modern Art Oxford, and Spike Island, Bristol, she built up a head of steam that saw her shortlisted, and eventually winning, the Turner Prize.

Nothing epitomizes the fetishization of the 1980s quite as much as the unprecedented and unbridled press adulation with which *The Place is Here* was greeted. Caroline Elbaor, writing for the website Artnet on 23 January 2017, reported,

> A major exhibition highlighting the work of black artists, writers, thinkers, and institutions in the 1980s in the UK is slated to open at Nottingham Contemporary on February 4, under the curation of Nick Aikens and Sam Thorne.
>
> *The Place is Here* will bring together over 100 works by 30 artists spanning the mediums of painting, sculpture, installation, photography, video, and archival displays from the 1980s, exploring, according to the press release, 'identity and representation, racism and colonial legacies.'
>
> Described as an 'intellectually fertile moment,' the institution aims to re-raise these conversations as they feel ever-relevant in the contemporary climate.
>
> '[The exhibition] takes as its starting point a period of divisive politics and inequality, which we see everywhere echoed today. Many works in the exhibition ask us to consider how we see ourselves as a society, a cultural community, and as the outcome of different historical processes. Thinking about these questions, and art's ability to articulate them, seems more vital than ever,' the curators of the exhibition told artnet News.[21]

Elbaor added, for good measure, 'Montage is to play a central role in the exhibition, and the show itself is to be understood as a montage itself.'

This though, was as nothing compared to the fulsome sentiments expressed by journalists such as Laura Cumming, who, writing in the *Observer* on 22 January 2017, declared, 'To describe this show as a revelation would be true, but an understatement', and

> The work here was often made when the artists were barely out of college. It is an art of protest, declaration, revelation, news; it is art as a form of public speech. But what's striking, too, is just how often it draws on art history. [Gavin] Jantjes is playing with pop conventions. Sonia Boyce's shattering four-part painting *Lay Back, Keep Quiet and Think of What Made Britain So Great* pits Britain's colonial past against the fetching patterns of William Morris. Rasheed Araeen's chillingly stylish grid, combining gleaming green panels with photomontages of Awacs surveillance planes in the first Gulf war, drives minimalism straight into politics.[22]

Cumming was joined in her hero worshipping of the exhibition by the likes of Veronica Simpson, who, writing for *Studio International* (21 February 2017), asserted that, 'The Place is Here resonates powerfully with today's cultural and political zeitgeist,'[23] before continuing,

> The timing of this show could hardly be better: an exploration of a period of great political unrest, characterised by widespread paranoia about

> immigration, stoked by politicians happy to appeal to people's worst instincts in order to win votes, amid huge disaffection with the political establishment. Sounds familiar? Well, that was then, not now: *The Place is Here* examines Britain in the 1980s through the prism of a group of young black and Asian artists who were trying to penetrate the impermeable crust of western art world complacency, via painting, photography, installation, sculpture and video.

Other equally generous press coverage was offered online by *Amuse* (8 February 2017), its coverage of *The Place is Here* declaring 'The exhibition surveys a decade of British past in which racial division and economic inequality were rife. But out of this hot bed of ideas came a new generation of thought.'[24] This coverage contrasted markedly and sharply with the pronounced lack of recognition of these artists and this work back in the 1980s. Further, as was perhaps typified by the antagonistic expressions of Sewell quoted earlier, much of the press and media were scornful of Black artists' work of/during the 1980s, particularly that which it read as having pronounced social, political or racial narratives.[25] The *Observer*'s now sister paper, the *Guardian*, had taken a piecemeal interest in Black British artists' exhibitions of the 1980s and its art critic, Waldemar Januszczak had declared himself something of a cheerleader for Sonia Boyce's work in particular. In 1985, Januszczak had responded to *The Thin Black Line* favourably, by reviewing it in the *Guardian*. Though his tone was supposedly generous, his review was located within the narrow and short-sighted confines of the notion that these artists were 'angry' and that this exhibition was a collective reflection of their agitated state of mind. In blatant disregard for the rules of journalism and a refusal to use a thesaurus, Januszczak used the word 'anger' or 'angry' four times and for good measure his review was titled 'Anger at Hand'. The subtitle of the review, too, left readers in no doubt as to how he summed up the show. It spoke of 'the barely controlled fury' of the exhibition. Elsewhere in the review, Januszczak gave the impression that he was discussing the activities of an uncontrollable mob, rather than art by artists who, for the most part, had passed through or were passing through, the higher education system.[26]

The previous year, Januszczak had reviewed *Into the Open*, an exhibition that had signalled an institutional embrace of Black artists, showcasing the work of some twenty-plus artists, and held at Sheffield's Mappin Art Gallery.[27] In his review for the *Guardian*, Januszczak conflated 'Black Art' as a distinct *politicized* type of practice that located particular theoretical and aesthetic framings at its core, with 'Black art' as a catch-all term to describe the work of non-white artists. This conflation typified a catastrophic failure of curators, exhibition organizers, critics, and others to respectfully differentiate between different types of artists and the individuality of their practices.

His review of the exhibition referenced many attitudes and assumptions that would in time be held in various quarters of the art establishment and come to blight the collective progress of Black artists. The exhibition was clearly titled *Into the Open*. Yet Januszczak or his sub-editor chose to call his review 'Black Art'.[28] Thus, he reflected and contributed to the arrival of a troublesome association that Black artists have not entirely managed to shake themselves free from. That is, the tendency to have their collective practices, irrespective of difference, irrespective of curatorial thesis, labelled by others as being 'Black Art'. One would not ordinarily expect an exhibition by any given number of non-Black artists to be labelled 'White Art', especially if a *bona fide* exhibition title was available and in use. The list of artists represented in the exhibition was noticeably diverse, in terms of their national origins, ethnicities and other backgrounds. Yet Januszczak or his sub-editor collapsed these diverse, almost eclectic identities into the inappropriate and misleading headline of 'Black Art'. This labelling of all work by all non-European artists as 'Black Art' has been a major contributing factor to the ongoing marginalization and pigeon-holing of Black artists.

Referring to the title of the exhibition, Januszczak suggested that 'The title clearly implies that black art is coming out of the ghetto.' Elsewhere, he asserted his view that 'what the exhibition underlines over and over again is that it is not enough to be noticed finally, you must also have something worthwhile to say.' Though a number of the artists whose work was enthusiastically celebrated when it was shown in *The Place is Here* had been included in *Into the Open*, Januszczak had dismissed, in 1984, the practices of these artists as lacking 'something worthwhile to say.' He considered the comprehensive scope of *Into the Open* to be 'a shame'. He did however, identify the 'Boyces' and 'Pipers' as being good enough for 'any' company. (For 'any', of course, read 'white'). Januszczak dismissed most of the *Into the Open* artists as not being good enough for 'any' company by referring to them as 'only' being 'here because of the colour of their skin.' Thirty-plus years ago the *Observer* had nothing to say about the work of the artists who made it into *The Place is Here*. And what coverage of these artists there was, by its sister paper, the *Guardian*, bordered on the derisive. Thirty-plus years later, Cumming, writing in the *Observer*, could hardly find enough words to praise what was in some respects a similar if not exact, body of work. Coverage of *The Place is Here* reflected a certain nostalgic framing of the 1980s, as a decade of righteous certainties vis-à-vis struggle. The memories of, or the imagined history of struggle against Margaret Thatcher and her hated Conservative government was after all so much more palatable, so much simpler, that the disappointments of tuition fees and the war in Iraq, that were the legacy of Tony Blair and his New Labour government. The struggle against apartheid was, again, after all so much more palatable, so much simpler, than the disappointments of the accusations of corruption and nepotism that swirled around the ANC government of Jacob Zuma.

The fetishization of the 1980s was hallmarked by a continued, somewhat wistful and sentiment *remembering* of the righteous activism of the 1980s. The Graves, in Sheffield, had contextualized its display of work by artists associated with the Blk Art Group with 'At a time when the Conservative government was outspokenly anti-immigrant, the British National Party was on the rise and the Brixton riots were shaking London, the Blk Art Group emerged as a creative force in Britain.'[29] This harking back to a pushback against Thatcherism as a way of framing Black artists of the 1980s, though somewhat partial and arguably disingenuous, had first been utilized in the framing of *Shades of Black: Assembling Black Arts in 1980s Britain*: 'In the 1980s – at the height of Thatcherism and in the wake of civil unrest and rioting in a number of British cities – the Black Arts Movement burst onto the British art scene with breathtaking intensity, changing the nature and perception of British culture irreversibly.'[30] Even the *Financial Times,* which although it had reviewed exhibitions such as *From Two Worlds*, had extended no specific attention to artists and exhibitions of the early 1980s, got in on the act. Its breathless review of *The Place is Here* included a narrative in which broader progressive initiatives were interwoven with what was taken to be the exhibition's resistance to Thatcherism:

> The 1980s in Britain was a febrile time: Margaret Thatcher was freshly in place as prime minister; there were riots in London and Liverpool in 1981, and again in 1985 in Brixton and Birmingham. There was enlightenment, too – campaigning commissioners at the new Channel 4, who invited groups like the film-making Black Audio Film Collective to create challenging new work (the 1986 Handsworth Songs, a fragmented and disturbing collage of riot footage, archival material and interviews, is being shown in Nottingham). Curators like Sandy Nairne at the ICA dared to put on a Robert Mapplethorpe show in 1983 (it got closed down, but not before it had opened a few eyes). Isaac Julien's experimental film Territories (1984), which looks at black identity through the lens of the annual Notting Hill Carnival, was even funded by the Police Committee.[31]

One of the most curious and (one might assume) self-defeating aspects of the fetishization of the 1980s was its extraordinarily pronounced partiality. The breadth of artists making cogent, highly engaging work during the 1980s was notably comprehensive. The 1980s were after all the decade that witnessed the first sizeable art school intake of Black British-born/raised youngsters, as much as it was the decade that saw the crystallizing of all manner of grievances of Black Britons. Given these factors, and a number of others,[32] one would have expected a curated *remembering* of the 1980s to embrace far more practitioners than the relatively select coterie of artists who tended to figure in initiatives that looked back on the decade. This is not the time or place to reflect in any depth on the breadth of artists who should, quite rightly be remembered, celebrated and recognized for their achievements and contributions made during the 1980s and beyond, but I'll take a moment to mention just three.

Sokari Douglas Camp is very much an artist who emerged into conspicuous and well recognized visibility in the 1980s. By the middle of the decade, Nigeria-born Douglas Camp had emerged as a bold and intriguing artistic presence in London, making a new and decidedly different kind of work. Her sculptures, when exhibited or displayed in galleries or public spaces, demanded to be seen (and in many instances, demanded to be heard) and forcefully required the viewer's attention. Her work boldly announced its presence, by the space it occupied, and in a number of instances, the *noises* it made. Simply put, indifference was not an option when faced with the work of this extraordinary artist, whose work was the subject of a number of important exhibitions around the country and further afield, from the 1980s onwards. Douglas Camp oftentimes used welded steel to create sculptures characterized by a formidable sense of presence, and frequently evoked the substantial frames of formidable African matriarchs. These sculptures pay particular homage to women whose fortitude, resilience, creativity, and indeed vulnerability, have frequently gone unremarked. This London-based artist had the distinction of having a substantial exhibition of sculpture, *Echoes of the Kalabari*, at the then newly-opened National Museum of African Art, Washington D.C., which was completed in 1987, just off the National Mall and adjacent to other Smithsonian museums. Douglas-Camp's exhibition took place from 11 November 1988 to 29 January 1989. In her *Echoes of the Kalabari* catalogue 'Introduction', Sylvia H. Williams, then-Director of the National Museum of African Art, Smithsonian Institution and Roy Sieber, Associate Director, wrote that this was

> the first showing in the United States of the sculpture of Sokari Douglas Camp, a Kalabari artist who has studied and lived in Europe and the United States. As is true of all artists, she draws upon a variety of her experiences in the creative process. Her sculpture exemplifies the universal search for artistic self-expression.
>
> Presented here are large constructions, some motorized, which evoke aspects of traditional Kalabari culture. Two sources emerge: the festival as a major cultural activity and funerary ceremonies. Hers is an aesthetic that combines the authenticity of its cultural past with contemporary artistic technologies. As a modern sculptor, she makes us aware by means of shape and rhythm of the aesthetic richness of her cultural legacy.

Another artist who can rightly identify the 1980s as the decade in which they established their practice and propelled themselves into public visibility is Denzil Forrester, one of the first Black British artists to graduate from art school with first and second degrees. Born in Grenada in 1956, Forrester came to England at the age of ten. After completing his BA at the Central School of Art and his MA at the Royal College of Art, he won the Rome Scholarship in 1983, followed by the Harkness Scholarship which took him to New York for eighteen months. Historically, Forrester has taken as his subject the twin themes of reggae/dub dance hall and the music, sights, sounds, and movement of carnival. At times, his work has touched on other themes, such as deaths in police custody. His canvasses – often large, oversize affairs – range from dark, brooding and sometimes menacing works, through to bright, liberated paintings resonating with bright and vibrant colours. Sometimes, the scenes he depicts are located in low light, almost tomb-like or nocturnal environments. On other occasions, much like carnival itself, Forrester takes the focus of his attention to the streets, allowing the sun and copious amounts of light, into his paintings.

Perhaps one of the most important features of Forrester's work is the way in which, inadvertently perhaps, it has created a series of historical documents related to the making of Black Britain. The mid to late 1970s and early 1980s saw the burgeoning of the British sound system – mobile, counter-cultural reggae enterprises characterized by dub music, MCs, DJs, and fiercely partisan followings of young Black people, primarily males. The clubs and other venues in which sound systems operated are graphically depicted and fondly recalled in Forrester's paintings. Similarly, Forrester's paintings have captured the tension and the menace of the intrusive and unwelcome policing that was often a feature of how society viewed Black cultural expressions, particularly those influenced by Rastafari and the attendant 'dread' lifestyle and habits. In his painting *Domino Hunters* Forrester depicts a club scene, complete with prancing revellers and carousing youth. The painting's unsettling elements take the form of two motionless police officers, menacingly and with no apology conducting surveillance; the embodiment of menace.

Forrester was one of a number of Black British artists to exhibit at the Bhownagree Gallery of the Commonwealth Institute, Kensington High Street, London, his exhibition taking place from 4 to 28 April 1986, some three years after he graduated from the RCA. The brief text on the accompanying exhibition poster/brochure was as follows:

> Denzil Forrester, who is originally from the West Indian island of Grenada, now lives and works in London. The contrast between grey, urbanised London and the colour of Grenada inspires him in his painting. Other influences include the London blues clubs that play Reggae music and the carnivals of Grenada with their crowds, noises and movements.
>
> In his works are crowded images with spaces between them that at times echo the music of blues clubs and at other times are reminiscent of blue sky as seen through a green, leafy forest. Tranquil moments occurring within a

complex and cluttered environment is a theme that runs throughout his paintings.

Whilst a number of Black artists of the 1980s embraced collage as their medium of choice, its cut and mix, tear and paste aesthetic being particularly suited to the conveying of these practitioners' exigent messages, other artists such as Douglas Camp and Forrester distinguished themselves as bona fide *sculptors* and *painters* respectively, though their practices were certainly no less diligent in the communicating of pressing, demanding, messages, conveyed with artistic maturity. The same can be said of Eugene Palmer, the third of a sizeable body of artists conspicuous by their absence from memorials to the 1980s. Like Forrester, Palmer was Caribbean-born, in his case, the island of Jamaica. Like Forrester, he too came to the UK as a child.

Palmer was one of the most accomplished and innovative painters to have emerged into practice during the period of the late 1970s to early 1980s. Born in Kingston, Jamaica in 1955, he came to England in 1966, completing an Art Foundation course in Birmingham in the mid-1970s, before going on to secure a degree from Wimbledon School of Art in 1978. This was followed, a few years later, with a Teaching Certificate from Garnett College, London, and an MA in Painting from Goldsmiths College, in the mid-1980s. A significant period of solo shows then followed, at venues including Bedford Hill Gallery, where Palmer exhibited in 1988 (this was the venue for Yinka Shonibare's debut solo exhibition, the following year). Palmer's work was, in the late 1970s, twice included in *The New Contemporaries*, and his paintings were included in a number of group exhibitions, including *Caribbean Expressions in Britain* in the mid-1980s and, a couple of years later, *Black Art: Plotting the Course*, which looked at the nature of Black artists' issue-based practice in the closing years of the 1980s decade.

Palmer's earliest works were excursions into the terrain of form, colour, composition and shape – non-figurative practice. Within time however, Palmer moved towards figuration, firstly in a fairly loose form, but increasingly, over the years, towards a tighter, more pronounced and explicit type of highly figurative painting. Within his work of the late 1980s, Palmer offered absorbing assessments and interpretations of Britain, Empire, history, and Black identity. As such, his practice was reflective of his own background, having been born in Jamaica at a time in which the island was, along with others in the Caribbean, a Crown colony. Within seven years of Palmer's birth, Jamaica was of course to secure its independence. But the links with Britain – political, sporting, cultural – among others – would continue through the artist's lifetime, in changing forms. To this end, the image of the British flag figured time and again within Palmer's paintings of this period. Palmer grew up in a period of independence and post-independence euphoria and optimism.

Given the pressing artistic concerns of practitioners such as these, *The Place is Here* contained not one jot or one tittle about Douglas Camp, Forrester, Palmer, et al. Their absences (and of course, those of many others) gave a somewhat accelerated and exaggerated profile to the artists collected together for the display. This point is not an argument for *The Place is Here* to have showcased a numerically greater body of practitioners than the thirty or so it represented. It is a curatorial (and indeed, a mathematical) fact that the greater the number of artists in an exhibition, the slimmer their individual contributions. My belief is that a radically different selection of the same or a lesser number of practitioners could just as easily lay claim to representing Black visual arts activity of the 1980s, particularly given that a number of artists in *The Place is Here* had seen to it that they were, year in, year out, ceaselessly associated with the decade. Related, the skewed selection of artists simultaneously threw into sharp relief the limitations of the archive and highlighted the degree to which, whoever owns the archive could be said to own history. *The Place is Here* had a display of contextualizing material drawn from the archives of the Blk Art Group Research Project; African-Caribbean, Asian & African Art in Britain Archive (Chelsea College of Arts Library, University of the Arts); the June Givanni Pan African Cinema Archive; the archive with which Himid was particularly associated, the Making Histories Visible Archive (housed at her own institution, the University of Central Lancashire); and the Stuart Hall Library, Iniva (Institute of International Visual Arts), London. In comprehending the vitrines of archival material, one sensed that again, sharp elbows had been in use, insofar as much of the material displayed was calculated to reinforce the idea that the 1980s belonged to the practices, histories and curatorial endeavours of certain artists alone. For certain, had the personal archives of artists such as Douglas Camp, Forrester, Palmer, Tam Joseph, et al. been used, the historical narratives presented would have been markedly different yet no less authoritative.

Beyond question, the artist who gained most from the fetishization of the 1980s was Himid, and *The Place is Here* pretty much functioned as a major outing of Himid's work, as much as, or more than, it might have functioned as a *group* exhibition. This much was evident to Louisa Buck, who, writing in the *Telegraph* on 17 February 2017, declared 'A trio of UK shows shines a light on the under-appreciated hero of black British art.'[33] As mentioned earlier, so ubiquitous was Himid's presence within *The Place is Here* that, together with concurrent displays of her work at Modern Art Oxford,[34] and Spike Island, Bristol[35] (which comprised the trio of exhibitions referred to by Buck), she built up a head of steam that saw her shortlisted for, and eventually winning, the Turner Prize. The oldest work in Himid's Spike Island exhibition dated back to 1999, though the major component was at its core, a work that dated from 2004 – *Naming the Money.* Given the consistency and largely undeviating aesthetics of Himid's work, from the early 1980s onwards, the awarding to her of the Turner

Prize in 2018 possibly said more about the fetishization of the 1980s than it did about any inherent developments in her practice. During the 1980s, the Museum of Modern Art, Oxford (the previous incarnation of Modern Art Oxford) distinguished itself by its steadfast refusal to acknowledge Black British artists, choosing instead to focus its energies on exhibiting the work of artists of colour drawn from elsewhere in the world, in a range of deeply problematic exhibitions.[36]

A couple of years after Himid's Modern Art Oxford exhibition, the gallery turned its attention to another artist seemingly shackled to the 1980s, Claudette Johnson. After an extended period of time during which her work was seen, enjoyed and appreciated by relatively few people, a major outing of her highly distinctive drawings took place during 2019 at Modern Art Oxford. *I Came to Dance* was heralded as 'Intimate, powerful and sometimes deliberately uncomfortable, Claudette Johnson's studies of black men and women demand attention and command respect. This show is an overview of one of the most accomplished figurative artists working in Britain today, and the first major institutional solo exhibition since 1990 of London-based artist Claudette Johnson (born 1959, Manchester).'[37] One of the principal problems with an exhibition such as *I Came to Dance* and the ways in which Modern Art Oxford described it was that, conspicuous by its absence, was any reference as to *why* Johnson's work had been subject to a nearly three decades long hiatus. What was it about Johnson's work that deprived gallery-going audiences, for the greater part of three decades, of substantial, stand-alone opportunities to see and appreciate her work? For numbers of Black British artists, sometime adulation might be order of the day, but frank honest reasons for years or decades in the wilderness amounting to a functional obscurity for certain artists, are pretty much impossible to come by, not least from those in control of gallery spaces such as Modern Art Oxford.

The tone of some of the essays in the accompanying catalogue didn't do much, if anything at all, to ask searching questions of Modern Art Oxford. Instead, several texts ramped up, excavated, and spun out Johnson's early 1980s moments, as if this period alone could offer defining context. One text reproduced page after page of the *The First National Black Art Convention* programme, even though it and other such material was freely available online. The catalogue's essays tended to leave us wondering why Johnson had been subject to such a bruising and invisible-izing decades-long career hibernation, and why (to mix metaphors) she had, momentarily at least, been brought in from the wilderness. It was as if the predictable rehashing of the 1980s was more than enough to contextualize the artist. 1980s. 'Nuff said.

The Turner Prize, Britain's most well-known award for contemporary artists, was established in the mid-1980s, at precisely the moment in which Black British artists of a younger generation were emerging into certain types of visibility. Even so, successive groups of Turner Prize judges remained steadfastly unimpressed or uninterested in what these artists were doing. Indeed, it took a while for the prize to be awarded to an artist who was not white (Anish Kapoor, 1991) and it took nearly a further decade for the prize to be awarded to British-born Black artists (Chris Ofili, 1998, and Steve McQueen, 1999, who were in many respects being rewarded for the distances they had created between themselves and many in the previous generation of Black artists).[38] Recognition of prolific practitioners of the 1980s 'Black Art' generation was in this respect, long overdue. (In 1997 I had reviewed Piper's then recent Iniva-sponsored midcareer retrospective at the Royal College of Art, Gulbenkian Galleries, that took place between 18 July and 13 August 1997. In my review, I had lamented, 'That the artist has never been shortlisted for the Turner Prize is shocking.')[39] What could though, be described as a retrospective awarding of the Turner Prize to Himid, an artist in her mid-sixties, owed more to changing art world attitudes to the 1980s than anything else. In the same ways in which the cultural zeitgeist declared 2012 to be the suitable moment in which to revisit a Black artists' gathering that had happened some thirty years previously, one understands that within the irrational but omnipresent moment of 1980s celebration, the time had come to recognize an artist who had, from the 1980s onwards, consistently presented herself in pronounced proximity to that particular decade.

The news of Himid's Turner Prize victory was greeted with widespread enthusiasm. Pretty much the only person to put his head above the parapet and express sentiments that oscillated between scepticism, indifference and condemnation was Rasheed Araeen. Of course, for decade after decade, Araeen had been tabling the view that all bar himself and perhaps a couple of Black artists had been making the wrong sort of progress, so his summation of Himid was perhaps to be expected. In an interview with Virginia Whiles in *Art Monthly*, February 2018, Araeen remained true to type, putting Himid in his crosshairs for failing his particular litmus test, and dismissing her Turner Prize victory as a manifestation of her 'unconditional loyalty to the system and the privileges thus obtain[ed] from it.'[40]

> Now, Himid – in my view, the Turner Prize has always been part of the media circus, which you have to enter to be a successful artist. Himid's success in this respect is not unusual. She has always wanted to be a successful artist, and I have no hesitation in wishing her good luck. But to confuse her success with a struggle for equality for all (black) women is a travesty, to say the least because this ignores an important background to her success.

Araeen continued to wax lyrical, citing the 1980s' context of the emergence of Himid's practice:

> In the 1980s, it was quite fashionable for some self-styled feminists to have a go at men instead of the system which produces and maintains male power.

> Himid's early work also emerged from this context, with some support from white liberals of the art establishment. She was subsequently awarded an MBE some years ago, an award particularly given to those 'BAME'[41] people who can act as functionaries of the system, if not the Empire, which is still there and is responsible for the catastrophe in the Middle East. I'm not saying that people like Himid may be aware of this connection or that they should be considered responsible for what the system does, particularly globally. However, when they are aware of this connection, they often maintain an ignorance or lack of understanding of it, so as to maintain their unconditional loyalty to the system and the privileges they thus obtain from it.[42]

Before moving on from Himid, Araeen (who had included her in his 1989 exhibition, *The Other Story*), couldn't resist tabling one final criticism, drawing Himid's success into dialogue with what he saw as the antics of the Tate. 'Himid is now being institutionally promoted because she is, racially, an African and a woman, and as an artist she creates what is expected from a black woman artist, which fits into Tate's 'cultural diversity' programme.'[43] If Araeen had been the only one to put his head above the parapet in his comments on Himid winning the Turner Prize, Richard Hylton was in turn the only one to put his head above the parapet in responding to Araeen's positioning of himself. Hylton responded to the interview with Araeen with a certain incredulity. Among his comments:

> Can it really be the case that, in terms in 'black consciousness' and 'the black struggle' in British art, all roads lead to one solitary figure? Not only does this position appear contradictory to the very notion of collective struggle, it also appears contradictory to the arguments and changes Araeen has so relentlessly pursued since the 1970s. At the present time, when historical revisionism vis-à-vis black British artists appears particularly, if only fleetingly, pronounced, would it not be more instructive to open up rather than close down ideas of history?[44]

For good measure, *Art Monthly* had appended a 'reply' to Hylton's letter, from Whiles, in which she conceded 'I agree full heartedly with your critique of my interview with Rasheed Araeen.'[45]

Nowhere in any of the adulation and fetishization of the 1980s was there any acknowledgement of a simple *uncomfortable truth*: that it was under the punishing, dreary and endlessly miserable years of Thatcherism and its cuts cuts cuts that Black British artists had a particularly fertile and creative period of activity. From Shaheen Merali's operating, between 1990 and 1993, of the One Spirit Batik Workshop and Gallery, in Haringey, North London, to Yinka Shonibare's early solo exhibition at the Bedford Hill Gallery in South London in 1989; from the founding of The Black-Art Gallery in Finsbury Park in 1983, to various exhibitions at Brixton Art Gallery at the other end of the Victoria Line, the 1980s was indeed a decade packed with no end of different types of Black artists' activity. These references are of course to a far broader range of artists than the skewed body of practitioners in *The Place is Here*, taken to represent a particular group of artists but in reality, doing no such thing. The attendant irony of the curatorial framing of *The Place is Here* was that, for all the mannerism of Tony Blair's New Labour government (taking over in 1997, after nearly two decades of Conservative rule), and its concerted attempts to foster a particularly British brand of multiculturalism, diversity and inclusivity, this contrived climate seemingly left very little in its wake worth reflecting on, as far as the practices of the wider body of Black British artists was concerned.[46]

Everywhere one turned in beholding fetishized manifestations of the 1980s, one came across the same small coterie of sharp-elbowed artists who seemingly had few if any questions to ask about the whereabouts of the art and artists who had been pushed to one side, forgotten or overlooked. These omissions were one of the most galling and troublesome aspects of the fetishization of the 1980s. The challenge is of course for art historians of the present and indeed, those of the future, not to be swayed or taken in by these caricatures of the 1980s and to pursue research that creates and offers altogether more nuanced, credible histories and sidesteps, rather than indulges, the self-appointed coterie of me me me artists.[47]

'The Fetishization of the 1980s' is a new, previously unpublished text.

Notes

1 See Ian Baucom, David A. Bailey and Sonia Boyce, 'Introduction', *Shades of Black: Assembling Black Arts in 1980s Britain*, Duke University Press in collaboration with Institute of International Visual Arts and African and Asian Visual Artists' Archive, 2005: xii.

2 See Baucom, Bailey, Boyce, *Shades of Black.*

3 In this respect, Keith Piper's then recent Iniva-sponsored midcareer retrospective at the Royal College of Art, Gulbenkian Galleries, was something of a last hurrah. Taking place between 18 July and 13 August 1997, this central London exhibition of Piper's work came with a substantial catalogue.

4 For a discussion of these changes see Eddie Chambers, *Things Done Change: The Cultural Politics of Recent Black Artists in Britain*, Amsterdam and New York: Rodopi, 2012. Chapter Three, 'Chris, Steve, and Yinka: We Run Tings' discusses the rise to fame, and respective artistic practices of Ofili, McQueen, and Shonibare.

5 *Evening Standard* – Thursday 4 January, 1990 p.25. Sewell's review drew a response from one John Binek, who penned a letter to the Evening Standard that was published on 9 January 1990. Given the heading of 'Art in black and white', Binek protested, 'I was saddened to read Brian Sewell's piece (Black pride and prejudice, 4 January) on *The Other Story* exhibition at the Hayward Gallery, I have seldom seen a review so prejudiced and in such bad taste. . . To those of us who do not have the opportunity to visit all galleries and museums Mr Sewell mentions it was an opportunity to see something new. Mr Sewell would have done better to tell us about the pictures and to spare us his bitterness. . . .'

6 Keith Piper, in his text for *Shades of Black*, was something of a lone voice in identifying and being troubled by the dominant framings of the 1980s that were, in 2005, beginning to take shape, gather pace, and become something of an unstoppable bandwagon. Wrote Piper, 'The 1980s [. . .] remains for us a difficult decade. They seem to be presented as the source of a fully formed and uncontested narrative package [. . .] Much less common is a presentation of the 1980s as a historical space that has yet to be fully narrativised and appraised by drawing on the multiple remembrances of those who were there and lived the decade. Particularly disturbing for me is the easy and profoundly unreflective use of two grand narrative terms: black art and the Black Arts Movement.' The first of a dozen short quotes that appeared on the poster/brochure accompanying *The Place Is Here*, Nottingham Contemporary, 4 February to 1 May 2017.

7 Caroline Roux, 'Visual Arts – Black British artists get recognition at last: A Nottingham show brings together work from the 1980s that reflects those times' https://www.ft.com/content/067eb27c-e7db-11e6-967b-c88452263daf accessed 3 March 2017.

8 Guy Brett, 'A Reputation Restored', *Tate International Arts and Culture* (March/April 2003), pp. 78–80. The article related to a display of Moody's work that took place at Tate Britain, 24 March–30 May 2003.

9 Roux, 'Visual Arts'.

10 The exhibitions were, *Five Black Women* at the Africa Centre (1983), *Black Woman Time Now* at Battersea Arts Centre (1983–4) and *the Thin Black Line* at the Institute for Contemporary Arts (1985).

11 One particular reviewer, Kelly Burton, had drawn attention to the arguably compromising spaces given to The Thin Black Line, with her review of exhibition, which had been titled 'Hemmed In', *Race Today* magazine, January 1986. p.26.

12 The Aicon Gallery exhibition ran from 29 June–24 July, 2010.

13 The other artists were: Rasheed Araeen, Sonia Boyce, Avinash Chandra, Uzo Egonu, Lubaina Himid, David Medalla, Keith Piper, Saleem Arif Quadri, A J Shemza, F N Souza, and Aubrey Williams.

14 Sonya Dyer, 'CLAUDETTE JOHNSON, Hollybush Gardens, London, UK', *Frieze*, March 2018: 181.

15 Several years after the 2012 gathering, another conference took place that looked to reflect on, and build on, art historical framings of 1980s activity amongst Black British artists. *Framing the Critical Decade: After the Black Arts Movement* conference, was held over two days at the University of Bristol in 2016.

16 The artists in *The Place is Here* were: Said Adrus, John Akomfrah, Rasheed Araeen, Martina Attille, David A. Bailey, Sutapa Biswas, Zarina Bhimji, Black Audio Film Collective, Sonia Boyce, Vanley Burke, Ceddo, Eddie Chambers, Rotimi Fani-Kayode, Joy Gregory, Sunil Gupta, Mona Hatoum, Lubaina Himid, Gavin Jantjes, Claudette Johnson, Isaac Julien, Chila Kumari Burman, Dave Lewis, Mowbray Odonkor, Pratibha Parmar, Maybelle Peters, Keith Piper, Ingrid Pollard, Donald Rodney, Veronica Ryan, Marlene Smith, Maud Sulter. The exhibition was curated by Nick Aikens and Sam Thorne, with Nicola Guy, and was an expanded version of an earlier display curated by Aikens at the Van Abbemuseum, Eindhoven, in 2016, titled *Thinking Back: A Montage of Black Art in Britain.*

17 https://www.nottinghamcontemporary.org/whats-on/the-place-is-here/ (accessed 27 June 2020).

18 Rasheed Araeen, *For Oluwale, 1971–73* (1975).

19 A couple of years after *The Place is Here* exhibition, a major publication bearing as its title the name of the exhibition, was brought out by Sternberg Press. Subtitled *The Work of Black Artists in 1980s Britain*, the weighty publication failed to cast its net wider than the painfully narrow body of the artists who had previously been featured in the exhibition itself.

20 The term originally referring to a man who epitomizes or represents a specified quality, cause, etc.

21 https://news.artnet.com/exhibitions/nottingham-contemporary-black-voices-1980s-uk-824666 accessed 16th May 2018.

22 https://www.theguardian.com/artanddesign/2017/feb/05/the-place-is-here-review-nottingham-contemporary-1980s-britain-black-art-movement accessed 16th May 2018.

23 http://www.studiointernational.com/index.php/the-place-is-here-review-black-british-artists accessed 16th May 2018.

24 https://amuse-i-d.vice.com/surveying-black-british-art-in-the-80s/ no longer accessible online.

25 An evaluation of the press and media's coverage of Black artists' exhibitions during the 1980s falls beyond the scope of this paper, but for a consideration of this subject, see my doctoral study, Eddie Chambers, *The Emergence and Development of Black Visual Arts Activity in England Between 1981 and 1986: Press and Public Responses*, Goldsmiths College, University of London, 1998.

26 Waldemar Januszczak, 'Anger at hand', review of *The Thin Black Line*, the *Guardian*, 27 November 1985, page 23.

27 *Into the Open: New Paintings Prints and Sculpture by Contemporary Black Artists* - Clement Bedeau, Sonia Boyce, Eddie Chambers, Pogus Caesar, Shakka Dedi, Uzo Egonu, Lubaina Himid, Gavin Jantjes, Claudette Johnson, Tom (as he was then known) Joseph, Juginder Lamba, Bill Ming, Tony Moo Young, Ossie Murray, Houria Niati, Ben Nsusha, Pitika Ntuli, Keith Piper, Ritchie Riley, Veronica Ryan and Jorge Santos. Mappin Art Gallery, 4 August–9 September 1984. The exhibition toured to two other venues, Castle Museum, Nottingham, 16 September–21 October 1984 and Newcastle Media Workshops, 2–30 November 1984.

28 Waldemar Januszczak, 'Black Art', review of *Into the Open*, the *Guardian*, 13 August 1984, p.9.

29 *Blk Art Group 1983–1984*, Graves Art Gallery, Sheffield, invitation card.

30 Such a framing was partial and ultimately disingenuous, because it failed to appreciate the degree to which it was the 1970s, rather than the 1980s, that generated so many of the terms of reference utilized by so many artists of the 1980s. The Brixton riots of 1981 had indeed shaken London, but it was the Ladbroke Grove riots in 1976 that shook not only London, but the country, and brought to the fore the grievances and fractious existences of so many Black British youngsters. The Conservative government was indeed outspokenly anti-immigrant, but Thatcher and her ilk had in many respects done little more than co-opt the language and the politics of the National Front, a far-right network (intent on *Keeping Britain White* and enacting repatriation) that was at a particularly prolonged moment of strength and influence in the mid to late 1970s – a time of a Labour government.

31 Roux, 'Visual Arts'.

32 For a discussion of the factors that led to the pronounced creativity of Black Britain during the 1980s, see Eddie Chambers, *Roots & Culture: Cultural Politics in the Making of Black Britain*, I B Tauris & Co. Ltd, London and New York, 2017.

33 https://www.telegraph.co.uk/luxury/art/lubaina-himid-trio-uk-shows-shines-light-under-appreciated-hero/?WT.mc_id=tmg_share_tw accessed 18 May 2018.

34 Lubaina Himid: *Invisible Strategies*, Modern Art Oxford, 21 January – 30 April 2017.

35 Lubaina Himid: *Navigation Charts*, Spike Island, Bristol, 20 January – 26 March 2017.

36 For a discussion of this, see an exhibition review by Eddie Chambers of 'Makonde' exhibition at Museum of Modern Art, Oxford, *Art Monthly*, London, Number 129, September 1989: 18–20. This review received hostile written responses from several people involved with the 'Makonde' exhibition. The sequence of post-review *Art Monthly* correspondence was as follows:

October 1989 issue: response from Jeremy Coote
November 1989 issue: responses from David Elliott and Michael Stephen
December 1989/January 1990 issue: my reply to Coote, Elliott and Stephen
February 1990: Elliott response to my reply

At this point, *Art Monthly* terminated the correspondence.

37 https://www.modernartoxford.org.uk/event/claudette-johnson/ (accessed 2 September 2019).

38 For more on this, see Eddie Chambers, *Things Done Change: The Cultural Politics of Recent Black Artists in Britain*, Amsterdam and New York: Rodopi, 2012. Chapter Four in particular, 'Coming in From the Cold: Some Black Artists Are Embraced' discusses Black artists and the Turner Prize.

39 Eddie Chambers, 'Keith Piper: Relocating the Remains', exhibition review of mid-career retrospective held at Upper and Lower Gulbenkian Galleries, Royal College of Art, London. *Art Monthly*, London, Number 209, September 1997: 43–44.

40 Rasheed Araeen Interviewed by Virginia Whiles, *Art Monthly* February 2018, No. 413, pages 1–5 (page 5).

41 BAME was an abbreviation of the latest government-sanctioned nomenclature to describe people of colour in Britain – 'Black and Minority Ethnic'.

42 Rasheed Araeen Interviewed by Virginia Whiles, pages 4–5.

43 Rasheed Araeen Interviewed by Virginia Whiles, page 5.

44 Richard Hylton, 'Letters', *Art Monthly* February 2018, No. 415, page 19.

45 Virginia Whiles, 'Letters', *Art Monthly* February 2018, No. 415, page 19.

46 For a consideration and chronicling of institutional and governmental funding of Black artists over several decades, and the undulating fortunes that resulted from this varying attention, see Richard Hylton, *The Nature of the Beast: Cultural Diversity and the Visual Arts Sector – A Study of Policies, Initiatives and Attitudes 1976–2006*, published by the Institute of Contemporary Interdisciplinary Arts, University of Bath, 2007.

47 For Black British artists caught up in the fetishization of the 1980s, this nostalgic, backward-looking, unimaginative reading of the period proved itself to be the only game in town, as regards opportunities to have their work seen. For more on the historical hemming in of Black artists' practices, see Eddie Chambers, *Things Done Change: The Cultural Politics of Recent Black Artists in Britain*, Amsterdam and New York: Rodopi, 2012, in particular, 'Introduction: You were the future once' and Chapter One, 'The only thing to look forward to . . . is the past'.

Chapter 6

Black-British Artists and Problems of Systemic Invisibility and Eradication: Creating Exhibition Histories of That Which Is Not There

I would like to begin by contextualizing my own involvement in the narratives I will discuss. I entered art school in the late 1970s, and shortly thereafter began to work with a loose association of young artists and art students, on a series of exhibitions and other activities that took place between 1981 and 1984. I came of age, and entered art school, at a time when tens of thousands of other young Black-British people were similarly emerging into adulthood, looking to make sense of their identities. We were the children of Caribbean migrants, who had been born and brought up as part of the British Empire. Coming to Britain, 'the Mother Country', these migrants – my parents, our parents – took up oftentimes unsettled residence in their adopted homeland. They gave birth to a generation of children who would be the first to grow up embodying an uneasy, curious, yet dynamic state of Black-Britishness. As much as anything else, my own personal history, and the history of tens of thousands of others, speaks of the formation and evolution of Black Britain. Given this, it is perhaps not surprising that so much of my own art, and the art of the others with whom I worked, touched upon pronounced notions of history and identity.

Being acutely aware of one's own 'history' leads, in some respects, to a wider consciousness of the ways in which a certain history is absent from dominant historical narratives. The widespread absence of Black artists from British art history is symptomatic of a wider invisible-ising of Black people from British history, society, presumed identity, and so on. Somewhat dispiritingly, it is largely in sports and entertainment that Black-British people achieve greatest visibility. The arenas of sport and music are where Black people most frequently acquire any sort of honorary Britishness. Consequently, there are formidable challenges facing those of us seeking to establish wider histories of postwar exhibition activity in Britain – histories that properly address and acknowledge the contributions made by not only my own generation of practitioners, but also preceding, and subsequent ones. One of the first things that might strike the would-be researcher is the extent to which the contributions made by Black artists are routinely, historically, systemically disregarded or omitted from dominant narratives. Such omissions are wholly out of sync with the realties of Black-British artists' contributions.

From the late-twentieth century onward, exhibition histories of Black-British artists reveal the extent to which they enjoyed periods of acclaim, exposure and acceptance.[1] At times, such as the early-1960s and the mid-1980s, it seemed as if such practitioners were well established, featuring, as they sometimes did, in important group exhibitions, solo shows, and so on. But Black-British artists – both immigrant and British-born – have found that within a few years of any given period of exposure, precious little 'evidence' relating to said exposure exists or remains. So exhibitions that took place in London in the early 1960s are as emphatically erased as the wider range of exhibitions that took place in the mid-1980s. How does one set about creating or establishing exhibition histories of that which is not there, or no longer there? With both artists and work being vulnerable to systemic omission from histories of exhibition activity, art historians such as myself are perhaps dealing with 'absence' as much as, or even more so, than that which has an irrefutable 'presence'.

These are by no means abstract concerns. The decade of the 1980s is widely regarded as a particular high point in the visibility of Black-British artists. Three examples to consider here: In 1985, Lubaina Himid presented 'The Thin Black Line' exhibition of work by Black women artists, at the ICA in Central London. Although the exhibition was presented in what some considered as peripheral spaces beyond the main ICA exhibition galleries, it was, nonetheless, the first time that this prestigious London venue had shown a considerable amount of work by Black-British artists. Within less than a year, the Whitechapel Art Gallery presented 'From Two Worlds', a gallery-wide exhibition that showcased contributions by those regarded as being at the forefront of Black-British artists' practice. This was the first time the Whitechapel had taken such a pronounced interest in this body of practitioners, which included Gavin Jantjes, Sokari Douglas Camp, Denzil Forrester and Keith Piper. In 1988, Sonia Boyce was the first ever Black-British artist to have a solo exhibition at the Whitechapel Art Gallery. Given the longstanding presence of Black artists in London, such 'firsts' have tended to be a long time coming. The first solo exhibition by a Black-British artist at the Serpentine Gallery was by Chris Ofili in 1998. The first one at the ICA was by Steve McQueen, in 1999. Somewhat ironically, although London is the home to the largest concentration of Black-British artists, London exhibition spaces have demonstrated the greatest resistance to embracing them, particularly as individual practitioners.

But while Ofili, McQueen and one or two others went on to ever greater levels of success and visibility within relatively short periods of time, precious little 'evidence' exists of the contributions made by the vast majority of Black-British artists. Many of them – some with once-impressive CVs – have passed into obscurity, or what I would describe as 'functioning obscurity'. While this might well be the fate of all manner of artists, the rendering invisible or peripheral of Black-British artists' exhibition activity not only has grave consequences, but also poses formidable challenges, for researchers and art historians alike.

The reasons for the apparent neglect of Black-British artists in so much of art history are seldom straightforward or easy to identify. In many respects, one has to begin by considering the extent to which only a very small proportion of artists ever achieve any sort of tangible recognition. At any one time, hundreds of thousands of people across the country would regard themselves as artists. If we look further afield, there are literally millions of people across the world who would regard themselves as artists, and aspire to have their work bought for collections, exhibited in important galleries, written about in adulatory terms in art journals, and be inscribed in the canon of art history. But the art world only ever recognises a few artists at a time: the favoured few achieve varying degrees of celebrity status, while the majority of artists struggle (often in vain) to achieve any visibility. It is when what we might call a *racial* dimension is brought to bear, that the results of this partiality create such adverse effects for Black-British artists.

Recovering Forgotten/Erased Histories

Black artists have seldom been accorded the right to simply be 'just' artists, and to be exhibited and interacted with accordingly. Instead of the art world adopting what we might call a 'colour-blindness,' it more often insists that Black artists can and must only show up in exhibitions and art projects that set them apart from the wider body of practitioners, and simultaneously de-emphasise their individuality. A number of artists have struggled to escape this ethnic quarantining, but it is an uncomfortable certainty that many Black artists have achieved their most pronounced visibility in 'Black' exhibitions, or in festivals and commemorations that have an explicit or implicit 'raced' agenda. In this sense, it could well be that the exhibitions referred to earlier – 'The Thin Black Line', and 'From Two Worlds' contained the seeds of their own marginalization; by presenting artists not as individual practitioners deserving of exposure, but as 'Black' artists somehow in need of separate (and group) treatment. White culture tends not to regard itself as 'raced' in the ways that Black culture is regarded, which leads to a systemic and perennial problem for individual Black artists – that of being perceived and utilised as apparent representatives of ethnicity and cultural practices that are supposedly reflective of their cultural or racial heritage, rather than simply being framed as 'artists' in their own right. The formidable and systemic framing of Black artists in this way means, in effect, that they are kept away from mainstream British art and art history.

Notwithstanding the skewed pathologies that saw the bulk of Black artists being accorded separate treatment, there are no acceptable reasons why they should have been so comprehensively left out of dominant histories of British art. But for Black artists' histories to assert or claim inclusion in British art history means that the would-be researcher has to do an almost inordinate amount of digging. One might assume that such investigation is not unusual for those who may have been practising in Britain a century or more ago. The reality is that Black artists of all periods – even very recent ones – have found themselves vulnerable to being ignored, forgotten or omitted. We might expect to do a certain amount of sleuthing to uncover information about Ronald Moody, the Jamaica-born sculptor who set up his studio in London, and then Paris, and then London again, in the 1930s and 1940s. But we might have to do a similar (or sadly, a greater) amount of it to uncover histories of artists practising in the 1970s, the 1980s, and even in the years since then. With all but a very small proportion of Black artists coming and going with barely a trace, trying to build a substantial history of Black-British artists is indeed a particularly difficult task.

The absence of Black artists from major books and catalogues of British art is a somewhat circular occurrence. The view, openly expressed up until the 1980s, was that Black artists didn't really exist. After all, how could they, when there was precious little 'evidence' of them in books, galleries and museums? Thus, Black artists have found their absence reinforced, time and again, leading to the persistent impression that they did not really 'exist'. The art world would look very different if successive generations of Black artists had not been kept out in the cold, decade after decade.

In seeking to contribute to the research and establishment of more substantial and credible histories of Black artists in the UK, one is faced with a number of difficulties and issues of not knowing. No one knows when the first artists of African, Asian or Caribbean origin made their way to Britain. It could have been 100 years ago, it could have been several centuries ago, it could have been earlier than that. Simply put, we don't know, because either no records were made, or no records were kept within reach of subsequent generations of researchers and scholars. There is a terrible burden of invisibility and eradication that history has bequeathed the Black-British artist. Setting aside what we don't know leaves us with what we do know, and we know for certain that a substantial history of Black artists practising in Britain can be traced back to at least as early as the 1920s, with the arrival in Britain of previously-mentioned Jamaican-born Ronald Moody, who would go on to become a much-respected pioneer figure in the sort of histories that are so vulnerable.

Perhaps most alarmingly, what might be called an erasure of Black-British artists continues right up to the present time. As both an example and a consequence of this, even many Black artists who emerged in the 1990s have disappeared from view. The overwhelming body of material and knowledge on Black-British artists remains subject to the same sorts of adverse pressures and conditions that have existed in this country for centuries, when it comes to the contributions of certain artists and people. The problem of the invisible-ising of Black-British artists has other, equally alarming dimensions. In a great many instances, not even the scantiest records of important exhibitions taking place in decades such as the 1970s, have been produced or kept in safe custody. While being mindful not to cast researchers and art historians as the sole gatekeepers of knowledge, it is certainly the case that a paucity of historical information on Black-British artists translates into, or corresponds with, a scarcity of general *awareness* of said artists.

Consequences and Implications of Erasure

Little is generally known, for example, about an important exhibition, 'Afro-Caribbean Art' that took place in 1978 in London and included work by Frank Bowling, Lubaina Himid (her first documented exhibition), Donald Locke, and Eugene Palmer. My earliest involvement in organising exhibitions dates, as mentioned earlier, to 1981, when, together with a small group of other young artists and art students, I organized an exhibition titled 'Black Art an' done' at Wolverhampton Art Gallery. The exhibition took place just a few years after 'Afro-Caribbean Art'. And yet, I knew absolutely nothing about that exhibition. *Not knowing* means that when it comes to the work of certain artists, every year is a sort of Year Zero. The history of Black artists' exhibitions in Britain might look significantly different if artists had more effectively been able to build upon, or acknowledge, what had gone before.

In excavating hidden, forgotten and obscured exhibition histories, one is struck by the extent to which Black and African artists are particularly vulnerable to periodically being cast as 'new'. Consequently, as mentioned earlier, Black artists suffer the vexatious consequences of problematic exhibitions of their work containing the seeds of their own marginalization: by presenting artists not simply as practitioners deserving of exposure, but as 'Black' artists somehow in need of separate and somewhat homogenized treatment. Take for example the notion of 'contemporary African art'. In 1969, an exhibition of that title took place at

Camden Art Centre in London. The exhibition cast its artists as pioneers, who through their work could assuage ignorance about Africa and its place in the modern world. But pretty much every large exhibition of contemporary African art that has taken place since 1969 has presented itself in the same sorts of terms. This by and large means that contemporary African art can never be left to exist on its own terms - as a consistent part of mainstream exhibition activity - but must instead wait to be exhibited as part of some or other spectacular undertaking of the 'new', every one or two decades.

This template of newness was liberally applied to the generation of Black-British artists to emerge during the 1980s. The consequences of this mirrored the consequences referred to earlier, of the ways in which contemporary African art has been framed. In 1984, Sheffield Mappin Art Gallery mounted what is recognized as the first major exhibition of Black-British artists to be presented by a major UK gallery. The exhibition was titled 'Into the Open' and featured work by some twenty practitioners. (Taking place outside of London, the exhibition lacked the profile and attention of the Black artists' exhibitions at the ICA and the Whitechapel Art Gallery, which took place one or two years later.) But three decades on, a great many of the artists in 'Into the Open' have now returned to, or are languishing in various degrees of obscurity, or the 'functioning obscurity' that I referred to earlier. Ultimately, Black-British artists have found that to be celebrated for newness is to be damned with faint praise.

In examining archival documents relating to Black-British artists, (particularly from the 1970s onwards) the question, 'Where are they now?' is never far from one's mind, such is the speed and regularity with which certain artists pass into relative or absolute obscurity. Other factors, equally dispiriting, must be brought into the consideration of the oftentimes-skewed ways in which so many Black-British artists are ignored or posthumously attended to. A relatively successful artist such as Maud Sulter could pass away with hardly anything in the way of acknowledgement and obituaries. Surprisingly perhaps, Sulter's death passed relatively unremarked, the most substantial obituary appearing in *The Herald*, Glasgow on 22 March 2008, a few weeks after her death. An accomplished and prolific photo-artist, she has effectively been 'invisible-ised' since her premature death. (Although, at the time of writing, a retrospective of her work is taking place at a gallery in Glasgow, assembled on a shoestring budget.)[2]

Another artist to suffer a similar fate of art historical obscurity and anonymity was Brenda Agard. She was born in 1961 and died in 2012, promptly entering into a pre-existing oblivion, as if her stellar contributions were somehow insignificant and unimportant. Agard was though, a familiar and consistent presence in the exhibitions of the mid-1980s that reflected the emergence of a new generation of Black-British artists, and deserves to be recognized as such. In effect, a large number of artists who have made important contributions to the history of Black

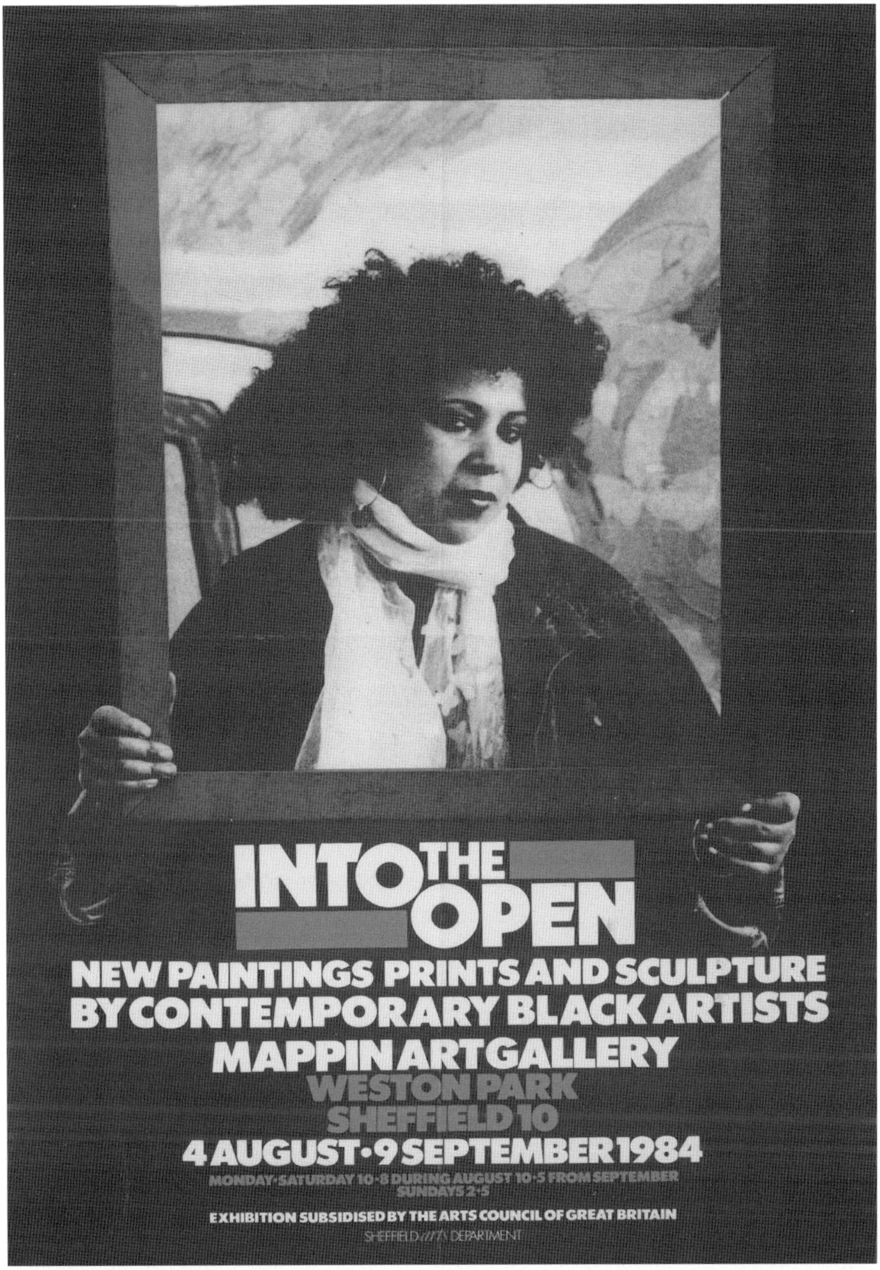

Figure 6.1 Poster with portrait of Houria Niati, for the exhibition *Into the Open: New paintings, prints and sculptures by contemporary Black artists*, Mappin Art Gallery, Sheffield, 1984, selected by Lubaina Himid and Pogus Caesar.

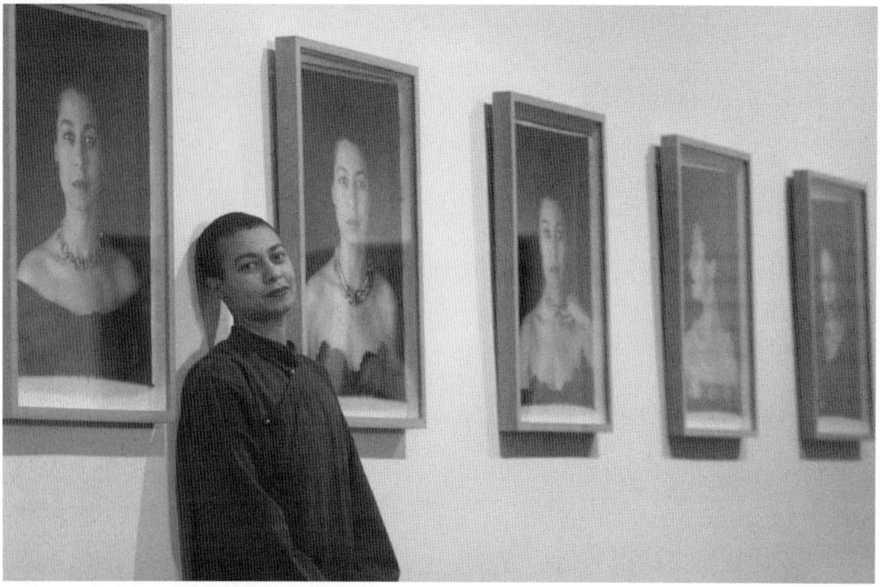

Figure 6.2 Photograph of Maud Sulter, used in the *Herald*, Glasgow, obituary of Sulter, written by Robyn Marsack, 22 March 2008. Image credit © the Herald and Times Group.

artists in Britain have passed into obscurity or disappeared from all vestiges of public and professional view. In this regard, Agard's fate is sadly typical.

There are profound consequences for the work of Black artists being accorded scant respect. One final example I wish to cite is The Black-Art Gallery, a space that existed for a period of a decade, between 1983 and 1993. It was located in Finsbury Park, North London and was the venue for significant solo exhibitions by artists such as Keith Piper, Donald Rodney, and Sonia Boyce. A few years ago, I sought to undertake research into the gallery and approached Islington Local History Centre. (The Black-Art Gallery had been revenue funded by Islington Borough Council.) I was told, in an email, that Islington Local History Centre held no records of the gallery. When it was forced to close in 1993, the entire contents of the gallery – its archives, its files, and its catalogues – were discarded or otherwise lost. This means that it is next to impossible for a history of this important gallery to ever be comprehensively assembled.[3]

Considering the dispiriting example of the erasure of any trace of The Black-Art Gallery in official archives, we can never regard any 'history' – be that of 'Black artists' or 'British art' – as being complete or accurate, at least until a process of fundamental art historical recalibration has taken place. In some regard, such progress can only be made when the major centres of learning that form such an important part of British art history start to more determinedly adopt radical revisionist practices that seek to *pluralise*. In addition, it will only happen when the leading curators and gallery/museum directors – and those at

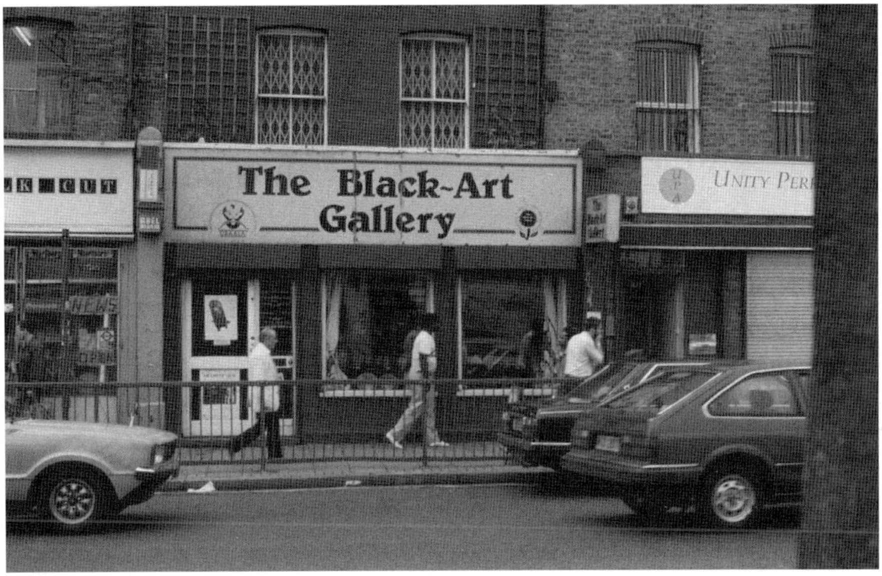

Figure 6.3 The Black-Art Gallery, Seven Sisters Road, Finsbury Park, London, circa mid-1980s, photograph by Eddie Chambers, © Eddie Chambers.

all levels below them – stop regarding Black artists in raced terms, and begin to treat them as individuals, who, irrespective of the content and nature of their work, simply wish to be regarded and treated on its merits.

'Black-British Artists and Problems of Systemic Invisibility and Erasure: Creating exhibition histories of that which is not there', was previously published as a chapter of *The Curatorial Conundrum: What to Study? What to Research? What to Practice?* Bard College Symposium papers, MIT Press/Copublished with the Center for Curatorial Studies Bard College/Luma Foundation, 2016.

Notes

1 Exhibitions and related catalogues such as 'The Other Story', and 'Transforming the Crown' were the earliest attempts to fashion histories of Black artists' practice that spanned several decades. 'The Other Story' was a landmark exhibition, which sought to outline a history of 'Afro-Asian artists in postwar Britain.' The exhibition was curated by Rasheed Araeen and organized by the Hayward Gallery and South Bank Centre, London, in 1989. It featured work of artists such as Araeen himself, Frank Bowling, Sonia Boyce, Uzo Egonu, Ronald Moody, Ahmed Parvez, Ivan Peries, and Li Yuan-chia. 'Transforming the Crown: African, Asian and Caribbean Artists in Britain 1966-1996' was an exhibition curated by Mora Beauchamp-Byrd, and presented by the Caribbean Cultural Center, New York. The exhibition was shown across three venues between October 1997 and March 1998. Several subsequent exhibitions have

sought to enhance understandings of the contributions of individual artists, and have highlighted the historically undulating fortunes of certain artists. See for example, Andrew Dempsey, Gilane Tawadros and Maridowa Williams (eds)., *Aubrey Williams* (London: Institute of International Visual Arts, 1998), and the Mel Gooding monograph, *Frank Bowling* (London: Royal Academy of Art, 2011).

2 *Maud Sulter: Passion*, selected by Deborah Cherry, Street Level Photoworks, Glasgow, 25 April – 21 June 2015. The exhibition was commemorated with a substantial catalogue, printed in an edition of 750, which now serves as an important document on a frequently forgotten artist.

3 Some three years after this text was published, a feature recalling the significance of The Black-Art Gallery was published by *Islington Gazette*, in November 2019. https://www.islingtongazette.co.uk/news/heritage/the-black-art-gallery-the-seven-sisters-road-gallery-at-the-centre-of-the-1980s-black-art-scene-1-6371797. (accessed 27 June 2020).

Chapter 7
Framing Black Art

In terms of its historical parameters, *No Colour Bar: Black British Art in Action 1960–1990* had two predecessors. The first was Rasheed Araeen's *The Other Story* (Hayward Gallery, London, 29 November 1989–4 February 1990), and the second was Mora Beauchamp-Byrd's *Transforming the Crown: African, Asian and Caribbean Artists in Britain 1966–1996* (presented by the Caribbean Cultural Center, New York and shown across three venues: 14 October 1997–15 March 1998, the Studio Museum in Harlem; 15 October 1997–15 March 1998, the Bronx Museum of the Arts; 16 October 1997–15 March 1998, and *Picturing England: The Photographic Narratives of Vanley Burke*, a component of *Transforming the Crown*, the Caribbean Cultural Center.) All three of these historical exhibitions were distinct and unique, though the gap of nearly two decades between *Transforming the Crown* and *No Colour Bar* (more than double the eight years between *The Other Story* and *Transforming the Crown*) possibly speaks to a curatorial ambivalence or a falling out of fashion of larger group exhibitions of Black artists' work that aimed at historical totality or breadth.

A great deal happened to Black artists between the end of the 1980s and the second decade of the 21st century, so it was in many respects correct and appropriate that an exhibition such as *No Colour Bar*, with its broad historical sweep, be presented, particularly since it was able to put forward its historical narratives to generations of artists, art students and gallery-going audiences for whom exhibitions such as *The Other Story* and *Transforming the Crown* were merely historical footnotes rather than active and present memories (if indeed they were known or remembered at all). Amongst the many developments involving Black British artists in the quarter of a century since *The Other Story* were significant solo exhibitions by the likes of Keith Piper; important group exhibitions such as *Mirage: Enigmas of Race, Difference & Desire*, held at the ICA (12 May–16 July 1995), featuring artists such as Steve McQueen showing alongside several African American practitioners; and perhaps most significant of all, the meteoric rise to art world superstardom of McQueen, Chris Ofili, and Yinka Shonibare. The success of these artists was, quite simply, unparalleled, and included Turner Prize wins, representing Britain at the Venice Biennale, and no end of media adulation. We can also put in the mix the establishment of the Arts Council-sponsored Institute of International Visual Arts, more commonly known by its acronym, Iniva, the letters being presented in varying assortments of upper- and/or lower-case letters. Such developments can in some respects be seen as providing a backdrop or context for *No Colour Bar.*

Transforming the Crown had taken as its parameters a three-decade period of the mid-1960s to the mid-1990s, so *No Colour Bar*'s embrace of a similar time frame had about it a certain familiarity. However, one of the unique features of *No Colour Bar* was the way in which it explicitly sought to interweave a narrative between the struggles of Black immigrants to Britain, and visual arts expressions, within the context of the physical exhibition. In seeking to create new art histories (or seeking to contribute to ones previously advanced), *No Colour Bar* refreshingly side-stepped or declined to position itself as any sort of definitive product, or last word undertaking. We might hope that curators of the future are similarly bold in offering histories of Black artists in Britain that admit to a certain partiality or incompleteness. An exhibition such as *No Colour Bar* reminded us of the extent to which history is there to be excavated, to be revisited and indeed, to be contested. In this regard, the strongest and most compelling contributions – curatorial, academic – are those that freely admit to the fragility of Black-British art histories and the extent to which erasure and partial memory are defining problems for curators and the researchers alike.

In appraising exhibitions such as *The Other Story* and *Transforming the Crown*, we are hugely aided by access to the thoughts and arguments of the respective curators, regarding the framing of their products. In this regard, both catalogues are indeed a treasure trove of ideas, histories, artworks, and references to artists, many of whom have been prone or vulnerable to the sorts of erasure mentioned previously. The documenting of Black artists' work is a challenge and a task of incalculable importance. In this regard, even modest catalogues are hugely significant documents and it can be asserted, with some certainty, that the paucity of good and credible published material has hampered efforts to advance the importance of Black British art histories. The recent arrival of a publication such as Sophie Orlando's *British Black Art: Debates on the Western Art History* (Dis Voir, 2016) may go some way to underlining the importance and necessity of troubling the complacent whiteness of British art history, although it must be similarly asserted that publications such as *Passion: Discourses On Blackwomen's Creativity* (edited by Maud Sulter, Urban Fox Press, 1990) or Rasheed Araeen's *Making Myself Visible* (Kala Press, 1984) very much deserve to be rescued from relative obscurity and put within easier reach of the present generation of art students and researchers keen to know more about Black British art histories.

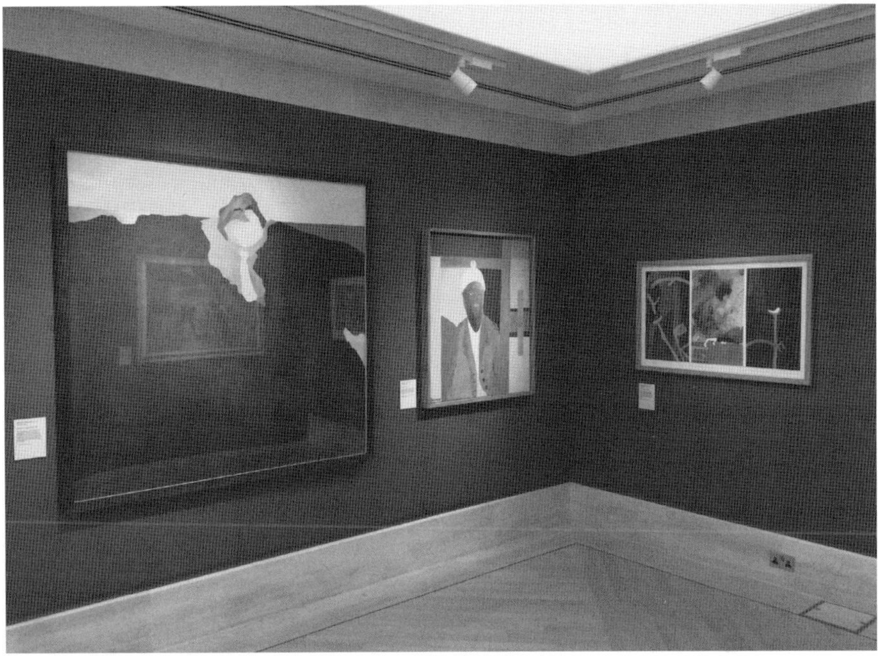

Figure 7.1 Installation view of paintings by Winston Branch, *No Colour Bar: Black British Art in Action 1960–1990*, Guildhall Art Gallery, London, 10 July 2015 – 24 January 2016. © Courtesy Guildhall Art Gallery, City of London, 2015.

To my mind, the central strength of *No Colour Bar* was the way in which it brought to our attention the work of artists who were, to some extent, conspicuous by their absence from an exhibition such as *The Other Story*. Of course, large scale group exhibitions can sometimes result in a relatively meagre representation of individual practitioners, so we should perhaps be thankful that 'The Other Story' or 'Transforming the Crown' (with, respectively, nearly 30 artists and nearly 60 artists) did not contain even greater numbers of practitioners.

One of many important works in *No Colour Bar* was Errol Lloyd's *The Lesson*, (1972, oil on canvas). In some respects, Lloyd's painting might take its place alongside a work such as fellow Jamaican artist Albert Huie's *The Counting Lesson* of 1938. This is largely on account of the ways in which such paintings asserted that literacy and numeracy are vitally important components in the challenge of nation-building and community-building, in the 20th century agendas for progress of peoples of the African diaspora. But whilst Huie's painting could be said to depict a young Black Jamaican girl using her fingers to count, or solve a mathematical puzzle, Lloyd's painting has about it the explicit air, feel and purpose of a distinctly Pan-African agenda of nation building and social advancement.

It is fair to say that Lloyd's painting was, until its recent showing, something of a hidden gem. It is a profound work which, in its own inimitable way, situates itself very much within art historical and social narratives of the early 1970s. The painting depicts a lesson in progress, with an older man as the teacher, and a much younger person as the learner. Seen from something of an aerial, or elevated view, they both occupy a sparse horizontal tricolor of orange-white-orange. The teacher, occupying the bulk of the lower part of the painting, looks on as his pupil, who occupies the upper-right portion of the painting, writes on a hand-held blackboard. Lloyd's painting brings to mind the iconic photograph by Earnest Cole of a young South African boy, determined to learn, as he squats in the somewhat challenging classroom environment, perspiring, but fixed on the endeavour of learning, and making use of his handheld blackboard. Cole's messages are clear: the child might be growing up in the most challenging of apartheid South Africa's circumstances, but he is determined to avail himself of learning as a means to individual, community, and national advancement. Lloyd's young learner has about him a similarly quiet determination, as his teacher looks on approvingly.

It is perhaps the distinctive tam[1] worn by the teacher that tells us much about the painting. Clearly, this is no ordinary teacher, but likely one of those individuals who worked without wider thanks and recognition to supplement the learning of

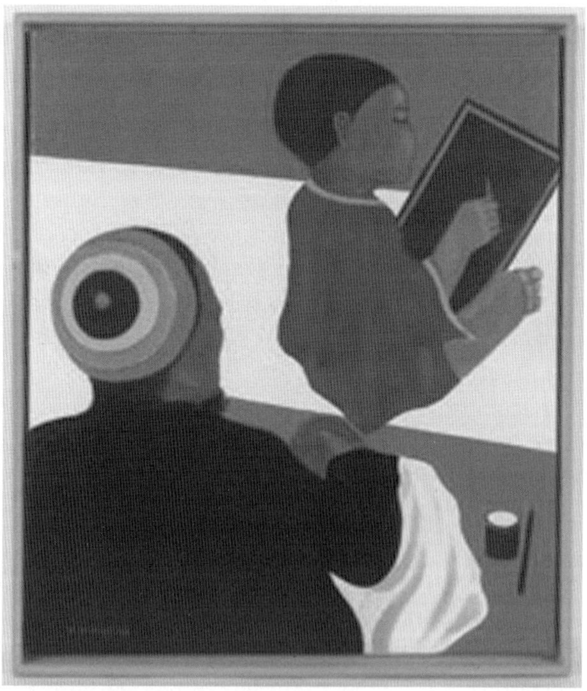

Figure 7.2 Errol Lloyd, *The Lesson*, 1972, oil on canvas, 76 x 61 cm. © Errol Lloyd.

Black children through Saturday schools or other such initiatives that were such an important dimension of Black Britain in the 1970s. It had not taken long for some African-Caribbean immigrants of the 1950s and 1960s to realize that there were things chronically wrong with the state education their children were receiving. Along with sectors such as housing, employment, and healthcare, education was a field in which Caribbean immigrants were being sorely failed. Why were so many children leaving school with such poor qualifications? Why did so many schools appear intent on expelling or suspending Black pupils?

And why was the education system seemingly so determined to exclude Black history from its curricula? These were the sorts of questions asked by many exasperated Black parents, and the Saturday school was perhaps the most familiar strategic response these parents fashioned. Simply put, such makeshift schools were environments where reading, writing and arithmetic were taught within the broader context of an Afrocentric consciousness. Some parents were attracted to the idea that teaching along the lines of what they themselves knew from their respective Caribbean countries was key to their children's educational advancement. Paradoxically perhaps, while many of these parents were convinced that classroom discipline such as they themselves had experienced was crucial to a child's success, they were also aware of the ways in which their children were seemingly singled out for punitive and disproportionate attention by teachers convinced that certain patterns of behaviour by Black children amounted to an insolence or non-conformity that needed to be punished. The Saturday or supplementary school was some parents' response to the miseducation of their children. It is such an environment of learning that Lloyd's singular painting depicts.

Simultaneously, we are obliged to consider the painting's art historical aspects. The teacher's tam puts us in the mind of the target motif, as popularized by American painter Jasper Johns in his iconic 1955 work *Target with Four Faces*. In this era-defining work, Johns utilised the somewhat familiar image of the shooting target, with its rings of concentric circles, but simultaneously gave the image no end of new and intriguing readings. Along with works such as Andy Warhol's *Campbell's Soup Cans* of 1962, Johns' *Target* utilised familiar everyday symbols of American popular and consumer culture to advance new truths and new ways of seeing, critically reading, and appreciating mid-century American conditions.

Lloyd was one of several artists who made work that, consciously or unconsciously, referenced Johns' defining contribution to American art of the mid-20th century. The concentric circles on the teacher's tam were the distinctive tricolour of red, gold and green, but embellished with a circle of black. At a (brush) stroke, Lloyd evoked not only a Rasta-esque sensibility, but also its (and indeed his own) Jamaican origins, the flag of Jamaica comprising the colours green yellow and black. At the time in which Lloyd painted *The Lesson* – the 1970s – red, gold and green had become instant signifiers of a particular type of Black presence. Not only had numerous flags of newly independent African states utilised red, gold and green in a variety of compositions, (primarily as horizontal or vertical tricolours) but the specific use of the colours within the Ethiopian flag (complete with the imperial Lion of Judah in the centre of the ensign), had led to the colours being so insistently worn, displayed and used as adornment by adherents of Rastafari, first in Jamaica and subsequently throughout the international Black world. Within the context of Rastafari and its attendant 'Dread' culture, the red, gold and green colours represented powerful symbolism: red (for the blood of the martyrs), green (for Africa's or Zion's abundant vegetation), and gold (for the wealth of Africa). When Rasta emerged in English cities in the early to mid-1970s, neighbourhoods, buildings and people, were all identified by the presence of these distinctive and dynamic colours. As one commentator noted, the wearing of the colours red, gold and green was a 'visible symbol which denotes the Rasta . . . Often the colours are worn in the form of a knitted hat, but they may also be worn as a badge, as epaulettes, or woven into a cord tied round the waist'.[2] Such sentiments bring us right back to Lloyd's painting; it depicts then, no ordinary teacher, but one steeped in a certain manifestation of Black consciousness. The 1970s were a time of profound racial consciousness, and Lloyd's *The Lesson* speaks to, and of, this consciousness. Lloyd's work was one of several gems within *No Colour Bar*, and it is the historical (coupled with the artistic) value of such works that made this such an important undertaking.

Since *No Colour Bar*, Black British artists have been the focus and attention of a number of initiatives. While successes can be identified, perennial problems of marginalization and vulnerability to erasure continue to be challenges faced by many practitioners. *No Colour Bar* was important in bringing together works that together created a compelling history of perseverance, creativity, and cultural identity.

'Framing Black Art', was first published as an essay in the catalogue *No Colour Bar: Black British Art in Action 1960–1990,* Guildhall Art Gallery, London, 10 July 2015–24 January 2016.

Notes

1 As endnoted in the Vanley Burke text reproduced in this volume, in the mid- to late-1970s (when this particular painting by Lloyd was produced) and for a while thereafter, tams were the preferred cap of choice for Rastas, dreads and males of a particularly Afrocentric inclination. A tam was a round woolen or cloth cap of Scottish origin, which sometimes had a pom-pom in the centre.

2 John Plummer, *Movement of Jah People: The Growth of the Rastafarians*, Birmingham: Press Gang, 1978, p. 38

SECTION TWO

History and Identity

Chapter 8
Section Two Introduction

For much of my work as a curator and writer of art criticism, and then a writer of art history, I found myself wedded to considering the importance of history and identity in the work of artists of the African Diaspora. Of course, other considerations, many other considerations, apply, but time and again, I turn to deliberations on the contexts offered up by history, and the centrality of identity in both the making and the appreciating, of art. The first time I consciously utilized these twin considerations was when I curated *History and identity: Seven Painters*, for Norwich Gallery in 1991. The exhibition brought together work by Said Adrus, Medina Hammad, Godfrey Lee, Mowbray Odonkor, Eugene Palmer, Tony Phillips and Lesley Sanderson. The exhibition marked a personal retreat from curating large-scale group exhibitions and was a staging post toward the solo exhibition format, to which I became, and remained, committed, as a means of presenting artists' work. The texts in this section each animate, in different dimensions, the ways in which history is of such central and foundational importance in framing many artists' practice, be those centuries-old histories or perhaps more recent, postwar histories. As mentioned in my Introduction to *World is Africa*, time and again, I find myself adopting and utilizing musical references, in the titling of some of my texts and other publications, and in the theoretical framing of some of my arguments. For example, I borrowed from the Notorious B.I.G's *Things Done Changed* for the titling and theoretical framing of my 2012 book, *Things Done Change: The Cultural Politics of Recent Black Artists in Britain*. And at the turn of the millennium, I reached for Roy Ayers Ubiquity's 1975 track *2000 Black* for '2000's Got to be Black', an essay in the catalogue for *Beyond the Pale 2000 Adelaide Biennial of Australian Art*, Art Gallery of South Australia, Adelaide, Australia.

Chapter 9
Handsworth Songs and the Archival Image

Seen from the perspective of 2006, *Handsworth Songs* remains a remarkable piece of filmmaking and an astonishingly important and relevant document of cinematography. London-based Black Audio Film Collective made it in 1986. The group's members (in the 1980s) were John Akomfrah (who directed *Handsworth Songs*), Reece Auguiste, Eddie George, Lina Goupaul, Avril Johnson, Trevor Mathison and David Lawson. They were a group of individuals committed to fashioning new types of filmic dialogues, reflective of social, cultural and political developments in 1980s Britain, and equally as importantly, committed to vigorously critiquing a number of then-existing orthodoxies. Such orthodoxies taken to task by Black Audio Film Collective (particularly within *Handsworth Songs*) included the format and the nature of the documentary film, and the privileging of certain accounts or perspectives arising out of the early- and mid- 1980s 'riots' in cities such as London, Birmingham and Liverpool.

The other highly important film and video workshop collective of the period was Sankofa, whose members were Martina Attille, Maureen Blackwood, Isaac Julien and Nadine Marsh Edwards. Together, these two collectives 'insisted on shifting the terms of avant-garde film theory and practice to include an ongoing engagement with the politics of race, combining a montage aesthetic with elements of personal reflection.' It is significant that groups such as Black Audio Film Collective and Sankofa in effect comprised a 'movement [which] was concerned to effect a shift to more collective modes of cultural production fully embracing Foucault's critique of the author name in favor of collective "authorship"'.[1]

To this end, *Handsworth Songs* was created as, and indeed remains, a complex, multi-layered sequence of narratives that defy linear, chronological and conventional historical readings and perhaps, most importantly, eschew the notion of the singular authentic, homogeneous Black voice, raised in protest against ongoing hardships and discrimination. The film, 'a nonnarrative, impressionistic documentary' was shown widely, in cinemas and film festivals in the UK and internationally, and has won a number of awards.[2] *Handsworth Songs* was also shown on Channel 4 and such is the film's enduring nature and reputation as a fresh and compelling example of film-making that it was included, some sixteen years after it was made, in *Documenta XI*, 2002, and more recently in *Making History, Art and Documentary in Britain from 1929 to Now* at Tate Liverpool in 2006.

With *Handsworth Songs*, Black Audio Film Collective marked themselves out as being one of the most perceptive and challenging groups of filmmakers working in the United Kingdom. Though they were not – in a conventional sense at least – documentary makers, their distinctive stock-in-trade was the archival image. They used archival footage as a means of animating and graphically illustrating potent debates and their own perceptions about culture, about history and identity, and how such concerns are irreversibly intertwined with (and indeed, affected by) the medium of film. One of the reasons *Handsworth Songs* is so compelling is because its makers took as a starting point for their practice the belief that the photograph or the documentary film can never simply be a dispassionate or unbiased visual representation.

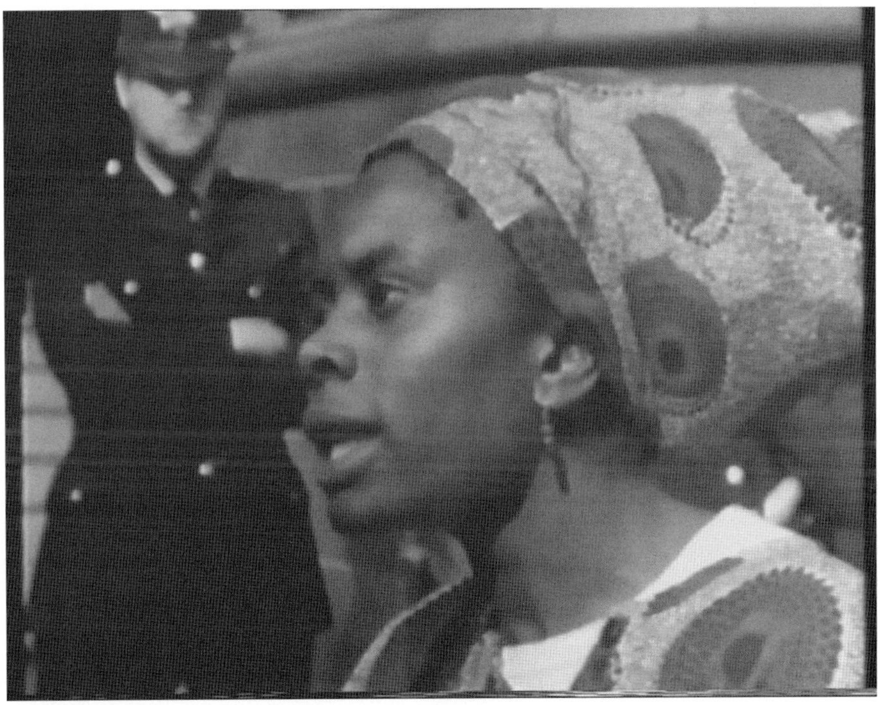

Figure 9.1 Black Audio Film Collective, *Handsworth Songs*, 1986, 16mm with sound, 57 min., film still. © Courtesy Smoking Dogs Films, London.

Black Audio Film Collective were aware that throughout the history of the medium, right up to the present day, lens-based representation in its various forms has often been used to objectify and demonise Black people, particularly by and within the mainstream media. Perhaps more accurately, we might speak of the photographic and film media being used to validate a wide range of troubling or problematic images of Black people. *Handsworth Songs* was, as much as anything, a critique of 'riot' newsreels that were generated during the disturbances of the early 1980s. Such mainstream media footage was often accepted, on face value, as authoritative, unbiased and even liberal. Yet the accumulative effect of the weight of this representation was to validate popular and ingrained racial prejudices. Black Audio Film Collective were acutely conscious of this tendency, and their work existed – in significant part at least – to critique, deconstruct and reconstruct the ways in which we look at and respond to photographs and the moving image, particularly as they relate to Black people. Especially worthy of note is the film's use of footage of camera crews and journalists. *Handsworth Songs* is decidedly critical of the ways in which legions of news media crews descended on Handsworth in the days following the riots, hungry for digestible soundbites and compliant stereotypes. As such, the film reveals 'an uneasy relationship between camera and subject.'[3] Within *Handsworth Songs* the acts of photography and filmmaking are implicated, almost as much as other sources of abuse and torment.

Whilst *Handsworth Songs* indulges no political perspectives, it is nevertheless important to look again at the act of 'rioting' and what the term and indeed the act, signified, over and above the generally accepted use of the word. In 1973 (in a song called *Burnin' and Lootin'*) Bob Marley had named and identified the riot as a positive act of purification, redemption and political integrity. This audacious and profoundly empathetic act struck an international chord with fractious Black British youngsters and Jamaican ghetto sufferers alike. Thereafter, rioting would never be considered by many as being the negative, destructive and anarchic act that others, particularly the mainstream media and the forces of 'law and order' took it to be. When Bob Marley and the Wailers sang 'That's why we're gonna be burnin' and a-lootin' tonight... burnin' all illusions tonight, burnin' all pollution tonight' rioting was, for some people at least, forevermore transformed from a violent expression of protest against perceived injustices, into an almost sacred act of righteousness, of purification, of judgment. Four years later, British reggae group Merger again celebrated the 'riot' in a song called *77*. Offering a transgressive alternative to the Queen's Silver Jubilee celebrations of 1977, they sang about the year being 'a festival of destruction time.'

The film's multiple strands, both aural and visual, combine to create a cinematic work of great depth and potency. Even setting aside, if we are able to, the images of violence that sporadically dominate the film, *Handsworth Songs* is by no means an easy or a comfortable piece of film-making with which to engage.

The film requires the viewer to undertake an almost bewildering, frame-by-frame process of absorbing its often bold and unflinching nuances, and to critique, deconstruct and reconstruct the film's various cycles. No two viewings of the film can ever be the same, simply because of the marked and profound sense of fluidity that the filmmakers brought to every aspect of the project. Within the work the idea of *meaning* becomes fiendishly elusive, as frame after frame throw up image, spectacle, and language that sit uncomfortably with the viewer and refuse to indulge any fixed meanings.

The fact that scenes of seemingly unequivocal violence, menace, prejudice and pathos dominate the film, makes this all the more remarkable. This elusiveness of certainties is perhaps best typified by the most striking words spoken in the film: 'There are no stories in the riots, only the ghosts of stories.' Coco Fusco discusses the film's rejection of 'monological explication' in favour of 'delicately interwoven visual fragments from the past and present, evoking larger histories and myths.'[4] Most central to the film's construction is its continuous and highly significant use of archival footage. Drawn from a wide variety of sources, the film amounts to an almost looped, never-ending, montage of archival voices and images that defy linear narratives and oblige us to fundamentally reconfigure what we mean by 'history' and how that 'history' might interplay with the 'present'.

The film looks at the lives, the communities, the people, the individuals and the personalities of the Handsworth district of Birmingham, in the aftermath of 'rioting' that left several people dead and numerous properties destroyed or severely damaged.

Birmingham, the largest provincial city in the country, was home to many people from the Commonwealth countries, and to their British-born/raised children. As such, Birmingham represented a heady mixture of elements that typified a changing face of 'inner-city' Britain.[5]

The children of these immigrants grew up in inner city areas of Birmingham that represented fascinating and heady contrasts and contradictions. Milkmen still delivered milk in hand-drawn carts, yet the deconsecrated church at the end of the street was now likely to be a Hindu temple, or a Gurdwara. Many people still lived in the sort of modest, working class terraced housing of which whole neighbourhoods had been built, yet the chippy at the end of the street was now likely to be a Chinese takeaway or an Indian restaurant. Many people still shopped locally, yet the high street was becoming reflective of the tastes and requirements of the city's new residents.

Together with Brixton, Handsworth had, during the course of the 1970s, come to symbolise territory that represented the unmistakable emergence and presence of Black Britain. To be sure, Handsworth was, as mentioned, home to many people from the Commonwealth countries, and to their British-born/raised children. Significantly the neighbourhood had gained a special and particular place in the

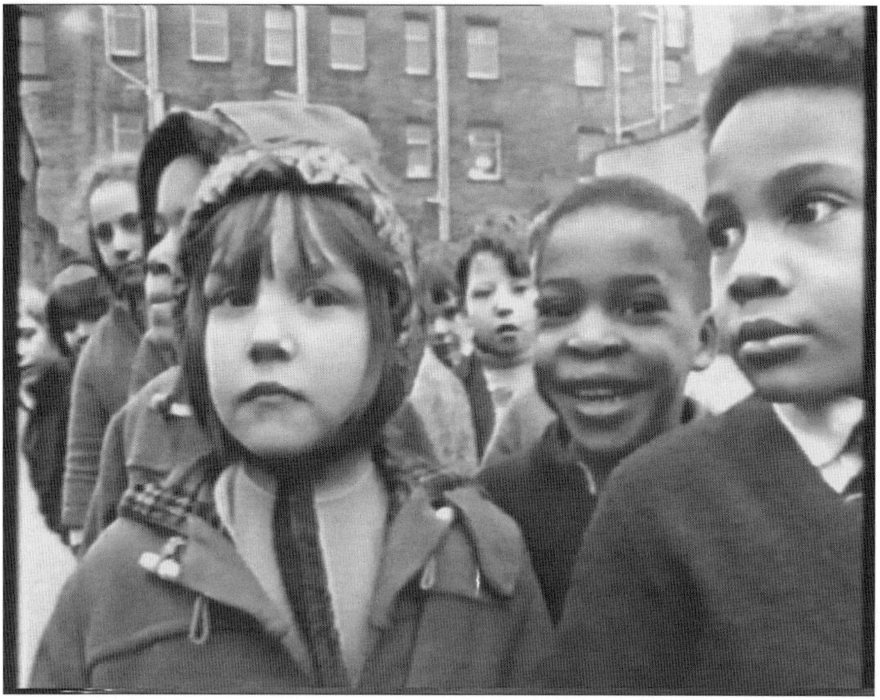

Figure 9.2 Black Audio Film Collective, *Handsworth Songs*, 1986, 16mm with sound, 57 min. film still. © Courtesy Smoking Dogs Films, London.

affections and empathies of younger Black British people. Steel Pulse had the measure of it when they sang (on their seminal 1978 Handsworth Revolution record) that 'Handsworth means us, the Black people, Handsworth means us, the Black people.' In the parlance of the time, along with areas such as Ladbroke Grove, St Paul's, and Brixton, Handsworth had achieved privileged 'frontline' status.

It might not be difficult to imagine the Birmingham of the early to mid-1980s as being a doomed landscape of hopeless contradictions and difficulties. Affluence seemed to be reserved for only parts of the city, whilst post-industrial unemployment had, since the late 1970s, become an almost inescapable fact of life for many younger people of other areas such as Handsworth. And yet, the conventional wisdom seemed to be that Birmingham represented the content, settled and colourful face of Britain's new multiculturalism. Just a few days before the Handsworth riots of 9–11 September 1985, the area played host to what had become an annual Carnival. Residents and visitors, young and old, people from different walks of life coming together to party and to celebrate Handsworth's apparently rich and vibrant cultural mix. The spectacle of large groups of dancing revellers, many in the brightly coloured costumes of carnival, gave some the sense that all was well and for Birmingham at least, 'race relations' were good.

It is perhaps necessary to provide a brief background into what apparently sparked the riots. On the late afternoon of Monday 9 September 1985, a Black man was arrested for an alleged traffic offence on Lozells Road, one of the main arteries of that part of Birmingham. A crowd gathered, demanding that the man be released. The arresting officers refused, an ugly situation turned uglier and somehow, on this occasion, a riot rapidly ensued. That night, and over much of the next two days, buildings were destroyed by arson, cars were set alight, shops looted, and in some instances, fearful residents left their homes or were prevented from returning to them. By the time the riot had ended, much property had been destroyed or damaged, many people had been arrested or hospitalised and two people were dead. The ensuing soul-searching by politicians, elements of the media and some residents themselves centred on questions such as 'Why Handsworth?' and 'Why now?'

In steps Black Audio Film Collective with a bold and deliberately uncomfortable work that attempts to explore different aspects of not only the riot itself, but also its aftermath and the lives of those affected by these events. The film has been described as 'a collage of reflections on the race riots that have shaken Thatcherite England, and the inadequacy of all institutional explanations of them – particularly those of the mass media. The filmmakers weave archival footage with reportage, interior monologue, and evocative music to evoke a gracefully orchestrated panopoly of signs and sounds that evoke Black British experiences.'[6]

Perhaps the most remarkable thing about *Handsworth Songs* is that it does not privilege any one voice, or community of voices. John Akomfrah and Black Audio Film Collective, in seeking to make a contemporary and challenging document, are determined to avoid anything that might lead, however inadvertently, to political sentimentality on the part of the viewer or indeed, the filmmakers themselves. *Handsworth Songs* offers no comfort zones, no free rides, least of all, perhaps, for those who might somehow expect Black Audio Film Collective to 'speak' for them or to 'tell' their stories. The film has no time for political complacency, choosing instead (in the words of its director) 'to reopen the questions rather than repeat the answers.'[7]

Though *Handsworth Songs* is ostensibly about riots in Birmingham and friction between the police and elements of the community, in a wider sense, the film is about the trauma of late 20th century shifts in the order of things. As Akomfrah stated, 'At a certain point, the nightmares which weigh on the brain are not necessarily historical ones - they are conjunctural ones. The fact of the matter is that a number of things were collapsing at a certain point. And the film in ways mirrors that collapse. It's not an avant-gardist intervention, in the sense that it doesn't frame a series of devices that would get us out of the crisis. It mirrors those forms collapsing, and it says what a shame.'[8]

The film uses the device of montage – the juxtaposing and overlayering of nearly sixty minutes of assorted still images and contemporary and archival moving image footage. (The moving image material is drawn from sources such as Archive Film Agency, Birmingham Central Library, the BBC, British Movietonenews Ltd. and Pathé Film Library. The film also makes eloquent use of the photographs of one of the first British-based Black people to distinguish themselves in the field of photography: Vanley Burke became responsible for producing many highly engaging photographs of Birmingham's Caribbean communities, through the course of the later decades of the 20th century, as such, becoming himself, a documenter, chronicler, and archivist.)[9]

This multi-layered storytelling avoids a single narrative that might be privileged by either journalistic 'objectivity' or (Black) community indignation. Consequently, it becomes difficult, if not impossible, for the viewer to regard some parts of the film as simply archival footage and other parts as having a more contemporary (and consequently, less historically nuanced) sourcing. For Coco Fusco, *Handsworth Songs* is a 'deconstruction of British colonial and postcolonial historiography' that 'attempts to render racial identities as effects of social and political formations and processes, to represent Black identities as products of diasporic history.'[10] Time and again, we are reminded that the past and the present are inextricably linked. The film denies us the opportunity for historical detachment. Within this work, the past and the present have a fascinating interplay; history, empire, immigration, industry, community, law and order, politics, and culture tussle with issues of identity, post colonialism and postmodernism. All of these issues, all of this interplay is presented to us through the consistent and insistent use of archival footage.

Possibly the most powerful archival material used in *Handsworth Songs* is the footage of the pioneering 'Windrush generation' of Caribbean migrants. The film draws liberally from cinematic records of the modern-day, Black presence in Britain, dating back to the years and decades immediately following the end of the Second World War. The bulk of these images consist of documentary and journalistic photographs and moving images of newly arrived Caribbean immigrants, either disembarking into seaport arrival halls, or waiting to be collected from boat-train transit terminals such as London Victoria station. Almost without exception, these images speak of an age when people dressed in their best clothes to travel, and to arrive. We see dapper suited young men and equally well-dressed young women. Nearly all of these people are wearing hats (without which, these people would have considered their dress to be incomplete). The messages from these photographs and newsreels carry a remarkable clarity: that these immigrants respect themselves, have full confidence in their own abilities to make good lives for themselves in 'the mother country', and have a corresponding confidence in the hospitality with which they expect to be treated.[11]

Coco Fusco has said that these images represent a 'poignant resurrection of the "50s immigrants" innocent faith in the "motherland"' and that the film resonates with 'psychological dilemmas in an expressive manner that transcends didactic illustration.'[12] The other powerful pieces of archival footage used in *Handsworth Songs* are scenes of police brutally (and apparently indiscriminately) arresting Black youth, and harrowing, sorrowful accounts of the maiming and death of Cherry Groce and Cynthia Jarrett respectively.[13] Another remarkable thing about *Handsworth Songs* is its use of unedited commentary by lay observers. In the present-day mass media culture of the sound bite, (lasting literally no more than a few seconds), the film distinguishes itself for the simple yet powerful ways in which it allows people the opportunity to say, in full, whatever it is they have to say. So we hear Black men and women recounting the origins and effects of the riots, in their own words and in their own time. Such material makes this a work of rare and profound empathy.

Alongside these individual expressions the film also gives us, in full, Margaret Thatcher's infamous comments that culminated in her expressing the view that 'I think it means that people are really rather afraid that this country might be rather swamped by people with a different culture. . .'[14]

The film is remembered not only for its new and very distinctive approach to its multiple subjects. It is also remembered for the decidedly mixed ways in which it was greeted by audiences and reviewers. Referring to this, John Akomfrah, stated '. . . the film was received as a transgressive text, because it didn't fall into line with the established concordat concerning the Black intelligensia and their discussion of race. That then makes the film an avant-garde text. Those who were willing to live with a more mixed economy of dialogue around figuration and race accepted it, and those who [weren't], didn't accept it.'[15]

Sankofa and Black Audio Film Collective 'effectively created a new genre, contesting the realism of both the British documentary movement and of fictional feature films...'[16] As such, *Handsworth Songs* was able to shift the terms of reference that were, up to the mid 1980s, universally employed in documentaries about Black people in Britain's inner cities. Likewise, the film shifted our approach to, and understanding of, the archival image of Black people in mid 20th century Britain. Within *Handsworth Songs*, these excerpts of archival newsreel footage ceased to be merely or simply 'historical'. They become instead important building blocks in our attempt to fashion an understanding of the postcolonial, post-modern condition.

'*Handsworth Songs* and the Archival Image' was previously published in *Ghosting: The Role of the Archive Within Contemporary Artists' Film and Video*, published by Picture This, Bristol, June 2006: 24–33.

Notes

1 Both of these quotes are from the entry by Mark Nash, 'Black Audio Film Collective' in *Documenta 11_Platform 5: Exhibition Short Guide*, (Hatje Cantz Verlag, 2002), p. 36.

2 Coco Fusco. 'A Black Avant-Garde?: Notes on Black Audio Film Collective and Sankofa'. *In Young British and Black: The Work of Sankofa and Black Audio Film Collective*, (Buffalo, NY: Hallwalls / Contemporary Art Center, 1988), p. 7.

3 Fusco. 'A Black Avant-Garde?', p. 18.

4 Fusco. 'A Black Avant-Garde?', p. 18.

5 The two largest groups of new Birmingham residents were those from the countries of South Asia – primarily India, Pakistan and Bangladesh, and those from the larger English-speaking islands of the Caribbean, such as Jamaica. Many other people, including those from the countries of Africa and elsewhere in Asia had made Birmingham their home during the decades following the end of the Second World War. These new immigrants were drawn to Birmingham and elsewhere in the West Midlands because of the region's industrial and manufacturing strength. Jobs were found in the factories of the 'Black Country' as well as on the railways, in the hospitals, and in those areas that required generally low-skilled, menial labour. For the entrepreneurial (drawn primarily from those of a South Asian background) the retail sector, the food/restaurant business and other aspects of the service sector also provided employment and income opportunities. Birmingham's 'Asian' presence was swelled in the early 1970s when the city became home to a number people expelled from Uganda by Idi Amin.

6 Fusco, 'A Black Avant-Garde?', p. 8. We observed a similar 'inadequacy of all institutional explanations' for the London riots, or England riots, of 2011.

7 John Akomfrah, in Coco Fusco. 'An Interview with Black Audio Film Collective: John Akomfrah, Reece Auguiste, Lina Gopaul and Avril Johnson' In *Young British and Black: The Work of Sankofa and Black Audio Film Collective*, p. 50.

8 Akomfrah, in Fusco. 'An Interview with Black Audio Film Collective', p. 51.

9 Born in Jamaica in 1951, Burke came to England in 1965, having received his first camera as a present for his tenth birthday a few years earlier. For him, 'Photography started to develop as a means of looking at people and how they lived.' Burke's photographs – depicting Black people at work, at play, at church, on the streets, and in their homes – have come to be regarded as key documents chronicling the lives of Black people in the country's second largest city. Through these images, we can chart the development, importance and the growing confidence of Black Britain. In Burke's photographs we see elderly Black men playing dominoes in a local pub, groups of young people hanging out in the park, baptisms by emersion, and burials. We see also confrontations between the police and Black youth, people dancing, portraits of college graduates and many other things illustrative of a vibrant, settled and multi-faceted community of Black British people.

10 Fusco, 'A Black Avant-Garde?', p. 9.

11 Incidentally perhaps, these photographs and newsreels, dating from the mid-late 1940s through to the early 1960s, give very good indications of the contemporary styles and fashions of not only the travellers themselves, but of the communities they left behind in the Caribbean. Perhaps the most celebrated photograph of newly

arriving Caribbean immigrants is that of the docking *Empire Windrush*, arriving at Tilbury docks in June 1948, bringing with her nearly 500 Jamaican and other Caribbean immigrants. This group were the first of a significant number of Caribbean immigrants seeking to start a new life in Britain. As such, the iconic photograph of the crowded bow of the *Empire Windrush* has come to graphically symbolise post-war immigration from the Caribbean and other parts of the Commonwealth.

12 Fusco, 'A Black Avant-Garde?', p. 11.

13 On Saturday 28 September 1985, Cherry Groce, a Black woman had been shot and paralysed during a police raid on her home in London. Groce was, allegedly, shot in her bed, by a member of a team of armed police officers who were looking for her son. Another, slightly divergent account has it that 'a team of armed officers went to the home of Mrs Cherry Groce in Brixton, South London, to arrest her son, Michael, who was wanted for [allegations of] armed robbery. In fact, Michael Groce no longer lived there. The officers smashed down the door with a sledge-hammer and then an inspector rushed in shouting 'armed' police'. Mrs Groce says the officer suddenly rushed at her, pointing a gun at her. She tried to run back but he shot her. She is now paralysed and confined to a wheelchair. (*Times*, 16 January 1987)'. Quoted in *Policing Against Black People* (London: Institute of Race Relations, London, 1987) p.26.

On Sunday 6 October 1985, just over a week after Groce sustained her horrific injuries, another Black woman, Cynthia Jarrett died of a heart attack during a police raid on her Tottenham home. Reports of Groce's injuries and Jarrett's death sparked widespread rioting throughout the Brixton area of South London and the Tottenham area of North London respectively. For more on these incidents and responses to them, see 'Riots and Rumours of Riots', a chapter in *'A Climate of Fear' The Murder of PC Blakelock and the Case of the Tottenham Three*, by David Rose, Bloomsbury Publishing Ltd. 1992 and 'Roll Call of Deaths', a chapter *in 'Deadly Silence' Black Deaths in Custody*, (London: Institute of Race Relations, 1991).

14 The quotation continues:

The British character has done so much for democracy, for law, and done so much throughout the world that if there's any fear that it might be swamped, people are going to react and be rather hostile to those coming in . . . We are a British nation with British characteristics. Every country can take some small minorities, and in many ways they add to the richness and variety of this country. The moment the minority threatens to become a big one, people get frightened.

From television interview with Margaret Thatcher cited in *Handsworth Songs*.

15 Akomfrah, in Fusco, 'A Black Avant-Garde?', p. 50. The film attracted a damning and negative review from Salman Rushdie, who reviewed it for the *Guardian* (12 January 1987), In response, Stuart Hall took 'issue' with Rushdie's review, in a letter that appeared in the *Guardian* a couple of days later. A couple of days after that, Darcus Howe wrote a letter to the newspaper in which he in turn wanted 'to take issue with Stuart Hall's attack'. These three heavyweight figures, each coming from different strands of the literary, sociological and activist firmaments respectively, all had choice words – oscillating between brickbats and bouquets – to say about *Handsworth Songs*. Such attention to a film was unprecedented. Nor has such attention been seen since.

16 Nash, 'Black Audio Film Collective', p. 36.

Chapter 10
Black British and Other African Diaspora Artists Visualizing Slavery

The generation of Black British artists that emerged in the early 1980s frequently made work that reflected and referenced the pungent cocktail of social and political factors that characterized the existence of themselves and the communities from which they emerged. While being mindful not to typecast all these artists as having the pursuit of social narratives as one of their core concerns, it is nevertheless safe to say that one of the elements of these new artists' practice that made their work so fascinating and distinctive was its frequent embrace of the figurative image, which tended to bring with it multiple, highly-charged social narratives. For good measure, much of this work made liberal use of text, thereby amplifying the sense in which these artists were communicating *messages*, even as they pursued careers as young artists. The work of these artists often had a dynamism, an urgency, a sense of *now is the time, and the time is now.* To this end, they used all manner of techniques and devices to push home their messages. Mention has already been made of the striking use of text within much of the work produced by these artists. But other techniques were employed in the creating of a new type of art that ably reflected the sense of urgency and the sense of destiny that these artists evoked. Techniques such as assemblage sculpture, photomontage, and collage were widely used by these artists, who tended to look with a certain skepticism on the hegemonic ways in which traditional methods and mediums tended to hold sway in the teaching of art at college level – the environment from which most of these artists, such as Marlene Smith, Claudette Johnson, Keith Piper, and Donald Rodney emerged. Simultaneously, other artists of the African diaspora, in countries such as Jamaica, made cogent, wonderful work that sought to describe, or comment on, the potent memory of slavery and its aftermath.

By the early 1980s it seemed that things had already gone spectacularly wrong for a new generation of Black-Britons. Growing up in cities such as London and the ex-industrial towns and cities of the Midlands and the North, these youngsters came of age just when the National Front, a far-right white nationalist party, was enjoying seemingly widespread appeal and support, even amongst those in the larger, Conservative and Labour parties. By far the most notorious anti-immigrant sentiment expressed by a mainstream politician was that spoken by Margaret Thatcher, who at the time (1978) was leader of the Conservative party in opposition. In words that seemed to give succor to the National Front (and tacit approval for the racial violence to which Black people were regularly subjected), Thatcher opined:

> Well now, look, let us try and start with a few figures as far as we know them, and I am the first to admit it is not easy to get clear figures from the Home Office about immigration, but there was a committee which looked at it and said that if we went on as we are then by the end of the century there would be four million people of the new Commonwealth or Pakistan here. Now, that is an awful lot and I think it means that people are really rather afraid that this country might be rather swamped by people with a different culture and, you know, the British character has done so much for democracy, for law and done so much throughout the world that if there is any fear that it might be swamped people are going to react and be rather hostile to those coming in.[1]

Openly racist in their platform, the National Front littered lampposts, letterboxes, park benches and other items in the built environment of Britain's towns and cities with stickers such as the ones declaring 'If They're Black . . . Send Them Back!' Racial violence was a regular occurrence in this grim period, as was a sense that young Black people were under the cosh of police brutality, societal alienation, and other ills.

When a number of emerging Black-British artists made work that referenced slavery, a distinct set of interlinked narratives could be perceived in these pieces. Slavery was treated not so much, or not only, as a traumatic but historical episode fixed in these artists' heritage, but rather as an emphatic signifier of discrete, ongoing Pan-African or African diasporic conditions. We are where we are because slavery existed. We are where we are because Britain was one of the world's leading slave-trading nations. We are where we are because how could we describe the effects of persistent demonization, vilification, and criminalization as anything other than the lingering effects of slavery's legacy? The memory and the visualizing of slavery became, in effect, a pertinent and arresting vehicle for understanding, making sense of, and above all, visualizing, ongoing torments and disappointments.

These Black-British artists tended to look outside of their geographic location and present-day existence, for images and philosophies that might bring meaning to their own lives, and mechanisms through which their condition could be communicated, and strategies for resistance and advancement formulated. One of the first ports of call for these artists, reflecting both empathy and a search for a political blueprint, was the history of Black struggle in the United States. Sojourner Truth, Malcolm X, Huey P. Newton, George Jackson, Angela Davis: the lives, writings, and struggles of these iconic figures consistently inspired these young Black-British artists. Elsewhere in the world, in the Caribbean and Jamaica in particular, the heady, potent and distinctly counter-cultural emergence of Rastafari and its attendant Dread subculture also distinctly influenced this new generation of practitioners. This was a time when reggae music was arguably at its most formidable, dominant, and influential in its ability to fashion an ideology of resistance and empowerment. Talk of Babylon, exile, exodus, righteous suffering, and redemption was a source of profound inspiration for these Black-British artists. It didn't hurt that many grew up in fundamentalist Christian households in which the decidedly biblical associations of Rasta-talk were recognized and well understood. Spinning the globe still further, this new generation of artists found common cause with the antiapartheid struggle and the defense of the so-called 'Frontline States' that so often came under attack by the army of racist South Africa.

In addition to these manifestations of Pan-African/African diasporic solidarity, young Black-British artists looked outside of their present-day existence by reaching back down into their history in search of means by which to make sense of present-day difficulties. In this regard, slavery stood unparalleled in its dramatic ability to crystallize aspects of Black Britain's late-twentieth century fractious and edgy existence. As was so often the case, reggae music provided a compelling blueprint for the ways in which history could be used to frame an understanding of present-day conditions and simultaneously chant down Babylon. Songs such as Burning Spear's *Slavery Days*, in which Winston Rodney challenged the listener with the insistent question, 'Do you remember the days of slavery?'; Culture's *Too Long in Slavery*; and perhaps most forceful of all, the Wailers' *Slave Driver,* in which Bob Marley conjoined a haunting, nightmarish memory of slavery with a telling assessment of the present-day economic woes of the Jamaican *sufferer*. 'Ev'ry time I hear the crack of the whip/my blood runs cold/I remember on the slave ship/how they brutalized our very soul/Today they say that we are free/only to be chained in poverty/Good God I think it's illiteracy . . .'

Keith Piper was one Black British artist who made extensive use of reproductions of lithographs of plans of slave ships, depicting their human cargo packed below deck like so many sardines in a tin. The origins of these drawings of slave ships (of which the *Brookes of Liverpool* is perhaps the most well-known and widely reproduced) and their awful contents date back to the abolitionist movements of the late eighteenth and early nineteenth centuries. The abolitionists had seized on this simple but effective graphic device as a means of driving home the horrors that had to be endured by captured Africans during the Middle Passage, the nightmarish journey by sea that took enslaved people from their homelands to slavery and death in the 'New World.' As Michael Jordan, one of slavery and the slave trade's many historians, notes:

> Members . . . also recognized the maxim that a picture paints a thousand words, particularly when trying to rouse public sentiment. One of the first positive moves in this direction was to approve the use of a seal depicting a black African supplicating in chains above a motto posing the question: 'Am I not a Man and a Brother?' This was to prove so successful in attracting attention that in March 1789 they settled upon a similar promotional venture in the shape of a sketch depicting the sections through a slave ship and revealing the excessively cramped conditions. Eventually, 500 of these, printed on wooden plaques, were delivered to members of the House of Commons, and another 500, more tastefully executed in copperplate, found their way to addresses of Their Lordships.[2]

In the above passage, Jordan references two distinct, and very different types of abolitionist *motifs*. The first, a kneeling slave, pleading for his humanity to be recognized; the second, an engineered, dispassionate plan of a slave ship, carrying unidentified and faceless captured Africans, each having been given less space than that ordinarily accorded to a dead body in a coffin. History would by and large decree that the first image, resonating as it did with humility, supplication and pleading, would be of little or no use to artists of the twentieth and twenty-first centuries, who were within their practice, intent on visualizing slavery. The second image, however – notwithstanding the calculating commodification of human beings that it sought to present – has intrigued and fascinated countless artists on both sides of the Atlantic. These powerful lithographs would in time take on a significance that went way beyond the abolitionist propaganda value of their day. The passage of time did little or nothing to diminish the memory of slavery in the collective and individual psyche of New World Africans and their descendants. Indeed, a century and a half after the abolition of slavery by the British, plans of laden slave ships were starting to become iconic shorthand graphic signifiers for the miserable, wretched history of slavery and the myriad ways in which that history spawned a thousand Black liberation struggles, in Africa and throughout the world. There are those who might regard slavery as something from the obscure crevices of history, but for many Black people the experience seared itself on the psyche in a way that few non-Black people could fully understand. And there was, apparently, no better *motif* to indicate the continued potency of the memory of slavery than the *Brookes of Liverpool* plan. For Black British artists, and other practitioners, slavery became a signifier of identity. In this regard, artists' use of the slave ship motif encapsulated and signified much in the way of Black history. The signifiers of enslavement, exploitation, bondage, torture and death were never far from their (and in turn, our) readings of the slave ship image. Nor were the redemptive signifiers of survival, perseverance and the struggle for humanity.

But Black British artists of the generation emerging in the early 1980s were not the only British artists to be drawn to the subject of slavery. Slightly older Caribbean-born artists, such as Tam Joseph (b. Dominica, 1947) and Eugene Palmer (b. Jamaica, 1955) also produced singular, compelling work that made intelligent, sensitive and complex commentary on the legacy and memory of slavery. One painting in particular, by Eugene Palmer, from the early 1990s, bears eloquent testimony to some of the ways in which references to slavery took their place alongside other signifiers of Black British history and identity. Palmer's *City Girl* depicts a young girl of African-Caribbean background, with a somewhat discomfited facial expression, standing in front of what looks to be a landscape painting. Significantly, the girl is depicted in front of, or outside of, the vista behind her. Within the painting, the landscape functions as a metaphor for English/British identity and the ways in which Black people are not, as a matter of course, included in constructs of Englishness/Britishness, as painted by artists such as Gainsborough and Constable. A small, discreet, but hugely important aspect of the painting is the paper boat – such as a child might make – that lies on the floor at the girl's feet. The boat functions as a metaphor for the seismic patterns of travel, migration, and movement which Black people were subject to and caught up in, over several hundred years. Some of this travel was to a great extent initiated by Black people themselves, such as those Caribbean migrants who sought better lives for themselves in the decades following World War II. But some of this travel also occurred as a result of the enslavement of African peoples.

In this regard, we might also consider the work of Mary Evans (b. Nigeria, 1963). Evans produced, in the mid-1990s, one of the most extraordinary works to utilize a plan of the slave ship. Given that contemporary African-American artists such as Dewey Crumpler and Hank Willis Thomas have been responsible for some astonishingly powerful work utilizing the plan of the slave ship, Evans' work is indeed a considerable achievement.

In 1792, Methodist preacher Samuel Bradburn (1751–1816), 'delivered a persuasive message to fellow Methodists in Manchester that the Negro was a fellow subject:'[3]

> Whatever may be the opinions of others, you, Brethren, believe that God hath made of one blood all nations of men, for to dwell on the face of the earth, and

hath determined the times before appointed, and the bounds of their habitation. Who then has any right to go, or to authorize others to go across a vast ocean, to enslave a free and in relation to us, a harmless people. None but the sovereign ruler of the universe has power to grant such a right. There is nothing plainer than that the Negroes have as good a right to invade Britain and make slaves of us, as we have to invade Africa and make slaves of them.[4]

It is this notion of Africans having as good a right to invade Britain and make slaves of white Britons, as white Britons have to invade Africa and make slaves of Africans, (meaning of course, that no-one has any such 'right') that lies at the heart of our understanding of Evans' *Wheel of Fortune,* produced by the artist in 1996. To create this fetching, imposing, engaging work, Evans painstakingly cut out of dark-colored paper, three times, the distinctive shapes – patterning even – of the plan of the slave ship. This was patient, meticulous work that one can imagine involved Evans' developing a particularly empathetic relationship with each

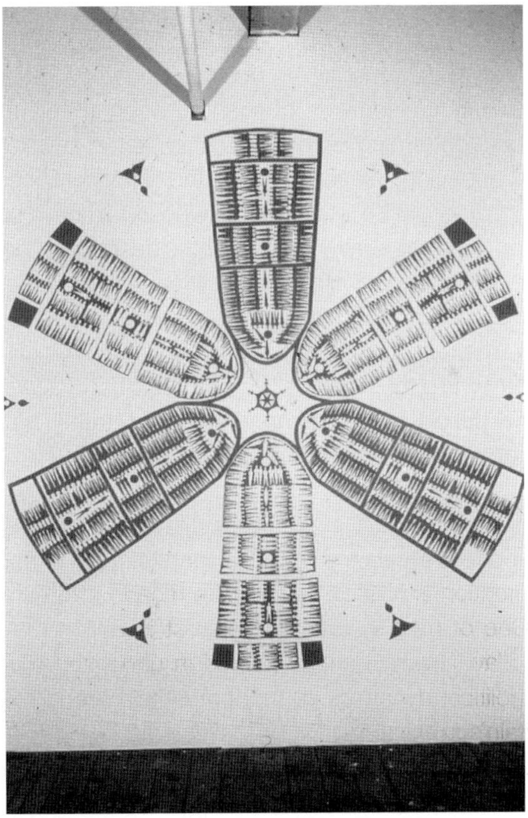

Figure 10.1 Mary Evans, *Wheel of Fortune*, 1996, Craftpaper, 250cm diameter, Photo: Patrick Gorma. © Mary Evans.

individual outline of a slave (and of course, the slave ship itself), as she took her time extricating whole fragile, delicate plans of slave ships from the pieces of paper she started with. For the three 'positive' outlines Evans secured for herself, she was left with three corresponding 'negative' pieces of paper. Evans then took these six pieces of paper and alternately placed them on a wall, forming a wheel of fortune, each ship with its bow located within the epicenter of the wheel of fortune.

In this work, Evans explores the idea of chance and slavery. The historic wheel of fortune, laden with fatal consequences for some, is spun, and *x* number of Africans are 'chosen' for capture and enslavement, their lives, the lives of their communities, families and indeed, their descendants, forevermore transformed through the horrific experiences of the transatlantic slave trade. The title of Evans's work, *Wheel of Fortune*, referenced a perennial American television game show in which contestants compete to solve word puzzles, such as those used in another word game, *Hangman*, to win money and other prizes supposedly determined by spinning something akin to a giant carnival or funfair wheel. Hardly deviating from its format, *Wheel of Fortune* is said to be the longest-running syndicated game show in US television history. By titling her piece as she did, Evans introduced a pointed, almost macabre, gallows humor into her commentary on history, fate, and enslavement. The cheery notion of a game show wheel of fortune, complete with its elements of chance, when coupled with an insistent and quite disturbing patterning of the slave ship, acted as a foil for what was a brave and almost audacious piece of work. If the historical shoe had been on the other foot, perhaps it would be white people who would have suffered, endured, and forced to find ways of surviving the death, destruction and disruption the Atlantic Slave Trade caused. While certain Africans of all ages and both sexes were captured into slavery, the effects of slavery deeply affected much of the African continent, the ramifications and effects of which are still being felt at the present time. What would the world be like if Africans had systematically enslaved Europeans over a period of several hundred years, rather than the other way around? Writing about *Wheel of Fortune*, Evans stated:

> Pattern is a strong leitmotif in my work. However, the work is rarely pure ornament, but often reveals the historical, architectural or social threads of its source. My intention is to look beyond the façade of ornament to see what lurks there. One of my key areas of interest is Britain's involvement in the Transatlantic Slave Trade. I am interested in understanding how the social, cultural and political dynamics of modern Britain are in many respects the legacy of Britain's imperial past. I am fascinated by the circuitous route via which people arrive and settle somewhere through emigration and joining the Diaspora; what affects people on those journeys; what they are forced to learn, and relearn; what they choose to remember and forget; and how they are irrevocably changed.[5]

Another British artist of West-African background, Godfried Donkor (b. Ghana, 1964), made fascinating use of images of the slave ship and other sea vessels evocative of African diasporic history in his celebrated *Slave to Champ* series. Metaphorically and literally rising out of these images of galleons and slave ship plans were the imposing figures of Black boxers – many of whom were heavyweight champions (perhaps the most well-known being the likes of Jack Johnson, Muhammad Ali and Mike Tyson). Ali and other boxers were in a number of instances depicted with heads crowned by a golden halo, bringing instant references to the poignant April 1968 *Esquire* magazine cover depiction of Ali in the pose of Saint Sebastian, shot through with arrows, martyred by the vindictive might of the US government that stripped him of his heavyweight crown and denied him the right to box because he would not fight against the Viet Cong in Vietnam. By montaging the slave ship motif with that of the Black boxer, Donkor was animating a range of narratives that centered on the political framing of the Black athlete. How far is the distance from slave to champ? How far is the distance from Africa to the New World? From Africa to Britain? From plantation to boxing ring? And while white American commentators demonized Ali as a loud-mouthed braggart, Donkor, through this depiction of Ali, seemed keen to overturn that notion by ascribing to this boxer, and others, the status of sainthood and all that that blessed state of being implied.

Within African, African-Caribbean and African American cultures, water is a particularly powerful symbol. One needs only think of songs such as *Wade in the Water, Take Me to the River,* and *You Don't Miss Your Water* to appreciate how deeply water runs through African American popular music. Gospel is full of countless references to the cleansing power of water, whether through baptism or the washing away of sin. Reggae, too, has no end of references to water's ability to replenish and bring forth life. But – mindful of the apocalyptic tale of the flood from which Noah escaped – there is much within these diasporic cultures to signify the destructive power of water, even as it washes away both wrongdoing and wrongdoers. It is this extraordinarily powerful interplay between water as a force of destruction and water as a source of life that lies at the core of singular pieces by two Caribbean-born artists – Dominica-born Tam Joseph, and Jamaica-born Charles Campbell. There are striking similarities between Joseph's *Under the Sea, Under the Sea* and Campbell's *Oceans*. These are haunting, meditative works that reveal different truths with each viewing. Perhaps one of the great successes of these paintings is that, on first encounter, they apparently make no direct or explicit reference to slavery. They are instead, at first glance at least, well-executed seascapes.

But water is of course as powerful a metaphor of slavery as the slave ship. Water was the means by which captured Africans were transported, and the means by which slaves chose to end their suffering in this life by jumping overboard when the opportunity presented itself. Some slaves, desperate to

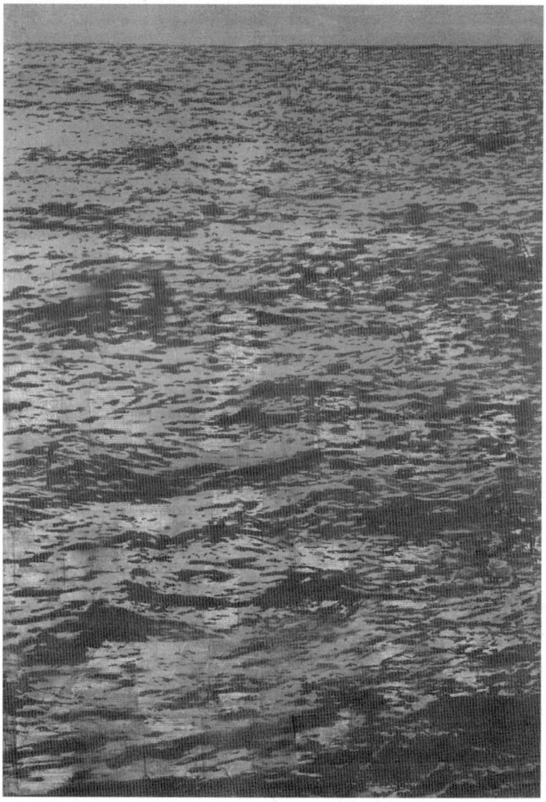

Figure 10.2 Tam Joseph, *Under the Sea, Under the Sea*, c. 1994, Acrylic paint on paper on canvas, approx. 244 x 168 cm. © Tam Joseph.

escape their torment, sought to return to the homelands by fleeing the wretched confines of the slave ship. To these incidents can be added the many instances of captured Africans being thrown over the sides of slave ships very much against their will. The sick, the dying, the supposedly belligerent, those who were deemed to be more trouble than they were worth – all these captured Africans – men, women, children and babies – found themselves being dumped overboard like so much inconsequential and damaged cargo.[6]

But water (and for that matter, the slave ship) is also a metaphor for redemption, salvation, survival and rebirth. For people of the African diaspora, the spiritual, the healing qualities of water are deeply cherished. Tam Joseph's work pays homage to those Africans who died in great violence during the course of the Middle Passage – those thrown overboard as well as those who chose to jump to certain death. And yet, alongside these meditations on great violence, there is, within *Under the Sea, Under the Sea*, a profound sense of the power of baptism by total immersion, redemption, salvation, and above all, survival. Joseph does not just celebrate survival; he also celebrates the power of the African diaspora to emerge from slavery and to live to tell the tale, in a range of ways that speak of a vigorous flourishing of creativity in the decades following slavery, through to the modern and contemporary eras.

Perhaps the most subtle, understated, and fascinating aspect of *Under the Sea, Under the Sea* and *Oceans* is the way in which the artists built survival and the resilience of New World African creativity into their paintings. Joseph adhered paper to the canvas, and then applied acrylic to the paper. The paper was in fact pages of books by towering figures of twentieth-century literature such as Toni Morrison, James Baldwin, Aimé Césaire, and Frantz Fanon. It is this sense of slavery's descendants living to tell the tale through beautiful, articulate, and poignant narratives of literature that gives the painting its subtle, understated strength and power. In its own way, the painting echoes Bob Marley's sentiment, expressed in *Survival* (1979) that we are the Black survivors.

'Black British and Other African Diaspora Artists Visualizing Slavery', was previously published in *Africa in the Arts: Migration, Improvisation, Exchange* Part III of Persephone Braham (ed) *African Diaspora in the Cultures of Latin America, the Caribbean, and the United States*, University of Delaware Press, 2014: 135–143.

Notes

1 'World in Action,' January 30, 1978, quoted in Trevor Russel, *The Tory Party: Its Policies, Divisions and Future* (Harmondsworth, UK: Penguin, 1978), 116.

2 Michael Jordan, *The Great Abolition Sham: The True Story of the End of the British Slave Trade* (Stroud: Sutton Publishing, 2005), 93.

3 Jordan, *The Great Abolition Sham*, p. 194.

4 Jordan, *The Great Abolition Sham*, p. 194.

5 http://www.africa.com/printblog?id=108 (originally accessed April 8, 2012, no longer online).

6 The most notorious recorded incident of living slaves being thrown overboard was the *Zong*. As Michael Jordan recounted, 'In March 1783, Gustavus Vasa, a black former crew member of a ship called the *Zong* visited Granville Sharp to recount an alleged case of mass murder. . . Vasa reported that 133 members of the captive human cargo of the *Zong* had been deliberately drowned in order to facilitate an insurance swindle.' (*The Great Abolition Sham*, 92). For a full account of this horrific incident, see James Walwin, *The Zong: a Massacre, the Law and the End of Slavery* (New Haven: Yale University Press, 2011).

Chapter 11

2000's Got to be Black

Herein lie buried many things which if read with patience may show the strange meaning of being black here in the dawning of the Twenty First Century. This meaning is not without interest to you, Gentle Reader; for the problem of the Twenty First Century is the problem of the color-line.

with sincere and respectful apologies to W. E. B. DU BOIS.

In a statement of profound optimism, focus and purpose, Roy Ayers (in a song written by Carl Clay and Wayne Garfield) sang '2000's got to be Black'. The record in question – '2000 Black' – was recorded and released a quarter of a century before the year 2000, thus signalling not only a belief in a bright liberated future for Black people, but also indicating the need for short, medium and long-term positive agendas, whereby we could confidently believe the future's bright, the future's Black. Looking back to the arguably unpromising period of mid 1970s America, we can appreciate something of the ways in which Clay and Garfield were looking beyond the then-contemporary position of Black people and envisioning a certain and inevitable achievement and fulfilment. The song was an invitation to Black people to 'think about the future' and anticipate (as well as actively plan for) happier, redemptive times. At much the same time as '2000 Black' was recorded, elsewhere in the African Diaspora, Bob Marley and the Wailers were exhorting us to 'make way for the positive day'.

It is no coincidence that both of these profound redemptive sentiments were articulated in the mid-1970s. For Black people around the world, that particular period signified much in the way of hope and optimism, in spite of present difficulties. In the United Kingdom, the mid-1970s saw the first signs of the coming of age of the 'Black Briton' – youngsters who were the children of Caribbean immigrants who had come to Britain over a period of a decade and a half from 1948 onwards. The 1980s saw a number of these youngsters developing significant careers and profiles as visual artists. Chief amongst them were the likes of Sonia Boyce and Keith Piper. Boyce, with her involved and ambitious oil pastel self-portraits and other depictions of Black women and men. Piper, with his vigorously-executed work that demonstrated what was, in a British context, a new Black attachment to distinct social and political narratives within art.

It could be said that across the globe, Black artists in the 1980s and 1990s made significant progress. In the New York of the early 1990s, thanks largely to the efforts of Thelma Golden, African-American artists were able, for a while at least, to storm the barricades of the Whitney Museum of American Art. In Sydney, Aboriginal and Torres Strait Islander artists were finally able to effectively demonstrate that their practice owed as much to modern/postmodern urban aesthetics as it did to the rural/dreamtime/dot paintings triangulation that often seemed to circumscribe the realities of their modern identities. In the London of the late 1990s, two of the capital's previously impregnable bastions of art establishment whiteness, the Serpentine and the Institute of Contemporary Arts (ICA) extended the ultimate validation – the solo exhibition – to two Black artists, Chris Ofili and Steve McQueen respectively.

These are necessarily brief, fleeting references, but much documentation exists, all over the place, to support and illustrate the progress that Black artists have made, over the past couple of decades. And yet, for Black artists and Black people alike, 2000 is far from being Black. Or, it's not as Black as we'd like it to be. Because, despite the progress we've been making, white folks are still ahead. Further, Black artists are in many ways (in the United Kingdom at least) currently in a collective and unbecoming position of disorderly retreat. Still marginalised, still excluded from almost anything you care to mention. Teaching positions, jobs in the visual arts, exhibition slots, etc. etc. What to do? What to do? What to do? 100 years ago, in the Forethought to his seminal publication, 'The Souls of Black Folk', W.E.B. Du Bois wrote that 'the problem of the Twentieth Century is the problem of the color-line.' It seems clear that in the 21st Century, within the visual arts and elsewhere, Black artists will continue to find that Du Bois' prescient observation has an unfortunately enduring application.

In Bruce Beresford's engaging filmic account of a chapter of the Boer War, 'Breaker Morant' [1979] the protagonist, Lieutenant Harry Morant makes an arresting observation about the apparently unorthodox military tactics employed by the British army. Mindful that the year in which the events in question took place – 1901 – heralded the beginning of a new century, Morant describes such military tactics as 'a new kind of war for a new century'. In other words, previously gentlemanly soldier-like campaigns were no use against a Boer enemy that fought a ruthless and tenacious guerrilla campaign resisting the British. This, Morant observed, was to be the way in which modern wars would be fought.

For Black artists, the struggle remains the same: art establishment racism firmly in place and white folks still ahead. The advent of a new century sees Black artists suffering from continued discrimination, but facing three additional, formidable obstacles, the workings of which have developed expeditiously over the past decade or so. Obstacles for which, as yet, Black artists have few, if any, effective responses. Strategies governing the art establishment's dealings with Black artists are characterised firstly, by white liberal posturing, secondly, by white political expediency and thirdly (possibly as an extension of the first and second) wretched equal opportunities policies. The pernicious and ruinous operating of these three things calls for new, more concerted tactics and original ideas in combating art establishment racism. For Black artists around the world, this has to be, in part at least, the agenda for the twenty first century. A new kind of struggle for a new century.

There is no agenda as totalitarian as the paternalistic liberal agenda that benevolently prescribes to Black people a rolling status of nature's children in regular though piecemeal need of 'discovery', 'support' or 'help' – always, always, always on white people's terms. Within the context of these notes, liberalism has one of its most warped embodiments in the 'international' exhibition wherein the Black/white racial polarisation corresponds with precisely the same dichotomy of those who are curated and those who curate. Those who are objectified and those who do the objectifying. Furthermore, such exhibitions establish uncomfortable relationships between groups of Black artists in different countries. Let me, Gentle Reader, explain what I mean.

Thus far, more than any other single entity, the international non-white exhibition has done more than anything else to compound the invisibility and gross marginalisation of Black British artists. The art establishment, having grown quickly bored with the wider body of Black artists, and finding no compelling reason for consistently acknowledging them, quickly and quietly reverted to a quota system which acknowledged the practice of only a tiny number of Black artists. But even this quota system has now been largely abandoned by an art establishment that has now turned its attentions overseas, towards the so-called 'international' arena.

For British galleries uncertain about how to deal with the problem of Black representation within their programmes, imported exhibitions have come as a godsend. The scenario, frequently repeated, sees white gallery directors attempting to demonstrate that they can do better than home-grown Black British artists' exhibitions, by allocating their 'ethnic' slots to what are perceived as being much more exotic, much more authentic, imported exhibitions.

Thus, Black artists in Britain rapidly came to find themselves considered to be obsolete and surplus to requirement, in comparison to a wide range of non-white artists whose most important characteristic was that they were not from the United Kingdom. The consensus among curators in the 1990s seemed to be that the most interesting art by coloured people was that being produced by artists in Africa or South Asia, or China, or the Pacific Rim, or Australasia, or wherever. Anywhere but here in Britain. During the 1990s we witnessed large scale group exhibitions from India, China, Aboriginal Australia, the 'Chicano' border states of the United States and one or two exhibitions that showcased the work of 'non-European' artists living in Europe. The only thing missing from the art galleries of Britain was similarly large or solo exhibitions of work by Black artists in Britain.

Within the context of the marginalisation of Black artists in Britain, these imported exhibitions effectively and rather unfortunately function along lines not dissimilar to strike-breaking 'scab' labour. These exhibitions are not a supplement or a compliment to Black British artists' exhibitions. They are instead, a brutal and cynical replacement/displacement. Every imported exhibition effectively serves to displace or dislodge Black British artists' claims on gallery space within the country of their birth and residence. Every exhibition such as 'Aratjara' or 'Cities on the Move' at the Hayward Gallery in London, hinders the programming of exhibitions of work by British-born Black artists and serves as a smokescreen for art establishment racism. Consider this, Gentle Reader: there has never ever been an exhibition at the Hayward Gallery dedicated to the work of British-born Black artists. I am not suggesting any sort of isolationist stance in which 'international' exhibitions have no place within Britain, but until Black artists are accorded proper status and attention in this country, imported exhibitions will remain a symptom of art establishment dysfunctionality. The arrival of these exhibitions spell nothing but trouble.

The most delinquent characteristic of these international group exhibitions is the way in which they were, by and large, curated by alien white curators from Europe or elsewhere who made their curatorial selections based on not much more than their own aesthetic prejudices, artificial empowerment and benevolent, liberal, Eurocentric agendas. So what we have seen is white curators literally flying off all over the place to pick and choose artists at their own idiosyncratic and self-centred discretion. One of the most problematic aspects of this curatorial practice is that it does little to genuinely empower curators within 'international' localities. The art establishment in Britain used to swear blindly 'that there aren't any black artists: black people don't make pictures'. This same art establishment seems to be demonstrating a similar blinkered view that there are no Black (or Aboriginal, or African, or Indian, or Chinese) curators who can be trusted to take a lead on curating major exhibitions of art from their respective parts of the world. The big shows of art from Africa and other continents that we see in Britain operate on the paternalistic notion that Daddy knows best. 'Daddy' being the big white boss man, ('Mommy' being the big white boss woman), armed with the pocketful of exhibition favours and the return flight ticket. Where Black curators have been employed on these international mega-exhibitions, they have invariably found themselves being involuntarily chaperoned and disempowered by Mommy or Daddy.

We need to be as aware as we can be about the problematic nature of internationally-gleaned exhibitions. We may be living in post-colonial times, but such exhibitions often work in the most markedly 'colonial' of ways. As the world's darker people, we have suffered the trauma of having already been colonised. We should be careful to avoid complicity in exhibitions that seek to colonise us twice over.

In 1995, the Royal Academy hosted a blockbuster exhibition called 'Africa – Art of a Continent'. The exhibition set out to present the finest examples of the totality of African 'art', from the year dot, right up to the beginning of the 20th century – the latter time period generally signalled by old-school African art historians as marking the end of 'real', 'authentic' African art. Although much of the work assembled came from collections within the country, 'Africa – Art of a Continent' nevertheless presented itself as a colonial exercise in bringing home, unpacking and showing off the spoils, the plunder, the trophies of empire.

Of course, traditional notions of 'African' art neatly dovetail into the British nation's collective, nostalgic, constructed remembrance of the glory days of the British Empire. Unfortunately, however, an indigenous exhibition from Australia such as Aratjara might function perfect well and trouble-free (in terms of its readings) within Australia. But within the 'colonial' context of the 'Mother Country', like 'Africa – Art of a Continent', it comes alarmingly close to being an exercise (inadvertently or otherwise) in bringing home the spoils. Adverse effects are a drag, aren't they?

But we need to be more than rightly critical of art establishment antics. We need to develop increasing numbers of respectful, mutually-supportive models of international exchange and dialogue that cut both liberals and old-time colonial duffers out of the picture. Furthermore, it's not just a case of making ourselves visible, but a matter of the ways in which we do so. It seems clear that large-scale exhibitions shipped from one country to another, circumscribe, rather than broaden the individuality of artists. Do we really want/need exhibitions that arrogantly aim to bring whole expansive areas of artistic practice to the attention of gallery-going audiences in one fell swoop? Exhibitions that aim to bring subjects, lock, stock and barrel, to the art world's high tables ought really to be avoided like the plague. Primarily for the simple reason that they fatally limit the viewer's ability to 'read' contemporary artists as individual practitioners, each with a unique approach to his/her own work.

As a barometer of the extent to which certain exhibitions suppress or exorcise artists' individuality, look out for the tell-tale sub-title. If the sub-title leans towards totality, walk the other way. Let me, Gentle Reader, explain what I mean by giving a couple of examples: For a start the Royal Academy's 'Africa' show, already burdened by a reductive one-word title, was supplemented by the impossibly grandiose 'Art of a Continent'. The Hayward Gallery recently played host to the previously-mentioned 'Cities on the Move'. The exhibition came with a real mouthful of a subtitle: 'Urban Chaos and Global Change East Asian Art, Architecture and Film Now'. And not long ago, New York audiences had an opportunity to see 'Transforming the Crown', an exhibition that came with the ambitious, confident sub-title of 'African, Asian & Caribbean Artists in Britain 1966–1996'.

The curator of 'Transforming the Crown' Mora J. Beauchamp-Byrd spent several years toing and froing across the Atlantic, working on the exhibition. Her aim was to introduce New York audiences to a major, wide-ranging look at the diversity, history and strength of visual arts practice amongst Britain's Black artists. Beauchamp-Byrd was of the opinion that such an ambition was best served by shipping in the biggest trundling roadshow exhibition that she could create. In her quest, no stone was to be left unturned, no artist to be left unconsidered. Despite the obvious flaws in such a strategy, Beauchamp-Bryd had decided that 'Transforming the Crown' was to be a fulsome, definitive introduction. Hence the burdensome sub-title.

And of course, Australians reading this will probably be familiar with Aratjara, an exhibition that referenced 40,000 years of Aboriginal and Torres Strait Islander history by sub-titling itself 'Art of the First Australians'. What these exhibitions have in common is that they consciously or otherwise prioritise particularly weighty notions of ethnicity over and above individual artistic content and ability. The ethnicity of the artist becomes everything, subservient to nothing, least of all the individuality and individual abilities of artists. A visitor leaving 'Transforming the Crown' would have been hard-pushed to recall, to any meaningful degree, the individual and specific practices of the many artists whose work had been corralled into one supposedly authoritative entity. Ditto 'Cities on the Move'. Ditto Aratjara

When I was last in Australia, the MCA was hosting 'Mao Goes Pop', an exhibition with another one of those overblown sub-titles, the scope of which was underlined by its frugality: 'China Post-1989'. One of the world's largest, and most populous countries, with an equally formidable diasporic presence (Chinese people being, quite literally, all over the place) found itself shoehorned into one solitary exhibition with absurd pretensions. Try as I might, I can't recall many (any?) of the nearly 30 artists by individual name or contribution, without reaching for my 'Mao Goes Pop' exhibition brochure. If I didn't have said brochure, chances are I wouldn't remember a damn thing, apart from the vaguest details of the exhibition.

The way forward must, I believe, be to demand that artists designated as 'international', or 'indigenous', or immigrant', or 'Black' etc. be given, in greater numbers, the ultimate validation and acknowledgement – such as that accorded Steve McQueen or Chris Ofili – the solo exhibition in the major gallery. This is not to say that artists should be in any way decontextualised from history, geography, language, culture or whatever. It is instead to demand the opportunity to look at the individuality of an artist's work – and assess or interact with it accordingly. White artists the world over can have big solo shows. Why can't we?

We not only need to resist jumbled up exhibitions like 'Cities on the Move', we need to be fully and actively aware of the racist mind-set that informs the programming (and, to a large extent, the curating) of such exhibitions. Additionally, Black curators need to advance to strategically important positions in the art establishment. We need to retire Mommy and Daddy to the bath chair on the porch, tie a bib around them to stem their dribbling, throw a blanket over their legs and leave them to enjoy the sunset. We then need to get on with the business of taking up our rightful positions within our galleries and museums, at all levels, particularly the curatorial ones. As long as we are on the outside, white folks will continue to run the show as they alone see fit. This means, I believe, vigorously rejecting equal opportunities policies that have done little or nothing for us.

With some opportunities clearly being more equal than others, it is time for an equal opportunities rethink. Time to include the issue of 'employment' as a key component of our 2000 struggle. We cannot possibly accept that equal opportunities policies are a good thing, because to do so is to accept that Black people are, when it comes to careers in the visual arts, inherently inferior and unsuitable. Consider the implications of the current application of equal opportunities: Jobs go to those considered to have the most relevant experience

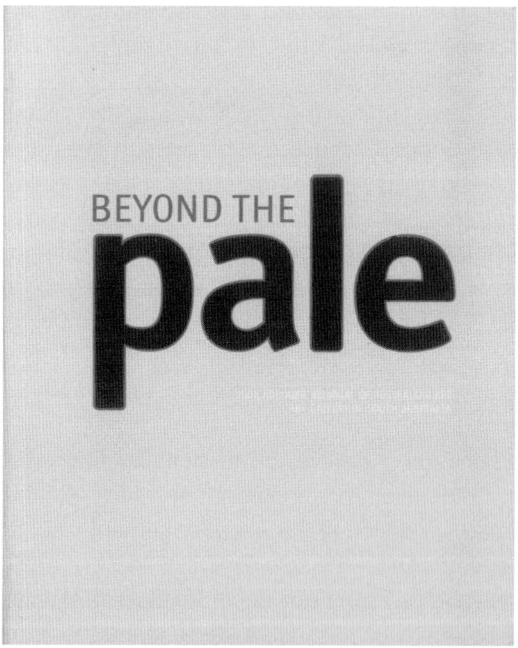

Figure 11.1 Catalogue cover, *Beyond the Pale*, Art Gallery of South Australia, Adelaide, 2000 Adelaide Biennial of Australian Art. Reproduced courtesy of Brenda L. Croft.

and who can otherwise demonstrate their suitability for the post. All but a few Black people consistently fail to get jobs in the visual arts. Therefore, according to the current culture of equal opportunities, Black people, despite being given sympathetic consideration by potential employers, simply do not have what it takes to work in the visual arts. The introduction of equal opportunities has had the effect of solidifying Black exclusion from visual arts jobs, whilst simultaneously giving the impression that everything is as it should be in the cozy benevolent white liberal world. We don't need equal opportunities policies. What we need is concerted anti-racism campaigns that expose and curtail white people's penchant for running the show themselves.

The last quarter century's polite beseechments were largely ineffectual against an international white art establishment tenaciously resisting change. Yes, Gentle Reader. For the 2000s to be well and truly Black, we need a new kind of struggle for a new century.

'2000's Got to be Black', was previously published as a catalogue essay, for *Beyond the Pale* (2000 Adelaide Biennial of Australian Art, Art Gallery of South Australia), Curated by Brenda L. Croft, 2000: 15–19.

Chapter 12

Next We Change Earth – New Art Exchange, Nottingham

Historical and cultural explorations of identity defined Nottingham's New Art Exchange's debut exhibition, a group show, with a particular focus on artists from Nottingham, or artists with substantial historical connections to the city. The exhibition reflected on issues faced by Black artists in the UK, and invited exchange around notions of culture, identity, time, space and home.

This exhibition, a bold and unique undertaking, features contributions from a range of artists with past, present or ongoing links to the East Midlands city. The artists represented in *Next We Change Earth* are: Said Adrus, Elshaday Berhane, Michael Forbes, Harjeet Kaur, Samson Kambalu, Hetain Patel, Keith Piper, Nazir Tanbouli and Andrew Wright. The exhibition also features a collaborative work by Gary Stewart, Trevor Mathison and Obinna Nwosu.

When credible histories of Black visual arts activity in England come to be written, Nottingham will be cited and acknowledged as having played a significant role in these narratives. Central to this role has been the part played by various artists, organisations and individuals concerned with the practice and profile of Black artists' work in the city over a period of several decades. Another important factor central to Nottingham's role in these narratives has been Trent Polytechnic (as it was, prior to becoming Nottingham Trent University) in offering places on its Fine Art courses to students such as Said Adrus and Keith Piper, from the early 1980s onwards, through to enrolment and graduation by Black students in more recent years. The artists represented in this exhibition have a variety of links with the city of Nottingham. As mentioned, a number were students at Trent Polytechnic or Nottingham Trent University. These artists come from a variety of backgrounds. Some were born and/or brought up in the UK, while others arrived in the city having been raised in countries such as Egypt, Ethiopia, Malawi, and Uganda.

The artists represent the multiple histories of immigration and settlement that are reflective of so many people in contemporary Britain. Simultaneously, these artists embrace and pursue a broad range of approaches to their practice, oftentimes eschewing (or moving on from) more conventional media such as 'painting', 'sculpture', 'printmaking' and so on. Loosely, we can describe much of these artists' practice as 'mixed media', but on closer inspection, we can ascertain that more importantly, what characterises these artists' practice is a desire and a determination to utilise a broad range of materials and approaches, in the making of their contributions and the telling of their stories. The artists' multiple histories of immigration and settlement referred to in this text are important for several reasons. These histories tell us something of why and how each of these artists pursues their interests.

Within the work of these artists, history is everything. History, identity, geography and location. These are the four cornerstones of their practice, but it is a sense of history, a (re) reading of history and a critiquing of history, which unmistakably dominates, and most defines what they do. History is (the) key to us availing ourselves of the fullest understandings of these artists' practice.

The period of the mid to late 1970s through to the early 1980s was without question one of the most politically, culturally and racially charged periods of Black British history. It was the time in which children of the pioneering generation of African, Caribbean and South Asian immigrants came of age. These immigrants came to the UK through a variety of routes and for a variety of reasons. In the case of Caribbean migrants, who comprised one of the biggest single groups of new post-war arrivals, some – a few – came to pursue and take up professional positions. The vast majority though, came to fill vacancies in manufacturing, healthcare and the service sectors. Broadly speaking, African and South Asian migrants came for much the same sorts of reasons, though South Asian communities were to be distinguished or characterised by the entrepreneurial elements amongst them who undertook to work in the retail, restaurant or manufacturing sectors. There was one other important factor that characterised the pioneering South Asian presence in towns and cities across the UK. South Asian immigrants had, for a variety of reasons often come via east African countries such as Uganda, Kenya and (perhaps to a somewhat lesser extent) Tanzania.

The children of these immigrants – for the most part either British born or raised in this country – found themselves coming of age in the late 1970s and early 1980s. The lives of these teenagers took a variety of routes. Then, as now, unemployment affected disproportionately large numbers of Black people. Some headed for the Labour Exchange. Reggae group, the Cimarons, were responsible for one of a number of songs lamenting the effect and experience of unemployment on Black British youth. Pointing the figure at society, the group sang 'You got me living on the dole. . .' Other youth took whatever jobs and apprenticeship opportunities they could find and got by as best they could. Aswad memorably summed up the route of delinquency and petty criminality taken by a few: 'Problem time like this I've seen youths who've turned to crime. They looking a way to keep their head above the water. . .' Some youngsters (such as Said Adrus, Keith Piper and Donald Rodney) went into further and higher education.

Then, perhaps less so now, only the comparative few from Britain's Black communities ventured into higher education and within this small number, only a comparative few undertook Fine Art courses. It is for researchers of the future to establish precise patterns of enrolment on the country's Fine Art courses by Black students, but the formidable impression exists that students such as Adrus, Piper and Rodney – plus those who had gone to other colleges before them – were truly breaking new ground in entering institutions of higher learning (such as Trent Polytechnic) to study Fine Art.

The early 1980s were intense, heady and potent times for Black people in England. They had by now established a particular and highly charged presence in various neighbourhoods and communities across the country, the districts in which they lived becoming synonymous with a sometimes fractious but nevertheless unmistakeable sense of place, space, and presence. These districts had, during the course of the 1970s, come to symbolise demarcated territory representing the unmistakeable emergence and presence of Black Britain. Within the local and national media, these areas would constantly be cast as quarters of menace, criminality and dysfunctionality. But to many Black people, these districts were, quite simply, home. London had Brixton and Ladbroke Grove ('the line'); Birmingham, the second city, had Handsworth; Leeds had Chapeltown, Bristol had St. Paul's; and Nottingham had Hyson Green. As mentioned, these areas were home to many people from the Commonwealth countries, and their British-born/raised children. Significantly these districts had all achieved – to varying degrees – 'frontline' status.

A number of elements characterised the existence and presence of Black Britain. Although the word was not fashionable at the time, there was a tangible sense of diaspora (with its multiplicity of attendant narratives, such as Black Power, Rastafari and the 'Dreadlocks' culture) and a feeling, or belief that Black youth were experiencing racism, disappointment, disaffection and what one sociologist poignantly referred to as 'endless pressure'.

Within the Hyson Greens and the Brixtons of the country, racism, educational under-achievement, unemployment, inter-generational conflict, homelessness or poor housing, and friction with the police were all experiences which, to varying degrees, typified young Black Britain. Time and again within their art practice, Adrus, Piper and Rodney would make work that referenced not only these troubled and vexatious conditions and experiences, but the variety of responses that they evoked and provoked.

The frustrations relating to these troubled and vexatious conditions and experiences were vented and given form in the 'rioting' that erupted during the mid-1970s and a few years later at the turn of the decade.

It was in these heady days of the early 1980s that the first of a number of exhibitions by younger Black artists, such as Keith Piper, took place. Within a short space of time of meeting Piper, Rodney joined him and others in contributing his work to these 'Black Art' exhibitions. For Piper, Rodney and other exhibitors still in further or higher education, the art school was as much a site of struggle as anywhere else. They took the view that Black art students could not afford to and should not insulate themselves from the more pressing realities of Black existence. The group often titled their exhibitions *The Pan-Afrikan Connection* and their position was effectively summarised in the catalogue introduction for one such exhibition in Nottingham:

> The exhibition title, *The Pan-Afrikan Connection*, has been used by the group since their second show as an expression of the solidarity which the artists feel with the struggles of all oppressed peoples of the world; be they in Africa, the Third World in general or the ghettoes of the capitalist West. Despite the fact that they are physically isolated from the centre of that struggle, insulated as they are within the liberal art school system, the group feel themselves to be connected to those struggles in so far that as long as international capitalism continues to use race as a basis for exploitation, then, all black people will remain its potential victims.

Between 1981 and 1984, the group of young artists and art students with which Piper and Rodney exhibited had shows and organised symposia across the towns and cities of Birmingham, Bristol, Coventry, London, Nottingham and Wolverhampton.

The group exhibited in Nottingham, [*The Pan-Afrikan Connection* took place at the Midland Group, 24–32 Carlton Street, in the city centre, 15 January – 12 February 1983] and subsequently organised Radical Black Art: a working Convention, which was held at the Ukaidi Centre, St Ann's, Nottingham on 28 March 1984. Amongst his brief comments included in the Midland Group catalogue, Piper stated: 'Understand also that we are not racists simply because race remains a factor in our analysis. A dialogue on racism will remain an issue in our struggle as long as its application remains a factor in their (or dare I say your) resistance.' With characteristic forthrightness, Rodney opened his contribution with the following comment: 'The work you shall see is fresh and cutting and black. The colour of our skin is the reason you are here, the colour of our skins is the reason that keeps us together and it is the colour of our skins that has made us produce this work.'

Piper and Rodney may well have felt themselves to be 'physically isolated from the centre of [black] struggle', but they were certainly living in the heart of the Black community. Their address was 3 Lindsey Walk, part of a modern housing development in Hyson Green meant to solve (or at least address) the housing needs of cities like Nottingham. It was the sort of place that aptly fitted Bob Marley's memorable description of one of Kingston, Jamaica's hardscrabble neighbourhoods – 'Concrete jungle, where the living is hardest. . .' By the mid to late 1970s Black people's urban existence was oftentimes characterised by having to live in problematic concrete environments such as Hyson Green.

We can start to get a sense of Trent Polytechnic's early significance as a destination for some of these artists when we look at the ways in which the art school is remembered and talked about by Rodney. Rodney, one of the most important and accomplished artists of his generation, is not represented in this exhibition, though he is, (with Keith Piper) to be the focus of one of the New Art Exchange's forthcoming exhibitions. After completing a foundation course at Bournville School of Art, Rodney went on to his Fine Art degree at Trent Polytechnic in Nottingham. He quickly fell in with Piper, also from Birmingham, who like Adrus, was a second-year student in the year above Rodney (Piper had undertaken his foundation course at Coventry Lanchester Polytechnic) and he and Rodney were to become lifelong friends and occasional collaborators.

On one particular programme from Channel 4's 1987 series *State of the Art*, Rodney suggested that it was Piper's influence – plus the apparent influence of one or two other Black art students – that steered him away from his early practice as what Rodney himself described as 'flower painting' towards a more politically robust, Black form of art practice.

Upon meeting Piper, the most prolific and accomplished figure of the 'Black Art' movement of the early 1980s, Rodney found himself being readily persuaded of the importance, validity and urgency of the Black Art/Black Power argument. In the course of several interviews – one of them for television (the aforementioned *State of the Art* programme) – Rodney made mention of Piper's profound effect on him, as Rodney himself explained: 'When I got to Trent [Polytechnic] I met Keith [whose] work was about the experience of being black . . . I suddenly became aware of what I wanted to say and who I wanted to say it to.'

[Though not himself an art student, mention should be made of Gary Stewart, currently [2008] inIVA's Head of Multimedia and one of the artists exhibiting in *Next We Change Earth*. A close friend of Piper's, Stewart, also from Birmingham (born there in 1961), went to Trent Polytechnic at the same time as Piper and Adrus. Stewart received his BSc in Electronics and Computing from Trent Polytechnic in 1984.]

Since the now distant days of the 1980s, Nottingham galleries have hosted a number of exhibitions of work by Black artists, and the city has seen the development and establishment of a number of dedicated visual arts initiatives. Of particular note was the creation of APNA Arts (Apna is Hindi for 'ours') and EMACA (East Midlands African Caribbean Arts), the former with a remit to cater to the needs of audiences with a South Asian background, the latter with a similar mission, though its focus was to be on artists and audiences of an African and

African Caribbean background. These two organisations joined together to develop the New Art Exchange, which has as its debut exhibition, *Next We Change Earth*. This exhibition consists of contributions by early to mid-1980s Trent Polytechnic graduates, plus contributions from a number of more recent graduates from the same institution and other artists with significant links to Nottingham. Some artists' contributions take the form of new commissions and recent work.

It seemed to the exhibition's curators – David Schischka Thomas and Michael Forbes – that the assembled artists' proposals were reflective of several overlapping themes and ideas, namely: time and space, home, culture and identity. In considering each of the artists' contributions, we can get a sense of how and why such themes and ideas might present themselves within the work of Said Adrus, Elshaday Berhane, Michael Forbes, Harjeet Kaur, Samson Kambalu, Hetain Patel, Keith Piper, Nazir Tanbouli, Andrew Wright, and the collaborative installation by Gary Stewart, Trevor Mathison and Obinna Nwosu.

Like a number of the other artists in the exhibition, Andrew Wright has a keen concern for issues of identity – though not just an individual's received, evolved or declared identity. In his work, Wright is engaged in a process of critiquing imposed or presumed identities. He is mindful of the ways in which negative and problematic racial attitudes affect not only those who perpetrate them, but also affect those on the receiving end of them. One of his recent bodies of work undertook to explore the image of the 'golliwog' and speculated on how this grotesque caricature contributed to the culture and climate of racism he saw himself as growing up in. Wright's assertion – that we are, to some extent, products of our environment – is thus given an international dimension, in this new work, in which he explores his relationship to Africa. It could be argued that little has changed since the Victorian framing of Africa as the 'Dark Continent'. Within much of the media and elsewhere, the image persists of Africa as a deeply dysfunctional, inherently backward-looking and technologically inept landmass, in which its innumerable cultural and language groupings are paradoxically perceived as being indistinguishable from each other and, simultaneously, perpetually in conflict. Troubled by the negative media stereotypes that so often depict Africa as a continent synonymous with the scourge of AIDS, famine and political and military conflict, Wright set out to see part of the continent himself, and visited Gambia, in West Africa. Through this journey, this pilgrimage, like other artists before him, he is engaged in the process of understanding, of making sense of Africa, and its complex relationship to himself, as someone of African descent, growing up and living in the UK. The paintings he has contributed to this exhibition explore these ideas.

Michael Forbes is also exercised by the notion that history has bequeathed Black people a troubled and problematic state of marginality and invisibility. Marginality because the legacy of slavery has, it could be argued, created and sustained a culture of racism that sees Black people as having less ability and less humanity than others within British/Western society. Invisibility because the presence and contributions of Black people have the unmistakable appearance of having been studiously erased from the shared sense of 'British' history held by the vast majority of white people in that country. Most people in this country would concede, or accept, that the African-Caribbean immigrants who made their way to Britain in the decades immediately following World War II created an unmistakable and irreversible Black presence. But comparatively few would accept, or even know, that the Black presence in Britain stretches back to Roman times. Within this work, *Coloured Black*, Forbes attempts to challenge not only the vindictive erasing of Black people from British history, but also the attendant self-image of cultural, historical and social superiority held – consciously or unconsciously – by white Europeans. The factors responsible for this are multiple and varied. We can blame history books, or the ways in which history has been taught in our schools. We might also blame the media, or at least, parts of it. Forbes has used the perhaps unlikely object of the china figurine in his attempts to critique the ingrained cultural sense of superiority that accompanies the pointed exclusion of Black people from Britain's history. He has bought, collected and acquired hundreds of porcelain figures, symbolic of a fictitious, but deeply held sense of a glorious, cultured and refined period of European and in particular, British greatness. Each gaudy figure evocative of, or from, the Georgian era, has then been repainted, the previous white skin of the ornaments becoming instead decidedly blacker. In so doing, Forbes, at a (brush) stroke, (re) creates a historical Black presence and a series of poignant and arresting narratives arising out of absence and presence.

Hetain Patel, like a number of the artists in this exhibition, has a pronounced interest in issues of cultural (that is, group or inherited) identity. His work for this exhibition is reflective of the process of critiquing the received or presumed identity of his Indian background. As the artist himself says,

> My practice took its beginnings from wanting to understand my Indian heritage. Not so much a factual historical timeline but rather through fighting the impossibility of being able to fully understand a mindset of a different context to the western one I was born and raised in.
>
> When my parents immigrated to the UK in the 1960s they brought with them an ideal of India. And as India continued to develop, this romanticized ideal is the one which was passed down to me. This is of course a common story amongst British born generations of immigrants. The dislocation of Indian culture naturally does not sit well with my British sensibilities. However, it is these very sensibilities that I wish to challenge. If the Western influence of my birthplace is embedded in my way of thinking and the physical mannerisms of my body, is it possible to retrain these ways of understanding the world with an Indian code. [?]

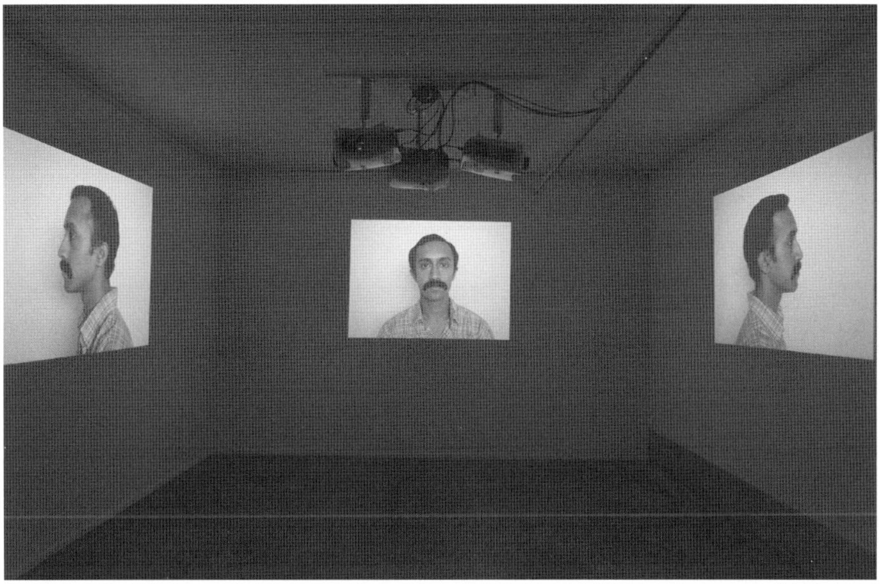

Figure 12.1 Installation view of Hetain Patel, *It's Growing On Me*, 2008, three-screen time-lapse video installation, in *Next We Change Earth*, the inaugural exhibition of New Art Exchange, Nottingham, 6 September – 28 October 2008. © New Art Exchange.

Like many other British artists of South Asian background, Patel is engaged in the critical and intriguing process of exploring cultural sensibilities which, whilst seemingly in conflict with each other (i.e. 'Indian-ness' versus 'British-ness') nevertheless coexist within the structure of his being. To an extent Patel is of course in his own way, reflective of the mixed-up-ness, which is so much a part of how we all are in contemporary Britain in particular, and indeed, in the wider world as well. Nevertheless, Patel is keen to critically engage with what he calls 'Indian signifiers' such as decorating his body with the sorts of pigments traditionally used in Hindu rituals, and learning to play the Indian tabla (hand drums). In so doing, he creates mechanisms through which he can consciously engage with Indian culture (rather than leaving unchallenged the often-unspoken assumptions that cultural identity is fixed, inherited and transferable from one location to another.)

As mentioned earlier, within these artists' work, history is everything. History, plus the accompanying elements of identity, geography, and location. History informs our sense of what and how our identity is constructed, and what and where we call home. In 21st-century Britain it is of course possible for each of us to embody multiple identities and to locate and regard several different places as being home. And of course, the sense of displacement that some of us carry with us (coupled with the realities of economic migration) might mean that belonging is an elusive state of being and we ultimately have little or no substantial sense of home – whether that be country, city or dwelling.

For Harjeet Kaur, home is not so much a place of solace and comfort, but more of an unsettled construct. Our migratory and at times nomadic lifestyles can often lead to a questioning of the idea of 'home', but also a questioning of our memories/experiences of it. Within her work, Kaur sets about the task of examining the ideal of 'home', through images that are both unswerving in their focus and evocative, in the responses that they elicit from the viewer. As viewers we are required to draw on, and question, our own memories and constructions of 'home'.

Notions of home and memories of childhood are of course inextricably linked and in this new work Kaur sensitively explores this coupling. Each of us has our own memories but Kaur's work allows each of us the possibility, and the chance, to explore/critique notions of home, particularly where these notions intersect with 'cultural identity'. 'One of the ways in which we are identified is through the idea of "home" which is used to perpetuate the myth of "home sweet home". I will examine the issues of identity and self through recovering past histories from our idea of home and its links to identity.'

As mentioned earlier, a number of these artists were born and/or brought up in various parts of the UK, including in the East Midlands, while others first came to Nottingham as adults having been raised in countries such as Egypt, Ethiopia, Malawi and Uganda. It is from Egypt that Nazir Tanbouli began a journey that brought him to Nottingham, as an accomplished artist whose work has been shown throughout Egypt and internationally, in countries as varied as Austria and Argentina. One of several painters in *Next We Change Earth*, Tanbouli's distinctive paintings in some ways depict home as a space and place of tension, discomfort and unease. In effect, Tanbouli's work disrupts and unsettles the frequently mythic notion of 'Home Sweet Home' alluded to by Kaur. The figures that occupy his paintings are decidedly and singularly strange. Oftentimes not quite human, not quite animal, the characters, even when embracing, present themselves to us as elements of a bad dream. The surreal aspect of the tension, discomfort and unease in Tanbouli's paintings is heightened by the highly decorative ways in which he renders and depicts the furnishings, walls and floorings of the domestic interiors in which the cast of characters exists.

As writer Judith Palmer has noted

> Here is a space where a freakshow of fantastical imaginings and down-home ordinariness co-exist in an uneasy truce. A snoring woman nods off on the sofa, oblivious to the snarling reptile padding across the lino. A man sprouts the head of a braying donkey, and his kitchen companion merely raises a polite eyebrow. Hemmed in by too-close walls and too-big personalities, the characters push against the edges of the paintings that struggle to contain them. All boundaries seem permeable and subject to collapse, as animate and inanimate objects exchange identities. The sitting room reptile adjusts to

its surroundings by camouflaging its skin to match the chintzy cushion-covers. The armchair looks livelier than the catatonic woman slumped in it.

Perhaps one of the most unusual contributions to this exhibition comes from Samson Kambalu, whose work has contributed to the titling of *Next We Change Earth*. Kambalu's work is characterised not only by its wit, but also more importantly, by the ways in which it obliges us to question things through its use of the familiar. In this regard, perhaps his most celebrated work is *Holy Ball*, a football covered in pages from the Bible. The work is particularly poignant, loaded and open-ended in its meanings and readings. Football as a sort of new religion, religion as a sort of plaything, desecration coupled with consecration, the word of the referee having the finality and the status of the word of God. In the artist's own words *Holy Ball*, like the rest of his art, is 'a question of how we create meaning for ourselves.'

This idea – of creating new meanings for ourselves – is central to this new work, which consists of an installation, *The New Art Exchange Creative Index*. The work is made of a number of bound volumes each containing hundreds of computer-generated anagrams of the words 'The New Art Exchange'. It may

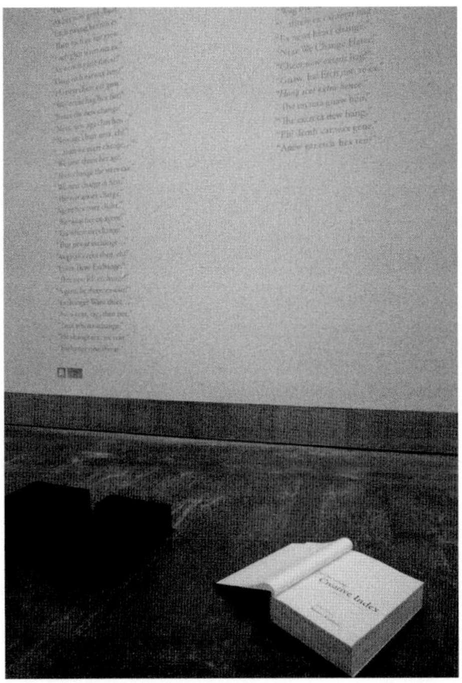

Figure 12.2 Installation view of Samson Kambalu, *Next We Change Earth* 2008, mixed media, in *Next We Change Earth*, the inaugural exhibition of New Art Exchange, Nottingham, 6 September – 28 October 2008. © New Art Exchange.

well be in the nature of anagrams, but I'm struck by the potential of the words generated to create new and powerful meanings and sentiments that at once tie them to, as well as liberate them from, The New Art Exchange and the multiplicity of things it represents. The anagram 'Next We Change Earth' is evocative of the exalted aspiration (articulated by the African-American poet Lucille Clifton) 'to make things happen and make them better'. Another anagram 'Next Teacher We Hang' seems to me to be a sentiment that might flow from Fela Kuti's powerful 'Teacher don't teach me nonsense', or Pink Floyd's memorable line 'we don't need no education.' Collectively, these bizarre, funny and poignant anagrams can be seen as a form of digital fortune telling in which the anagrams are reflective of a range of signifiers, as unpredictable as the artist's practice itself.

Like a number of other artists in this exhibition, Elshaday Berhane secured her degree from Nottingham Trent University. Originally from Ethiopia, Berhane came to Nottingham by way of London, where she completed a foundation course at Camberwell Art College. I had earlier made mention of the ways in which notions of home and memories of childhood are inextricably linked in the new work by Harjeet Kaur. We might in some ways advance the same sentiments in discussing this new work by Berhane, which seeks to explore childhood dreams by creating distinctive pieces of sculpture utilising broken and discarded toys found on the streets around her home.

In so doing, Berhane establishes a working relationship to her neighbourhood, her area, her district, of inner-city Nottingham. In this sense, location is of immense importance. In the artist's own words

> While living in Hyson Green and Forest Fields, a highly multicultural inner-city area of Nottingham, situated within a small distance of the New Art Exchange, I collected bits of toys that were discarded by children playing on the streets. I will be incorporating some of these found toys in the sculpture. These are often found in crowded inner-city areas where families have very little space in the home and children often play outside on the streets. I will use these broken and discarded pieces of toys, to inspire the forms I make. These toys are the leftover ghosts of a world imagined by a child's daily play, reminder of dreams, fantasy and escapism.

Through this process of salvaging the discarded debris of broken toys, Berhane introduces critical (and critically important) ideas of class and its intersections with race. In Berhane's work, a broken toy becomes a signifier of 'no backyard for the children to play' (a line from Aswad's 'African Children', a song protesting the inequities of living in poor housing conditions). Within this work, perhaps more than the other contributions to this exhibition, social and economic stratification and disadvantage come to the fore.

In 'A Cemetery in Ilford' (a chapter in the Bookworks publication *I'll get my coat*) Sukhdev Sandhu makes the telling observation that 'It is hard to escape the thought that immigrants are never so deep a part of the English landscape as when they die.' Said Adrus' latest work takes as its starting point the Muslim Burial Ground in Woking, Surrey, a Grade II listed site located in a corner of Woking's Horsell Common. Enclosed within ornate brick walls, the cemetery has a domed archway entrance reflecting the design of the nearby Shah Jehan Mosque, said to be Britain's first purpose-built mosque, erected in 1889.

The Muslim Burial Ground was apparently built during the First World War to receive burials of Indian Army soldiers who, having fought and been wounded fighting for the British Empire, died at the dedicated hospital established for them in Brighton Pavilion. During the 1960s, the bodies of the fallen were exhumed and reinterred in the Military Cemetery at Brookwood, about 30 miles from London. According to Adrus, the work exists, in part at least, to highlight 'issues about War, Empire, and Islamic Architecture in the South East of England and notions of contemporary landscape in the Home Counties.'

I mentioned earlier that history is (the) key to us availing ourselves of the fullest understandings of these artists' practice. As much as with any other artist in *Next We Change Earth*, we can apply this idea of history to Adrus's practice. We learn from him that 'my own father had been part of the British Army in Kenya during the Second World War.' Within this work, Adrus creates his own 'memorial' – not just to the often forgotten and overlooked soldiers of the colonies who gave their lives fighting for the interests of this country, but also a memorial to history itself, and the multiple ways in which history impacts our contemporary lives.

Keith Piper was, as mentioned earlier, by far the most prolific and accomplished figure of the 'Black Art' movement of the early 1980s. More than any other Black artist of his generation, it was his fiery brand of racially charged and assertive images and text that announced the arrival of a new generation of Black artists, a new type of Black artist. There were many things that were new, fresh and different about Piper's work and the ways it seemed to be wholly in step with the more progressive and militant aspirations and sensibilities of Black Britain. Piper's practice was characterised by what was, in a British context, a new attachment to social and political narratives. These narratives were expressed through the mechanisms of Pop Art, assemblage sculpture, mixed media and a variety of other aesthetic (p)references.

For this exhibition, Piper will return to Nottingham, the city in which he gained his first-class degree in Fine Art, to produce a series of video studies of the landscape of Nottingham, interweaving it with a multiplicity of attendant and related narratives. In this work Piper considers the built environment of the city, and the ways in which town planners sought to retain a sense of pastoral England in the heart of an expanding urban mass. As Piper himself opined:

> A key, and recurring aspect of the Nineteenth century expansion of urban space was the need on the part of town planners to constantly evoke the memory of the idyllic and the pastoral. This is true of the development of the city of Nottingham in which place names such as Hyson Green, Sherwood and Forest Fields carry with them the echo of some long-lost rural idyll which has long since been bricked and concreted over with the forward march of the urban.

To these fascinating considerations Piper adds an element of perhaps inevitable conflict when studiously affected urban constructs of rural Englishness run headlong into what Piper calls 'the shadows cast by the contemporary mythologisation of Nottingham as a site of danger, crime and threat.'

Considerations of rural Englishness are important because 'Englishness' tends to be evoked by rural, wide-open spaces, rather than by urban environments. In this sense, the centre of Piper's home city of Birmingham is not 'England' (even though it is located at the epicentre of the West Midlands) but the nearby, yet altogether more rural and monocultural area of the Cotswolds is. We need look no further than the official Cotswolds website, which tells us 'Popular with both the English themselves and visitors from all over the world, the Cotswolds are well-known for gentle hillsides ("wolds"), sleepy villages and for being so "typically English"'.

Though Piper bridles against what he calls the 'mythologisation of Nottingham as a site of danger, crime and threat', recent crime figures, for what they're worth, show many types of crime in Nottingham to be above the national average. Notwithstanding the current media hysteria over gun and knife crime, Gary Stewart, Trevor Mathison and Obinna Nwosu take as their subject the reality of incidences of homicidal deaths in Nottingham and elsewhere. This is an issue of genuine concern that forms the starting point for their contribution to this exhibition. *Bitter Thickest Blood* will be what the artists have called 'an interactive sonic installation interrogating the traces of evidence, meanings and conclusions formed as a consequence of teenage deaths at the hands of their peers.' The work is an attempt to go beyond the predictable, banal and fleeting attention paid to incidences of murder amongst young people, and to produce a response, or a memorial which is much more textured, layered, nuanced and engaging. Emitting from speakers will be a cacophony of audio clips comprising 'voice overs created from various text sources and interviews with young people, family friends, legal staff, lawyers, police, courts, youth workers, sociologists, journalists & politicians.' In addition, speakers will emit 'Extracts from memorial websites. Field recordings from the murder sites and newly created sonic soundtracks and atmospheres made specifically in response to the content and material. Fragments of selected published music and spoken word.'

This is a work which, in its own way, critiques the often trite and sensationalised media news stories of teenage homicide deaths. *Bitter Thickest Blood* offers the viewer/listener a set of altogether more serious and intelligent mechanisms for engaging with this sobering reality and its implications and manifestations.

Next We Change Earth offers gallery-going audiences an absorbing and engaging set of snapshots of 'Nottingham Past, Present and Future', as seen through the work of a range of artists with corresponding past, present or ongoing links to the city. The contributions of each artist stand in marked contrast to those of the other exhibitors. In this regard, the exhibition offers the potential to be a fascinating encounter. *Next We Change Earth* may well offer clues as to the sort of exhibition programme that residents of the city (and visitors to Nottingham) can expect from the New Art Exchange. It is for art historians and cultural historians of the future to determine the longer-term successes or otherwise of Nottingham's latest visual arts initiative. One senses that at the present time, the great unknowable is the extent to which the New Art Exchange is willing and able to develop and maintain healthy and ongoing relationships with arts organizations and audiences across the city, beyond its supposed or presumed 'core' constituencies of artists and audiences.

'*Next We Change Earth*' was previously published in the catalogue to accompany the exhibition *Next We Change Earth*, the inaugural exhibition of New Art Exchange, Nottingham, 6 September–28 October 2008: 10–71.

Chapter 13

Keith Piper, Donald Rodney and the Artists' Response to the Archive

This article will look at how two artists – Keith Piper and Donald Rodney – have used archival images within their practice. Within this text I'll be considering the making of one particular piece of work by Piper, in 1981 and one piece of work by the pair, in 1987. As someone with my own interest in the archive, I'm especially interested in the ways in which artists respond to the notion of 'history', and their place within that 'history'. Within the specific pieces under consideration – as well as in other work the artists made – they have in effect created history by responding to what were, at the time, contemporary events, realising perhaps, their 'historical' significance.

Artists themselves are, on occasion, great collectors of material and ephemera. To all intents and purposes these artists are themselves not only archivists, but archives and repositories of knowledge and information. This text will seek to explore some of the ways in which Piper and Rodney sought to utilise this material in the making of their work. I'd also like to consider the ways in which they attempted to reinscribe history. Not rewrite it, but unpick it and reassemble it, being mindful of the ways in which certain people have been written out of history, or have been the victims of historians' (and society's) prejudices and ignorance.

'History' is of immense importance to certain artists, as can be witnessed by the fascinating ways in which they historicize contemporary events, or repurpose archival images within their practice. This text will also, in part, be a consideration of what notions and constructs such as the 'archive' and 'history' meant to Piper and Rodney. It is also my intention to consider the idea of 'history' as cultural memory and the ways in which this counters abusive or discriminatory hegemonic accounts of it.

When it comes to ideas of the artist as archivist, Donald Rodney would take some beating. Rodney, who died in 1998, was a prolific collector of newspapers, magazines, books, gadgets, and much much more. In fact, Rodney was a collector of stuff, stuff that took many forms. Amongst the 'stuff' he had amassed was a collection of globes of the world. All sorts of sizes and all sorts of ages. Being bed-bound and hospitalised for weeks and months at a time did not prevent or limit Rodney's compulsion to get his hands on and collect an almost bewildering assortment of material. For her contribution to the catalogue accompanying Rodney's *9 Night in Eldorado* exhibition,[1] artist Virginia Nimarkoh created an exhaustive inventory of the 'Contents of [his] Bed space, Kings College Hospital, 29.5.97'. Nimarkoh divided Rodney's impromptu, bedside archive into a number of sections: Books, Computer Games, CDs, Equipment, Magazines, Materials, Newspapers and finally, Videos. Rodney's newspaper stash included the previous day's *Evening Standard*, as well as recent and current copies of the *Guardian* and the *Sun* newspapers.

Rodney's scrapbooks were full, not only of sketches and ideas for work, but also full of clippings of newspaper articles that interested him. In this regard, he found the *Sun* to be an invaluable source of material, as much as, if not more so than the *Guardian* or any other newspaper or magazine. Rodney would comb his newspapers not just for stories or articles on Black people, but more importantly, he would scour these newspapers for indications of the ways in which 'race' was animated. A wide range of articles and news stories tickled, exercised and intrigued him. He was for example, interested in the ways in which Mike Tyson, one of the towering personalities of the 1980s and 1990s was consistently caricatured and vilified within sections of the mass media as a near sub-human beast and an incorrigible delinquent. Likewise, the ways in which certain newspapers caricatured young Black males as inherently inclined to criminality was of great interest to him. Further to this, the interplay between 'race', 'immigration' and the Black British experience fascinated him. With both cynicism and wit, Rodney would make good use of his newspaper cuttings, and frequently, these articles, cartoons and pictures made their way into his artwork.

Rodney's embrace of the archive and history was nothing new, or recent. From the moment he developed a serious interest in painting, he began to familiarise himself with the medium's history. Speaking in 1987, about embarking on a fine art degree course some six or so years earlier, Rodney recalled that 'When I went to Trent, I'd been brought up in the tradition of painting. I knew how to paint. I knew the history of painting. I knew my Picassos; my everything.'[2] In knowing this history, Rodney sought not to make work that merely stood outside of this history. Instead, he sought to make work that critiqued that history, whilst simultaneously demanding for himself a place within it. This multiple act – of critiquing history, whilst simultaneously seeking a place within it – was a strategy that lay at the heart of his embrace of the archive.

Arriving at Trent Polytechnic in 1981, Rodney met, in the year above him, Keith Piper. Embracing both the aesthetics of pop art and the ideology of 'Black Art' (that is, a socially dynamic visual art practice, closely aligned to militant political and cultural agendas of progress for Black people), Piper's practice even as a student was sharp, witty, powerful and engaging. Piper had argued that the work of Black artist/art student should speak to 'the Black experience'. To this end, Piper's work touched on the experiences of Black people in the United States, Africa, and elsewhere in the world. Rodney found himself charmed and persuaded by Piper's position and practice, the two going on to collaborate on a number of occasions. The work and the exhibitions they produced together represented a decisive meeting of minds. In 1987, they issued a statement called 'Piper & Rodney On Theory'. Its opening paragraph read

> In Britains (sic) art schools, where the mythology of individual self-expression is held at a premium, collaborative activity is discouraged. Apart from throwing a spanner into bureaucratic machinery geared to assess the virtuoso, collaborative activities begin to counter many of the negative effects of an individualism which leaves the art student isolated and vulnerable. Supporting collaborative activity has therefore never been in the interest of the art school hierarchy, as many students expressing an interest in working collaboratively have learned to their cost.

Piper was, even by 1981, a highly skilled and effective user of archival material. An artist with a particularly keen eye, he sourced an astonishingly broad range of material for the making of his art. The range of imagery and paraphernalia Piper sourced for his work included many images from the ongoing history of the fight against apartheid. Throughout the 1980s and well into the 1990s, the struggle against the racist system of apartheid in South Africa consumed the creative and political energies of many people. Within this context, Piper produced numerous works that sought not only to expose the barbarity and criminality of apartheid, but also the hypocrisy of apartheid's friends in the upper echelons of British society. To this end, Piper made good use of the hugely important archive of images chronicling the victims of – and resistance to – apartheid. Similarly, Piper sourced a number of images from the documentation of the years of the transatlantic slave trade, which occurred between the 17th and 19th centuries. But he was also interested in decidedly local concerns and to this end also sourced his imagery from British contexts. Indeed, one of his collaborations with Rodney was a 1987 exhibition called *Adventures Close To Home*.

Politically, these were heady and difficult days for Black people. Piper knew how to visualise the trauma and dynamism of the times and to this end, he produced some remarkable work. One particular example is his 1981 mixed media piece, *13 Killed*. 1981 was the year of the New Cross Massacre, in which thirteen Black youngsters, attending a birthday party, lost their lives in a suspicious house fire. This was an horrific incident that galvanised the Black community, acutely increasing its sense of identity and purpose. Mystery surrounded the cause of the fire and, in Black circles at least, speculation was rife. There were those who felt that the fire pointed to the work of racist arsonists. After all, arson attacks on the homes of Black and Asian people were not uncommon. In other quarters, an accident or the malicious work of a disgruntled party-goer were cited as possible causes. One thing however, was certain. The aftermath of the tragedy threw into sharp focus an apparent widespread indifference shown to the deaths by the mainstream news media, and important religious or political figures of the day. Even the Queen had no declaration of condolences for the bereaved. This comprehensive expression of indifference deeply offended many within the Black community. Furthermore, there existed the disturbing perception that any efforts made by the police to establish the fire's cause, or to apprehend possible suspects, appeared unconvincing. In the aftermath of the fire, there existed the sobering realisation that the British establishment appeared indifferent to the sufferings and traumas of Black people.

In *13 Killed*, Piper cut up and collaged a newspaper report of the tragedy, overlayering image and text on a powerful background that consisted of a recreation of a burned and charred wallpaper and skirting board reminiscent of a typical 'West Indian' domestic environment. Using found materials in such a strikingly original and emotive way, Piper gave form to Black people's tragedy, grief and outrage. This was a work of the most profound empathy, in which Piper paid homage to lives lived and lives lost. Using plain household postcards, Piper penned messages to each of the fire's victims, naming them all and attaching portraits of them to each message. This effectively restored to each victim a humanity and an individuality that seemed robbed from them, not only by the fire itself but by the subsequent apparent indifference. The party at which the tragedy occurred was held to celebrate the birthday of 16-year-old Yvonne Ruddock. Piper's message to her read 'SEND THIS ONE BACK TO THE PEOPLE! SISTER YVONNE SURVIVED 15 YEARS WITH US IN BABYLON. ON THE DAWN OF HER 16TH YEAR BABYLON SNUFFED HER OUT. SEND THIS ONE BACK TO THE PEOPLE + LET THEM DEMAND AN ANSWER!' Similar messages were penned for the other victims, namely Humphrey Brown, 18, Peter Campbell, 18, Steve Collins, 17, Patrick Cummings, 16, Gerry Francis, 17, Andrew Gooding, 14, Lloyd Richard Hall, 20, Patricia Denise Johnston, 15, Rosalind Henry, 16, Glenton Powell, 15, Paul Ruddock, 22, and Owen Thompson, 16. An infamous episode of history occurred in January 1981. Piper benchmarked that history with a truly remarkable piece of work.

One of Piper and Rodney's most compelling and successful collaborations was *The Next Turn of the Screw*. Like Piper's own *13 Killed*, *The Next Turn of the*

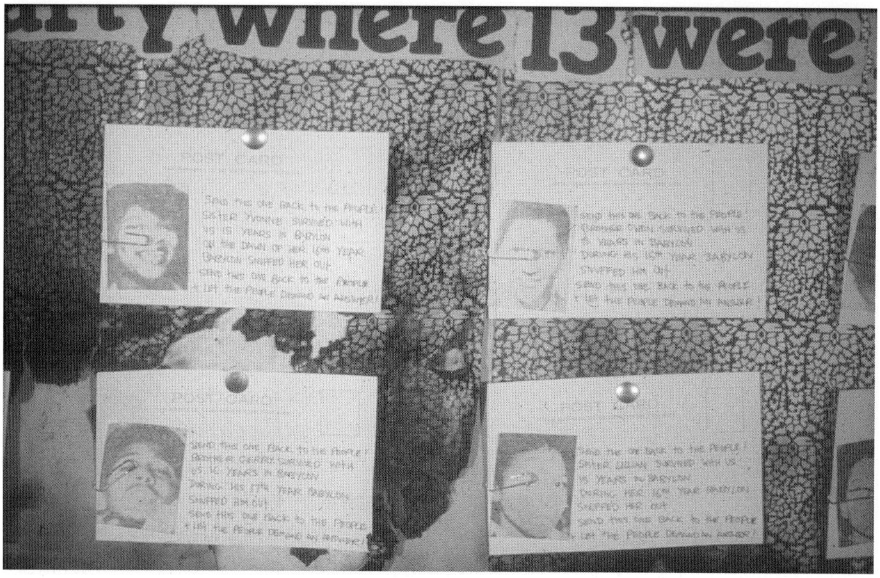

Figure 13.1 Keith Piper *13 Killed*, mixed media, 1981. Detail © Keith Piper.

Screw was in effect a homage to lives lost or damaged in acts of great violence. The work took the form of an installation, painted and built in the gallery area of Chelsea School of Art. This work was part of a larger group show, titled *The Devil's Feast* that featured work by Zarina Bhimji, Chila Burman, Jennifer Comrie, Allan de Souza, Keith Piper and Donald Rodney. The exhibition took place in April and May of 1987. In some ways, the catalyst for the piece was yet another 'death by misadventure'. Clinton McCurbin, a young Black man, died whilst being arrested and subdued by the police, in Wolverhampton town centre, in February 1987. But McCurbin's violent death was only one of the most recent of a number of similar tragedies.

For example, on Saturday 28 September 1985, Cherry Groce, a Black woman had been shot and paralysed during a police raid on her home in London. Groce was, allegedly, shot in her bed, by a member of a team of armed police officers who were looking for her son. Another, slightly divergent account has it that 'a team of armed officers went to the home of Mrs Cherry Groce in Brixton, South London, to arrest her son, Michael, who was wanted for [allegations of] armed robbery. In fact, Michael Groce no longer lived there. The officers smashed down the door with a sledge-hammer and then an inspector rushed in 'shouting armed' police. Mrs Groce says the officer suddenly rushed at her, pointing a gun at her. She tried to run back but he shot her. She is now paralysed and confined to a wheelchair. (*Times*, 16 January 1987)'.[3] On Sunday 6 October 1985, just over a week after Groce sustained her horrific injuries, another Black woman, Cynthia

Jarrett died of a heart attack during a police raid on her Tottenham home.[4] There were others, many others.

Piper and Rodney were determined that these deaths would not go unremarked. To this end, they set about creating a work of profound empathy. *The Next Turn of the Screw* featured, in part, painted portraits of six unfortunate people, each one a victim of alleged police brutality. The unhappy roll call featured, chronologically, Colin Roach, Jackie Beverley, the aforementioned Cherry Groce and Cynthia Jarrett, Trevor Monerville and finally, the aforementioned Clinton McCurbin. What was remarkable about *The Next Turn of the Screw* was that the artists had to collect and rely on decidedly scrappy source material. The nature of these archival images threw into sharp relief the violence that blighted the lives of these sorry individuals. Colin Roach is shown smiling, the portraits of Jackie Beverley and Trevor Monerville are incomplete – evidence of the ways in which their likenesses were sourced from what one artist has called 'other people's photographs'. By far the most poignant image is that of Cherry Groce. The only image of her that was circulated within the press and media in the aftermath of her injuries was lifted from a wedding photograph. The cropped photograph – taken several decades earlier – showed her as a bride, wearing her wedding day finery. No other pictures of the hapless victim recent – or otherwise – were available. Beneath each portrait the artists had, almost by way of an epitaph, written a brief description of the violence that had befallen the six.

The Next Turn of the Screw is in effect 'history' as cultural memory, history as remembrance. To profound and deeply sobering effect, the artists used archival images to create something that is in itself an archival document. The piece was only ever shown as part of *The Devil's Feast* exhibition[5] and, upon the close of the exhibition, was dismantled and the six portraits executed directly on to the gallery wall were painted over.

Relatively little has been written about the 1980s emergence of a new generation of Black artists in England. And much of what has been written has been shallow and reductive. Historians and researchers have yet to substantially undertake a process of critical examination of the broader body of artists of the period, according their work individual and focussed attention. A great many works have been lost, or lost to history, so the task of researching art practice of the recent past is an urgent and important one. Paradoxically, given the sophistication with which a number of artists have sourced and used archival material, accessible documentation of their work remains patchy. There is still much to be done in fashioning a substantial and tangible history of the emergence of artists such as Piper and Rodney.

'Keith Piper, Donald Rodney and the Artists' Response to the Archive' was first published on the axisweb.org website, circa late 1990s. It is no longer online.

Notes

1 *9 Night in Eldorado* South London Gallery 10 September–12 October 1997. Kesewa Hennessy, in conversation with Donald Rodney explained that the exhibition title was 'named after the Jamaican tradition of people meeting, drinking and reminiscing for nine nights after the death of a family member'. And that furthermore 'it represents the nine nights Donald was unable to attend after the death of his own father.' [The feature on Rodney was titled 'Sweet as sculpture' and was part of a regular series of interviews that went out under the weekly heading Answer the Question. The *Voice* newspaper, September 1 1997].

2 Donald Rodney in conversation with Lubaina Himid, *State of the Art*, Channel 4/ Illuminations (Television) Ltd television programme, 1987.

3 Quoted in *Policing Against Black People*, Institute of Race Relations, London, 1987: 26.

4 For more on these incidents and responses to them, see 'Riots and Rumours of Riots', a chapter in *A Climate of Fear: The Murder of PC Blakelock and the Case of the Tottenham Three* by David Rose, Bloomsbury Publishing Ltd. 1992 and 'Roll Call of Deaths', a chapter in *Deadly Silence: Black Deaths in Police Custody*, Institute of Race Relations, London, 1991.

5 *The Devil's Feast* was a group exhibition held at the foyer gallery of Chelsea School of Art. The exhibition featured Zarina Bhimji, Chila Burman, Jennifer Comrie, Allan de Souza, and Keith Piper and Donald Rodney, 27 April–8 May 1987. For a review of the exhibition, see Eddie Chambers, 'Problematic Space', *Race Today*, Vol. 17 No. 5, June/July 1987 p. 27.

Chapter 14
Photography

The first substantial body of photographic images of the black presence in Britain date back to the years and decades immediately following the end of the Second World War.

1. Documenting migration and communities: 1940s–1970s
2. Vanley Burke
3. Armet Francis
4. Horace Ové
5. The 1980s onwards

1 Documenting migration and communities: 1940s–1970s

The bulk of these photographic images consist of documentary and journalistic photographs of newly arrived Caribbean migrants, either disembarking into seaport arrival halls, or waiting to be collected from boat-train transit terminals such as London's Victoria Station. Almost without exception, these photographs show people dressed in their finest clothes. Such pictures speak of an age when people wore their best clothes to travel, and similarly dressed to arrive. We see dapper-suited young men and equally well-dressed young women, nearly all of whom wear hats, without which they would have considered themselves to be incompletely dressed. The message conveyed by these photographs is remarkably clear: these immigrants respect themselves, have full confidence in their own abilities to make good lives for themselves in 'the mother country', and have a corresponding confidence in the hospitality which they expect to receive. The photographs, dating from the mid to late 1940s to the early 1960s, give a very good indication of the contemporary styles not only of the travelers themselves, but in the communities they left behind in the Caribbean. Perhaps the most celebrated photograph of newly arrived Caribbean migrants is that of the *Empire Windrush* arriving at Tilbury docks in 1948, bringing nearly 500 Caribbean immigrants. This group were the first of a significant number of Caribbean immigrants seeking to start a new life in Britain. As such, the iconic photograph of the crowded bow of the *Empire Windrush* has become a graphic symbol of post-war immigration from the Caribbean and other parts of the Commonwealth.

The next body of photographs that act as benchmarks of the post-war presence of Caribbean immigrants are studio portraits. These images, primarily dating from the 1960s and 1970s, were produced by numerous high street photographers who drew much of their patronage from the immigrant communities. The portraits invariably consisted of individuals or small groups of family members, again dressed in their finest clothes, or their professional uniforms, against a variety of studio backdrops. Caribbean immigrants and their families in effect commissioned portraits that indicated a real or imagined sense of career development and individual prosperity. Sitters were frequently photographed wearing the uniforms of their professions, such as transport or nursing. At a time when very few Caribbean migrants could afford to have telephones in their homes, many were photographed speaking into the mouthpieces of the heavy, distinctive Bakelite telephones that were standard GPO – General Post Office – issue at the time. These images were frequently sent to family and friends back 'home'. High street photographers provided an invaluable service to their patrons, who could ill-afford their own cameras and processing equipment and materials. Various factors contributed to the demise of the high street photographer, and by the late 1970s such studios had become a rarity, though correspondingly perhaps, a sense of black British photography had begun to emerge and develop.

2 Vanley Burke

One of the first British-based black people to distinguish themselves in the field of photography was Vanley Burke. Born in Jamaica in 1952, Burke came to England in 1965, having received his first camera as a present for his tenth birthday a few years earlier. For him, 'Photography started to develop as a means of looking at people and how they lived.' To this end, he became responsible for producing many highly engaging photographs of Birmingham's Caribbean communities, through the course of the later 20th century. These photographs – depicting black people at work, at play, at church, on the streets, and in their homes – have come to be regarded as key documents chronicling the lives of black people in the country's second city. Through these images we can chart the development, importance, and growing confidence of black Britain. In Burke's photographs, we see elderly black men playing dominoes in a local pub, groups of young men hanging out in the park, baptisms, weddings, and burials. We see also confrontations between the police and young blacks, people dancing, portraits of college graduates, and many other things that illustrate of a vibrant, confident, and multifaceted community of black British people. Burke's pictures oftentimes perfectly composed, are an extraordinarily important document of the growth and coming of age of black Britain. Simultaneously they have become a highly significant record of the changing cultures, demographics, and lifestyles of the peoples of Birmingham. Year on year, Burke's photographs are increasingly being recognized and appreciated.

3 Armet Francis

Another important practitioner who must be regarded as a pioneer of black British photography is Armet Francis. Born in Jamaica in 1945, by the early 1970s Francis had become an important chronicler not only of black people in Britain but of people of African origin throughout the world. His most celebrated work was *The Black Triangle*, a seminal exhibition and publishing project of the mid-1980s. The book comprised three pictorial sections, each consisting of photographs taken by Francis on his travels through Africa (Kenya, Nigeria, Senegal, and Zimbabwe), the Caribbean (Barbados and Jamaica), and Britain and the United States. Taken between 1969 and 1981, these photographs offer an invaluable insight into aspects of the late 20th-century African diaspora. In Francis's photographs, we can chart the dynamic rise of Rastafari and the attendant 'dread' culture as it developed amongst communities in Jamaica and the United Kingdom. We see dancers and performers in Lagos, in London and in New York. We also see portraits of what we might call ordinary people, proud, confident, self-assured witnesses to the post-independence years of hope and optimism that typified continental and diasporic African identities throughout the 1960s and 1970s. Celebrated too, within Francis's photographs is the new independence of Zimbabwe.

4 Horace Ové

Horace Ové must also be considered a pioneering figure of black British photography. He was born in Trinidad and Tobago and came to London as a young man. Over the course of the 1970s he became known as one of a small number of leading black independent film-makers to emerge in Britain. He is widely respected for his pioneering and ground-breaking work as a director of films such as *Pressure*. Made in 1975, the film tackles the issues that came to shape and influence the lives of a new generation of black Britons. A timely, engaging, and deeply empathetic work, *Pressure* was, and remains, a gritty and dynamic study of a generation in crisis.

Equally important is Ové's work as a photographer. During his time in London in the politically and culturally heady days of the 1960s and 1970s, he became responsible for some of the most remarkable and candid photographs reflecting the emergence of black Britain. He photographed important black literary, political, and cultural figures of the period, both British, such as C. L. R. James and Darcus Howe, and American, such as James Baldwin. He also captured a rare spectacle – Stokely Carmichael, Allan Ginsberg, and Michael X at an early Black Power gathering in London in 1967.

Ové was responsible for the most compelling documentation of the development of a uniquely British element of African diasporic cultural identity. He photographed Samuel Selvon, Andrew Salkey and John La Rose, the founding members of the Caribbean Artists Movement. He also photographed the birth and development of the Notting Hill Carnival and the growing importance of reggae music to British youth. Like others before and alongside him, we see in Ové's work copious and fascinating evidence of black British fashion from the 1960s onwards. Perhaps his most remarkable photographs are his studies of the self-styled firebrand Michael X. The historical significance and importance of the photographic body of work produced by Ové cannot be overstated.

Several other very important and pioneering black British photographers include figures such as Dennis Morris and Neil Kenlock. Both of these photographers were responsible for wonderfully crafted portraits of black people that told important stories of lives being lived, particularly at a time when the mainstream media and dominant society seemed particularly reluctant to recognize the depth, the humanity, the challenges, the cultures, of black Londoners' lives.

5 The 1980s onwards

Since the mid-1980s new generations of black British photographers have emerged. By and large these are British-born, art-school-trained practitioners, keen to work with the medium of photography in a marked range and variety of ways. This new generation includes photographers such as Faisal Abdu'Allah, Ajamu, Rotimi Fani-Kayode, Joy Gregory, Sunil Gupta, Mumtaz Karimjee, Roshini Kempadoo, Dave Lewis, Ingrid Pollard, and Franklyn Rodgers. The practice of these artists reflects the ways in which photography has become a compelling and indelible element of a wider fine art practice. As such, their work has been exhibited at art galleries across the United Kingdom and further afield.

Complementing this group of photographers are those fine artists whose practice incorporates elements of photography. The practice of such artists (for example, Keith Piper and Yinka Shonibare) focuses, to varying degrees, on what we might refer to as narratives of 'race' and 'representation'. It might perhaps be more accurate to describe these artists as using photography, rather than being photographers. They employ the photographic medium as a means of animating and graphically illustrating potent debates about culture, history, and identity, and the ways in which such concerns are reflective of the black experience and African diasporic sensibilities and aesthetics.

Mention should also be made of Autograph, the Association of Black Photographers. Formed in London in the late 1980s, Autograph ABP is a photographic arts agency with a brief to support and promote the work of black British photographers 'and to advocate their inclusion in all areas of exhibition, publishing, education and commerce in the visual arts'.

'Photography' was previously published as an entry in David Dabydeen, John Gilmore, and Cecily Jones (eds), *Oxford Companion to Black British History*, Oxford University Press, 2007: 363–6.

SECTION THREE

On Artists

Chapter 15
Section Three Introduction

I had made mention, in my introductory notes to the previous section, of the ways in which my 1991 exhibition, *History and identity: Seven Painters*, for Norwich Gallery in 1991 had marked a personal retreat from curating large-scale group exhibitions and was a staging post toward the solo exhibition format, to which I became, and remained, committed, as a means of presenting artists' work. During the early to mid-1990s it increasingly dawned on me that solo exhibitions perhaps went some way to creating the conditions whereby an artist of colour's work could be engaged with solely on the basis of her or his practice itself. In this regard, the solo exhibition was perhaps the ultimate validation of an artist's practice. The texts in this section reflect the general gravitation of my writing toward discussions of individual artists and the specificities of her or his particular practice. Several texts aside, the writing in this section consists in the main of essays in catalogues, to accompany solo exhibitions, or reviews of projects relating to individual practitioners. From 'Three Songs on Pain Light & Time', a review of a film about British artist Donald Rodney, made by Trevor Mathison and Edward George for the Black Audio Film Collective, that appeared in *Art Monthly*, London, Number 200, October 1996, to 'Jonathan Jones: untitled (the tyranny of distance)' a text for the exhibition catalogue for *Jonathan Jones: untitled (the tyranny of distance)*, Sherman Galleries, Sydney, Australia, 2008. The section also contains two new pieces of writing, 'Frank Bowling and the Enigma of Guyana', and 'Charles White's 10- and 12-Inch Vinyl Messages.'

Chapter 16
Sokari Douglas Camp, CBE

1:54 offers a number of us a privileged opportunity to remind ourselves what an important and accomplished sculptor Sokari Douglas Camp is. Working from her studio, she has, over the course of a number of decades, produced a vast and compelling body of work, for the most part characterised by her large figurative metal sculptures. Born in Rivers State, Nigeria, and educated at art schools in California and London, Douglas Camp has been able to convincingly and with great cultural dexterity, make work that reflects not only the richness of her particular cultural heritage, but simultaneously embraces no end of references to the wider world around her.

By the mid-1980s, Douglas Camp had emerged as a bold new presence in London, making a new and decidedly different kind of work. Her sculptures, when exhibited or displayed in galleries or public spaces, demand to be seen (and in many instances, demand to be heard) and forcefully require our attention. Her work boldly announces its presence, by the space it occupies. Simply put, indifference is not an option when faced with the work of this extraordinary artist. Her sculptures are characterised by a formidable sense of presence. Gradually, over time, Douglas Camp's work came to strikingly embrace many aspects of history and events in the wider cultural, social and political arena that have given her work renewed relevance to its audiences. Her sculptures have frequently evoked the substantial frames of formidable African matriarchs. These sculptures pay particular homage to women whose fortitude, resilience and creativity have frequently gone unremarked. In recent years Douglas Camp has dramatically renewed her interest in the lives and histories of the men, women and children of Africa and its Diasporas, whose existence has not only gone unnoticed, but whose stories of survival have seldom been told.

The formidable group of figures *All the world is now richer*, 2010 that Douglas Camp made around the time of the anniversary of and heightened reflection on the passing of, the parliamentary bill to abolish the slave trade is a compelling case in point. Each of these dramatic figures represented or symbolised an individual caught up in highly charged narratives of the slave trade, slavery, abolition, emancipation, and the making of the African Diaspora. Each of these figures simultaneously came to represent different phases of history, the movement of peoples, survival, resilience and the triumph of the human spirit in the face of indifference, adversity and affliction. But these sculptures were also, in a range of ways, compelling sculptural investigations into form, shape, space and balance. In this regard, whilst we can consider this work as being culturally specific or evocative of the trauma heaped on Africa and its peoples, these considerations are interwoven with other impulses that give the work a universal application.

Douglas Camp wants to, in her words, 'have a world conversation.' This desire, poignantly expressed, represents a quiet yet determined refusal to be perceived in constraining terms. Whilst frequently having very particular cultural reference points, her work is more fully appreciated when more open-minded

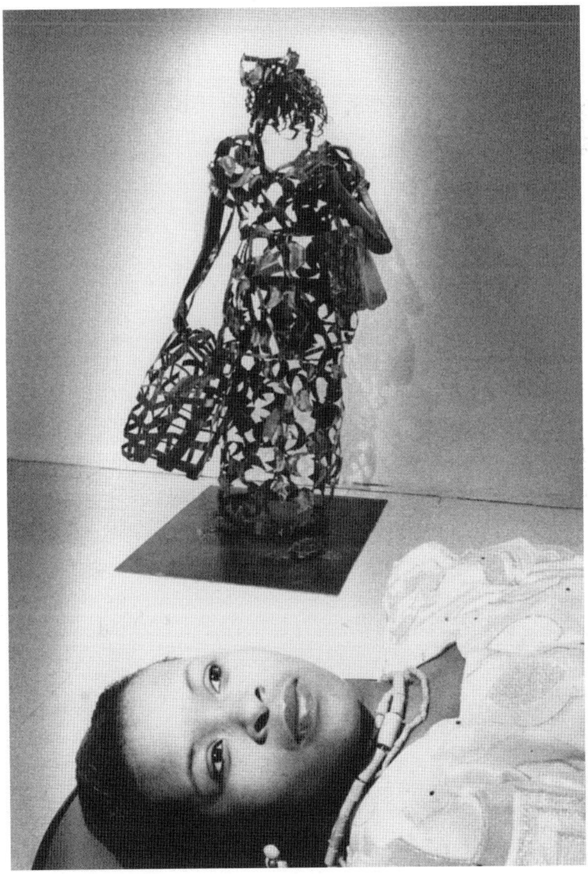

Figure 16.1 Sokari Douglas Camp portrait with *Nigerian Woman Shopping*, 1990, Steel, Sculpture, 180 × 66 × 83 cm, photograph by Simon Norfolk. © Simon Norfolk.

considerations are brought to bear in our viewing and reading of it. Douglas Camp's 'wanting to have a conversation that isn't Western' should be taken as an invitation to all of us to appreciate her wonderful work on its own, decidedly universal terms.

Notwithstanding the often-weighty subject matter, that she does not shy away from embracing, much of her work retains a pronounced playfulness that reflects both her impressive skills as a sculptor and her commitment to spectacle. It is a measure of her talent as a sculptor that her structurally solid pieces nevertheless evoke an infectious playfulness and vivid agility. Sometimes, her works are kinetic, and strongly evocative of movement, transport and journeying. They simultaneously demand to be both seen and heard, as they emit their discordant yet rhythmic sounds. But Douglas Camp's non-kinetic sculptures make similar demands on our attention as they seek to engage our various senses. In this regard, even her imposing figures of welded and manipulated steel, though silent, require an engagement that goes way beyond the visual.

We need to be reminded, and we need to remind ourselves, what an important and remarkable sculptor Douglas Camp is. Her work is truly unique and is deserving of ever-increased levels of visibility. More than that, it continues to evolve, develop and to fashion new dialogues with the world around it.

'Sokari Douglas Camp, CBE' was first published as a brochure accompanying an exhibition taking place at the artist's studio, Saturday 18 October 2014, coinciding with *1-54 Contemporary African Art Fair*, London, 2014.

Chapter 17
William Kentridge: The Main Complaint

William Kentridge has established himself as one of the weightiest players within South African contemporary art. Time and time again, all sorts of curators have found themselves drawn to and engaging with Kentridge's work. In the United Kingdom, his work has been included in two of the three major group exhibitions of South African art that have taken place during this decade.

Kentridge's work was featured in *Art From South Africa* at the Museum of Modern Art, Oxford, back in 1990. Five years later, Kentridge was one of ten artists whose work made up the *Transitions* exhibition at the Hotbath Gallery, Bath, and Ormeau Baths Gallery, Belfast. He has also been busy on the home front: his work was included in both Johannesburg Biennales – 1995 and 1997.

Despite having long become a darling of the biennale/mega-exhibition circuit and the South African group show, the current Serpentine exhibition is the first opportunity that gallery-going audiences within reach of London have had to see a substantial body of his work. The exhibition consists of two parts: there are the wall-based drawings and other works on paper, such as etchings, and there are the animated films. Much of the gallery space has been given over to the latter, with no fewer than three separate areas in which are projected a number of films, made by the artist over a ten-year period.

Kentridge is a talented and able draughtsman, and he has developed a fascinating process of making animated films by working and reworking wall-based charcoal drawings. But interesting though Kentridge's work is, the most significant debates it raises relate to questions of how and why as a South African artist, he has managed to achieve the celebrated status he enjoys. Kentridge's success as an artist, particularly beyond South Africa, throws up disturbing reminders of the ways in which issues of racial hierarchies and their attendant cultural and political orthodoxies have taken a seemingly irreversible hold on the world during the course of this century.

Make no mistake, in international curatorial circles, Kentridge has come to represent, officially or otherwise, South Africa. Or, more accurately, he represents those elements of South Africa of which we approve. When David Elliott curated *Art From South Africa*, white artists like Kentridge were presented to us as representing liberal South Africa's considered and serious resistance to apartheid and a concurrent willingness to engage artistically with the realities of that country's odious and self-destructive programme of 'separate development'. Witness Kentridge in the *Art From South Africa* catalogue:

> I have never tried to make illustrations of apartheid, but the drawings are certainly spawned by and feed off the brutalised society left in its wake. I am interested in a political art, that is to say an art of ambiguity, contradiction, uncompleted gestures and uncertain endings. An art [and a politics] in which my optimism is kept in check and my nihilism at bay.

That was then. This is now. Now, with apartheid, formally and officially at least, a thing of the past, Kentridge's projected self-image has shifted slightly, but significantly. He is now taken to represent the new supposedly non-racial, liberal, non-hierarchical South Africa. His work is taken to represent not only the cathartic process of post-apartheid healing, but also the image of South Africa as a forward-looking country, wholly in step with Western liberal values and aesthetics.

What is significant about the evolution of Kentridge's profile as an artist over the course of this decade, is that it is he, a white male (artist), who has been selected by an international coterie of curators to represent intelligent, considered and acceptably dispassionate resistance to apartheid. This self-image then evolved into one in which Kentridge, again as a white male (artist) is embraced and curatorially celebrated as representing the new South Africa.

The evolution of Kentridge's profile points to not much other than racial business as usual. Of the South African population of about 38 million, some 29 million are black, roughly five million are white, three million are so-called 'coloured'/'mixed race' and approximately one million are of Indian descent. Yet no black South African artist has any sort of profile that remotely comes close to that of Kentridge. The same must be said of South Africa's so-called 'coloured' artists. Such is the emphatic eclipsing by white South African artists of all other ethnic groupings that, as well informed as we might consider ourselves to be, most of us would be hard pushed to name even one South African artist of Indian origin who has successfully made it into the international exhibiting arena. In other words, the 29 million majority, along with South Africa's 'coloured' and Indian populations have found themselves being represented, in the world's art galleries, by a small impregnable clique of white, primarily male South African artists, of which William Kentridge is the prime example.

This scenario is wholly consistent with the racial hierarchies and their attendant ideologies that have, during the course of this century, established themselves the world over. Presumably, in showing the Kentridge exhibition, the Serpentine is seeking to embrace and acknowledge South Africa as a new member of the international (artistic) community. But it has chosen to do so by ignoring those people and artists who much more readily qualify as credible (artistic) representatives of South Africa's struggle to heal and rebuild itself.

Kentridge's biographical details attest to the ease with which white males such as he can choose their career options, their higher education, to live in South Africa, or travel beyond it. For example, Kentridge studied Politics and African Studies at the University of Witwatersrand in the early to mid-1970s, when it was, essentially, a 'white' university. He was then a student and a teacher at the Johannesburg Art Foundation. From teaching etching, Kentridge then studied mime and theatre in Paris. And so it goes on. Film-making, theatre, puppetry, opera, acting, writing, directing. Meanwhile, many black South Africans, finding themselves with virtually no life choices or career options, continue to live in poverty. And so it is that the curators of the world readily, and happily, embrace one of South Africa's most privileged minority as one whose 'work raises powerful issues that bear on the human condition in general – victimisation and suffering, guilt and confession, domination and emancipation.'

Unless you include the damage of repetitive strain injury brought on by endless liberal hand wringing, people like Kentridge – artists like Kentridge – have not done badly out of South Africa and are the clear beneficiaries of whatever that country was and now is – both in its previous condition and its new, so-called 'post-apartheid' state. Kentridge's technical skills, in drawing, in etching, in animation, in film-making are beyond doubt. What is doubtful is the extent to which his work can honestly be said to effectively engage any sort of self-criticality. He occupies much the same space as that taken, elsewhere in the world, by artists such as Alfredo Jaar. Such artists are happy, anxious even, to present themselves as acknowledging the political conditions of the wretched of the earth, whilst critiquing the antics of their tormentors. Yet these same artists seem reluctant to acknowledge, in any way, the bountiful privileges of their social, racial and economic status. After all, Kentridge's work continues the well-established tradition in which white South African artists are able to produce lavish, expensive, expansive work, while their black counterparts are only able to produce more modest works.

And yet, within Kentridge's work, there are interesting flashes of tension and inspired creativity. Take for example the animation 'Johannesburg – 2nd Greatest City after Paris' in which the artist developed a fascinating technique. To quote him directly: 'The film was made in my studio; a drawing on the wall at one end and a wind up bolex camera at the other. I would draw, walk across the room, shoot off two frames of film, walk back to the drawing, so at the end of the film

I was left with about twenty rather beaten drawings.' The film chronicles the battle between two characters, Soho Eckstein and Felix Teitlebaum for the hearts and minds of Johannesburg and the affections of Eckstein's wife. In this film, the image of Soho Eckstein, a property magnate who buys up half of Johannesburg, is presented as a bloated, avaricious and exploitative figure.

The Serpentine press release informs us that the character of Eckstein is in actuality based on the artist's grandfather and that Teitlebaum, who always appears naked, is modelled on Kentridge himself. Thus, what at first sight appears to be a dark, brooding, menacing series of animations exploring South Africa's body politic, turns out to have some sort of grand autobiographical narrative or reading.

'The Main Complaint' was first published as a critique of an exhibition by William Kentridge (South Africa), Serpentine Gallery, London. *Art Monthly*, London, Number 227, June 1999: 1–4.

Chapter 18
Hurvin Anderson: Double Consciousness

Birmingham, Britain's second city, has given rise to a number of important artists of Caribbean background, amongst them Vanley Burke, Keith Piper, Donald Rodney, Barbara Walker and Hurvin Anderson. Anderson is one of the most accomplished painters of his generation, respected for his unique vision, emerging into prominence during the 1990s, and since then has garnered much attention in the international arena. Some of his paintings are singular compositions which achieve, to some extent, the unlikely combination of being investigations into colour, shape and form, and unsentimental explorations of cultural and socially-charged spaces such as the Black barbershop, and places in Jamaica, the Caribbean island from which his parents had emigrated.

Typical of Anderson's representation of the Black barbershop is *Jersey*, a painting of 2008 now in the Tate collection. Like other paintings by him it is a study of the interplay between figurative and non-figurative elements, and the fascinating results that ensue when the painter's brushstrokes are used to create what are in effect *collages*. *Jersey* (from the artist's *Barbershop Series*) depicts a barbershop, in which two empty barbers' chairs – perhaps recently vacated – occupy an unusual type of environment. The notable presence of abstraction within the painting decisively prevents it from being merely a painterly study of a space of congregation for Black males, who would often find themselves with few other social spaces to which they could gravitate. The painting is dominated by a light blue wall, onto which, or in front of which, has been placed rectangles of assorted sizes and colours. In this way, Anderson has created an astonishingly ambiguous depth of field, rendering the viewer uncertain as to whether the barbershop existed within walls or whether it was instead located in a kind of indeterminate space filled with floating rectangles of colour. Such infinite possibilities of space have uncanny echoes of the feeling one gets when standing on a beach, facing the sea, giving rise to 'a sense of disorientation and displacement.'[1]

When the Windrush generation of Caribbean migrants arrived in Britain, from the late 1940s through to the mid-1960s, they rapidly responded to the challenges and peculiarities of the often frosty and unwelcoming environments they encountered. Instead of attending decidedly unfriendly white churches, they set up their own congregations, first meeting in each other's flats and houses, then meeting halls, before finally establishing their own churches. Instead of existing bars, public houses and dancehalls hostile to their patronage, they set up their own *blues* parties, again at home, before West Indian Social or Sports Clubs and other more formally constituted spaces were established. And in response to the reluctance of white barbers to cut Black people's hair (and a corresponding lack of faith in the services offered by white hairdressers) Black hair salons and barbershops were established, either as cottage industries or in premises more publicly located. The Black barbershop thus represented more than a much-needed amenity. Instead, it represented a space of comfort, affirmation of self, and a certain double consciousness. Within the Black barbershop, such topics as current affairs, sport, and music in the UK could be passionately discussed and argued over at the same time that equally nuanced observations were being made on current affairs, sport, and music in the Caribbean. Many Black people in Britain found that a substantial sense of self could only be maintained if they continually availed themselves of understandings of aspects of the country to which they had migrated, alongside corresponding familiarities with the cultural life they had left behind. White British people were, by and large, under no such pressures and often baldly stated their ignorance of geographies and history of the Caribbean, including those countries that were or had been part of the British Empire. Consequently, the Black barbershop became, and indeed remains, a space for sharing news, opinions and information about activities particularly pertinent to the Black communities.

Back in the early 1980s, Tam Joseph, the London-based, Dominica-born artist painted a scene in which a barber makes the final gesture of showing his client (with the aid of a mirror) the results of his labour. It abounds with cultural references to the ways in which certain notions of grooming, and indeed, the Black barbershop itself, are of immense and particular significance for African-Caribbean people. Entitled *Is It Okay at the Back?*, the painting stands as a key work in acknowledging a space that is, despite half a century or more of varying degrees of assimilation, still a cornerstone of whatever we might call 'the Black community'. In the mid-1990s, Faisal Abdu'Allah (like Anderson, a graduate of the Royal College of Art) produced a remarkable series of works – screenprints on etched steel – that celebrated the Black barbershop as a space of *diasporic* cultural affirmation and referenced the artistry of the barbers themselves.

Like these artists before him, it was the *space* of the Black barbershop that Anderson sought to commemorate in the *Barbershop* and *Peter's* series, and in so doing he has produced a remarkable body of work. *Jersey* has a luminous and optimistic disposition, with its combination of a bright, light pastel blue, and rectangular shapes of lilac and other small patches of colour painted or affixed to a wall, such as homemakers might live with before deciding on a final colour scheme for a room at home. In this way, with such an emphasis on decor, *Jersey* effectively problematises dominant societal notions of African-Caribbean males. In referencing elements of the modernist grid, colour field painting and Black male grooming, Anderson has produced a work of great sophistication, capable of telling no end of stories.

There is an insistent oscillation between abstraction and figuration in Anderson's work, consequently imbuing it with a wealth of artistic, cultural and historical narratives. His series of prints, *Mrs. S. Keita*, from 2010 is typical. The central and recurring image is that of a clearly very stylish Black woman. Though she appears in silhouette, her fashionable dress, likely from the 1960s or early 1970s, is clearly discernible, as is her neat Afro hairstyle. She stands elegantly, made all the more so by the brightness of the colour backgrounds that Anderson gives her, together with the treatments of loose mark-making, almost to the point of abstraction, that occupy the areas of her short dress, her legs, and the side table on which her right hand casually rests. The image is reminiscent of Sonia Boyce's *Aunt Enid, the Pose*, depicting as it does a modern young Black woman of the 1960s dressed up for the sort of portrait photograph that was such a familiar feature of Caribbean homes. But Anderson, through the title of the print, is making a more specific reference to the studio portraits taken by Malian photographer Seydou Keita between the 1940s and 1960s.

The Windrush generation gave rise to an incredible body of photographic work that became a benchmark for the post-war presence of Caribbean immigrants. These are studio portraits, primarily dating from the 1960s and 1970s, produced by numerous high street photographers located within reach of Britain's Black immigrant communities. Anderson sensed the profound interaction between this legacy of Caribbean photography in Britain, and equivalent types of portraiture as practised by the likes of Keita. More than anything, it is this that most informs work such as *Mrs. S. Keita*. And making another bold reference to art historical reference, the prints of *Mrs. S. Keita* were executed with a variety of Warholesque backgrounds and colours, at once emphasising uniformity and difference. Having been variously rendered, they were then given titles such as *Mrs. S. Keita – Blue, Mrs. S. Keita – Purple, Mrs. S. Keita – Solid Gold*, and so on.

Anderson makes wonderfully complex paintings, rich with meaning and symbolism that excavate a range of histories. The painterly beauty of his work, with its arresting manifestations of colour, shape, patterning and collage, acts as a foil for the subtlety of the stories he tells and in this respect, *Hope Gardens*, 2005, is typical. The painting takes as its subject the main entrance to Hope Botanical Gardens, in its heyday a magnificent botanical haven on the edge of Kingston, Jamaica, modelled to some extent on London's Kew Gardens. It depicts a verdant collage of trees of varying heights and sizes, rising above the brick walls and entrance, against a rich, pale blue sky. When writing about this work, artist-curator Cameron Irving not only alludes to some discernible strategy, but also offers a compelling description:

> a Caribbean park enveloped by a turreted redbrick wall. Behind it lies a bounty of foliage with trees that shoot up beyond the canvas frame. Anderson's work incorporates bold vertical marks, a visual technique to draw the eye to the paint dripping back down and flooding into the foreground. Here, greenery morphs from its figurative representation of foliage and becomes a wash of green paint, leaving the foreground and background to meet on a plane that hovers between abstraction and figuration. Stenciled letters showing no concern for formal perspective spell out its ambiguous name/message: HOPE GARDENS, and alerts us to its colonial context. More wistfully, it does not indicate any clear future; instead we are left in a situation that resides in an awkward state of uncertainty.[2]

It is his use of bold, confident painterly gestures to generate a sense of *uncertainty* that makes Anderson such an extraordinarily accomplished painter.

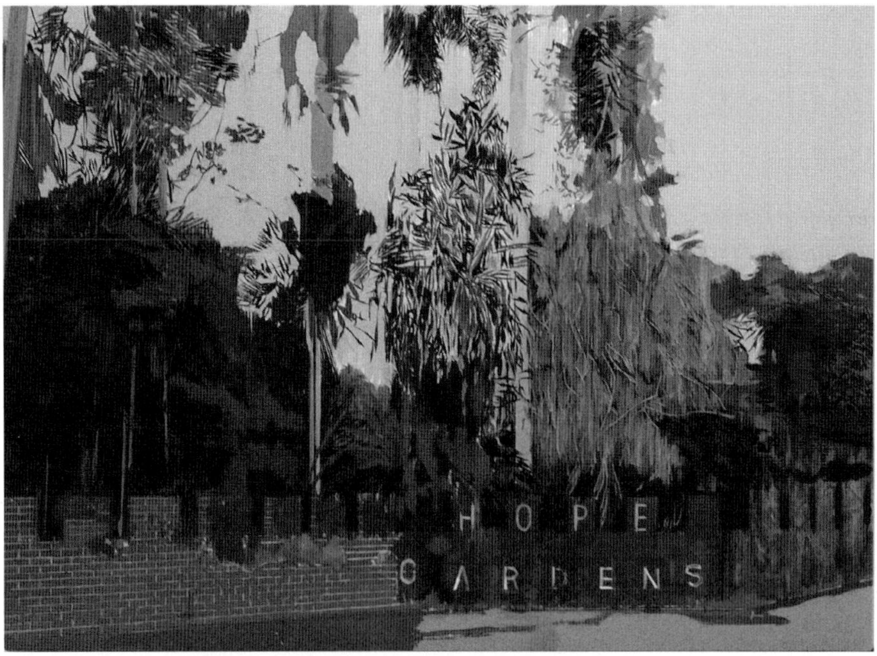

Figure 18.1 Hurvin Anderson, *Hope Gardens*, 2005, Oil on canvas, 130 × 173 cm. © Hurvin Anderson. All Rights Reserved, DACS/Artimage 2020.

Hope Gardens was originally part of Hope Estate, which was owned by Richard Hope, an officer in the British army who was gifted the estates by the Crown as a reward for helping Britain to wrestle control of Jamaica from the Spanish in the mid-17th century. Originally a sugar plantation, by the late 19th century some 200 acres of the estate were purchased by the colonial government to establish an experimental garden for growing foreign species. Following Queen Elizabeth II's visit to Jamaica in 1953, the gardens became known as the Royal Botanical Gardens, Hope, before eventually reverting to being known as Hope Gardens. Nothing in Jamaica – not even the supposedly innocuous growing of exotic flora – exists without reference to wider social histories and narratives.

Hope Gardens was first the preserve of Jamaica's privileged white minority, including colonial expatriates. Control, or occupancy of this particular territory then passed to foreign tourists, at a time when Kingston was very much a port of call for cruise ships and a destination for holidaymakers to the island. Thereafter, it fell into dramatic disrepair, unloved by government, tourists, and local residents alike. In this uncultivated state, the gardens became a metaphor for wider problems faced by the Caribbean island and so, within this painting, Anderson animates not only these complex and layered histories, but also conveys the 'awkward state of uncertainty' that Hope Gardens represents, notwithstanding the restoration initiatives in place since the mid-1990s. Is Anderson depicting Hope Gardens in an earlier state of pronounced dilapidation and abandonment? Or does he show us an optimistic space of fecundity? Does it seem to be a place resonating with colonial nostalgia, or a once elitist environment, now transformed and open to everyone? Does his rendering of Hope Gardens make it a foreboding or a welcoming place?

Anderson's work is, above all else, about an intriguing visual interaction between such things as memory, perception, geography, location, history, and identity. This is an interplay that enables him, according to Cameron Irving, 'to assemble new viewpoints'[3] visualised through his refreshing and singular compositions. Travelling to Jamaica, since he was in his mid-teens, he came to notice the ubiquitous presence of security grilles on the windows of its residential and commercial properties. For Anderson Jamaica is very different to that enjoyed by holidaymakers from the US or Europe, who, with rare exception, effectively barricade themselves into beach resorts. His Jamaica might appear to be very similar, in the ways in which people live, work and socialise, but instead, for Black British people of local heritage, it is loaded with an unsettling ambivalence signified by the security devices used by almost all Jamaican householders. And by noticing them, Anderson came to paint a remarkable series of pictures.

The paintings – known as the *Welcome Series* – are both a highly-charged visual investigation into the ubiquity of security grilles in countries such as Jamaica, and an exploration of their geometric patterning. In making them, Anderson also triggered considerations of security, exclusion, and what we see,

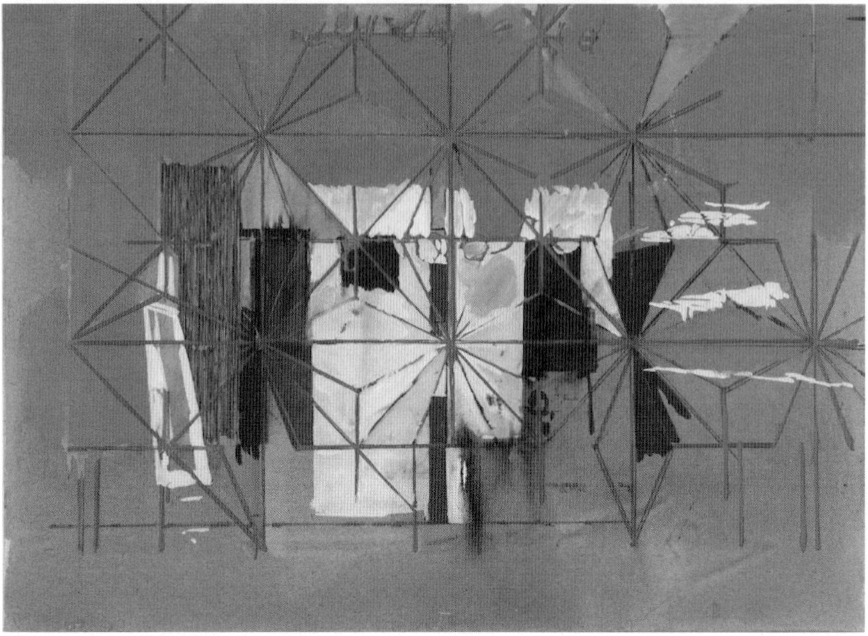

Figure 18.2 Hurvin Anderson, *Original Welcome*, 2002, Oil on canvas, 71.3 × 97cm.

or what we imagine we can see, when we look through other people's grilles, into their homes and lives. Perhaps by beautifying grilles (designed primarily to stop criminals from breaking into private property) manufacturers were creating architectural features that evoked the decorative rather than the altogether blunter consideration of security against burglars. More or less all verandas, windows and doors of houses and flats in Jamaica and elsewhere in the Caribbean are grilled. Ground floor, first floor, front door, back door. Householders fear that any opening left ungrilled will attract the attention of burglars.

The irony of the *Welcome Series* arises out of Anderson's superimposition of grilles onto his characteristic investigations into shapes, forms, colours, and other figurative and non-figurative elements. In *Some People (Welcome Series)*, 2004, for example, the intricately welded triangles of steel combine to create a variety of diamond-like formations, punctuated by starbursts, formed at the point at which the triangles converge. Towards the top of the grille – at the top of the painting – Anderson has included the word 'welcome' which has, doubtless with unintended irony, been welded on to the diamond bars he depicts. The range of attractive geometric configurations is fascinating, but that fascination is intensified by what can be seen, when we look through that which is there to keep us out. Like Anderson's subsequent *Peter's* series, this painting involves a somewhat disconcerting depth of field, rendering the viewer uncertain as to what might lie immediately behind the patterned grille. It depicts a kind of indeterminate space in which a range of elements, including what appear to be human figures, occupy a private universe decidedly different from that occupied by the viewer. Again, it is this loaded sense of distance, or otherworldliness, that is pervasive in Anderson's work, where conventional rules of perspective and structure are emphatically challenged. From the 1990s through to the present time, Anderson has infused painting with a new dynamism. Nothing about his work is merely descriptive, or merely illustrative, and yet, paradoxically, it offers a compelling assortment of clues to help us understand his disquiet.

'Double Consciousness', was first published as a catalogue essay for the exhibition, *Hurvin Anderson: Reporting Back,* Ikon Gallery, Birmingham, England, 25 September–10 November 2013: 71–77.

Notes

1 http://www.saatchigallery.com/artists/hurvin_anderson.htm.

2 https://cameronirving.wordpress.com/2012/02/09/selected-magazine-reviews-2-untitled-magazine2005/.

3 https://cameronirving.wordpress.com/2012/02/09/selected-magazine-reviews-2-untitled-magazine2005/.

Chapter 19

Jonathan Jones: *untitled (the tyranny of distance)*

Within the practice of Jonathan Jones, one of the most original artists of his generation, nothing is incidental, everything is considered and deliberate and, consequently, meaning, inference and interpretation all become vitally important. Works such as *homeland illuminations*, 2007 (with Ruark Lewis),[1] *white lines*, 2005, and *trade mark*, 2007, open up an assortment of potent and fascinating means by which we can consider history and identity and how these have impacted upon this young, Sydney-based artist of the Kamilaroi and Wiradjuri indigenous peoples, as well as on ourselves and our own thought processes.

At first glance it may appear that Jones has an attachment to, or a pronounced interest in, the symbolism, tools and aesthetics of modernism. But we must look deeper, or closer, if we wish to avail ourselves of a broader grasp of Jones's practice. A few years ago, Jones created an installation titled *blue poles*, 2004 echoing, none too subtly, Jackson Pollock, abstract expressionism, and the consequences and implications of Pollock's *Blue Poles*, 1952, being a foundation work in the National Gallery of Australia's collection of twentieth-century American art. We might also consider that Jones's blue poles resonated with wider musings on art history, Australian art practice, and ever-relevant, ever-present dualities of inclusion and exclusion. It seems clear that in knowing art history, in referencing in such explicit and implicit ways this art history, Jones has sought not so much to make work that merely or simply stands outside of, or alongside that history. Instead, he has, we might conclude, sought to make work that intelligently critiques the problematic nuances of that history, whilst simultaneously demanding for himself a place and a space well within it.

As Blair French has written:

> Jones deploys certain materials and forms associated with Euro-American modernism to draw upon the seductive familiarity of its aesthetic conventions while subtly critiquing its broader historical purview. The formal construction

> of Jones's work should alert us to the manner in which, rather than simply being conditioned by or located within a space of play or dialogue (or indeed a gulf) between cultures, the work itself animates that space, encouraging reflection upon that space, but also acting to destabilise our experience of it.[2]

Abstract expressionism (together with jazz, blues and other forms of music) may indeed be among America's gifts to the world. But within Australia, the ways in which the country has received, embraced and understood abstract expressionism in particular and modernism in general cannot, as far as Jones is concerned, be kept separate from the politics of Aboriginal experience and identity (and what is, for him, an attendant quest for artistic independence). The art historians and curators of the United States, Australia and Europe have tended to interpret and present modernism in decidedly blinkered ways that have steadfastly refused to embrace wider concerns and wider constituencies of people and artists. Yet within Jones's work we see an artist who is intent on using the aesthetics of modernism whilst attempting to subtly and quietly disrupt what rapidly became its dominant ethos or hegemonic meaning historically and traditionally attached to it. In other words, Jones (much like British-Chinese artist Anthony Key) is 'interested in minimalism with lots of meaning'.[3] This is important because art historians traditionally describe modernism as being void of what might be referred to as socio-political references. It seems to me that both Key and Jones take issue with this, seeing modernism in much more animated, pertinent and engaging terms. Katrina Schwarz posited the view that: 'Jones. . . finds in appropriation a means of empowerment – a challenge to the representation of indigeneity as "other"'.[4] It seems to me that reading Jones's strategy as being one of appropriation as a means of political empowerment and a rebuttal of the prejudices associated with *indigeneity* is, at the very least, a misreading and perhaps insufficiently nuanced. Jones is after all utilising a set of aesthetics available to all artists, irrespective of the artist's perceived or actual identity. We need not regard Jones's way of working as being somehow symptomatic of attempts to sidestep or challenge otherness. As a contemporary artist, Jones is free to make good use of whatever influences he chooses, from whatever quarter those influences emerge.

Incidentally, during precisely the same time period in which Pollock and others were most creative, related matters were concerning and preoccupying artists of African and Asian origin, who were busy relocating from their respective countries to what were, at the time, the major metropolitan art centres of London and Paris. Rasheed Araeen has argued that these 'Afro-Asian' artists laid claim to modernism as much as (and in much the same ways as) the artists of the United States, Europe and Australia:

> I would like to assert that the movement of artists from Asia, Africa and the Caribbean to the West was also not between different cultures but a movement

> within the same culture defined and constructed by modernity. In the early twentieth century, modernism travelled from Paris to other countries of Europe, triggering other movements in many countries (Futurism, Constructivism, Suprematism, etc), and to the Americas, but it also moved to the colonies in Asia, Africa and the Caribbean (as well as to the countries of Latin America). When AfroAsian artists from different parts of the world arrived in Europe, they were not entering another culture but a different level of the same culture which they had left behind.[5]

Modernism had a global reach and a global embrace. Likewise, in the twenty-first century, to discuss Jones's practice as merely emerging from, or addressing some sort of schism that constructs aboriginality and modernity as being *naturally* (my emphasis) mutually exclusive is to largely misrepresent and limit his art and misread art-historical movements such as modernism.

If, as Araeen asserts, 'Modernism. . . signifies that broad philosophical framework within which the modern art movement has taken place in the twentieth century, with all its diversity and disunity of forms and styles, and which also provides theoretical discourse for the evaluation and legitimisation of modern works of art',[6] then there can be no possible reason for Jones's practice not to be located at the heart of the canon. Furthermore, looking at Jones's work we might conclude that it puts art history (or more accurately, hegemonic interpretations of it) on trial. The development of African-American art in the twentieth century is inextricably interwoven with the development of modernism in the United States in the twentieth century. But few (white) art historians have acknowledged or taken any interest in this. In this sense, *art history* has failed diversity, plurality, and has failed *people*. Jones's work tells us this and other stories.[7]

Earlier I made mention of Jones's *blue poles* having resonated with, amongst other things, the ever-relevant, ever-present dualities in inclusion and exclusion. The same could be said of several of Jones's other installations, including this new undertaking at Sherman Contemporary Art Foundation. Much has been written about the elliptical grid formations and regimented patterning of Jones's installations such as *white lines*, 2005, and *under the aegis*, 2006. For example, Blair French says: 'the repeated patterns of [Jones's] works recall traditional forms carved on weapons and shields and trees, or marked on possum-skin coats'. And, 'Jones's patterning of fluorescent light is akin to attempting to knit together a sense of community. But at the same time it is drawn from a traditional shield design. It asserts cultural identity while acting as protective cover to the self. It is an invitation to breach cross-cultural divides, while remaining hard and impenetrable – an invitation and a challenge broached with a formal beauty.'[8] Hetti Perkins has noted: 'In Aboriginal ceremonial life, where participation is structured according to the position of the individual in the community, cultural affirmation is conducted and achieved through iteration.'[9] Katrina Schwarz has echoed and embellished some of these sentiments with the proposition that the fluorescent tubes of Jones's blue poles, 'glowed in a geometry derived from the patterns of the Kamilaroi/Wiradjuri – carvings on wooden objects, weapons and the designs of possum-skin coats.'[10] If we bring together these assorted interpretations of geometric patterning we might conclude, in much the same way as Andrew Frost, that a 'notion of dual meaning of materials. . . informs much of Jones's work.'[11] But the materials Jones uses, much like the work itself, have more than simple 'dual' meanings. Jones's grids, though seemingly strong, pronounced and deliberate structures, nevertheless have much in the way of ambiguity. Grids represent an imposition of a certain (type of) order and structure, but this order can only be achieved by each shape within the grid being created by, and relying on, all those around it. A grid can create bold and decisive patterns, but simultaneously, a grid homogenises and in some ways limits and is constrained by its own patterning. A grid establishes seemingly formidable barriers, boundaries and borders. Yet spatially and visually, these things can really only exist as long as the grid itself does. A grid (like the patterning which is such a distinctive feature of so much Islamic art and architecture) can be a thing of great beauty. But a grid can represent confinement, compartmentalisation and a kind of regimented fragmentation.

Andrew Sayers has commented that, 'Jones's materials are. . . simple in substance and equally complex in meaning.'[12] It seems to me that what Jones seeks to do in his practice is, above all else, not to present us with a range of meanings but to *disrupt* meaning and to *interrupt* our inherited and assumed ways of seeing. In entering his installations, we may think or believe that we know what we are looking at (or indeed, what we are looking *for*), but Jones has other ideas. Much like Aikido (the Japanese martial-arts form in which an opponent's strength is used against him), any complacency we may bring to our reading of Jones's work can trip us up and will more than likely be used against us. Within the artist's statement that accompanied Jones's 2003 installation *volta a crociera*, single words, groupings of words and even, on occasion, single letters within words are, at seemingly random intervals, rendered in bold. Likewise, within his text, single words and groupings of words are lightly underlined in red. Read together, the text in bold forms a sort of stream of consciousness, though the words underlined in red have clear and precise inferences: 'domestic', 'creating meditative environments', 'other indigenous communities across the world', and so on. The two columns of text are effectively and categorically presented in such a way as to disrupt an easy reading. Jones makes sure that our reading of the text is *difficult*. In so doing he *disrupts* any presupposed sets of meaning we might be minded or tempted to bring to the text. As such (and as previously mentioned) Jones seeks to *interrupt* our inherited ways of seeing.

Jones also writes in his statement: 'To give you an idea of my artistic interests, the subject central to my practice is the symbiotic relationship of community to the individual, and the individual to the community. The two are inseparable, though I believe the two factors are fictions.'[13] We would do well to bring such clarity (and such caution) to our readings of this new work by Jones. Within the Sherman Contemporary Art Foundation exhibition space are a number of rectangular, freestanding walls, each of equal size, each on the same slight diagonal and each closely spaced in proximity and relation to the others. The gallery visitor has room to walk around the assembled and constructed walls but not pass *within* the installation, between the walls themselves. This point – about a *physical* lack of access *within* the work – is of great significance because, paradoxically, it is by limiting our access that Jones wishes us to open up our understanding of what is happening in the restricted spaces. As Jones himself has stated, 'I tend to look at the spaces in between things.'[14] He would like us to do the same.

Within an instant we might recall Jones's comments about his work having as its central theme 'the symbiotic relationship of community to the individual, and the individual to the community'. But even here we must be careful. For as Jones states: 'The notion of a community in many ways is an impossibility, as there is no group of people who are exactly the same constituting a community. Therefore, all communities can be broken down to individuals.' Jones goes on to

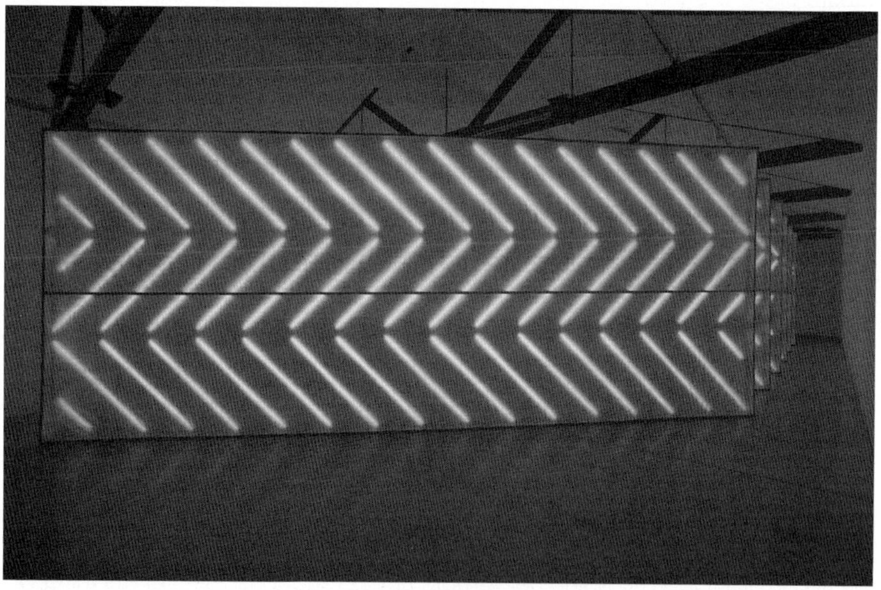

Figure 19.1 Installation view, Jonathan Jones: *untitled (the tyranny of distance)*, Commissioned by the Sherman Contemporary Art Foundation (SCAF), Sydney, Australia, in conjunction with Jonathan Jones: *untitled (the tyranny of distance)*, August 14 – October 11 2008. Image reproduced © courtesy of Jonathan Jones and Dr Gene Sherman AM, SCCI (Sherman Centre for Culture and Ideas).

flip this proviso on its head by asserting that: 'The individual by itself is a further impossibility, as all individuals are products of their community and must relate to the powers of each other.'[15] If we read the rectangular walls as people, we are struck by their sameness, their apparent homogeneity. This leads us – inevitably – to a symbiotic discussion of community belonging versus the historical and contemporary realities of 'racial' prejudice. One of the defining features of racism is its inability (or refusal) to attribute any sort of *individuality* to those it regards as a group sharing the same characteristics, a group in which each member is in essence indistinguishable from the others. Racism robs its victims of their *perceived* individuality, the perpetrator preferring instead to rely on prejudicial certainties, amounting to 'they're all the same.'

Yet simultaneously, *untitled (the tyranny of distance)* resonates with an insistent, determined and profound sense of what we might call communal empathy in light of, and in the face of adverse circumstances. If the blocks can in some ways be read as people, then the grouping resonates with a discernibly bold and articulate sense of shared experiences in the face of wider societal hostility or indifference. Within these two conflicting yet symbiotic readings we can clearly detect what I have referred to as the ever-relevant, ever-present dualities of inclusion and exclusion. Entering the space of this new work, the viewer ascertains in some ways an awkwardness, a discomfort, almost as much as he or she might ascertain a sense of harmony and order. The blocks might form their own *community*, but they simultaneously form a *quarantined* environment. This might be called a 'dynamic of intimacy versus exclusion.'[16] Within many countries of the world, the late nineteenth- and early twentieth-century wholesale movement of labouring people from the *country* to the *town* brought with it new realities. In country after country, profound demographic shifts occurred as a result of mass labour becoming, by and large, surplus to requirement in agrarian societies. When this new *working class* (which was often poor, dispossessed and homeless) settled in urban areas, these communities rapidly became framed and perceived as undesirable centres of deviance, dysfunction, poverty and squalor. Over the course of the twentieth century many of these communities became absorbed into the general fabric of society and the urban environment. Other such communities – particularly in so-called *underdeveloped* countries (or, in wealthier countries, those communities regarded as *underdeveloped*) fared less well, falling victim to an apparently indelible societal, political and economic marginalisation. In this sense, the town and the city became, for its ghetto *sufferers*, what Bob Marley so aptly, so poetically described as a *concrete jungle*.[17] As such, the concrete jungle functioned as a dispiriting and constraining space (though simultaneously, a space resonating with hope, optimism and a certain indomitable spirit). With its connotations of resourceful, rudimentary and makeshift sheltering (signified by the blue tarpaulin with which the structures are covered), each of us will have our

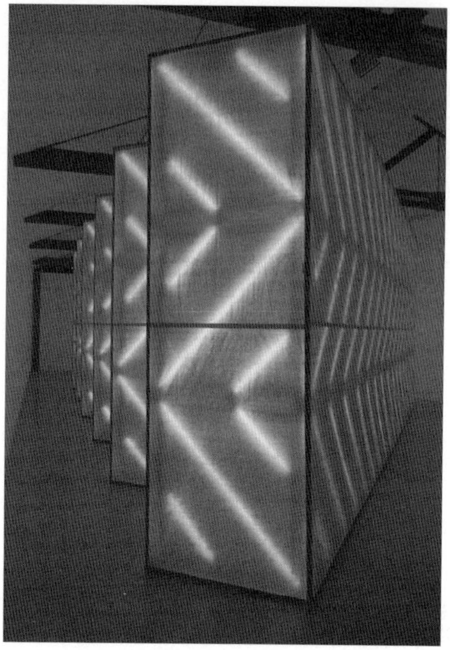

Figure 19.2 Installation view, Jonathan Jones: *untitled (the tyranny of distance)*, Commissioned by the Sherman Contemporary Art Foundation (SCAF), Sydney, Australia, in conjunction with Jonathan Jones: *untitled (the tyranny of distance)*, August 14 – October 11 2008. Image reproduced © courtesy of Jonathan Jones and Dr Gene Sherman AM, SCCI (Sherman Centre for Culture and Ideas).

own visual, cultural and mental access points to this installation. 'Concrete Jungle' is one of mine.

Visitors to the installation will find that they are, 'unable to fully participate in the sculpture – they [are] able to walk around the outside of the walls but not between them.'[18] In this regard, the notion of *limited participation* takes on a particular wider relevance and poignancy. Again, each of us will have our own visual, cultural and mental entrance to this sense of denial, refusal, limited opportunity and limited participation. For some, the effects might be (or might include), 'alienation, longing, cultural claustrophobia, hidden spaces and lost or secret histories.'[19] However we approach this work, and whatever cultural reference points we might bring to it, we ought at all times to be mindful of Jones's penchant for disrupting meaning. In this regard, his new work, like much that has gone before it, is 'at once delightfully simple and profoundly complex'.[20]

'Jonathan Jones: *untitled (the tyranny of distance)*' was first published as a text for the exhibition catalogue for *Jonathan Jones: untitled (the tyranny of distance)*, Sherman Galleries, Sydney, Australia, August 14–October 11 2008: 8–11.

Notes

1 Homeland illuminations was based on Jonathan Jones's (Pa's) narratives of country and culture.

2 Blair French, 'Jonathan Jones', *Adventures with Form in Space*, Art Gallery of New South Wales, Sydney, 2006, pp. 34–35.

3 Walcot Chapel, 2002, video on anthonykey.net.

4 Katrina Schwarz, 'Jonathan Jones: ANZ/Art & Australia Emerging Artists Program', *Art & Australia*, vol. 43. No. 2, summer 2005, p.320.

5 Rasheed Araeen, *Third Text*, 'A New Beginning Beyond Postcolonial Cultural Theory and Identity Politics' no. 50, Spring 2000.

6 Rasheed Araeen, 'In the citadel of modernism', 'The Other Story: Afro-Asian Artists in Post-War Britain', South Bank Centre, London, 1989, pp. 16–49. See this chapter for further discussions by Araeen on modernism's links to the artists of Africa, Asia and the Caribbean.

7 See, for example, *African-American Artists, 1929–1945: Prints, Drawings, and Paintings in the Metropolitan Museum of Art*, New York, 2003.

8 French, 'Jonathan Jones', *Adventures with Form in Space*.

9 Hetti Perkins, 'Jonathan Jones: lumination', *Jonathan Jones*, exhibition catalogue, Gallery Barry Keldoulis, Sydney, September 2003.

10 Schwarz, 'Jonathan Jones: ANZ/Art & Australia Emerging Artists Program'.

11 Andrew Frost, 'Afraid of the dark', *Australian Art Collector*, issue 42, October to December 2007, pp. 132–141.

12 Andrew Sayers, 'Jonathan Jones: white lines', *Jonathan Jones*, exhibition catalogue, Gallery Barry Keldoulis, Sydney, June 2005.

13 Jonathan Jones, *volta a crociera*, exhibition catalogue, Gallery Barry Keldoulis, Sydney, July 2003.

14 Jonathan Jones, email communication with the author, 10 October 2007.

15 Jones, *volta a crociera*.

16 Laura Murray Cree, email communication with author, 25 October 2007.

17 'Concrete jungle where the living is hardest. . . No chains around my feet, but I'm not free, I know I am bound here, in captivity. . .' Bob Marley, *Concrete Jungle*, from 'Catch a Fire', Island Records, 1973. Marley was referring to one particular hardscrabble neighbourhood of Kingston, Jamaica, as much as he was referring to the alienating modern city spaces of office blocks, business, and high end commerce - zones from which the poor were emphatically excluded and unwanted.

18 Murray Cree, email communication with author.

19 Murray Cree, email communication with author.

20 Lisa Slade, 'New acquisition: Jonathan Jones 68 Fletcher, Bondi, 20:20, 8.6.03' *Artemis*, vol. 38, no. 1, July 2007 pp. 10–11.

Chapter 20

Vanley Burke: An Inglan Story, An Inglan History

Within the next decade or so, people so inclined will be celebrating, or commemorating, the 75th anniversary of the arrival at Tilbury Docks of the *Empire Windrush* that carried 500 or so Caribbean immigrants to Britain, in 1948. It was the arrival of this pioneering generation of immigrants that heralded the beginning of what was a unique moment in the country's post-war history. Whilst the African presence in Britain dates back several millennia, and whilst British cities such as Cardiff and Liverpool are long-established homes to Black people from across the world, it was not until the relatively recent post war period that particular neighbourhoods in other, primarily English towns and cities developed what were, for a while, distinct and recognisable 'Black communities'. Answering the call from 'the Mother Country' to fill labour vacancies, hundreds of thousands of migrants from all over the Caribbean made their way to Britain.

Black people had of course been making their way to Britain for centuries, some coming of their own free will, others – particularly during the many years of Britain's association with the Atlantic slave trade – coming very much against their will. But it was not until the relatively recent post-war arrival of Caribbean immigrants that Britain's Black population swelled significantly and emphatically. Within months and years of settling, Caribbean immigrants started to establish families in their adopted country. Many of these Caribbean immigrants left children behind, in the care of grandparents or other members of their immediate or extended families. In time, when conditions and circumstances allowed, Caribbean immigrants began to 'send for' these children. Simultaneously, other immigrants started to have children and build families in communities across the country.

These two groups of children – those born in the Caribbean and coming to Britain as children, and those of Caribbean parentage born here – grew up to become the new generation of 'Black British' youngsters. Never before had Britain been home to such people who embodied a heady and intriguing fusion of Blackness and Britishness. These children (for a period euphemistically described as 'West Indians') would in time become the cornerstone of Black Britain. The children of Caribbean migrants to Britain represented an entirely new body of people. These new 'British' people were here as toddlers and infants in the 1950s. In the 1960s, they were here as children. By the early to mid-1970s, their collective presence was unmistakable and conspicuous – they were here as teenagers, on the verge of an oftentimes fractious adulthood. The Black British youngster – born, schooled and raised in Britain – had arrived. What's more, for close on four decades Vanley Burke was there to create and provide a fascinating photographic record of the complexities, the nuances and the political realities of this new Black presence.

Vanley Burke was one of the first British-based Black people to distinguish themselves in the field of photography. As such, he occupies a central and elevated position in the history of Black photography in Britain. Born in Jamaica in 1951, Burke came to England in 1965, one of the 'sent for' children mentioned earlier. He received his first camera as a present for his tenth birthday, perhaps little knowing where such a present would lead him. For Burke, 'Photography started to develop as a means of looking at people and how they lived.' To this end, he became responsible for producing many highly engaging photographs of Birmingham's Caribbean communities, through the course of the later decades of the 20th century. These photographs – depicting Black people at work, at play, at church, on the streets, and in their homes – have become key documents chronicling the lives of Black people in the country's second largest city. Through these images we can chart the development, importance and growing confidence of Black Britain. In Burke's photographs we see elderly Black men playing dominoes in a local pub, groups of young people hanging out in a park, and occasions like baptisms, weddings, and burials. We see confrontations between the police and members of the Black community, people dancing, portraits of college graduates, and many other images illustrative of a vibrant, confident, and multifaceted community of Black British people, some of whose local accents are laced with a Jamaican twang.

The Britain of the present time represents a unified grouping of countries that have in many respects changed beyond measure since the middle of the last century. Perhaps Vanley Burke's greatest contribution has been the way in which he has reminded us, or made us aware, of the ways in which Black Britain has similarly changed beyond measure. In looking at, and in considering, Burke's photographs, we are obliged to reflect on the evolving face of Black Britain, as well as the ever-changing nuances of Diaspora that are so compelling in these photographs. Many of Burke's photographs of the mid-1970s through to the early 1980s conclusively point to the unmistakable influence of Rastafari on young Black Britain. Casting around for ideas with which to make sense of its Britishness, and finding, or seeing, little to nothing in the way of indigenous

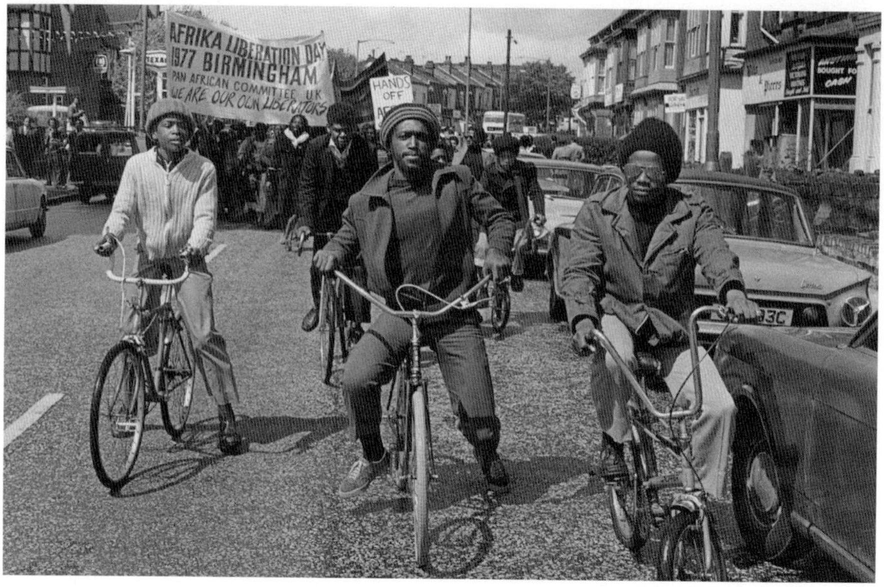

Figure 20.1 Vanley Burke, *Outriders head the Africa Liberation Day rally, Rookery Road, Handsworth, 1977*. © Vanley Burke.

sensibilities to aid it in this purpose, significant numbers of British-Caribbean youth embraced the intriguing ideology of Rastafari, a decidedly countercultural set of beliefs that first emerged in Jamaica in the early decades of the 20th century. Those Black youngsters, who fell someway short of declaring themselves to be Rasta, nevertheless immersed themselves in the music and other cultural aspects of the Dread way of life that frequently accompanied Rastafari.

Consider, if you will, one of Burke's great crowd scene photographs, taken in Handsworth Park at an Africa Liberation Day rally in the late 1970s. Perhaps counter intuitively, Burke has made the focus of the photograph not the people addressing the multitude, but the multitude itself. In this sense, though the focus of the gathered throng's attention is located somewhere beyond, or outside of, the right side of the image, Burke chooses to make the attentive crowd the subject of his picture. To successfully photograph large numbers of people gathered together in one place is one of the most difficult of tasks for a photographer. And yet, within this image, Burke produced a compelling and remarkably cogent document of an especially culturally and politically charged moment in Black British history. The majestic, panoramic photograph effortlessly evokes Bob Marley's sentiment, expressed in his challenge and admonition to the Black people of the world, to 'Wake Up and Live'. Within the song, Marley declares – as Burke's photograph does – that 'we're more than the sand of the sea shore, we're more than number'. The mass of blessed yout in the photograph are indeed 'more than number', and they nearly all – to a man, to a woman –

betray about them or their person some evidence of the influence of Rastafari. Dreadlocks abound, as do tams[1], wraps and numerous other signs of Rasta. As with all great photographs of crowd scenes, we see not so much a crowd, or a multitude, but a group of individuals. And in beholding or appraising individual people 'more than number', we are able to consider such things as the facial expressions, body language, and clothing that make each of these people distinctive, particular, and in one or two instances, idiosyncratic or eccentric.

In the far reaches of the photograph, at the edge of the crowd, can be seen the massive speaker boxes of the sound system there to entertain the crowd. The speakers have fallen silent while speechmakers address the upful and noble gathering; but within time, shortly after the photograph was taken one imagines, the speaker boxes would again be pumping out the potent, infectious, righteous, judgmental brand of roots and culture message-laden reggae music that was popular at the time. By the mid to late 1980s Rastafari had loosened its grip on young Black Britain. Similarly, reggae music – the message from the King – was giving way to rap music and hip-hop. Now, in 2012, were it not for photographs such as these by Burke, our memories of this moment in time would be so much dimmer, if indeed they existed at all. History happens right under our noses, and the best and most successful historians take upon themselves the task of resurrecting those histories – oftentimes quite recent histories that we'd almost forgotten we had. In this regard, Burke's photographs present us with an Inglan story, an Inglan history.

As mentioned earlier, present-day Britain has in many respects changed beyond measure since the middle of the last century. And Burke is here to remind us, through his astonishing photographs, that Black people have been agents of that change just as much as they have found themselves caught up in it. It is perhaps fortuitous that Burke should have made his home in Birmingham, one of the great cities of the British Empire. A central hub of the Industrial Revolution, Birmingham's wealth, power and influence were legendary. During the height of Empire, for many residents and visitors alike, Birmingham represented a blessed city, and nothing reflected that more than characteristics such as its industrial output, its solid working-class communities, and the grandness of its civic architecture.

But with the decline of the British Empire came a dramatic slide in the fortunes of cities such as Birmingham, which, despite prestige-building projects such as the original Bull Ring, had lost much of its economic greatness. As such, by the later decades of the 20th century Birmingham came to represent a heady mixture of elements that typified a changing city, in a changing country. By now, citizens of the Commonwealth and former British Empire had well and truly come to Birmingham, reflecting the extent to which Birmingham had gone out to the Empire. Added to this, areas such as the Black Country and Birmingham itself were in effect laid low by the rapid decline of manufacturing and other areas of traditional working-class employment such as mining. The post-industrial era found, or left, Birmingham in crisis, unsure of itself and insecure about its future.

And again, Burke was there to record significant moments of a city in crisis, such as the riots that shook and devastated parts of Birmingham in the mid-1980s. Inner-city areas of Birmingham, such as those that bore the brunt of the 1985 riots witnessed fascinating changes. Reflecting a nationwide decline in the centrality of organized religion in the lives of white British people, deconsecrated churches in these neighbourhoods were, by the mid-1980s, now Hindu temples, Sikh gurdwaras, or Muslim mosques. Many people still lived in the sort of modest, working class terraced housing of which whole neighbourhoods had been built, yet the traditional chip shop at the end of the street was now likely to be a Chinese or Caribbean takeaway or an Indian restaurant. Many people still shopped locally, yet the high street was becoming reflective of the tastes and requirements of the neighbourhood's newest residents. Many of Burke's photographs of the mid-1980s bear witness to the profound changes visited on Birmingham by waves of immigration from the former colonies, and countries of the Commonwealth. Burke's photographs had the astonishing ability to visualise the extent to which Birmingham had become home to one of the largest concentrations of African-Caribbean migrants anywhere outside of the capital. Likewise, his images became invaluable records of Birmingham's built environment and the passing styles and fashions of the city's residents.

Together with areas such as Brixton, during the course of the 1970s Handsworth had come to symbolise territory that represented the unmistakable emergence and presence of Black Britain. To be sure, Handsworth was, as mentioned, home to many people from the Commonwealth countries, and to their British-born and British-raised children. Significantly the neighbourhood had gained a special and particular place in the affections and empathies of younger Black British people. The reggae band Steel Pulse had the measure of it when they sang [on their seminal and epoch-defining manifesto of resistance, the 1978 record 'Handsworth Revolution']: 'Handsworth means us, the Black people, Handsworth means us, the Black people. . .' For better or for worse, Handsworth became synonymous with Birmingham's Black people. In the parlance of the time, along with areas such as Brixton and Ladbroke Grove in London, Moss Side in Manchester, Toxteth in Liverpool, Hyson Green in Nottingham, and St Paul's in Bristol, areas like Handsworth had attained somewhat privileged 'frontline' status, and in this, Handsworth was aided in no small measure by Burke's photographs – in this instance those images capturing the decidedly fractious and oftentimes violent exchanges between the police and Black youth.

But the Birmingham of the early to mid-1980s, as pictured by Burke, was far more than a doomed landscape of hopeless contradictions and difficulties. Though affluence seemed to be reserved only for parts of the city – just as surely as unemployment, endless pressure, and distinct patterns of discrimination had,

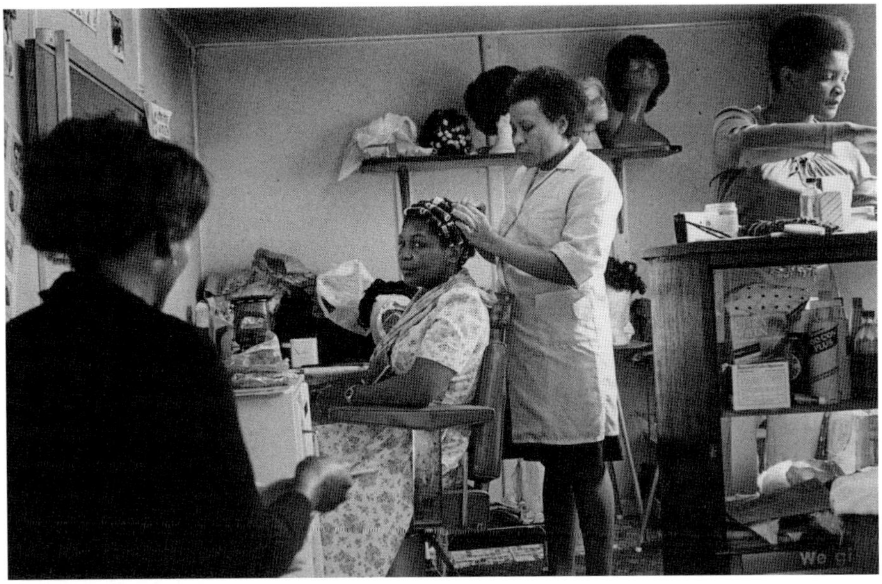

Figure 20.2 Vanley Burke, *Mrs Walker and her customers at her hairdresser's shop, Rookery Road, 1979*. © Vanley Burke.

over time, become seemingly reserved for other, less well favoured parts of the city, such as Handsworth and Lozells – Birmingham nevertheless provided Burke with a compelling backdrop and context for his assiduous work in documenting the different faces of Black Britain. Time and time again Burke's photographs remind us of the fascinating and intriguing ways in which particular new forms of British identity have been created by Black Britons. One of his particularly arresting images – one of many – is a photograph of a gentleman, sitting alone on a bench in an open expanse of city parkland, garlanded by mature trees. The man sits watching a game of cricket, that most quintessentially English of sports. In actuality, the racial identities of the cricketers are not particularly apparent to us; neither for that matter is the racial identity of the lone cricket-watcher. But in many ways, the strength of the image lies in the associations that we as viewers bring to the picture. We identify the cricket watcher as a Black Brummie, and we invest the photograph with all manner of the cricketing analogies, metaphors, histories and reminiscences so memorably crafted by CLR James in his influential and groundbreaking book, *Beyond a Boundary*.

There is, within Burke's photographs, a distinct, reassuring and quite unmistakable sense of empathy. He is gifted with an almost extraordinary ability to engage and charm even the most casual of acquaintances, and from there it is but a short hop, skip and a jump to these acquaintances considering themselves to be firm friends of the photographer, if only for the duration of these chance, or brief, encounters. Burke is a familiar, respected and indeed loved figure within the communities and neighbourhoods of his upbringing and residence. His remarkable ability to engage people has resulted in no end of touching, sensitive and striking portraits – both literal and metaphorical – of a people. To this end, for evidence of this empathy, we can look at *No Time for Flowers*, his important series of photographs of Black South African people very much under the cosh of economic and social misfortune. Burke offers empathy, and his subjects in return offer their trust and immediate affection.

Consider, if you will, one of Burke's great group portraits, taken in the children's play area of a local Birmingham park. The photograph depicts a group of young men, some of whom are in the adolescent age group, having commandeered a seesaw for the purposes of the photograph or communal conversing. The boys, the young men, are all relaxed, and are charming and charmed in equal measure as they pose for the camera. The photograph is a beautiful study of, and celebration of, 'youtman', but the photograph is also a sociological study of boys inheriting a world with seemingly few options beyond the ones they create for themselves. Unemployment and underemployment are apparently compounded by a paucity of social spaces in which these young men can congregate away from the judgmental eyes of their parents and the police alike. These youngsters have little or no option but to head to the park for social contact with each other, and for affirmation of their individual and group identity. City parks were of course created for just such a societal purpose, but these portraits by Burke speak of

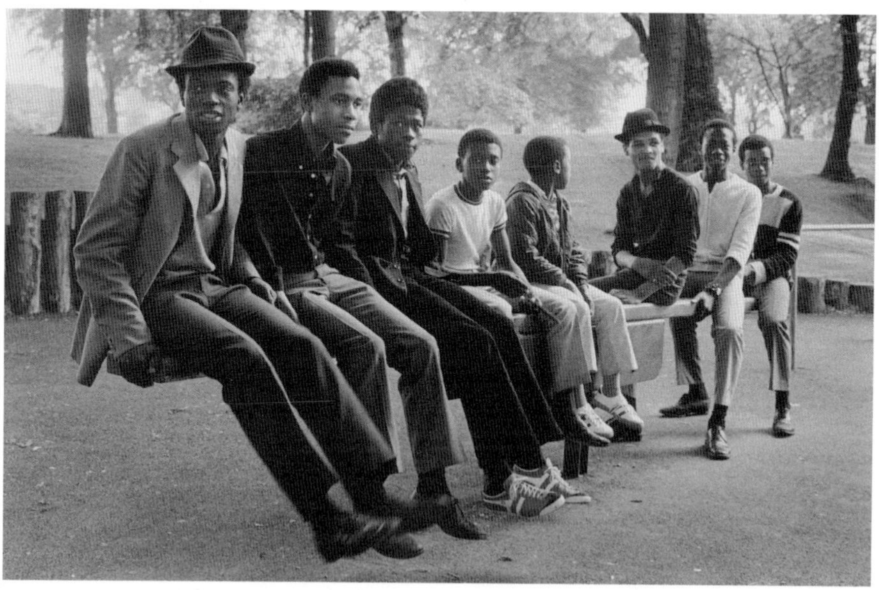

Figure 20.3 Vanley Burke, *Young men on a Seesaw in Handsworth Park, 1984*. © Vanley Burke.

people alienated from society, much more than they see themselves, or feel themselves to be included in it.

Burke has what amounts to an extraordinary ability to frame his subjects and compose his photographs. Within so many of his images, composition is the defining element of the picture's greatness and success. The picture of the 'youtman' on the seesaw is a case in point. Burke's remarkable and quite exceptional ability to frame and compose his subjects is a reflection of the respect he has for them. And it is this sense of respect that leads us as viewers to look, as if with fresh or new eyes, at the people he photographs. In this regard, one of my favourite photographs of Burke's is his wonderful portrait of a woman – the proprietor perhaps – behind the counter of a Caribbean takeaway. Amongst Black people, apocryphal tales abound, of surly and begrudging service received in Caribbean takeaways, particularly if we are not immediately known to those serving us. But here we see that Burke has, improbably perhaps, or, in his own inimitable way put the proprietor at her ease, and she smiles for the camera, a slight smile, but nevertheless a smile born of a wonderful combination of quiet self-confidence and service to her clientele.

One of Burke's great gifts is to encourage us, oblige us even, to look at people and things we might not otherwise see, notice or look at. So his portrait of the takeaway proprietor obliges us to consider the tantalising assortment of Caribbean food available on the menu, written with chalk on the blackboard behind her. The writing is neat, methodical and patient, and speaks to us of the rudiments of writing having been impressed upon her as a child in the Caribbean. This is a captivating and enchanting photograph by a remarkable photographer. Perhaps the highest compliment that the peeps of Birminam have paid to Burke is to regard him as a trusted documenter of their lives, their triumphs, their tragedies, their frustrations, their challenges, and their achievements. In sum, Burke has, over time, become a custodian of the history and the cultural memory of Black Birmingham. As such, his photographs amount to an extraordinarily important chronicle of the growth and coming of age of Black Britain.

'An Inglan Story, An Inglan History', was first published as a catalogue text for *By the Rivers of Birminam*, a retrospective exhibition by Jamaican-British photographer Vanley Burke, mac (Midlands Arts Centre), Birmingham, 22 September–18 November 2012: 11–14.

Notes

1 In the mid to late 1970s and for a while thereafter, tams were the preferred cap of choice for Rastas and dreads. A tam was a round woolen or cloth cap of Scottish origin, which sometimes had a pom-pom in the centre.

Chapter 21
Helen Wilson: Painting for a Brighter Future

News reports of the mid 1990s bequeathed us several new journalistic buzzwords that have entered the lexicon of everyday speech. Chief amongst them perhaps, is the term 'ethnic cleansing'; coined in a journalistic attempt to neatly and succinctly describe the motivation behind, and the effect of, the massacres that were allowed to happen in countries such as Bosnia and Rwanda. The western news media, struggling to effectively explain these late 20th century outbreaks of orchestrated genocidal savagery, sought to present these massacres as latter-day holocausts, motivated by, and summed up in, the neat turn of phrase, 'ethnic cleansing': This euphemism became the standard means by which 'the mass expulsion or extermination of members of a particular ethnic or religious group in a certain area' was explained.

Looking at Helen Wilson's paintings is a sobering and poignant experience, because her work reminds us that a term such as 'ethnic cleansing' does nothing but reduce the horrors of genocide in the most facile, irreverent and disrespectful of ways. In Rwanda, people were not 'ethnically cleansed', they were massacred in their hundreds of thousands. (Within the space of several months, militia and death squads systematically massacred an estimated 500,000 to 1,000,000 people.) Regions of the country were not 'cleansed'; they were soiled and tainted by the gratuitously shed blood of innocents. Death, with grotesque abandon, was visited on what Helen describes as 'a very beautiful country.'

Within the popular imagination, the continent of Africa is faithfully regarded as being – and constructed as – a wholly dysfunctional continent racked by interminable and incomprehensible tribal and ethnic tensions and conflicts that pathologically lead African people to kill each other. The common and popular view has it that Africans just can't help killing each other, in a bewildering array of 'conflicts' that rumble on, year in, year out, in various parts of the continent. The effect of this mindset is to engender another, equally troubling and problematic one. That is; that African lives are of a lesser value than the lives of people in other parts of the world. That African humanity is a less tangible entity than European humanity, or [white] American humanity. Disrespectful and insensitive media coverage of Africa's problems exacerbates this sense that the African continent is fully deserving of its status as the world's basket case, but not (to any meaningful degree) deserving of the world's sympathy and support.

Helen is an extraordinary artist with an important, compelling and compassionate mission: to tell and retell the story of Rwanda's genocide in ways that underline and emphasize the dignity, resilience and humanity of the genocide victims – both those whose lives were lost and those who survived. Helen's interest in Rwanda began in the mid-1990s. A news item on television about the genocide caught her attention. It made mention – in barely comprehensible terms – of the flight of 800,000 refugees into neighboring Zaire, to escape the genocide. The news item struck a chord with Helen, who found herself to be profoundly affected by the plight of this wretched and miserable sea of abandoned and frightened humanity. What, Helen wondered, might that volume of people look like? [To give some idea, try to imagine the population of Bristol, twice over, fleeing the city en masse, in abject terror, panic, confusion and chaos.] The plight of these refugees struck a sympathetic and empathetic cord with Helen. And so began her remarkable quest to remind her children, to remind the world and to remind herself that each murder, each displacement represented unspeakable violence meted out to real people. People like her boys, people like her. Speaking about her compulsion to paint the often-forgotten victims of Rwanda's genocide, Helen said 'I just want to paint these images in a way that can communicate with children, people that I know, people in Easton, my family . . .'

There is however nothing shrill, hectoring or gratuitous about Helen's Rwanda paintings. It is the absence of these things that makes Helen such an intelligent and remarkable artist. Mindful that the genocide victims have been robbed of their humanity – first by the death squads and then by the fleeting attention of the world's media – Helen is adamant that her paintings will not heap further abuse on the Rwandan victims. It would after all not be surprising if Helen's paintings featured bloody and hideous nightmare depictions of prolonged slaughter. But it is precisely the breezy ways in which such television images are mundanely paraded before us for teatime viewing that cause Helen so much discomfort. She was, in her own words 'so used to seeing images of Ethiopian children starving to death or carnage in Sierra Leone on the TV.' Had she painted gratuitous depictions of the unspeakable savagery that took place in Rwanda, though well intentioned, such paintings would in effect have been no different from or no better than the grotesque mid-1980s spectacle of well-fed foreign reporters telling the world what a tragedy it was that Ethiopian people were dying of starvation.

As a human being and as an artist, Helen is mindful of her responsibilities and obligations towards the individuals depicted in her paintings. Whilst not for a moment wishing to downplay the horrors of what took place in Rwanda, Helen's paintings seek to restore to the genocide's victims and survivors a critical sense of acknowledgement and humanity. In reverential ways, her paintings prompt us to remember the forgotten, those who died as well as those who survived. And these people are remembered not as a faceless generic mass, but as individual people, each with their own stories to tell.

These paintings constantly challenge us to locate the source of Helen's empathy towards Rwanda's victims. It is perhaps not surprising that these people should find in Helen such a worthy, committed and sympathetic chronicler of their suffering. Her paintings are a visually arresting fusion of what we might ordinarily regard as mutually exclusive impulses: the beautiful and the disturbing, the violent and the cathartic, the painful and the optimistic. It might seem strange to us that Helen's pictures, in recalling the 1994 massacres, contain much that is beautiful. But for her it's important to remember that, pre-1994, Rwanda was a beautiful country. In time, it may well be beautiful again, if and when the process of healing takes full effect. Rwanda deserves to be healed. After all, as Helen observed 'what I saw in Rwanda was incredibly beautiful. The beauty just hit me when I arrived'. She has, very consciously, painted beautiful pictures, some based on photographs that were taken during the course of a visit to Rwanda that Helen made in 2002. But this is not superficial or surface beauty. This is the beauty of personal dignity, courage and survival. The beauty of people determined to carry on living.

Helen's work invites us to consider our own place within the wider scenarios being played out and depicted in these paintings. In one of her most haunting works, several shadowy, sinister specters take part in (or are about to become victims of) a massacre. One ghoul is seen executing its fiendish work, with a raised machete in one hand, standing or kneeling over the prone body of a lifeless victim. But what disturbs most about this painting are the two young men to the right of the foreground, passively observing the hideous scenario. Perhaps they felt themselves to be powerless and unable to intervene. Perhaps they were being forced to watch the summary butchering of loved ones. Though Helen makes effective and discomforting use of ambiguity within this and other paintings, she nevertheless unequivocally challenges us to consider ourselves in the place of the two motionless observers. This painting asks the question: if we as individuals observe inhumanity and do nothing, what does that say about us? What does that make us? The most powerful nations in the world observed the Rwanda genocide and did nothing. Just another genocide, in just another African country that no one can locate on a map of the continent.

Despite its sobering and ominous subject matter, there is, within Helen's paintings, much in the way of hope and optimism. One painting in particular shows four children, each one in their own way a victim of the genocide. Children caught up in the horrors of 1994 saw things and did things that no adult – let

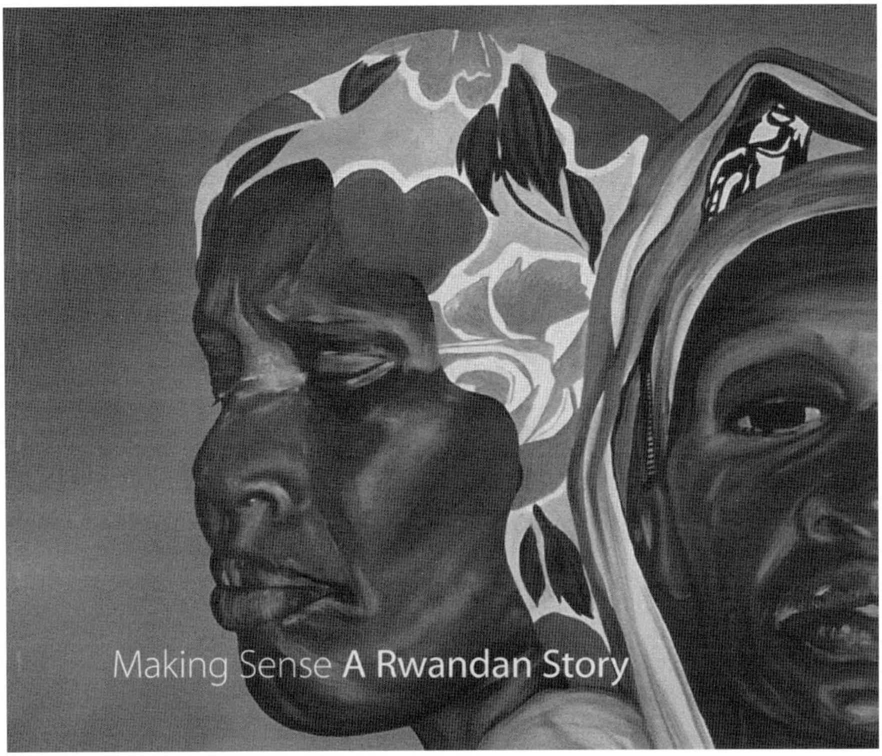

Figure 21.1 Catalogue cover, Helen Wilson: *Making Sense: A Rwandan Story*, Bristol City Museum and Art Gallery, September/November 2003. © Helen Wilson-Roe.

alone children – should ever have to see or do. So a very necessary part of the healing and reconstruction process is enabling, as much as possible, Rwanda's children to live their lives as ordinary children rather than as battle-scarred refugees. The painting shows the four youngsters diligently painting pictures, engaged in what some might regard as art therapy. The children exude a quiet strength and a determination to learn, to paint, to be creative. To be children. Though the painting is executed in bright colours, the weight of much sadness accompanies our reading it. And yet, despite this sadness, it is reassuringly evident that these children are engaged in a necessary (and necessarily) cathartic process; almost literally, painting for themselves a brighter future.

'Painting for a Brighter Future' was first published as a catalogue essay for *Making Sense: A Rwandan Story*, an exhibition by Helen Wilson, Bristol City Museum and Art Gallery, September/November 2003: 4–5.

Chapter 22
Barbara Walker: *Private Face*

Barbara Walker is an unfashionable artist. Unfashionable because in this age of instant imagery – typified by the digital camera and the computer scanner – her work presents itself as the very antithesis of contemporary image making. Her work, exclusively painting, requires a significant degree of skill, commitment and dedication, as well as a considerable amount of patience and labour. Good paintings like these cannot be produced in a hurry. They speak to us of long and varied periods of engagement and gestation, before an image is committed to canvas and the physical work of 'painting' begins.

There is nothing particularly methodical about the ways in which Walker works. An image may lie dormant in her mind for extended periods of time before she commits a version of it to canvas. She sometimes has to work hard to win the trust and confidence of her subjects before she can begin to sketch or otherwise document these people and their everyday or regular activities. Doubts have to be overcome – not just by those the artist wishes to sketch and paint – but doubts of the artist herself and of those closest to her. For everyone involved, not least Walker herself, the right to paint familiar subject matter has been earned. Having earned that right, it has to be nurtured, protected and never abused.

Walker does more than simply 'paint' her community, her family, her friends and herself. She is in effect a chronicler, a faithful and friendly documenter of the lives and culture of African-Caribbean people around her in her native Birmingham. Her work is not merely social documentation, important though social documentation is, for it effortlessly exudes a warmth, a familiarity and a humanity seldom within genuine reach of even the most accomplished and empathic photographer. Walker has grown up in, as well as grown out of, the 'community' that she takes as the subject matter of her work. Born into an African-Caribbean family in Birmingham, itself a solid home to many of Britain's post-war Caribbean Immigrants. Walker grew up in the Pentecostal church, one of many predominately or exclusively 'Black' churches that practice baptism by total immersion. She grew up with a familiarity with the reggae dance hall and many other social or religious environments in which African-Caribbean people congregate, worship and socialise.

Miscellaneous attempts to 'document' Black life are of course very familiar to us. However, these images, primarily photographic, often lack the familiarity and the intimacy of Walker's work. Being very much a 'local' person obviously helps Walker to paint these pictures. She is in no sense of the word an 'outsider' to the scenes she depicts. Having raised three children to adulthood within Birmingham, Walker is very much at home within the community she depicts. Yet, familiarity itself could never be enough to guarantee Walker the access she has needed in order to paint these pictures. Her paintings speak of a trust between herself and her subject matter. Too often Black people have found themselves the objects rather than the subjects of people's image-making but Walker's work contains none of the brutal and harsh objectifying that has tended to characterise the social documentation of Black people. Walker makes clear to her subjects that they and their images are 'safe' with her. That she will do nothing to brutalise or dehumanise them.

The importance of this point cannot easily be overstated. Though Black people have been in this country for a long time, within the mass media images of them still exist in decidedly problematic ways. You would have imagined by now that a range of pressures would have mitigated against the continuing circulation of images of Black people as being socially dysfunctional,

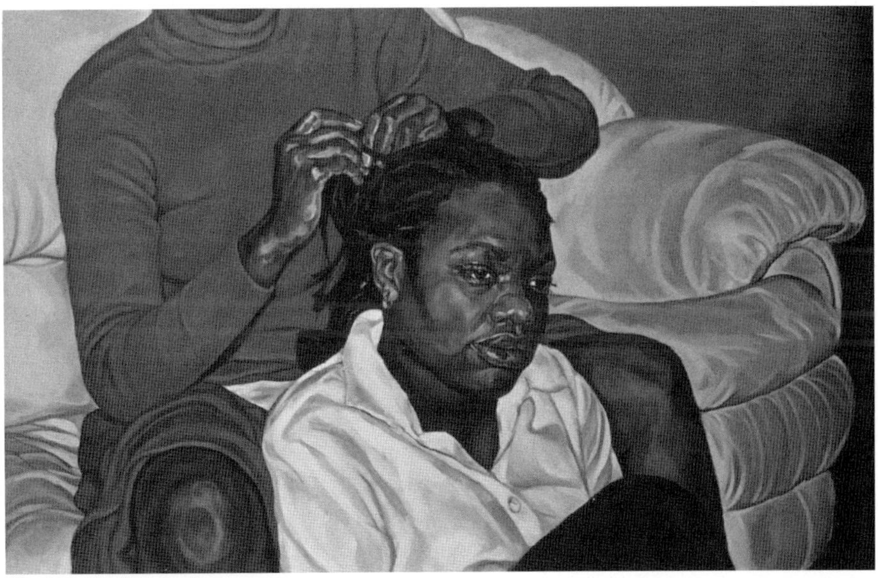

Figure 22.1 Barbara Walker, *The Sitter*, 2002 oil on canvas, 182 × 122 cm. © Barbara Walker.

under-achieving and criminally minded. Yet within the media, these racist stereotypes doggedly persist, to be interrupted only by equally problematic images of Black British sports personalities wrapping themselves in the Union Flag.

Walker does much good to undermine these corrosive and negative images. Through her paintings, she ensures that the ways in which we see ourselves and the way in which others see us avoid what we might bluntly call the 'racist' stereotype. The people in Walker's painting have real lives, real relationships and real needs. In other words, they are real people – people to whom we can, quite effortlessly, relate. They go to church, they have their hair cut, they play dominoes (of course they play dominoes!). Real people, real lives. Within her work, Walker is paying homage to, as well as building on, the work of other Black artists. As such, she is contributing to an important and worthy canon as she herself acknowledges, 'I want to challenge the stereotyping and misunderstanding that abounds, and offer a sophisticated and positive alternative in a mainstream setting, as a number of other Black artists have tried to do.' For good measure, and adding another dimension, Walker has added, 'I am interested in the quality of painting and what it uniquely has to offer.'[1] In many ways, what painting uniquely has to offer to both Walker and the subjects of her paintings is gravitas, status and respect. By painting in frequently subdued and restrained colours and palettes, Walker lays quiet claim to the tradition and the belief that to be painted is to be made visible in a range of profoundly respectful ways. Her characters have a quiet but determined dignity. Only painting – good figurative painting – can do this.

Perhaps without her consciously knowing it, Walker's paintings depict history, or more specifically, contemporary history, if we can use such a term. Her paintings represent something more than, something other than history book history. They represent instead a living, breathing historical document of the modern-day Black Birmingham resident: relatives in Jamaica, roots in Africa, home in Balsall Heath. Or Edgbaston or Handsworth or Erdington or Moseley. Residents whose accents are local, yet at the same time resonate with a range of diasporic twangs. These are valuable paintings because they provide us with copious evidence that the contemporary Black presence in England's second city is not – as the mainstream media would oftentimes have us to believe – a fractious and dysfunctional presence. It is instead a settled presence, typified by ordinary people, living ordinary lives, going about their day to day business – and being painted by an extraordinary artist.

As one commentator has recorded, 'Walker sees herself not (just) as a portrait painter, but rather as a commentator of the histories and experiences of people she knows and the Birmingham community in which they live. . . Walker is a contemporary history painter. . .'[2] In years to come, as much as at present time, we will thank Walker for these paintings.

'Barbara Walker, Private Face' was first published in the catalogue accompanying an exhibition *Barbara Walker, Private Face* at mac (Midlands Arts Centre), Birmingham, May/June 2002: 5–11.

Notes

1 *Private Face* – Artist's Statement, December 2001.

2 Gen Doy, 'The subject of painting: works by Barbara Walker and Eugene Palmer', *Visual Communication*, Volume 1 Issue 1, February 2002: 46.

Chapter 23
Barbara Walker: 'It's a Bit Much'

In 1986 a group of London-based filmmakers, the Black Audio Film Collective, made what proved to be a seminal film that examined the broad historical background and the aftermath, of the 'riots' that had flared up in inner city Birmingham in September of the previous year. The rioting – apparently triggered by community discontentment and sparked by an altercation between police officers and members of the public – rocked not just Birmingham itself but also London's political establishment. The film, *Handsworth Songs*, is an engaging document that consists, in part at least, of an overlapping series of archival images and contemporary footage of Handsworth streets, and the surrounding neighbourhoods. One of the most disturbing aspects of this contemporary footage is the way in which areas like Handsworth are shown as being, in effect, territory which is *occupied* by the police, as much as it is occupied by regular people going about their normal day to day activities. This sense of Handsworth and surrounding areas being virtually under siege by the police is reinforced, time and time again, by newsreel and by the recounted experiences and opinions of aggrieved and frustrated residents. Within *Handsworth Songs* we hear from a variety of Birmingham's Black residents who are sick and tired of being perceived as drug dealers and other criminals, and who resent the intrusive, disruptive and aggressive policing that they feel targets them.

Along with surveillance and a generally intimidating, almost militaristic police presence, the principal tactic of this policing, as residents complained, was the widespread and enthusiastic use of 'stop and search'. In the period leading up to the disturbances of September 1985, hundreds of Black youth were subject to summary stop and search whilst going about their legitimate business. In one of many of *Handsworth Songs'* particularly sobering passages, one noticeably aggrieved woman, employing poignant understatement, describes and condemns such police tactics as being 'a bit much.'

Two decades later, the intrusive and corrosive effects of stop and search are still being felt, in Birmingham and elsewhere in the country. In 2006, Black youth, many of whom were born in the 1980s and 1990s find themselves, effectively harassed by a similarly new generation of police officers. Behind each stop and search statistic there lies an individual human being who has, for whatever reason, been targeted as 'someone of interest' to whatever police officers or patrol car happens to be passing. Stop and search is in effect racial profiling, as these stopped individuals, these luckless pedestrians, tend to be of a certain ethnic background (African Caribbean), tend to be of a certain gender (male) and tend to be of a certain age group (young). Beyond that, a range of equally subjective and often bizarre variables is employed by the police, in their decisions to target a given individual and mess up his day.

Enter Barbara Walker, who has for this exhibition produced a body of work that unflinchingly and intelligently explores the impact that stop and search has had, and continues to have, on her son, Solomon, as well as on herself as a mother. Barbara is one of the most talented, productive and committed artists of her generation and over the course of the past few years she has established and distinguished herself as an important chronicler of the lives of her family and her community in and around her native Birmingham. Her work – painting and drawing – is marked by its profound empathy for its subject matter as much as its distinctive style. Within her pictures, there is great honesty, an honesty that speaks of (as well as to) the human condition in many of its forms. Like the great African American artist Charles White, Barbara's pictures are 'images of dignity' and because her work is highly figurative, we all have uncommon access to its multiple and pronounced social narratives.

Astonishingly perhaps, though this body of work speaks of a mother's love and protectiveness towards her son, there is nothing sentimental about these images. Neither is there any hint of the shrill or the hectoring. If any single element is discernible, it may well be dismay and what Elizabeth Catlett, in titling one of her most famous woodcuts, referred to as 'a special fear for my loved ones.'

'Louder Than Words' consists of a series of deeply arresting (no pun intended) drawings that directly address the personal, social and political implications of the police obsession with stopping and searching those hapless young Black men deemed to be *suspicious* in appearance or behaviour. As a parent, an artist, and a life-long resident of Britain's second city, Barbara has used her formidable drawing ability to explore the impact of stop and search on her son Solomon who has, on a number of occasions been stopped by the police, questioned and searched. To this unwarranted act of intrusion and aggression was added the curiously modern and thoroughly bizarre act of being issued with a *record* of the stop and search. It is now apparently required by law that at the end of a stop and search encounter the time waster presents the one whose time is being comprehensively wasted with a duplicate or carbon copy of an official form relating to the stop and search. For Barbara (perhaps even more so than Solomon) these small, almost unassuming and sometimes barely legible pieces

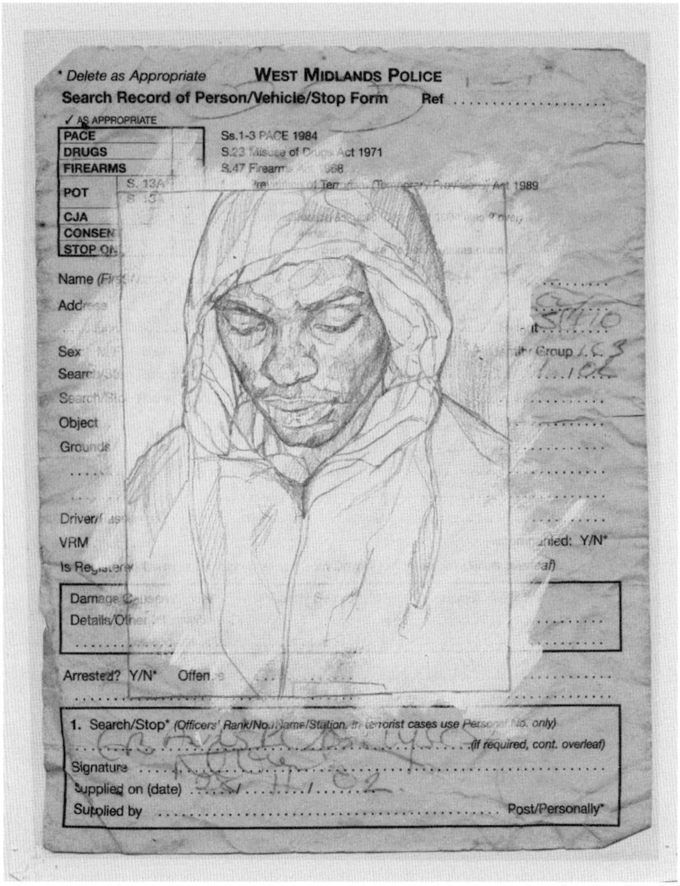

Figure 23.1 Barbara Walker, *Untitled*, 2006, mixed media on digital image, 114 × 85cm. © Barbara Walker.

of crumpled paper took on a sinister life of their own. Humiliation and intrusiveness reduced to obligatory rituals of bureaucratic form filling and box ticking. It's difficult to know just what those stopped and searched are supposed to do with these *souvenirs*. Curious about these incidents affecting and involving her son, Barbara began to collect these carbon copies issued to Solomon. As an artist whose practice has, for some years now, sought to document the lives of Birmingham's Black communities, Barbara wanted to find ways in which she could address what was happening to her son on the streets of his home city.

Perhaps more than anything, 'Louder Than Words' gives us a chance to consider this question: given that Solomon has, apparently, while going about his lawful business or leisure, given the police 'suspicions' and given that these 'suspicions' have led to him being stopped and searched on a number of occasions, what are the consequences and the implications of being a young

Black male in British society today? Furthermore, what on God's earth informs this curious negative stereotype that insists that young Black men are somehow perpetually 'suspicious' and worthy of police scrutiny? What is it that apparently makes them such a threat to society or community? Just what is it that makes the police so convinced that young Black males such as Solomon must have either criminal intent or criminal experience (or both)?

The 'special fear' mentioned earlier alludes, in this instance, to the worry that after years of baseless police suspicions, Solomon might simply have had enough and *resist* questioning and *resist* being searched. There are after all many many mothers grieving for sons who have died in what are euphemistically referred to as 'suspicious circumstances' involving police officers. It is often after being handcuffed that an innocent detainee's day can go from bad to worse. Commenting on one man's fatal encounter with the police, Tom Robinson wisely cautioned that 'If you figure on stayin' alive, button your lip and just swallow your pride/ and don't make trouble when your hands are tied . . .' Barbara's other fear may well be that sooner or later, the police will come looking for Solomon simply because his stop and search details have been entered, one too many times, into some police computer, even though no criminality whatsoever, on his part has taken place.

The crumpled yellow bits of paper given to him at the end of his encounters with the police symbolise these questions, these concerns, fears, and worries. Likewise of course, the crumpled yellow bits of paper have in their own ways come to reflect and represent Solomon's own frustration, displeasure and above all fear. Barbara takes as her starting point for this work these scrunched up bits of paper. She has had them digitally enlarged and used them as a base on which to execute drawings of Solomon and paintings of street scenes depicting the neighbourhood in which he lives. The very same neighbourhood in which he is stopped and searched. These paintings by Barbara are particularly powerful, as through the device of depicting a pleasant, near innocuous street scene, she reveals her neighbourhood not to be an environment of comfort, safety and domesticity, but an environment in which there lurks a terror that might, quite literally, descend at any given moment. Within this work, Barbara reminds us that our homes offer little safety or shelter from the perils of the police attention. Just ask Cynthia Jarrett or Cherry Groce.*

Other work within this new series consists of sensitive drawings of Solomon himself. These compositions capture his image, his facial features and expression,

---

* On Saturday 28 September 1985, Cherry Groce, a Black woman was shot and paralysed during a police raid on her home in London. Cherry Groce was, allegedly, shot in bed, by a member of a team of armed police officers who were looking for her son. Another, slightly divergent account has it that

> 'a team of armed officers went to the home of Mrs Cherry Groce in Brixton, South London, to arrest her son, Michael, who was wanted for [allegations of] armed robbery. In fact, Michael Groce no longer lived there. The officers smashed down the door with a sledge-hammer and then an

his identity, and his personality. The intention of this work, in part at least, is to raise the question 'what does one who is seen as a menace to society look like?' Or to put it another way, how can Barbara's beloved, law-abiding son be seen as a threat to civil order time and time again? This series of drawings prompts this further enquiry: what are the consequences and implications of living in a world in which an individual such as Solomon is often judged by others (particularly those with power and in power) by the way they look, rather than by what or who they actually are.

'It's a Bit Much' was first published in the brochure to accompany the exhibition *Louder Than Words* by Barbara Walker, at Unit 2 Gallery, London Metropolitan University, London, November 18–December 16, 2006.

---

inspector rushed in shouting "armed police". Mrs Groce says the officer suddenly rushed at her, pointing a gun at her. She tried to run back but he shot her. She is now paralysed and confined to a wheelchair. (*Times*, 16 January 1987)'.

Quoted in *Policing Against Black People* (London: Institute of Race Relations, London, 1987) p.26.

On Sunday 6 October 1985, just over a week after Cherry Groce sustained her horrific injuries, another Black woman, Cynthia Jarrett died of a heart attack during a police raid on her Tottenham home. Reports of Cherry Groce's injuries and Cynthia Jarrett's death sparked widespread rioting throughout the Brixton area of South London and the Tottenham area of North London respectively.

These incidences figured prominently in *Handsworth Songs*. For more on these incidents and responses to them, see 'Riots and Rumours of Riots', a chapter in *'A Climate of Fear' The Murder of PC Blakelock and the Case of the Tottenham Three*, by David Rose, Bloomsbury Publishing Ltd. 1992 and 'Roll Call of Deaths', a chapter in *'Deadly Silence' Black Deaths in Custody*, (London: Institute of Race Relations, 1991).

Chapter 24
Reviewpiece: Ajamu and Sunil Gupta

Why have these two photographers been brought together in the same show? What does their work have in common? Looking at the work assembled for this exhibition, the answer to this question might be: very little. In looking for commonality, we might be on firmer ground when considering their individual profiles and identities. One is a man of African ancestry, the other is a man of Asian background. Both have, within the official publicity accompanying the exhibition, been described as 'gay' or 'queer'. But having family roots that lie beyond Europe and being gay are as far as their commonality goes, because these photographers have presented very different and contrasting bodies of work. Having said that, if these two artists are happy to be curatorially paired-off with each other, it may not be for us to question the wisdom of the arrangement.

Ajamu presents us with reworked antique, archival photographs of 'freaks' of nature – a three-legged man, another man, armless and legless, and so on. The power of the images is magnified by the diminutive (suddenly, that word becomes so loaded) size of the photographs – they are not much bigger than playing cards.

By contrast, Gupta's work is decidedly colourful, though I use the word advisedly. He has produced a series of colour diptychs that alternately show the exteriors of 'gay scene' night clubs and intimate self-portraits. Not 'intimate' as in cozy, but intimate in that they reveal not just the physical body of the artist himself, but elements of his attitudes towards his (to quote the exhibition brochure) 'own "condition" – as someone living with HIV, and as an Asian gay man'.

The problem is, one body of work has only the most opaque relevance to the other. Possibly the only tangible relation that the bodies of work have to each other is one of a troubling and problematic contamination. Two distinct and separate solo exhibitions would, I'm sure, have been better and more respectful of each photographer's practice. After all, within this exhibition, politically potent debates about gay identity, HIV/AIDS etc. are involuntarily cross-referenced with questions about the historical/contemporary depiction of 'freaks' of nature.

There is no reference anywhere in the exhibition press release or brochure to the show's curator. But whoever it was, it may be that they are of the view that historically, to be 'gay' was to be considered a 'freak'. But if that is the case, where is the sense in dredging up ancient prejudices? This question also applies to the gay=freak/freak=gay correlation that the exhibition press-gangs us into considering. The question also applies to the peculiar body of work presented here by Ajamu. Titles like *Auto Portrait as armless and legless wonder*, *Three Legged Wonder in a study by Ajamu* and *Unknown tailed boy in a study by Ajamu* will give the reader a sense of what he/she can expect to see in Ajamu's section of the exhibition. We are told that Ajamu has based 'his portraits on unearthed archives of American freaks'. But such photographs, with all their brutal objectification, have been removed from public consumption for a raft of good reasons.

Ajamu has manipulated archival photographs to produce computer generated prints. But the essential elements of these photographs – the 'freakishness' of the subjects – remain intact. What is the difference between people voyeuristically visiting a Victorian-era freak show and gawping at these latter-day, two-dimensional versions, presented in the supposedly rarefied and enlightened context of the art gallery? Both the exhibition and the brochure essay, worthy and earnest as it is, leave the question unaddressed and unattended to.

Gupta's body of work is altogether more successful. Within the exhibition brochure, Emmanuel Cooper concludes his short text on Gupta with a muddled sentence, badly in need of some editing: 'In finding the courage and mettle to turn the camera on his own life, to contemplate eternity, Gupta holds up a two way mirror, offering revelations that challenge and disturb – though in the reality that Gupta defines[,] eternity seems a long way off.' Cooper seems to be suggesting that for Gupta 'eternity seems a long way off'. Within these photographs, it seems clear however, that Gupta's musings on illness, disease and mortality suggest that he considers 'eternity' to be close at hand. (How else could we account for *Shroud* – a self-portrait of Gupta laid out as in death?)

These are, in the main, engaging and thoughtful photographs. The six pictures of the clubs are as much a critique of such establishments as they are anything else. A photograph of one club *Attitude* shows the wonderfully ambiguous words BOOK THIS VENUE written across its doors. On the one hand, this is obviously an invitation to hire the premises. But the verb to 'book' is also a soccer term referring to a player being yellow-carded – a formal warning about decidedly unacceptable behaviour that results in the player being closely scrutinised by the referee for further misdemeanours. Is Gupta inviting us to critique the mannerisms of the 'commercial gay scene in south London'? After all, each of Gupta's photographs locates him firmly on the outside of these establishments. Gupta invites us to further critical scrutiny in his photograph of another club *Hoist*, which is photographed with the entrance doorway conspicuously embellished by two perfectly symmetric surveillance cameras.

The other six photographs are melancholic portrayals of a man coming to terms with living with HIV. There is a poignant yet oppressive weight to these photographs. In *Christmas* we see Gupta standing naked with his back to us, next to a decorated Christmas tree. But there is no hint of joy, no hint of Christmas spirit within the picture.

Reviewpiece: Ajamu and Sunil Gupta was first published as a review of an exhibition, *Sunil Gupta: From Here to Eternity* and *Ajamu Anti/Bodies: A Spectacle of Strangeness*, organized by Autograph and shown at Standpoint Gallery, Coronet Street, London N1. The review appeared in *Creative Camera*, Oct/Nov 1999: 36–37.

Chapter 25
Pat Ward Williams: *Isolated Incidents*

Pat Ward Williams is one of the most perceptive and challenging image-makers working in the United States. Though she is not – in a conventional sense at least – a photographer, her stock in trade is the photographic image. She uses photographs as a means of animating and graphically illustrating potent debates and her own unique perceptions about culture, about history and identity, and how such concerns are irreversibly intertwined with the photographic medium. One of the reasons her work is so compelling is that she consistently takes as the starting point for her practice the belief that the photograph can never simply be a dispassionate or unbiased visual representation. Instead photography is perhaps the most loaded of mediums, frequently used against particular groups of people.

Notwithstanding the formidable work of early- to mid-twentieth-century photographers such as Richard Samuel Roberts, James Van Der Zee and Roy DeCarava, throughout the medium's history, lens-based representation in its various forms has frequently been used to objectify and demonize African American people, particularly by and within the mainstream media. Perhaps more accurately, we might speak of the photographic medium being used to validate a wide range of spurious or problematic images of African American people. Mainstream media photographs of African American people have often been accepted, on face value, as authoritative, unbiased and even liberal. Yet the accumulative effect of the weight of this photographic representation has been to validate popular and ingrained racial prejudices. Ward Williams is very much aware of this tendency, and her work exists – largely – to critique, deconstruct and reconstruct the ways in which we look at and respond to photographs.

To this end, Ward Williams has been responsible for some particularly important pieces of work that examine the position, treatment and societal perceptions of African American people. Widely celebrated, in this regard, is her 1992 piece *What You Lookn At*, a large-scale work, combining photography and text, and variously exhibited within and outside of art galleries. Though we might take issue with her use of the word 'menacing' Thelma Golden nevertheless offers us a succinct and useful summary of the work: 'Marked by poise and attitude, they [the group of five males featured in the piece] create the menacing tableau usually mediated by the media. Williams adds text [the work's title], which functions specifically as voice, giving her subjects the ability to subvert the proverbial gaze and pierce their societal silencing.'[1]

But perhaps we should be careful not to typecast Ward Williams as an artist whose practice deals solely with racial matters, important though these things unquestionably are. The same artist who brought to our attention the seminal work *Accused/Blowtorch/Padlock* has latterly been responsible for some compelling examinations of the landscape and the climate of the South, particularly as it compares and contrasts to both the northern environment of Philadelphia, in which she was born and raised and the urban sprawl of Los

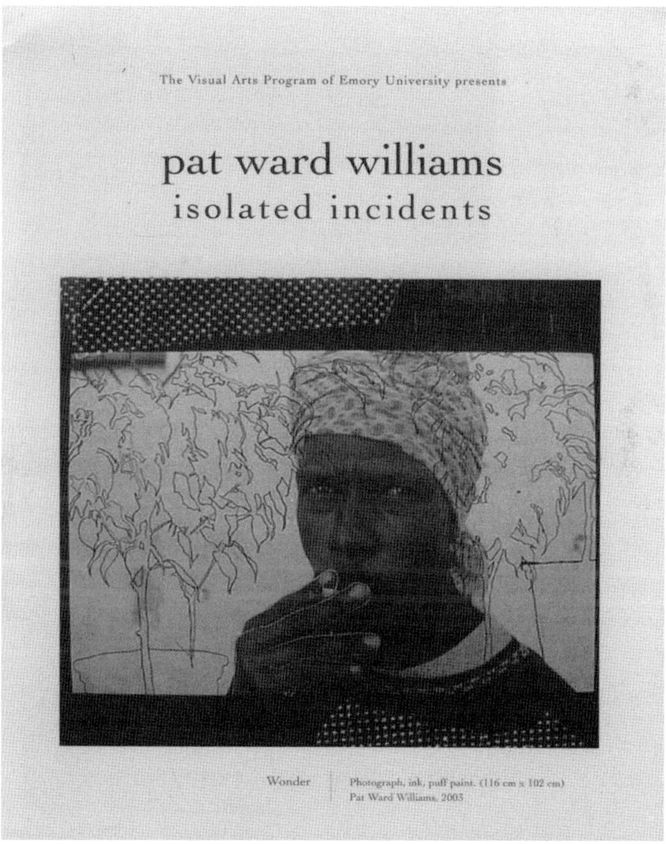

Figure 25.1 Brochure cover, Pat Ward Williams: *Isolated Incidents*, Gallery, Visual Arts Building, Emory University, March/April 2005, courtesy Pat Ward Williams.

Angeles in which she spent a significant number of years. Currently living in Tallahassee, Florida, Ward Williams describes the natural environment there as 'unrelentingly Floridian: not just trees and grass but unyielding heat and humidity, mammoth creepy crawly things. This group of landscape photographs reflects my undefinable relationship to this natural Floridian environment. Through text, image, and a love of darkroom processes I try to express my experiences here.'[2]

This exhibition brings together a range of pieces that span several decades of the artist's practice, from earlier works through to more recent examples. As such, it represents a valuable opportunity for gallery-going audiences in Atlanta to see work by one of the most acclaimed American artists, working within what we might call the medium of photo (re)construction.

'Pat Ward Williams: *Isolated Incidents*' was previously published in an exhibition brochure to accompany *Pat Ward Williams: Isolated Incidents*, the inaugural exhibition in the gallery of the Visual Arts Building, Emory University, Atlanta, 21 March–15 April 2005.

Notes

1. Thelma Golden 'What's White?' essay in catalogue for 1993 Biennial Exhibition, Whitney Museum of American Art, 1993: 32.
2. Email correspondence with the curator of this exhibition, November 2004.

Chapter 26

Donald Rodney: *Three Songs on Pain, Time & Light*

In 1990, Emmanuel Cooper, an exhibition reviewer committed the most terrible *faux pas*. Somehow, somewhere, he had got hold of the idea that the artist Donald Rodney had departed this life, on the eve of his work being included in a group exhibition in Bristol. In *20/20*, the short-lived magazine launched by *Time Out*, Cooper wrote 'Rodney, who suffered from a rare blood disease, did not live to see his work in the show, which adds a poignant note to his plea for tolerance and understanding'. An accompanying byline reiterated the message that the artist was no longer with us. 'Work by the late Donald Rodney can be seen in Bristol'. At the time, I remember thinking that it wasn't much of an obituary – not because Donald Rodney was dead – I knew he wasn't – but because, well, it just was not much of an obituary.

Six years later, and the Black Audio Film Collective have produced a film about Rodney. Perhaps mindful of Cooper's appalling blunder, Black Audio and/or the Arts Council of England (who funded the film) seem to be hedging their bets as to Rodney's longevity. The official blurb about the film tells us that 'Donald Rodney is an artist whose bones are being eaten away by sickle cell anaemia, a disabling disease that will eventually kill him'. So, there you have it, medical diagnosis, morbid prediction and film press release, all rolled into one.

Donald Rodney was born in 1961 and studied at Trent Polytechnic and the Slade School of Fine Art. He has exhibited widely, including solo exhibitions at Chisenhale Gallery, Camerawork and Rochdale Art Gallery. Despite nearly fifteen years of consistent exhibition activity, Rodney remains something of an enigma, possibly 'known' as much for having 'sickle cell' as for any of the bold, thoughtful and engaging art he has produced. *Three Songs* is an uncomfortable reminder of the extent to which Rodney the artist and Rodney the sickle cell sufferer have become one and the same in the minds of many people. It is true that it was Rodney himself, back in the 1980s, who started to make extensive use of discarded medical X-rays in his work. But he himself was always careful to maintain an intelligent and critical distance between himself and his illness. He attempted to show 'disease' in the human body as a metaphor to represent political or societal 'disease' in local, national or international contexts.

Diseases – cancer, leukemia, Parkinson's disease etc. are, to an extent, afflictions that pay no heed to racial or national boundaries. This is important because in an age where 'identity' has become the slipperiest of constructs, 'sickle cell' has become a rock-solid signifier of blackness and black people. All black people might not develop sickle cell, but only black people will develop sickle cell. And because only black people are affected by it, the government, the medical profession and the nation at large accord sickle cell scant recognition. At least, that seems to be the prevalent view of the moment. So those who suffer from sickle cell become living barometers of 'woe is me' racial injustice, whether they want to be or not. Enter *Three Songs on Pain, Time & Light*.

Three Songs is a wide-ranging film. Perhaps because Donald Rodney is a wide-ranging artist. The film offers a potted history of Rodney's work, from the late 1980s through to the work he made for the recent 'Care and Control' project at Hackney Hospital. It's a pleasure to see these works again, albeit fleetingly. These brief glimpses of work such as *Self-Portrait as Clinton McCurbin*, *Black Man Public Enemy*, *The House That Jack Built*, and *Middle Passage* remind us how little we have seen of Rodney's work and how much we would benefit from, and enjoy a major showing of these and other pieces.

Stylistically, *Three Songs* is a sequence of filmic, photographic and video montages. Interspersed with super 8 film shot by Rodney from his hospital bed, we have visual documentation of past work, conversations with the artist himself, three 'video postcards', and lots and lots of film of sunflowers. Sunflowers in fields and bunches of sunflowers being held by family and friends of the artist. Apart from enigmatic, almost cameo appearances by Edward George and Trevor Mathison, the film's directors, *Three Songs* is embellished entirely by women. Women nursing him, a woman assisting him and a woman (curator) talking to him. The film gives the distinct impression that it is women alone who support and acknowledge Rodney. The absence of male voices is of some consequence because so much of Rodney's work deals with assorted issues relating to perceptions of black masculinity. And so, intentionally or not, issues relating to black masculinity (or more specifically, the presence/absence of black men) are played out within *Three Songs* itself. The video postcards are delivered by Marlene Smith, Brenda Agard and Sonia Boyce. These contributions are distinctly melancholic and mournful, almost being delivered as eulogies. Inadvertently perhaps, Smith, Agard and Boyce all speak to Rodney as if he has been laid out in a chapel of rest or about to flatline on a life-support machine. It is almost as if they've been talking to Emmanuel Cooper.

Ten years ago, a fresh-faced Donald Rodney was seen on television (State of the Art) rather sheepishly telling Lubaina Himid that until he met Keith Piper, he had painted flowers, but with his consciousness now elevated, flowers were out and black struggle was in. Rodney became possibly the foremost advocate and practitioner of the black Art/black Strength manifesto. Times change, and the 'Road to Damascus' is now interspersed with U turn signs and mini-roundabouts. In *Three Songs*, Rodney tells us that he now sees himself returning to flower painting, flowers being rich with metaphoric readings and art historical references.

Three Songs is a useful and valuable film, because it is a substantial, dignified and considered look at the work and life of one of the most interesting artists of his generation. To the credit of Black Audio, they steer clear of overloading the film with extraneous racial narratives, leaving Rodney's voice largely unfettered. In this regard, the film successfully navigates potentially difficult and hazardous territory, even if it does manage to cast a distinctly morbid shadow over the artist, his life and his work.

'Donald Rodney: *Three Songs on Pain Light & Time*' (film about British artist Donald Rodney) made by Trevor Mathison and Edward George (Black Audio Film Collective), colour, sound, Digibeta, 25 mins, 1995, was previously published as a film review, *Art Monthly*, London, Number 200, October 1996: 65–66.

Chapter 27

Ben Jones: *In the Spirit, In the Flesh*

Gallery-going audiences in London rarely have the opportunity to see for themselves anything of the remarkable body of work produced by African American artists of the present time, or previous eras. Such exhibitions are few, but when they occur, they remind us that there is much we can learn from these artists, and much visual pleasure to be taken in these opportunities. This is in fact Ben Jones' second exhibition in London; the first having taken place at the 198 Gallery the greater part of nearly two decades ago. Ben Jones' return to London is indeed to be celebrated, enjoyed, and widely acknowledged. Active as an artist for many decades, he has established himself as perhaps one of the most respected senior figures of contemporary African American art, whose practice emerged in the artistically, culturally and politically turbulent period of the late 1960s, and continued, with notable rigour and constantly maturing creativity, through the decades right up to the present day. A native and lifelong resident of New Jersey, Ben Jones has spent significant periods of his life travelling to different continents and countries of the world. This travel, this meaningful interaction with different peoples of the world, has gifted his visual art practice a remarkable breadth and depth of vision.

Ben Jones makes beautiful, often highly decorative wall-based pieces and installations, that frequently have male figures or faces as their central element. I use the word beautiful deliberately, because it tends to be a word society withholds – and indeed on occasion, we ourselves withhold, from Black males. (Stereo) typical images of the Black male do not, as a matter of course, reflect notions of beauty. As such, Jones' work exists as a profound gesture of rehumanising that which has been demonised, and presenting complex, layered imagery that seeks to evoke celebratory and life-affirming sensibilities. The figures in his work resonate with exuberance, aspiration, and triumph, in ways that few artists attempt, let alone achieve. And yet, his work simultaneously reaches deep into African history and culture, in the most singular of ways. As such, we can perceive, and indeed track, a grand majestic historical sweep within Jones' work; a sweep that stretches from the earliest stirrings and manifestations of Yoruba culture, through to the hopes, dreams, aspirations and experiences of present-day African American peoples and those in other parts of the African diaspora.

It is through his use of symbols such as the Ankh and the two-headed axe that is the symbol of the mighty Yoruba deity Shango, that Jones most graphically evokes his connection to Africa and the spirits of his ancestors. In one of his recent pieces, both of these symbols are amongst those used to decorate a patterned work that repeats other images and symbols, most noticeably, the visage of Malcolm X. Slain though he is, Jones resurrects and evokes Malcolm X in a way that is joyful, celebratory, affirming and instructive. The Ankh, for millennia regarded as the key to life, was the ancient Egyptian hieroglyphic symbol equating to the notion of eternal life. Other symbols proliferate within the work. Pairs of eyes resonate with references to the wheel of Ashoka and most challenging perhaps, love hearts are included in the blended mix of images. This is deeply moving work that not only presents us with a wonderful panorama of the beauty of the diaspora, but also bravely seeks to draw the still-powerful image of Malcolm X closer to explicit feelings of love and affection.

As one summary on the artist noted

> Jones's interest in the god Shango is both aesthetic and political. As the god of thunder and lightning for the Yoruba people, Shango is honoured wherever descendants of the Yoruba live in the African diaspora. The colours red and white [which dominate in Jones' Malcolm X piece] are closely associated with the deity, and these colours frequently appear in Jones's works. For Jones, Shango is not just an element in the context of his art but also a metaphor for the empowerment of African peoples.

Ben Jones has, within his practice, a declared respect and love for African cultures, in a wide variety of manifestations. Not just those aspects that can be traced back to continental Africa, but those with much more recent manifestations, within the diaspora. Notable in this regard is his work from the mid-1990s which uses shapes that are clearly evocative of purpose-made hand-held fans traditionally used by members of the congregation of African American churches during hot spells. The saintly portrait of Reverend Dr Martin Luther King sometimes adorned these fans. But in *Shango/Chango Fans*, Jones uses images of regular Black males, to be embellished, decorated and beautified with a wonderful range of brightly coloured mark making. Then, as now, the artist invites us, compels us even, to see these often-maligned men as fitting embodiments and recipients of our love and affection.

As Jones himself commented

> One of the spiritual influences in my art is the Yoruba culture in Africa, Cuba and Brazil. In these countries I have absorbed and participated in African-influenced rituals, religions, culture, and art. Another influence is the Black church – its rituals and their similarities to some of the ritual traditions in African societies. Faith, spiritual healing, renewal, and hope are the force. The heart and the mind as one.

Away from his ongoing explorations, a new body of work deals with ecological concerns, triggered perhaps by the recent BP oil spill in the Gulf of Mexico. Though oil companies have been wreaking havoc on the environment for decades – most noticeably perhaps, the oil fields of the Niger Delta – it was the BP spill which caught the world's and the media's attention. The sight of thick oil belching uncontrollably from the depths of the earth, on the ocean floor, was a graphic image, almost biblical in its resonances. Like a great many people, Jones was disturbed by this ecological carnage and out of this concern sprang a new body of work, several pieces of which are included in this exhibition. In one work, consisting of three panels, he presents a study of delicate marine life, almost as if seen through a microscope. Within the piece we sense something of the

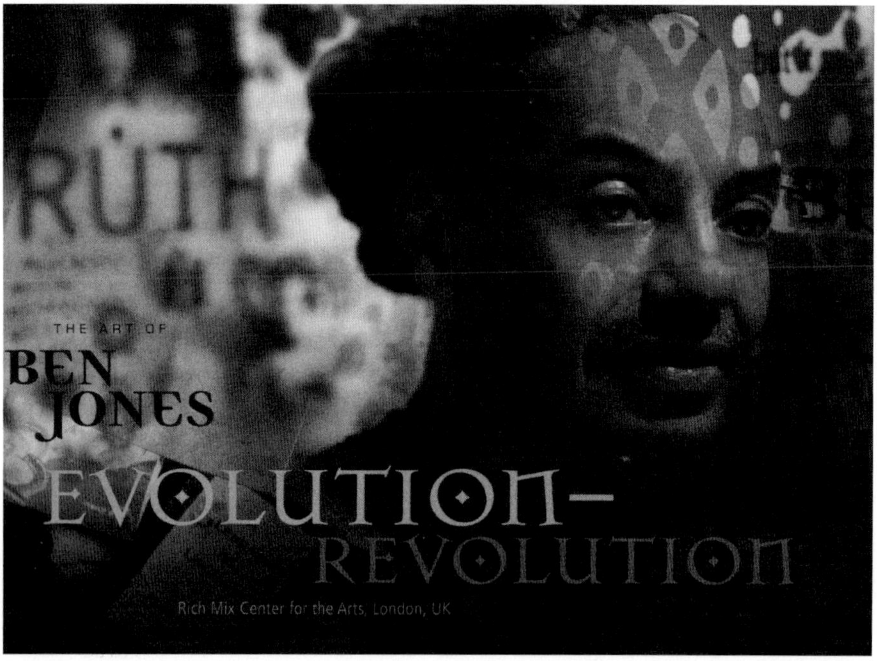

Figure 27.1 Catalogue cover for Ben Jones' solo exhibition, *The Art of Ben Jones: Evolution – Revolution at Rich Mix Centre for the Arts, London*, 13 January – 24 February 2011.

incredible ways in which all manner of sea life exists in the oceans of the world, affirming perhaps the primeval belief that the oceans represent life, no less than other prehistoric elements.

The work may well lean towards a delicate abstraction, but the shapes created by Jones' mark making remind us of seahorses, marine plant life, and so on. And yet, his piece is not a benign representation. The enlarged microscopic forms, if we read them as such, appear to be in the process of being targeted by rifle rangefinder scopes. The red wash, and the sporadic placing of more intense mark making, again in red, reinforce the sense that we are witnessing a scene of calculated and targeted destruction, made all the more real by the work's subtle associations with blood and killing. The oil that spilled out into the Gulf spread out in concentric circles of death and destruction, brought to mind by the artist's use of rings and circles within the piece, pollution subtly but insistently referenced. Most uncomfortably perhaps, the viewer is to an extent implicated in the work. We become the ones not only looking through the lens, but also the rifle crosshairs. This is subtle, haunting work in keeping with Ben Jones' oeuvre of beautiful, delicate mark making.

'Ben Jones: *In the Spirit, In the Flesh*', was first published as a catalogue text for Ben Jones' solo exhibition, *The Art of Ben Jones: Evolution – Revolution* at Rich Mix Centre for the Arts, London, 13 January–24 February 2011: 13–25.

Chapter 28

'There's No Place Like Home': The Enigma of Guyana in Frank Bowling's Map Paintings

This text concerns itself with what I have termed the *enigma of Guyana*. A small country – only some 215,000 km^2 – Guyana is located on the northern coast of South America, bordered to the south and southwest by Brazil, and to the west by Venezuela[1], and is an enigma for several reasons. In the first instance, it is emphatically regarded as being a 'Caribbean' country, though nearly all of its Caribbean neighbours are islands of various sizes, stretching from the western to the eastern Caribbean, united and divided by the Caribbean Sea. That Guyana should be commonly regarded as part of the Caribbean, rather than as part of Latin America is what this text concerns itself with. There are clear historical reasons for the designating of Guyana as a Caribbean country, which go hand-in-hand with a pointed refusal by Latin Americanists to accept the idea of Guyana having an active and important place in contemporary constructions of Latin America. Previously a British colony, and at that time known as British Guiana, the country has declared itself (and indeed, been declared) culturally part of the Anglophone Caribbean. With English being the official language, Guyana is at once different from the majority of countries of Latin America, in which Spanish and Portuguese are the dominant languages. English, Spanish and Portuguese may well all be European languages, but it is the speaking of Spanish, and Portuguese, which are the dominant definers of Latin American identity. Consequently, Cuba, the giant of the Caribbean, is a presumed component of Latin America, whereas its very near neighbours of Jamaica and Haiti, are emphatically not. The emphasis on linguistic dominance as a criterion for inclusion/exclusion is hugely problematic, as it papers over, or disregards, the presence of Spanish-speaking people in countries such as Trinidad or Jamaica, as much as it fails to heed the presence of English-speaking people in countries such as Argentina and Chile.

Demographics also account for Guyana's differences with Latin America. Numbering significantly less than a million, the two main ethnic groups in the country are those of *Indian* decent, who have their roots in the indentured labourers imported by the British, and those of African descent, whose roots lie amongst those victims of the Atlantic slave trade, brought to Guyana and elsewhere in South America in chains. Whilst both groups – particularly those of African descent – are far from uncommon throughout South America, their visibility is to some extent compromised by the more numerous and socially and politically dominant South Americans of European descent. Simply put, Guyana is a *Black* country, whereas (protestations of multiculturalism, racial democracy, and diversity aside), the rest of South America looks (and seemingly wants to look) decidedly *white* in comparison. I should again stress that this is not to advance the view that the Black presence in South America is negligible. Instead, I am arguing that, as is the case across a number of other continents, those of European background have positioned themselves at the centre of constructions of nationhood, at the expense of those of a darker hue. Black-skinned and English-speaking, Guyana doesn't fit with the dominant perceptions and pre-eminent images of the South America of which it is part.

With only limited exceptions, Latin Americanists have historically held themselves apart from the African element in their midst. As well as the pathology in which decidedly white manifestations of Latin Americanness take centre stage, this tendency towards cultural quarantining is possibly a consequence of the ever-more pronounced *Balkanising* of academia. Latin American art and Caribbean art have a potted and erratic history of being put together under the same umbrella, clumsily indicating more than a passing commonality. But as textbooks, exhibitions, and catalogues have multiplied, and the respective disciplines have grown, the Caribbean and Latin Americas have tended to go their separate ways. Latin American art and Caribbean art may well have been, until recently, the unloved and unwanted stepsiblings of European and American art history, but as they've become an increasingly familiar component of the curricular at various American universities, they've tended to exist in mutually exclusive spheres, denying the indelible and dynamic interplay that exists between as well as within these two conjoined regions. The 'problem' of presenting Latin American art as being wholly separate and distinct from Caribbean art dates back to the middle of the twentieth century, when the Museum of Modern Art presented 'The Latin-American Collection of the MoMA' in 1943. Within several years of this exhibition, the study of Latin American art began to develop, along the unmistakeable lines of a self-referencing entity that occasionally reached out to embrace certain Caribbean countries, on a somewhat erratic basis. In 1950, the Pan-American Union of Washington published its *Art in Latin America* series of essays, which included one on the art of Haiti. In addition to the perhaps predictable countries of South and Central America, its bibliography contained material on the Caribbean countries of Cuba, Dominican Republic, and Haiti.

In 1970 the Free Press published Gilbert Chase's *Contemporary Art in Latin America*, described as 'a pioneering work. . . the first book in any language to concentrate on the major contemporary art forms and major artists in the whole of Latin America.' The second of the book's six chapters was 'the Caribbean and Central America' which looked at the art of Haiti and Cuba alongside that of countries such as Guatemala, Nicaragua and Panama, amongst others. A certain irrationality characterized Chase's approach to his Caribbean coverage. Jamaica takes its place alongside Cuba and Haiti as being a Caribbean country with a formidable history of visual arts practice, albeit one that, according to a number of Jamaica's art historians, stretches back only to the early part of the twentieth century. Yet there was in Chase's thinking no room for Jamaica, even though the country had a rich and pronounced history of a Spanish presence (and indeed, the Spanish had ceded control of the island to the British in the second half of the seventeenth century. In Chase's book, room was found however, for Haiti, a country in which the dominant languages were French and a localized Creole. Given the subsequent insistent separating of Caribbean and Latin American art that has occurred since the book was published, its muddled nod towards the Caribbean was nevertheless notable. Ultimately though the author's tendency was towards needlessly compartmentalizing or culturally tidying up the region, rather than accepting that a range of formidable historical factors had created the most singular manifestation of diversity and plurality that was the Caribbean and Latin America. Furthermore, that such diversity and plurality were most fully understood when simply accepted as a consequence of historical shifts including migration, the slave trade, colonialism, etc. Chase's tendency towards compartmentalizing the region was masked, or complicated, by an admission of arbitrariness on his part. Wrote Chase,

> The several countries of Central America and the Caribbean area – a rather loosely defined geographical entity – are somewhat arbitrarily grouped here without any claim to cultural or historical unity. The arts of Cuba and Haiti have in common an Afro-American heritage (shared in part by Panama) but in Cuba this heritage has perhaps been more prominent in music and poetry than in the visual arts (though there are of course, some exceptions).[2]

Chase would have done better to simply have accepted that 'an Afro' heritage exists and is discernible throughout Latin America, and that a distinct range of ethnicities and respective cultural influences have come together in each of the countries of the Caribbean and South America, and that isolating or disregarding certain countries makes no academic sense whatsoever.

In 2000, Phaidon published a weighty volume, *Latin American Art in the Twentieth Century*, in which Cuba, the Dominican Republic and Puerto Rico were its favoured Caribbean nations. Mention should also be made of one or two publications that attempted to forge an interplay, though somewhat hesitant and insecure, between the regions of Latin America and the Caribbean. In 2004 the Museum of Modern Art, New York collaborated with El Museo del Barrio, to create the exhibition, 'MoMA at El Museo: Latin American and Caribbean Art from the Collection of The Museum of Modern Art'. The exhibition presented some 100 or more paintings, drawings, sculptures, prints, and other artworks produced by artists from Latin America and the Caribbean. The exhibition, which was accompanied by a substantial catalogue, featured work by artists practicing across the twentieth century: Antonio Berni, José Clemente Orozco, Diego Rivera, and David Alfaro Siqueiros in the 1930s; Roberto Berdecio, Wifredo Lam, Roberto Matta, and Joaquín Torres-García in the 1940s; Rafael Montañez Ortiz, Jesús Rafael Soto, Marisol Escobar, and Fernando Botero in the 1960s; and Jean-Michel Basquiat, Los Carpinteros, and Vik Muniz in more recent times. Because the exhibits were drawn from MoMA's collection, and because the works were, on this occasion, shown at a gallery supposedly existing to attend to the cultural needs of New York's Hispanic and Latino 'communities', 'MoMA at El Museo' had a perhaps timid and predictable composition.

The *Encyclopedia of Latin American and Caribbean Art* (2006) represents, to date, the most substantial attempt to art historically conjoin the two neighbouring regions. Inadvertently perhaps, the *Encyclopedia of Latin American and Caribbean Art* represents a marriage of convenience between two self-referencing, and self-interested partners, more than a union with a more credible and intellectually challenging basis.

To return to the question of Guyana, it is without question, alongside Haiti and Cuba, one of the countries of the Cirum-Caribbean region to put itself on the map, in terms of art history. Yet the strength and vibrancy of Guyana's modern and contemporary art histories have been consistently ignored by scholars of Latin American art, who have tended to read their subject through a decidedly Eurocentric prism. Two of the dominant artistic personalities to emerge from Guyana in the mid twentieth century were Aubrey Williams[3] and Frank Bowling,[4] both of whom have had important and compelling things to say – in their respective practices as painters – about South American identity.[5]

Williams was born in Georgetown, British Guiana's capital, in 1926. After settling in London in his late twenties, he enrolled at St Martin's School of Art and soon thereafter, established a career as a prolific and widely exhibited artist. An active member of the Caribbean Artists Movement, Williams came to be closely associated with the presence of Caribbean art/artists in London and his work was featured in a significant number of Caribbean art exhibitions, as well as other group and solo shows.

A passionate believer in art and culture in its many and varied forms, Williams was responsible for a substantial body of work and his paintings have latterly found their way into a number of important collections, including that of the Tate Collection and the Arts Council Collection, London. It might in some ways be difficult to characterize Williams' work, as the painting for which he is perhaps best known and celebrated contains both figurative and non-figurative elements. On the one hand, his paintings reflected his interests in such things as aboriginal South American culture, cosmology, and the music of the Russian composer Dmitri Shostakovich. On the other hand, his work also declared an interest in form, shape, colour and composition. Longtime admirer of Aubrey Williams' work, London-based critic Guy Brett noted, 'Williams' painting fluctuates between representational references and abstraction.'[6] Alongside such paintings there exists Williams' sensitive and faithful renderings of bird life. In concluding remarks in one of his essays on Williams, Brett cautions against the instinct to typecast Williams' practice.

> It may be futile to try to explain [his] painting. But it is also true that to merely name a motif in Williams' painting as 'pre-Columbian' or Mayan does not suggest the complicated life it leads in its changed form within his work, where it moves between past and present, between natural and artificial beauty, between excitement and warning. To grant Aubrey Williams' paintings their enigma only awakens one to their links with the actual, contemporary world.[7]

In 1986, British filmmaker Imruh Caesar made *Mark of the Hand*, a documentary that looked at the life and work of Williams, who as mentioned was a major force amongst Caribbean artists living and working in the UK during the second half of the twentieth century. The film followed Williams as he left his home in London and returned to his native Guyana to restore one of his murals, located on an outside wall of the capital's airport terminal building; be honoured for his contributions to art and culture by the Guyanese government, and make a journey deep into the country's interior, to revisit the places and the indigenous people he knew and worked amongst before he left the country. As much as anything else, the film was a look at the consequences of relocation, migration, memory, return and the difficulties and disappointments that can come from these things. Further to this, *Mark of the Hand* gave valuable insights into Williams' strikingly original practice as a painter whose work was frequently, but by no means exclusively, characterized by the range of figurative and non-figurative elements referred to earlier. The film was a pioneering work and to this day, sympathetic and sensitive documentary film studies of artists, such as *Mark of the Hand*, remain a rarity. One hugely important aspect of the film is the exploration of Williams' respect and fondness for the indigenous peoples of the Guyana interior. In this regard, the film positively complicates and challenges assumed notions of Caribbean and Latin American identity, which frequently ride roughshod over the existence, and contemporary cultural contributions of the aboriginal peoples of the region. Furthermore, the film stands in marked contrast to the somewhat Eurocentric mindset dominating chronicles of Latin American art, in which the contributions of indigenous peoples are relegated or confined to the historical/ahistorical realms of crafts and the decorative arts, whilst the work of artists of European background is elevated to the status of high art.

It is though, a discussion of the paintings of Frank Bowling that comprises the central element of this text. Bowling is an artist who has been painting for well over five decades, and like Williams, he was born in what was then British Guiana (now Guyana). Bowling first came to London in his teens, to complete his schooling. He was first a poet, eventually turning to painting in his late teens. After periods of study at art colleges in London, his career as a painter began in earnest with solo exhibitions in London in the early 1960s. Bowling has come to be widely known and respected for his abstract paintings, often-large expansive affairs rich with colour and texture. He came to abstract art via figurative painting, at the beginning of the 1970s. Before that time, his art of the late 1950s and 1960s was figurative and resonated with distinct narratives of figurative representation.

By the mid 1960s Bowling had taken the first of the innumerable transatlantic flights that enabled him to maintain studios in New York and London. Having decamped to the United States, it was in New York, around 1966, that Bowling met, engaged with, and was influenced by abstract artists, both African-American and European-American. Thus began Bowling's enduring love affair with modernism, something to which he has remained steadfastly loyal, decade after decade. The central and pivotal esteem in which Bowling places modernism is evidenced by his statement that 'I believe that the Black soul, if there can be such a thing, belongs to modernism'[8].

Whilst Williams had provocative and perceptive comments to make about the modern and historical presence of indigenous peoples in South America, it is to Frank Bowling's map paintings that we must turn, for the most singular evidence of a Black, Guyanese-born artist's complex reflections on his South American identity. Bowling's map paintings were produced at a time when he was moving away from explicit figuration within his painting, but had not yet adopted the non-figuration with which he is now most commonly associated. In an essay on Bowling's map paintings, Kobena Mercer suggested that they

> come from a key moment of transition. Produced between 1967 and 1971, the works have been acknowledged as a distinct strand in his oeuvre that

arose out of a shift from figurative painting to post-painterly abstraction during the artist's relocation from London to New York in this period.[9]

Positing that Bowling's map paintings were 'perhaps an attempt to recover an identity that he had tried to suppress in the past', Rasheed Araeen has described these paintings as 'a mixture of colour fields superimposed upon iconographic allusions to his mother's house in Guyana, maps of South America with Guyana emphasized, maps of Africa, etc.'[10] Three of the most remarkable aspects of Bowling's map paintings are firstly, the ways in which they seek to visually craft the biography, the identity of this African-Caribbean person around and within the motif of the outline of the South American continent, on which he himself was born. Secondly, the map paintings create a South America visually charged with and by pronounced signifiers of Pan-African, or African Diasporic, identity. And thirdly, Bowling's map paintings lay claim to, or declare themselves a part of, a modernist tradition in which South America is included. It may have been a keenness on the artist's part for his work to engage in a dialogue with Pan-Latin Americanism that lead him, in the early 1970s, to exhibit at the Center for Inter-American Relations, 680 Park Avenue, New York.[11]

Scholarship and curatorial interest in Bowling has of late increased exponentially, with Okwui Enwezor's *Mappa Mundi* (Haus der Kunst, Munich)

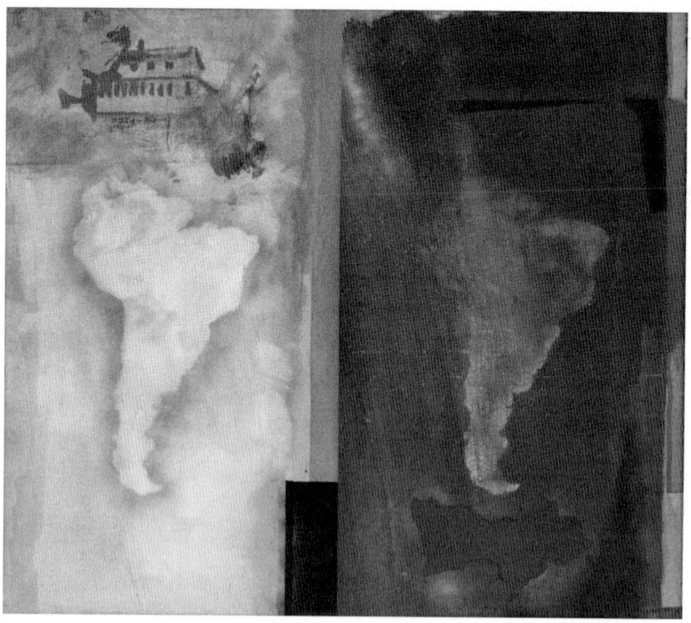

Figure 28.1 Frank Bowling, *Plus Mother's House*, 1968. Oil on canvas, 210 × 232 cm Courtesy of Frank Bowling OBE RA. © Frank Bowling. All Rights Reserved, DACS 2020.

and Elena Crippa's *Frank Bowling* (Tate Britain, London). Until one or two decades ago, the most significant showing of Bowling's map paintings was his solo show at Whitney Museum of American Art, towards the end of 1971.[12] Several years later, the Whitney exhibition was summarized by one art critic as follows:

> The Whitney show consisted of large scale, more or less monochromatic (or so they appeared) stained paintings which contained stencilled images of maps. Since then his paintings have been built on color alone. If the Whitney paintings suggested a nebulous view of the world the newer ones evoke a color atmosphere that has a more *felt* relationship to nature.[13]

But whilst a number of Bowling's map paintings may indeed have appeared nebulous, as if partially obscured by cloud or haze, the outline of the South American continent often appeared clear and unambiguous, almost as if Guyana, and the South America of which it was a part, were the cornerstones of Bowling's world view, and the central element of these singular paintings. After all, a striking feature of a number of Bowling's map paintings is the way in which they embody, or envisage, a world made over in the artist's own image. To accept the

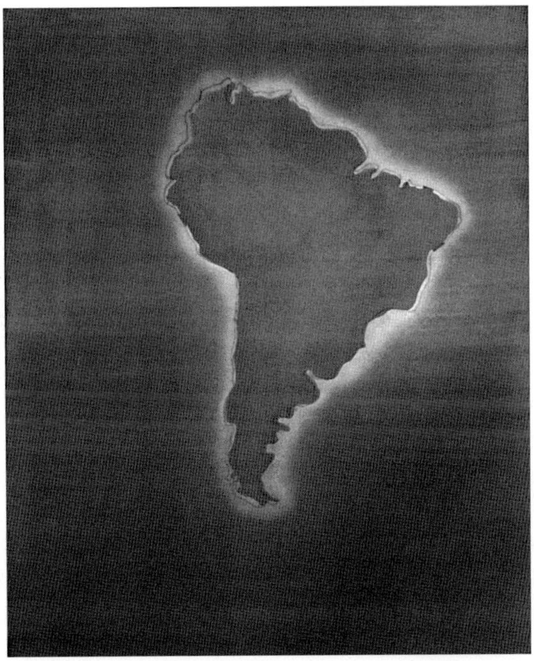

Figure 28.2 Frank Bowling, *False Start*, 1967, acrylic on canvas, 161.9 × 129.5 cm. Courtesy of Frank Bowling OBE RA. © Frank Bowling. All Rights Reserved, DACS 2020.

hegemonic world cartography that presents itself to us at every turn is arguably to accept the world as it is, to accept the consequences of its sordid and bloody episodes, and to accept its endemic pathologies that brutalize so many of the world's people. Bowling rejects the world as it is by frequently depicting, within his map paintings, a world literally turned on its head. In this regard, some of his map paintings offer more than a passing nod to the iconic illustration of South America by the Uruguayan modernist Joaquín Torres-García,[14] sometimes referred to as the *Upside-down Map* (1943).

Torres-García's striking map occupies a central position in Latin America's attempts to assert itself as a continent with a pronounced destiny on the world's stage, a destiny that contrasted markedly with the marginalization and subservience with which it was frequently treated by its more dominant and powerful neighbour to the north. In a singular gesture of revision that envisioned as it were, a new world order, Torres-García inverted the map of South America, and placed the South Pole at the top of the earth. In so doing, Torres-García forcefully proposed a seemingly simple, yet profound visual representation of the importance of the South American continent. At the time of the *Upside-down Map*'s making, it was centres such as Paris or New York that had come to typify, or embody, the spirit of modernism, and it was to cities such as these that artists, philosophers, poets and others gravitated, as the twentieth century took shape. Torres-García proposed the bold and provocative view that Latin America had every right to see itself, and to be regarded, as embodying progressive values and ideas about art and culture. This making over of the world in Torres-García's image, this attempt to embody the hopes and aspirations and sense of purpose of an entire continent; these impulses were present in Frank Bowling's map paintings, as much as they were in Torres-García's *Upside-down Map.*

One of Bowling's map paintings was his 1968 work, *Who's Afraid of Barney Newman?* The painting was, in some ways, a profound homage to one of the giants of American abstract expressionism, and his seminal painting of 1948, *Onement, I.*[15] The title of Bowling's homage casually reflected a familiarity on Bowling's part with the dominant personalities of contemporary art, who had made New York their home, in much the same way as Bowling himself had. But the title also gives more than a passing nod to another of Newman's works, *Who's Afraid of Red, Yellow and Blue II*[16], as well as to the critically acclaimed film, starring Elizabeth Taylor and Richard Burton that had been released in 1966, *Who's Afraid of Virginia Woolf?*[17]

Newman's painting used what was to become his trademark approach to structuring vertical blocks of colour, in this instance demarcated by a slim fissure of a contrasting band of pigment. *Onement, I* was a hugely important work, breaking as it did so many of the conventions that dominated the practice of painting before the coming of abstract expressionism. Newman's painting was in many ways a precise, disciplined and highly structured affair that confirmed him as a great American talent. Bowling's painting featured several discernible outlines of his beloved South America, overlaid with Newmanesque vertical *zips* of green, yellow and red, creating a highly charged and bold exploration of history and identity. The colours Bowling used related directly (or had a direct relation to) the powerful symbolism of the tricolour of red, gold and green. Since the 1970s the colours had become instant signifiers of a particular type of Black presence. Numerous African flags utilized the red, gold and green colours in a variety of compositions, but primarily as horizontal or vertical tricolours, including Senegal, Ethiopia, Ghana, Rwanda, Benin, Cameroon, Guinea Bissau, Guinea, Mali, and Congo.[18]

It was though, the use of the red, gold and green colours in the Ethiopian flag, complete with the imperial Lion of Judah in the centre of the ensign, that led to the colours being so insistently used, worn, displayed and used as adornment by adherents of Rastafari, first in Jamaica and subsequently, throughout the international Black world.[19] In English cities such as Liverpool, signs denoting street names in 'frontline' districts were painted in the colours, thereby decisively demarcating the territory. This though, was simply a version of what had long since been happening in Jamaica. 'Every Rastafarian commune is identifiable by these colors which appear everywhere, even painted on the trunks of trees in the yards.'[20]

The colours came to signify a particularly 'conscious' type of Black presence. When worn on an individual, the colours confirmed that the wearer aspired to 'upful' living. When adorning musical instruments such as drums, the colours signified that the drums in question were employed in the righteous task of 'chanting down Babylon'. And when the red gold and green colours adorned dwellings, the message went out that no 'weakheart cannot enter'. Thus, Bowling's use of the colours evoked a multiplicity of diasporic readings that casually collided with his pronounced embrace of modernism and his respect for abstract expressionism.

The Black presence in South America may have been consistently denigrated, marginalized or even rendered less than visible, but in *Who's Afraid of Barney Newman*, the South American land mass, as distinctive in its outline as the shape of Africa, was imagined as an unmistakably Black diasporic space. It would though, be a serious error to suggest that *Who's Afraid of Barney Newman* and other map paintings by Bowling were in any way merely illustrative, or explicit examples of pronounced social narratives. These paintings left an incredible amount to the imagination, because whilst the outlines of continents such as South America were unmistakable, other outlines of landmasses in these paintings emphatically defied conventional recognition. In this regard, Bowling not only created his own worlds by reconfiguring the world that already existed, he also created imagined new land masses, that, try as we might, we could never quite recognise as familiar parts of conventional world maps. Furthermore, whilst in Torres-García's *Upside-down Map*, South America was inverted, in a number of Bowling's map paintings, South America sometimes appeared to have been reversed, thereby creating something that appeared at once familiar, yet not quite familiar. Whether or not Bowling's maps were indeed reversed is a matter of visual conjecture or speculation. What is unquestionable however, is the extent to which his map paintings destabilize seemingly emphatic or monolithic constructions of the world, (or, as is the case in many instances, monolithic constructions of South America and South American identity). In other map paintings, Bowling goes further in challenging our sense of familiar cartography by presenting outlines of landmasses that look a lot like amalgamations of the outlines of the African and South American continents. And in so doing, Bowling again proposes a provocative and primary interplay between Africa and Latin America.

This interplay between Africa and Latin America is central to the haunting painting of 1968–9, *Night Journey*. Despite the red, yellow, green and blue that dominate, this is a brooding work, having a nocturnal quality that well reflects the painting's sombre title. The outlines of South America and Africa dominate the painting, though they emerge from, or lie behind, cloud or haze. Numerous artists – most of them Black – have tackled issues relating to slavery and the slave trade, but by far the strongest examples of this work are the pieces that reference slavery indirectly, eschewing the explicit symbolism of chains, slave ships, whips, branding irons, and bondage. *Night Journey* is a majestic, sombre work that references the Middle Passage – the nightmarish journey by sea that took captured Africans from their homelands to slavery and death in the 'New World'. Described by Mercer as one of Bowling's 'most important paintings', he also maintains that *Night Journey*'s:

> sombre darkness evokes the unrepresentable terror of the Middle Passage. Whether exploring the historical violence that inaugurated the experience of diaspora – which transported bodies and culture out of Africa into the Americas – or giving over the vast expanses of his canvases to an almost geological enquiry into the imperceptibly slow time of continental drift, Bowling was fully part of a cultural moment whose cumulative effect was to decentre the planisphere projection of the globe that had been taken for granted ever since the Renaissance.[21]

One of the strengths of the painting is the way in which it fuses two visual tensions. Though evocative of a lateral dialogue, or movement, from east to west, from Africa to South America, a dominant tension in the painting is the downward pull of the messy blocks of colour, poignantly and mournfully applied by Bowling. It's as if some terrible corrosive, acid-like substance has been poured over a bright and colourful world, resulting in a horrendous, ghastly and shocking disfigurement.

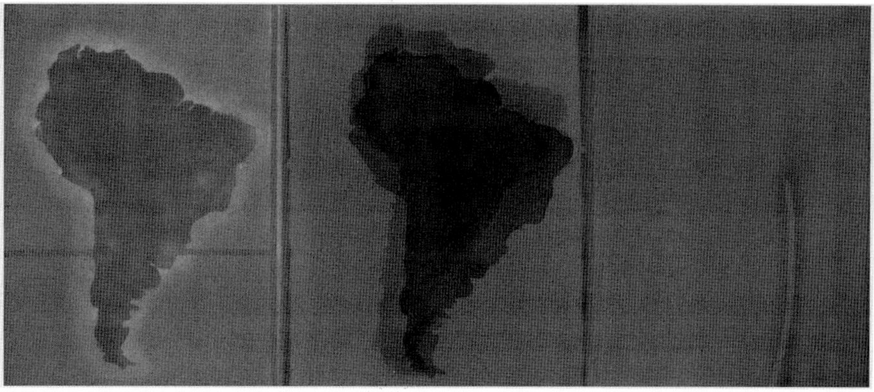

Figure 28.3 Frank Bowling, *South America × 3 at root 2 puce*, 1967, acrylic on canvas, 121 × 271 cm. Courtesy of Frank Bowling OBE RA. © Frank Bowling. All Rights Reserved, DACS 2020.

Though slavery on US soil is better known, researched, visualized and recalled, Bowling's painting seeks to draw particular attention to the ways in which South America was as much a part of the Atlantic slave trade as the US or the Caribbean region. Indeed, slavery in Brazil continued until well near the end of the nineteenth century, several decades after its abolition in the US and the Caribbean. Within *Night Journey*, North America is effectively obscured, leaving its southern neighbour as one of the painting's key focal points. Packed into lightless, airless holds, in a nightmare seemingly without end, the darkness of the experience, the cloak of death that surrounded slavery's victims, these things are convincingly referenced in the painting and its title. In *Night Journey*, Bowling appears to have attempted to obscure the world map as we know it, by a menacing use of brush strokes of the reds, yellows, greens and blues mentioned earlier. Slavery established a formidable bond between Africa and South America, a bond that endures through the presence of South Americans – just like Bowling – of African descent throughout the continent. *Night Journey* is a beautiful painting, despite the profound melancholy of its implied subject matter, and despite its arresting visualization of a world disfigured by slavery.

Bowling's map paintings lend themselves to no end of perceptive, intelligent interpretations; evidence of their profound ability to animate powerful subject matter in ways that eschew didacticism on one hand, and formalism on the other. Though only about 160 words in length, the brief review of Bowling's Whitney exhibition that appeared in *ARTnews* of December 1971, contained many pointers to the striking nature of these paintings.

> Frank Bowling [Whitney Museum; to Dec. 6] shows big, acrylic-stained color-field canvases, the bright red and orangey, over-heated color fields of which

> ebb around, illuminate and otherwise obscure their basic world-map imagery. In Bowling's big, lyrically messy maps, much of the world at large is missing, the bulk outlines of countries other than North and South America and Africa have been replaced by sweeping, amorphous continents of almost relief-like light and shades. The countries that do show up are, for all their densely hard-edge delineation, well-kept secrets, as if the artist were giving us a strictly literal reading of the old saw, 'There's no place like home.' The only home Bowling would seem to know is painting; the dark, hidden continents of his planetary maps hover and beckon on the canvas, but in the end it is the style of these works through which one travels, a style that is a kind of cartography, sensitively, colourfully and accurately awry. GH[22]

Whilst scholars, writers, artists and others have variously proposed and explored the links between Latin America and modernism, several of Bowling's map paintings give compelling form to these links, particularly his enigmatically titled painting, *South America Squared*. The title's interpretations are severalfold. One inference is that, being a native-born South American, Bowling has the measure of the enigma of that continent. So long framed by many Latin Americanists, as well as by unthinking and uncritical persons throughout the world, along frequently narrow, unimaginative and skewed lines, Bowling boldly suggests that in this series of paintings, and in this work in particular he has put to rights, rectified, or remedied the misrepresentation and marginalizing of South America. He does so by casting the continent in an entirely unfettered vein, as a region of the world that ought, rightfully and correctly, to have modernism and a distinct and recognizable African presence at the core of its twentieth-century identity. In *South America Squared*, a dramatic, South America appears on a plane of fiery reds and oranges, almost as if back lit by sun or some other such searing light source. The poured acid effect, utilized so effectively in *Night Journey*, is present, but this time the aesthetic evoked is altogether more life affirming and optimistic. The continent appears contained within a rectangle. Not one that traps or constrains it, but one that evokes the modernist grid. For good measure, two other rectangles – minus dramatic contents – are partially visible, at different levels, in the upper left- and right-hand corners of the canvas. The minimalist grid is in many ways the cornerstone of modernism. Emphatically dispensing with what had become the tyranny and indeed, the dullness of classicism, the grid became, for early modernists, the mainstay of their practice. It conclusively circumvented hierarchy in a picture, thereby creating multiple focal points, and in some instances, removing the very idea of focal points and replacing such tyrannies with a whole new language of seeing. The grid enabled ideas – often complex and challenging ones – to be coolly and dispassionately presented. The modernist grid imposed, or allowed for, certain creative, angled structures to have their day. *South America Squared* was a decisive message – that the continent was as much of a home to modernism as other parts of the world seemingly more associated with it. In the painting, Bowling's beloved South America unashamedly takes centre stage, and simultaneously lays the strongest of claims to modernism. In this regard, Bowling's vision critically engages with the judgement that 'The belated onset of modernism might be the leitmotif' of Latin American Art of the Twentieth Century.[23]

Such declarations of modernism also lie at the heart of *Mother's House on South America*, in which a decidedly verdant South America appears – in its upper section at least – held in place by a supporting square. Both continent and square appear in washes of green, against a background of contrasting colours. To borrow from Guy Brett, 'these map paintings of Bowling contain, within each canvas, fluctuations between representational references and abstraction.'[24]

Bowling again proposes a provocative interplay between Africa and South America in his painting, *Bartica Born*. Referencing the artist's place of birth, Bartica, Essequibo is a town on the left bank of the Essequibo River, lying at the confluence of the Cuyuni and Mazaruni Rivers with the Essequibo River. It is, both literally and metaphorically, in the heart of Guyana. And yet, no map of South America is present. Instead, it is the bold, the emotive, the unmistakable outline of the mighty African continent that dominates the painting. There are in fact two outlines of Africa, the dominant one rendered in light blues, and gently streaked by running rivers of reds, that pour down from the vicinity of the other Africa, located higher up the canvas. Bartica born Bowling may be, but Africa still dominates, or figures boldly, in this painting. Other map paintings provide us with ample evidence of the artist's singular attempts to give visual form to the complexities of his identity, particular the centrality of South America. In some of these paintings, South America is laid on its side, as if by so doing the continent is better able to bear the weight of Bowling's childhood memories, particularly the neighbourhood store run by his mother.

Whilst a significant number of artists – including Horacio Zavala, Anna Bella Geiger, and Alfredo Jaar – have executed important work featuring the maps of South America, the world, or specific countries, no other single South American artist – with the possible exception of Torres-García – has worked so single-mindedly to challenge, refute and interrogate what we think we understand by the motif of the South American continent. Whilst Joaquín Torres-García envisaged a South America that had emerged from apologetic shadows and taken up its rightful place at the centre of the world's stage, Frank Bowling used the map of South America to make sense of his own existence, and in so doing, presented us with bold and imaginative new ways of looking at Latin American identity. It is in many ways the duty or work of an artist to prompt questions, rather than merely providing emphatic statements or declarations. In this regard, Bowling's maps engage, with relish, in the multiple acts of what Mercer calls the 'searching, questioning and journeying' typical of the work of other artists who have, like Bowling, sought to challenge the vexing hegemony of the world map as we have known it, and its accompanying prescriptive and lumpish assumptions of space, place, location and identity. Wrote Mercer (of the period in which Bowling painted these pictures), 'Frank Bowling's trajectory through this moment shares the sense of searching, questioning and journeying evoked by other artists who also approached maps as a critical surface upon which new uncertainties had emerged.'[25] Mercer also opined that, 'it could be suggested that it has taken over thirty years for Frank Bowling's map paintings to reveal their hidden riches.'

We might each have our own starting points, or access points, for appreciating Bowling's map paintings. For me, some of these paintings' most challenging dimensions, and some of their most important, valuable, and enduring contributions are the ways in which they challenge dominant constructions of Latin American identity. In recent years (and indeed, at the present time) Bowling's map paintings are an increasingly respected, (though previously unremembered) dimension of his oeuvre. With each viewing, from a show such as *Frank Bowling: The Map Paintings 1967–1971* (16 September to 23 November 2013, Hales Gallery), to a couple of years later, *Frank Bowling: Map Paintings* (20 February to 2 August 2015, at the Dallas Museum of Art), or more recently, *Frank Bowling: Mappa Mundi* (24 March–8 July 2018, Irish Museum of Modern Art), Bowling's map paintings lose none of their intrigue and fascination. Indeed, ever more poignant readings and considerations seem to come to the fore. And with each outing of this extraordinary series, questions continue to emerge, not only about the visualizing of Guyana and South America, but questions about how this work unsettles dominant, though problematic assumptions about Latin American art.

'"There's no place like home": The Enigma of Guyana in Frank Bowling's Map Paintings' is a new, previously unpublished text.

Notes

1 There are in fact three *Guyanas,* Guyana itself, and to its immediate east, Suriname, then to the east of Suriname, French Guiana. Within the dominant mindset that frames South America, all of these relatively small countries have been discarded by Latin Americanists. This text though, focuses on Guyana, previously known as British Guiana.

2 Gilbert Chase, *Contemporary Art in Latin America*, New York: The Free Press, 1970, Chapter 2, 'The Caribbean and Central America', p. 39.

3 For material on Aubrey Williams see Rasheed Araeen's, 'Conversation with Aubrey Williams', in *Third Text*, No. 2, London, Winter 1987–88. See also Andrew Dempsey, Gilane Tawadros and Maridowa Williams (eds), *Aubrey Williams*, (exh. cat., 12 June–16 August 1998; London: Whitechapel Art Gallery, 1998), and Anne Walmsley (ed), *Guyana Dreaming: The Art of Aubrey Williams*, Coventry: Dangaroo, 1990.

4 For material on Frank Bowling see Mel Gooding, *Frank Bowling*, London: Royal Academy of Arts, 2011.

5 Mention should also be made of Donald Locke, another Guyana-born artist of international stature. Locke was born in September 1930, in Stewartville, Guyana and died in December 2010, in Atlanta, Georgia. He began painting in 1947 under the legendary E R Burrowes, who ran the Working People's Art Class in Georgetown, Guyana's capital. Locke was awarded a British Council Scholarship in 1954, leading Locke to study at Bath Academy of Art in England. In 1959 he was awarded a Guyana Government Award to study in Edinburgh, Scotland. It was in Edinburgh that Locke's son Hew was born. Hew Locke has himself gone on to establish a successful career as a sculptor.

6 Guy Brett, 'A Tragic Excitement', *Aubrey Williams*, Whitechapel, 12 June–16 August 1998, catalogue, p. 24.

7 Guy Brett, 'Introduction', *Aubrey Williams*, Shibuya Tokyu Plaza, Japan, 1988, catalogue, unpaginated.

8 'Frank Bowling & Bill Thompson: a conversation between two painters', *Art International*, December 1976. Quoted in Rasheed Araeen, *The Other Story: Afro-Asian artists in post-war Britain*, Hayward Gallery London, 1989: 40.

9 Kobena Mercer, 'Frank Bowling's Map Paintings', in Gilane Tawadros and Sarah Campbell (eds) *Fault Lines: Contemporary African Art and Shifting Landscapes*, inIVA, London, 2003: 140.

10 Rasheed Araeen, *The Other Story: Afro-Asian artists in post-war Britain*, Hayward Gallery, London, 1989: 40.

11 The exhibition's dates were 28 November 1973–13 January 1974.

12 *Frank Bowling*, 4 November–6 December 1971, Whitney Museum of America Art, 945 Madison Avenue, New York, New York 10021.

13 Jeanne Siegel, *Art International The Art Spectrum*, Volume XIX/5, 15 May 1975. This Whitney exhibition was discussed in a section of Kellie Jones, 'It's Not Enough to Say "Black is Beautiful": Abstraction at the Whitney, 1969–1974', in *Discrepant Abstraction*, inIVA and MIT Press, 2006. The section in question was 'Frank Bowling: 4 November–6 December 1971'.

14 For more on Joaquín Torres-García (1874–1949), see Margit Rowell, *Joaquín Torres-García*, Ediciones Poligrafa, 2009. Torres-García was one of Latin America's most intelligent, perceptive, innovative and significant artists of the early to mid twentieth century. One of the most original figures of his generation, Torres-García is now regarded as a particularly important and influential early modernist pioneers to have emerged from South America, a continent, like Africa, frequently relegated to the margins of modernism by European and North American curators, art historians, and university professors. Torres-García is celebrated for his work as a modernist painter, though he was also a distinguished teacher, and art theorist.

15 Barnett Newman (American, 1905–1970). *Onement, I*, 1948. Oil on canvas and oil on masking tape on canvas, 69.2 × 41.2 cm. In the collection of the Museum of Modern Art, New York.

16 There were several paintings by Newman with this title, each one numbered I, II, III, IV. 'Who's Afraid of Red, Yellow and Blue II, 1967, was acrylic on canvas, 305 x 259 cm.

17 From the Internet Movie Data Base, 'George and Martha are a middle-aged married couple, whose charged relationship is defined by vitriolic verbal battles, which underlies what seems like an emotional dependence upon each other. This verbal abuse is fuelled by an excessive consumption of alcohol. George being an associate History professor in a New Carthage university where Martha's father is the President adds an extra dimension to their relationship. Late one Saturday evening after a faculty mixer, Martha invites Nick and Honey, an ambitious young Biology professor new to the university and his mousy wife, over for a nightcap. As the evening progresses, Nick and Honey, plied with more alcohol, get caught up in George and Martha's games of needing to hurt each other and everyone around them. The ultimate abuse comes in the form of talk of George and Martha's unseen sixteen-year-old son, whose birthday is tomorrow.' http://www.imdb.com/title/tt0061184/ accessed 16 November 2011.

18 In the case of a country such as Rwanda, the country's red, yellow and green vertical tricolour, complete with capital R in the centre band, was replaced after the horrific period of genocide that the country went through in the mid 1990s. The replacing of the old Rwanda flag was part of the country's attempts to shed associations with that violent and traumatic episode of its existence.

19 In the iconography of Rastafari, 'The Lion of Judah' symbolises the Emperor Haile Selassie I of Ethiopia, who was crowned in 1930, taking the titles King of Kings, Lord of Lords, Conquering Lion of the Tribe of Judah, Elect of God and Power of the Trinity. Rastafarians hold Haile Selassie in the highest esteem, believing him to be a direct descendant of the Israelite Tribe of Judah, tracing his lineage through the line of King David and Solomon. Further, Rastafarians assert that Haile Selassie is the personage of the Lion of Judah mentioned in the New Testament Book of Revelation.

20 Leonard E Barrett, *The Rastafarians: The Dreadlocks of Jamaica*, Heinemann/Sangsters, 1977 (1982 edition), 143.

21 Mercer, 'Frank Bowling's Map Paintings', p. 141.

22 *ARTnews* December 1971: 13.

23 Edward Sullivan (ed) *Latin American Art in the Twentieth Century*, Phaidon, 2000. Jacket publicity.

24 Brett, 'A Tragic Excitement', p. 24.

25 Mercer, 'Frank Bowling's Map Paintings', p. 141.

Chapter 29

Charles White's 10- and 12-Inch Vinyl Messages

Looking at the range of Charles White's art, a clear, strong and profound interplay with the music of Black America is ever-present. Indeed, this may well have been a contributory factor to the consistent ways in which White's illustrations were used on record sleeves, throughout his career and after his passing. White's work *spoke* to people. And people reciprocated with love and pronounced affection for the artist and his work. That much was evident when Nikki Giovanni, the renowned creator of such extraordinarily soulful, spiritual poetry, penned a homage to White. Who else but White could be serenaded with such endearment and fondness? Referencing the reproduce-ability of White's work, Giovanni's paean included the lines,

> Charles White and his art were introduced to me through magazines and books – that's why I love them[1]

During the 1950s White began a particularly fertile period as an artist whose work appeared on records of the Vanguard label. Vanguard was a particularly innovative record label, founded in 1949 by Seymour Solomon and his younger brother Maynard Solomon in New York City, at a time when jazz music was entering a dynamic period of becoming as much a form of music listened to through recordings and on the radio, as a form of music performed live in clubs and other venues. The Vanguard label grew to become one of America's leading independent labels. White supplied drawings and illustrations for a number of Vanguard records, for the most part with 10-inch sleeves. Many of these were jazz recordings, but in one or two instances his illustrations were used for other types of recordings, such as opera.

White's drawings for record sleeves were, with limited exception, of African Americans. This might not be surprising, given that many of the musicians and all of the singers creating these recordings were themselves African American. But in his renderings of African Americans, White chose, in a great many instances, not to depict faithful likenesses of these musicians, but to create generic images that thereby had a wider and much more profound engagement with the record-buying and record-listening audience. From the period in which White's work emerged into wider visibility and appreciation, he was intent on countering the images of African American favoured and indeed, generated, by the dominant culture. These images insisted on depicting African Americans as on the one hand, comical, and obsessed with the consumption of watermelons, and on the other hand, as sinister, delinquent, and criminal-minded. The time in which White was born and raised saw a continued manifestation of blackface, and the seemingly endemic culture of minstrelsy. To these humiliations and abuses could be added the widespread criminalization and incarceration of large numbers of African Americans, particularly males. The most visible aspect of this criminalization and incarceration was the chain gang, a group of convicts chained together while working outside the prison, in agriculture, railroad construction, road building and so on, the prisoners frequently obliged to wear distinctive horizontally striped clothing.[2] In time, White would seek to draw the sting from this particularly degrading manifestation of American racism in his album sleeve renderings of Huddie William Ledbetter (the legendary American folk and blues musician better known as Lead Belly, the name commonly rendered as Leadbelly). In his renderings of African Americans, White sought not only to challenge the dominant society's visualizing of Black people, but also, along with countless other people, to challenge and resist the lack of civil rights, the dominance of Jim Crow throughout the South and beyond, and other manifestations of American racism. A measure of the challenging times in which White and other African American artists worked was the ongoing problem of lynching, which was to continue for all but the last decade or so of White's life.

In the early 1950s White was commissioned by Vanguard Recording Company, Inc., to produce a series of drawings to be used, primarily, in relation to its Jazz Showcase releases. The commission came at a time when White was receiving significant accolades for his art. As those responsible for issuing the records never tired of informing their purchasers, White had recently 'won an Academy of Arts and Letters award in 1952, and, that same year, a National Prize of the Metropolitan Museum of Art in New York.' Furthermore, 'His work is represented in the Whitney Museum, Library of Congress, and other famous collections.'

In 1954, White provided an illustration for the cover of the eponymously titled *Sir Charles Thompson Trio*. The record was released on the Vanguard label as part of its Vanguard Jazz Showcase. As was the case for many record releases of the mid-twentieth century, this was a 10-inch mono recording. Sir Charles Thompson was an American swing and bebop pianist, organist, composer, and arranger and the cover of *Sir Charles Thompson Trio* featured a drawing of a pianist. The drawing was not signed by White and neither did the record sleeve contain any references to him. More often than not, White's drawings were appended by a signature and the last two digits of the year. Additionally, the notes on the sleeves for which White provided drawings frequently, though not always, contained biographical references to White. Typical, in this regard, was,

> ABOUT THE COVER The drawing on the cover is one of a series commissioned by Vanguard Recording Company, Inc., from the distinguished artist, Charles White. Mr. White won an Academy of Arts and Letters award in 1952, and, that same year, a National Prize of the Metropolitan Museum of Art in New York. His work is represented in the Whitney Museum, Library of Congress, and other famous collections. The drawing does not portray any of the actual performers on this session, but rather reveals the human experiences out of which jazz comes.[3]

White's drawing was of a contemplative piano player, the fingers of both of his seemingly oversized hands resting on the keyboard. Head angled to one side, leaning back on his stool, the musician's suit was drawn without colour, the only marks for his clothing being the outline of his jacket and trousers, plus the creases and folds of these garments. The only colour about his person was a splash of yellow in the area of his tie, and a splash of yellow on the handkerchief in his left breast pocket. The following year, 1955, White provided another illustration, this time for *Sir Charles Thompson and his band featuring Coleman Hawkins*. This time, White's drawing was of an altogether more animated piano player, his hands caught in the time and space between the musician's fingers striking the keyboard. On this occasion, sheets of music were open in front of the pianist, further emphasizing his musical training, talents and abilities. As mentioned earlier, 'The drawing does not portray any of the actual performers on this session, but rather reveals the human experiences out of which jazz comes.' in his renderings of African Americans, White frequently chose not to depict faithful likenesses of musicians, but to create generic images that had a particular fluidity in their assigned uses. The pianist on the cover of *Sir Charles Thompson Trio*, for example, was also used (alongside another drawing by White, of a trumpet player) on the cover of *2 part inventions in jazz*, featuring the music of another piano player, Ellis Larkins, playing alongside Ruby Braff, a trumpet player.

There was a certain versatility and flexibility in the use of White's drawings of jazz musicians. The image of the trumpet player used in the bringing together of two drawings for *2 part inventions in jazz* (Ellis Larkins and Ruby Braff) was also used on the cover of *Joe Newman and his band*. In this instance, the trumpet player's shirt was rendered in ways previously mentioned in this text, that is, drawn without colour, the only marks for his clothing being the outline of his shirt, plus its creases and folds, energetically rendered by White in marks that were, in turn, precise, loose, angled, or straight. Only the musician's hands, playing the trumpet, and his face, were more substantially attended to. This artistic strategy had the effect of drawing greater attention to the instrument itself, the mouth of which was pointing to the upper left corner of the sleeve, the musician having angled his trumpet upwards, as he played it. There was, unmistakably, something heraldic about this cover, as if the trumpeter were offering his audiences something more than music, or, perhaps, a special kind of music. The musician depicted carried more than a passing resemblance to the actual Joe Newman, who was African American. And though Ruby Braff was white, the same drawing had, as mentioned earlier, been used as part of the cover of Braff's recording, with Ellis Larkins. Jazz was in essence music that respected no colour line, with its musicians, devotees, and aficionados alike coming from many different ethnicities and social backgrounds. As a lover of music, White breezily used his drawings of Black musicians in a variety of ways, perhaps playfully yet determinedly challenging the ways in which, in the US, *black* and *white* were decidedly unstable categories.

White's drawing for another release of the eponymously titled *Sir Charles Thompson Trio* album was of a pair of hands, touching, with sensitivity and purpose, the keys of a piano. The hands took up pretty much the whole of the record cover and as such, accentuated an understanding that a pianist's skills lay for the most part in their hands and fingers. This was an exquisite drawing which was somehow able to communicate a sense that a passage was being played which required particular attention, focus and care. There was an otherworldly dimension to the image, as it appeared as if the pianist (whose disembodied hands played with such delicacy and intent) was submerged in water, as was the piano being played. It was thus possible to read White's illustrations such as this as distinctly *interpretive*.

In 1954, White provided an illustration for the covers of *Buck Meets Ruby* (Ruby Braff, trumpet and Buck Clayton, trumpet), on the Vanguard label as part of its Vanguard Jazz Showcase. The covers featured a drawing of two trumpet players, a younger player, sitting next to an old-timer. The album notes stressed some of the ideas behind White's drawing: 'The drawing does not portray any of the actual performers on this session, but rather reveals the human experiences out of which jazz comes, in this case symbolizing the young student of the horn and the old veteran.' There was, in White's work, a characteristic respect for African American elders, and all that they had been through. See for example, one of White's drawings of this mid-1950s period *I've been 'buked and I've been scorned,* 1956, charcoal on paper, 114.3 x 91.44 cm. Of this distinctive drawing, Andrea D. Barnwell wrote that it was,

> inspired by the spiritual of that title [and] underscored the systematic rejection black people continually encountered. With her hand outstretched, a proud lone subject encapsulated the lyrics of the song but showed that, despite continuing efforts to disenfranchise blacks, armed with her unyielding faith

> they would overcome seemingly insurmountable impoverishment and endure the rigors of a treacherous journey.[4]

White's commitment to such imagery is not surprising, given that so many of the grandparents of his generation had been born into slavery. The centenary of slavery's abolition in the US was to be commemorated during the course of White's lifetime, but in the mid-1950s, many African Americans were just one or two generations removed from slavery. Furthermore, the wretched experience of sharecropping, to which so many African Americans across the South continued to be shackled, was an ever-present reminder of slavery that locked sharecroppers into economic and social servitude.

In the mid-1950s (the exact year is not specified on the recording), White provided an illustration for the cover of *Urbie Green and his band*. The cover of *Urbie Green and his band* featured a drawing of a trombone player, the trombone being Green's instrument. The drawing was signed by White and dated '54', though there were no further references to White in the notes on the back of the record cover. The trombonist depicted was framed on the sleeve by a red-coloured surround, though it appeared as if the musician was emerging from (and not in the least bit constrained by) the border. What was remarkable about the depiction, however, was that White chose to render the musician with darker skin, giving him the distinct appearance of being African American. Green was in actuality white, and White's rendering of him spoke of the artist's determination to create and place *positive* images of Black people whenever and wherever he was able to. White's commitment to positively portraying Black people was something noted and commented on by a great many writers.

> White's art did more than simply celebrate the dignity and beauty of black people: he reminded viewers of the long shadows that slavery cast over his country and challenged Americans not just to fight for racial equality, but also to reject the stereotypes that pervaded their culture. Drawn to art for its potential to effect social change, White's work communicated 'love, hope, courage, freedom, dignity – the full gamut of the human spirit. When I work, though, I think of my own people . . . their history, their culture, their struggle to survive in this, a racist country'.[5]

It was perhaps White's determination to portray *his* people that led him to a highly original approach to the sleeve he created for Vanguard's release of music by Sam Most, a young American jazz flautist, clarinettist and tenor saxophonist in the mid-1950s. Like Green, Most was white and it was perhaps this consideration that lead White to provide his commissioners with a drawing of a pair of disembodied Black hands, playing a flute. Slightly angled, the top and bottom of the flute extended beyond the top and bottom of the sleeve, with a hand on the instrument, in both sections of the cover. It was perhaps in the manner of Winold Reiss's portrait drawings, from several decades earlier, of African Americans wearing white suits or clothes that accentuated the beauty of their black skins, White's black hands on the Most sleeve gave the appearance of the flautist as also wearing white clothing, suggested by nothing more than cuffs, one of which is buttoned. In another version of this recording by the Sam Most Sextet, the imagery of the disembodied black hands playing a flute was duplicated, the two instruments crossing to create a dramatic V shape.

In 1954 the Vanguard record label released *Brother John Sellers Sings Blues and Folk Songs*. The record was subsequently reissued some four years later. Versions of the two 1950s releases carried different renderings of a drawing by White. The record was released in Britain on the Fontana label and again, the sleeve carried a version of the White drawing, though the drawing carried no signature and the Fontana bore no references to the artist. White's drawing was of an African American man, sitting, relaxed, his left hand on his left knee and his right hand emphasizing a passage, or a sentiment, of whatever song is being sung. On the first iteration of the recording, the man is depicted wearing a red shirt, though his trousers were colourless and rendered with the type of gestural marks White had used for his drawing of a pianist for *Sir Charles Thompson Trio*. That is, the only marks for his trousers were their outline, plus creases and folds. The striking use of red was again deployed on the 1958 release, though on this occasion as a background to the singer, who now appeared with both his shirt

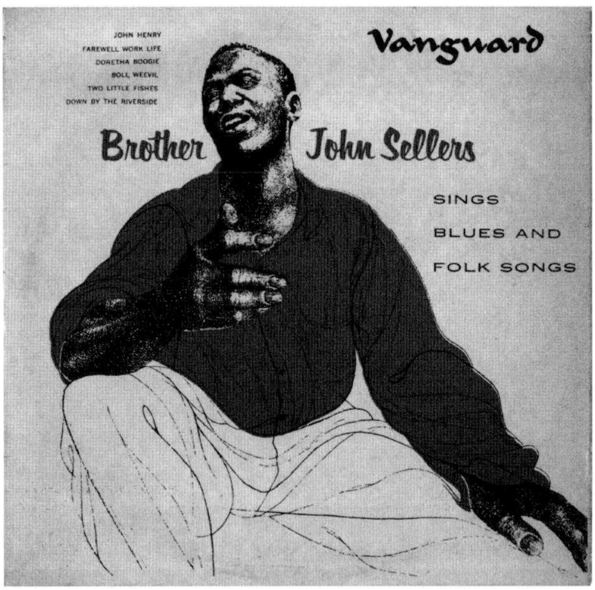

Figure 29.1 *Brother John Sellers Sings Blues and Folk Songs*, Vanguard label, 1956, PPT 12008 Courtesy of Concord Music Group, Inc.

and his trousers colourless. It's worth noting that whilst Reiss's trademark technique of depicting African Americans in white clothing conferred or implied social status, the attire of the singer on the Brother John Sellers recording, when shorn of colour, rendered the garments altogether more unrefined, simple and unpretentious. Here was a man who, in singing his blues and folk songs, had come from an environment that signified the *soil*.

From the uncredited sleeve notes:

> Brother John Sellers was born a little over thirty years ago in Clarksdale, Mississippi. As a child he sang gospel songs in the Church of God in Christ, the members of which traditionally address each other as 'brother' and 'sister'. Mississippi has one of the largest Negro populations of any state, and most of this population lives under conditions of extreme hardship and poverty. This life is reflected in the music, and Mississippi is one of the richest centres of folk music of the Negro people. The music is full of poignance, but also found in it is strength, dignity and love of life. It takes many forms: gospel or church songs, spirituals, children's game songs, traditional story ballads, blues or a solo, improvised 'minstrel' music. Much of this music infused jazz, as it developed. But to those who knew and felt its origins, and understood its styles, these strands of music were not to be lightly confused with one another. Gospel songs and spirituals were a serious and sacred music. Blues and ballads were a different music, secular, sometimes 'sinful'. Jazz was something else again, a music often using the blues, but with a different beat, born in the cities rather than in the countryside where the blues had arisen. It is not surprising that some of the greatest Negro folk singers were Mississippi born, like the blues singer Big Bill Broonzy. All this music was familiar to John Sellers from childhood.

As mentioned earlier, illustrations such as these decisively pointed to a clear, strong and profound interplay with the music of Black America, an aspect of African American culture for which White had profound respect and regard. The year 1954 also saw the release of Brother John Sellers – *Jack Of Diamonds (And Other Folk Songs And Blues)*. On this occasion, White provided a crosshatched rendering of a young person's face, their hands clapping, lost in the ecstasy of the moment. White was keen to ensure that his illustrations for record sleeves not only worked to promote the records themselves, but also worked to make visible the *folk*, the *ordinary* people, the biblically derived *salt of the earth*, the types of people from which musical forms such as blues, gospel and folk music had itself emerged. Around the time White was commissioned to produce these drawings for Vanguard, he had created *Songs of Life* (1953–4) (pen and brown and black ink w/gouache additions and ink wash, on illustration board, 73.66 x 101.6 cm). The drawing depicted five African Americans, several of them with what looked

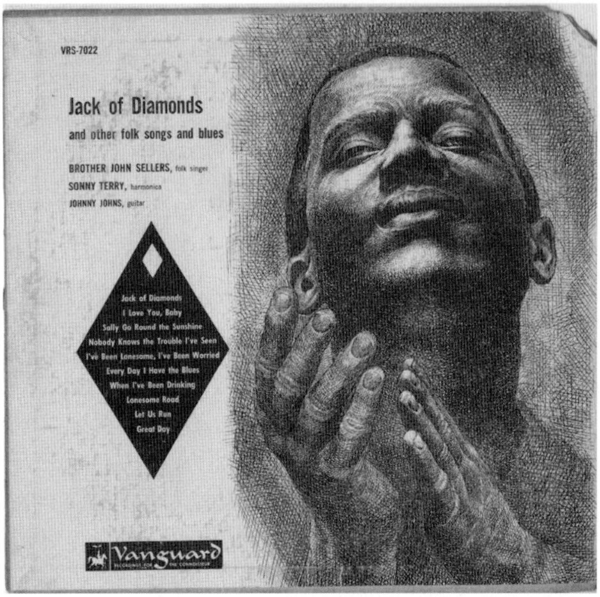

Figure 29.2 Brother John Sellers, folk singer, Sonny Terry, harmonica, Johnny Johns, guitar, *Jack of Diamonds and other folk songs and blues*, Vanguard label, 1954, VRS-7022 Courtesy of Concord Music Group, Inc.

to be hymnals in hand, exuberantly, triumphantly, singing their *Songs of Life* (the title of the hymnal, clearly visible on the cover of the volume in the right hand of the singer nearest to us viewers). One of the singers in the group bears more than a passing resemblance to the youngster depicted on the cover of *Jack Of Diamonds (And Other Folk Songs And Blues)*. There was a great deal happening across the US in the mid-1950s for an artist such as White to react to. In May of 1954, in its *Brown v. Board of Education* ruling, the US Supreme Court unanimously agreed that segregated schools were unconstitutional. The emerging civil rights movement may have regarded this ruling as a quantum step forward for America, but the most vicious setback to the cause of American societal progress occurred the following year, with the brutal murder of Emmett Till. The headiness of the times, and the purposeful stride of the civil rights movement were further emphasized by the Montgomery bus boycott, initiated towards the end of 1955. In the midst of such extraordinary adversity, turbulence and drama, White was able to advance the cause of humanity and the indomitable spirit of his people through record sleeves such as *Jack Of Diamonds (And Other Folk Songs And Blues)*.

Recorded in 1953, Vanguard Jazz Showcase released *Vic Dickenson Septet*, a four-volume set of records. Charles White provided an illustration that was used on the four covers. The drawing of an African American trombone player (the trombone being Dickenson's instrument) was signed 'Charles White '55'.

There was perhaps something visually playful in the design of the four covers. In the first instance, a colour coding differentiated each of the four records. The cover of Volume 1 for example, featured two rectangular blocks of yellow, one to the left and one at the top of the sleeve, with the drawing of the trombone player overlaid, while Volume 4 had the drawing of the musician differently overlaid, in this instance across two different sized rectangular white blocks situated on a blue background.[6]

In 1955, White provided an illustration for the cover of *Jimmy Rushing sings the blues*. Again, the record was released on the Vanguard label as part of its Vanguard Jazz Showcase, and again, it was a 10-inch mono recording. Jimmy Rushing was an American blues and jazz singer who had worked closely with Count Basie's orchestra from the mid-1930s to mid-1940s. The cover of *Jimmy Rushing sings the blues* featured a drawing of two guitar-carrying musicians, though again, the sleeve notes stressed the generic nature of the drawing, and the ways in which it was perhaps characteristic of or related to a certain demographic within the African American population. 'The drawing does not portray any of the performers on this record, but attempts to capture the human experiences out of which the blues arose.' The clothing of the two men was again line-drawn, emphasizing the creases, contours and folds of their garments. It is though, clear to us that one of the musicians wears a shirt with vertical stripes. Within the drawing, both men look to their left and on closer inspection, we see that behind the two men, White has included a line drawing of a railroad stop/go signal, raised, as if to allow a train to pass through, and obliging pedestrians and other road users to halt at a junction where the road intersects with the railroad. The post bearing the stop/go signal device carries the vertical number and letters 9XX, meaning perhaps, that the train itself or perhaps the railroad line is dedicated to Foreign Railroad Haulage.

In an instant, White evokes the culture of poorer Americans, including of course African Americans, as itinerant travellers, obliged to seek their living from place to place, particularly during the economically challenging years of the 1930s Great Depression. The symbolism of the African American balladeer, or peripatetic troubadour, coupled with the symbolism of the railroad, was profound indeed. Whether these guitar players – one whose instrument is in a case, one whose instrument is not – are waiting for a train to pass so that they can resume their traversing, or waiting for a freight train onto which they can clamber, is unknown to us. The sense that these musicians are hemmed in by their circumstances is perhaps reinforced by fencing, emphatically rendered in solid black lines, behind the men and against which one man and his guitar case rests his right knee nonchalantly, with his feet presumably resting on one of the fence's horizontal bars.

This record cover might bring to mind Romare Bearden's *Folk Musicians*, 1941–2.[7] The work depicts three people, the middle figure carrying a guitar, all resting, or standing at the corner of a red brick building. The men look for all the world like they are trying to eke out a living as itinerant musicians, metaphorically singing for their supper. That they are located in the South is perhaps hinted at by the dried, barren and broken trees located in the background to their left. The barren tree is in many instances a recurring trope, or motif, in the work of African American artists of the mid-twentieth century, including of course, White himself. The withered tree was a very compelling signifier of land cursed by slavery and the continued economic impoverishment of so many African Americans. White's figures however, on the cover of *Jimmy Rushing sings the blues* had faces that resonated with dignity and purpose, even as these musicians sought a living under the most difficult of circumstances – such as during the years of the Great Depression, in which White was a teenager.

In 1954 Vanguard released *Alexander Nevsky* – a cantana (a medium-length narrative piece of music for voices with instrumental accompaniment, typically with solos, chorus, and orchestra), an opus by Russian composer Sergei Prokofiev (1891–1953). Alexander Nevsky was a revered thirteenth-century Russian leader (1219–63), prince of Novgorod and then grand prince of Vladimir. He was an outstanding military leader and statesman who earned his surname from a victory over the Swedes at the Neva River. Sung in Russian, the music was performed by the Vienna State Opera Orchestra and Chorus, conducted by Mario Rossi. Ana Maria Iriarte was mezzo soprano. The record cover featured a montage, part of which was a rendering of Nevsky drawn by White, and dated '54'. Though the gatefold sleeve contained extensive notes when opened up, there was nothing about White.

Perhaps the most unusual sleeve commissioned from White was the one he produced for *Sandhog, a folk opera* devised and executed by Earl Robinson, singer and pianist, and Waldo Salt, narrator. Miscellaneous notes by I S Horowitz, in the *Billboard* magazine of 26 February 1955, noted that, 'Vanguard Records will soon cut its first L.P. in a new series of show albums. The initial set will be a "special composers' performance" of *Sandhog*, with Earl Robinson and Waldo Salt featured. The work was recently introduced in New York.'[8] A 'sandhog' was the informal term traditionally given to miners, and those construction workers toiling underground on excavation projects in cities such as New York. *Sandhog* was the brainchild of Robinson and Salt. Both were (to coin a phrase) blacklisted (on account of their apparent or perceived left-leaning sympathies) during the McCarthy era, during which time hundreds of Americans, many of whom were artists, writers or otherwise involved in the creative industries were accused of being communists or communist sympathizers and became the focus of aggressive investigations and questioning before government or private industry panels, committees and agencies. It was as a consequence of this targeting that figures such as Salt and Robinson came to be (again, to coin a phrase) blacklisted.[9]

The record, (an opera-like musical) for which White provided a fascinating cover was about a *sandhog* (as mentioned, a tunnel digger in cities such as New York) named Johnny O'Sullivan, set in the late nineteenth century. Characteristically, the opera celebrated the common people, and the labouring man. White's sleeve featured a sympathetically drawn portrait of a sandhog, shirt sleeves rolled up, with industrial safety goggles perched on his forehead. His muscular arms dominated the lower part of the portrait, and as with other renderings by White, the man's shirt was suggested by a series of sometimes briskly executed lines. The sandhog gazed, somewhat wistfully, out of the frame, suggesting, in the clearest yet unspoken terms, that although this man lived by the sweat of his brow, he was, even so, capable of deep thought and singular intellect. He was, very much, in a manner of speaking, 'a gentle giant'. It was though, the delicate line drawing of a little girl jumping rope, in the upper left corner of the record sleeve, that reinscribed this depiction of humanity. The girl was drawn with her knees bent, as the jump rope passed beneath her, the folds of the rope momentarily joining the folds of the sandhog's shirt. Robinson and Salt's wish to celebrate the humble labourer was echoed by White's drawing, including his simple, fetching depiction of a carefree little girl, skipping, her hair in unpretentious, simple, pigtails.

In 1965 one of White's pieces was used to illustrate the cover of an album by Morton Gould, the American pianist, composer, conductor and arranger, and the legendary American composer, Aaron Copland. The record was *Gould: Spirituals For Orchestra/Copland: Dance Symphony*, the Chicago Symphony Orchestra, Morton Gould conducting. The piece of White's work used was perhaps ideal for use on a record cover, in that it was circular and on the Gould/Copland sleeve, stood very much as a symbol of the record itself, and the music to be enjoyed, when the record was played. The work in question was *J'Accuse!* No. 14, a work in charcoal. It was in every respect a perfect choice, depicting as it did a portrait of a young African American person, their facial expression, closed eyes, and slightly intertwined hands deeply evocative of earnest contemplation and destiny. Perhaps in view of its use on a record sleeve, a feature on White in *Negro Digest* of June 1967 stated that, 'The drawing was nominated for an award by the National Academy of Recording Arts and Sciences in 1966. It is also called *Spirituals.*'[10]

In 1976 Charles White provided a drawn rendering of Leadbelly for the record that accompanied the eponymously titled biopic of the singer's life, directed by Gordon Parks. This was not the first drawing of Leadbelly that White had produced. He had produced a significant number of drawings of African American guitar players, signifying the extent to which White saw within African American music much that sustained and reflected the lives of his people. The drawing of Leadbelly on the record sleeve depicted a man sitting atop a pile of rocks (themselves evocative of the chain gang, mentioned earlier in this paper), strumming his guitar. Not surprisingly, given that the man – a prisoner wearing distinctive striped trousers that were at one time regulation prison attire – is manacled at his bare feet, the guitar player carries a somewhat pained expression on his face.

Within the film itself, the life of legendary blues and folk singer Huddie Ledbetter, (as mentioned earlier in this text, nicknamed Leadbelly) is recounted. Much of the film is set within the context of Leadbelly's life in prisons and the chain gangs that were such a dreaded aspect of incarceration. With Roger E. Mosley playing the part of Huddie Ledbetter, Parks' film emerged alongside a significant number of the Blaxploitation films common at the time. Indeed, several years earlier, Parks was responsible for directing the defining film of the Blaxploitation era, *Shaft*, a 1971 American action-crime film which revolved around a private detective named John Shaft, who is hired by a Harlem mobster to rescue his daughter from the Italian gangsters who have kidnapped her. Amongst the credits on the back of this 1976 release by ABC records is 'Cover illustration: Charles White'.

The attendant poster for the Leadbelly film presented a drawn image of the guitarist looking every inch the figure of John Henry, the legendary railroad worker who did heroic battle with the steam drill, winning, but dying, in the process. White was himself responsible for a particularly compelling portrait of John Henry that appeared on the cover of *A Man Ain't Nothing But a Man: The Adventures of John Henry*, written by John Oliver Killens.[11]

White's most productive and income-generating period of record sleeve illustration occurred with Vanguard during the mid-1950s. After his passing in 1979, Charles White's images would still be used to illustrate record sleeves. To this end, the sleeve of a 1981 release, *Love Byrd*, by Donald Byrd and 125th Street, NYC, featured a work by White. The piece in question was *Silent Song #2 (Nocturne)*, 1969, an etching on heavy cream wove paper, measuring 32.4 × 35.1 cm. On the sleeve notes, the illustration (here untitled) was credited to White, though no other details were given. Although *Silent Song #2 (Nocturne)* dated from 1969, beneath the bottom left corner of the image there appeared a small copyright symbol followed by 1961 Heritage Gallery. At the time of the release of *Love Byrd*, all bar a very small number of the records featuring illustrations by White had been released on the Vanguard label.

In 2002 Harry Belafonte was finally able to release his visionary work, a multi CD box set titled *The Long Road To Freedom: An Anthology Of Black Music.* This extraordinary collection emphasizing the history and the heritage of African American music came in a substantial casing, complete with a full-size portrait of Leadbelly that was, for many years, owned by Belafonte himself. In the entire history of African American art, no other artist contributed more art for record sleeves than White. Others, such as Elizabeth Catlett (to whom White was briefly married), Jacob Lawrence and Romare Bearden, were responsible for no end of magazine covers, book illustrations, and so on, but White alone is distinguished by the extent to which he readily made his art available for record sleeves and other illustrations, underlining, with some emphasis, the extent to which he believed in his art being disseminated to multiple audiences.

'Charles White's 10- and 12- Inch Vinyl Messages' is a new, previously unpublished text.

Notes

1 'Charles White', *The Selected Poems of Nikki Giovanni*, New York: William Morrow and company, Inc, 1996: 257–258.

2 We tend to associate the chain gang with punishing, physically exhausting tasks such as breaking rocks, but prison governors also hired out convicts for tasks such as road sweeping.

3 From the cover of *Sir Charles Thompson and his band featuring Coleman Hawkins*, Vanguard Jazz Showcase – VRS-8009.

4 Andrea D. Barnwell, *Charles White* (The David C. Driskell Series of African American Art: Volume I), Pomegranate, 2002: 60.

5 R. Blakeslee Gilpin 'Love Letters to Black America: Charles White's Art for the People', *Slavery & Abolition*, Vol. 34, No. 2 (2013), 281. The White quote was from Jeffrey Elliot, 'Charles White: Artist', *Negro History Bulletin* 41, no. 3 (1978): 825.

6 My research for this text uncovered five different record sleeves, not four. These can be viewed at http://www.eddiechambers.com/charles-white/

7 gouache on paper, 90 × 115.5 cm.

8 I S Horowitz, 'Liner Notes', *Billboard* magazine, 26 February, 1955: 38.

9 Charles White's own left-leaning impulses and his art work that reflected these impulses were chronicled in Mary Helen Washington's *The Other Blacklist: The African American Literary and Cultural Left of the 1950s* [Columbia University Press, 2014]. Andrew Hemingway, *Artists on the Left: American Artists and the Communist Movement, 1926–1956*, [Yale University Press, 2002] also documents the left-leaning aspects of White's practice.

10 'Images of Dignity: A Portfolio of Drawings by Chares White', *Negro Digest*, June 1967: 47.

11 Published by Little, Brown, Boston (1975).

Chapter 30
Hew Locke's Depictions of Royalty: Some Considerations

In 2019, it is without doubt the case that Black British artists have the most pronounced proximity to the British monarchy than they have ever had at any time in these artists' or indeed, the monarchy's history. There has, over the course of the past couple of decades or so been what looks like an accelerated pace of the bestowing of honours on Black artists in the bi-annual lists released by the British government Cabinet Office. British artists of *minority* ethnicities are now a periodic feature of these lists, and recently, such recipients (of African or Caribbean background) have included Frank Bowling, Sonia Boyce, Sokari Douglas Camp, Lubaina Himid, and Yinka Shonibare. In considering the types of honours bestowed, the career trajectories of a number of these practitioners might also tell their stories. British-born, Nigeria-raised Yinka Shonibare, and British-born Steve McQueen were, in the early 2000s, recipients of an MBE (Member of the Order of the British Empire), and an OBE (Officer of the Order of the British Empire) respectively. Shonibare secured a CBE (Commander of the Most Excellent Order of the British Empire), a decade and a half later, and McQueen was created CBE, about a decade after receiving his earlier honour. Certain Black British artists have found that their stock just keeps on rising, with their career trajectories noted by, or brought to the attention of, the Cabinet Office.

A select number of male practitioners from *minority* ethnic backgrounds accepting such honors have received the highest accolade, a knighthood. For example, David Adjaye, the architect and the painter Chris Ofili's sometime collaborator, was awarded one of these supreme (male) 'gongs' as they are colloquially known, entitling him, as a knight of the realm, to be both addressed as and referred to as 'Sir David.' The not insignificant number of other Black British artists, photographers, filmmakers, and arts workers, upon whom Her Majesty the Queen, or her representative, have bestowed honours includes John Akomfrah, David A. Bailey, Gus Casely-Hayford (who was for a time the director of the Smithsonian's National Museum of African Art), Isaac Julien, Mark Sealy, and Barbara Walker.

An artist who has set about the task of establishing a different type of proximity to the British monarchy – by way of his distinctive art practices – is British-born, Guyana-raised, Hew Locke. This text looks at several of Locke's decidedly and deliberately odd, peculiar and unsettling depictions of Her Majesty the Queen. One such work was included in London's National Portrait Gallery's touring exhibition, *The Queen: Art and Image*. Traditionally of course, there were (notwithstanding the occasional artistic parody or even mocking of monarchs throughout British history) pronounced reverential aspects to most artists' depictions of royalty. As well there might be, as the consequences of a monarch's displeasure at the way in which he or she had been depicted might, in centuries past, have caused severe difficulties for the artist.

Pronounced reverence for the institution of the monarchy itself has waned markedly over the decades, and perhaps this waning is reflected in the work of an artist such as Locke, as we perceive within his work a relaxation of the constraints under which an artist painting or sculpting their monarch was placed, in times gone by. The changing nature of depictions of Her Majesty was noted, somewhat sorrowfully, by Britain's ultra-conservative newspaper, *The Daily Telegraph*, which ran a review of *The Queen: Art and Image*. Alastair Smart, the reviewer, wrote 'Held to celebrate the Diamond Jubilee with 60 chronological images (one for each year of the reign), this exhibition sets out to show how depictions of Queen Elizabeth have shifted from the formal to the familiar down the decades – as a reflection of changes in society.' Locke's contribution was one of the pieces singled out for attention by Smart. 'Perhaps the most telling work is *Medusa* (2008) by Guyana's Hew Locke: a brightly coloured sculpture of the Queen's face made from beads, plastic flowers and voodoo toys. Unwittingly it suggests the fate of any artist who has ever tackled Her Majesty: immediately turning them to stone.'[1]

Like the plays of William Shakespeare, Greek mythology is full of characters we might know considerable amounts about, or we might know little to nothing about them. Chances are though, we will at least have heard of them and sensed their importance and significance. In Greek mythology, Medusa was one such character. Medusa was a monster, a Gorgon, (frequently described as a winged human female with frightening, living venomous snakes in place of hair). As alluded to by Smart, it was said that those who gazed upon her face would be turned to stone. She was beheaded by Perseus, who then proceeded to use Medusa's decapitated head as a weapon, as it still possessed its deadly ability to turn onlookers to stone. It's difficult not to bring some of these associations to our readings of Locke's *Medusa*. This is though, not the only work by Locke depicting royalty that resonates with a grotesque beauty. It might even appear to viewers that this sculptural depiction of Her Majesty is, quite literally, in the

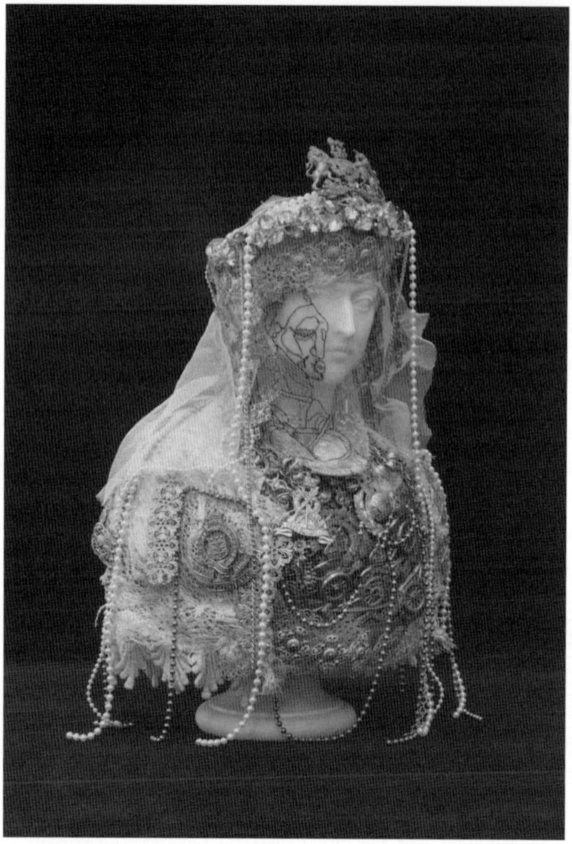

Figure 30.1 Hew Locke, *Souvenir 1 (Queen Victoria)*, 2018, Mixed media on antique Parian Ware, h 36 cm × w 24 cm × d 19 cm. Photo by Angus Mills, Courtesy Hales Gallery, London, © Hew Locke/Hales Gallery.

process of disintegration, as it has the appearance of dripping off the wall, the face unable to maintain, or keep in place, the cheap, brightly-coloured plastic materials such as beads and trinkets, from which it is made.

There is a fascinating cultural contradiction on which these pieces by Locke thrive. Across the world, we all grow up, from infancy onwards, with no end of signifiers that kings and queens, princes and princesses, are, or have been, 'special' people, the subjects of fairy tales and gripping pages of school history books alike. And we in Britain (and its colonies, including the British Guiana/Guyana in which Locke grew up) cannot escape the ubiquitous presence of the monarch, particularly in everyday or commonplace items such as postage stamps and currency, both paper and coins. Despite the modernism brought on by the 20th century, sections of the British populace still cling to a reverence for the monarchy that, while anachronistic, maintains a decidedly historical and archaic notion that a king or a queen is worthy of profound respect. And yet, in making his artworks of British royalty, Locke purposefully uses the cheapest, most worthless plastic knick-knacks he can get his hands on. The abundance of these ultimately valueless trinkets, when repurposed for the making of portraits of Her Majesty, are not exactly transformed, but instead contribute to work in which the previously mentioned cultural contradiction – of making images of someone who ceremonially rules over us – from the nastiest, most inexpensive plastic that in most cases are particularly close to being polluting detritus or landfill.

Make no mistake, Locke's portraits are a world away, an age away, from famed painter and sculptor Ben Enwonwu's mid-1950s sculptural depiction of the Queen. Born in Nigeria, at a time when the West African country was a British colony, Enwonwu came to prominence as an artist on account of his prolific and notable output, as well as the depth, breadth and integrity of his practice.[2] His bronze portrait of Her Majesty, from 1956, was one of his most notable creations.[3] As with images of royalty that were popular at the time, Enwonwu's sculptural depiction – commanding, reverential, assured – contained none of the freewheeling decidedly *different* depictions of Her Majesty from half a century later, such as Locke's *Medusa*. It's not difficult for us to consider the awarding of Enwonwu's MBE, in the mid-1950s as having a relationship to his greatest commission. Sylvester Ogbechie, in his wonderful study of Enwonwu, noted the significance of the commission. 'The fact that the commission was agreed upon at all was historical in terms of the political relations between the British Empire and its colonial domains. The image of the queen, representative of the Empire's continued relevance in the affairs of African states even after independence.'[4]

We might not have a clue how or where Smart came by his reference to 'voodoo toys', but there is admittedly, something decidedly otherworldly in Locke's *Medusa*. A certain evocation of death and decay characterizes this and other such works by Locke. He has been fond of depicting royalty through using flowers, whether drawn, or the sculptural use of cheap plastic ones. The use of flowers is fascinating, as they are of course, when purchased by us from florists, gifts that we pass on to loved ones, or objects of our affection or respect. But ironically perhaps, as soon as flowers are cut and packaged for consumer use, they begin a process of decay that is only stalled for a matter of days, when said blossoms are kept in water. Should water not be used, the deterioration of flowers can indeed be quite rapid. The link between flowers and royalty was particularly strong in the wake of the death of Diana, Princess of Wales, in 1997. In an unprecedented public, somewhat theatrical outpouring of grief, many people converged on the most accessible, and visible symbol of the British monarchy, Buckingham Palace. Bizarrely, the crowds, through the media, conveyed demanding messages to Buckingham Palace that were at once a nonsense and a profound breach of protocol. They in effect ordered that the

Union flag over Buckingham Palace be lowered to half-mast.[5] But the weeping distraught crowds also brought flowers, in never before seen abundance. So dense was the floral sea, that crowds in effect had to retreat from the Palace gates, as more and more flowers were laid. Within a short time, the expanse of flowers began to rot, giving off that familiar fetid smell we recognize when dead or dying flowers are removed from a vase containing days-old water.

This association between flowers, as a bountiful, affectionate gift to the esteemed, in life or in death, and flowers as rotting, decaying, fermenting, putrefying matter is another of those visual, cultural, and evocative contradictions on which Locke's images of royalty thrive. The plastic flowers used in some of the artist's depictions of Her Majesty might not rot and putrefy, but the associations with that which will ultimately be thrown away, are there all the same. Furthermore, Locke's works such as *Black Queen* (2004) and *Koh-I-Noor* (2005) in many ways represent his attempts to artistically replicate the decidedly tacky, tawdry, trashy and cheap pop-up memorials to Princess Diana, in the wake of her death. Recalled Locke,

> I went regularly to have a look at public manifestations of grief over Diana . . . I thought it was incredible, especially the altars that seemed to spring up all over the place . . . There were jam jar bottles . . . with candles with Di and Dodi on them . . . There were teddy bears garroted to railings, little girls' ballet shoes, mock Andy Warhol images of Di, Japanese paper cranes, Hindu texts, rosaries along with floppy toys and queen cards. There was something about this: it was crude, powerful, quite bizarre.[6]

Some of Locke's most successful depictions of the monarch have about them a distinct, and tangible aspect that is, simultaneously powerful, and quite bizarre in its crafting, and melding of yet more knick-knacks that one would not typically associate with regal subject matter.

Is Locke depicting the royal family in a state of dissolution or decay? Is fun being poked at the monarch, perhaps recalling historical parodies? Might we read these fascinating pieces by Locke as pointing one way, towards republican (abolition of the monarchy) sentiments? Or perhaps pointing another way, towards royalist sympathies? The artist leaves these questions or these interpretations to us. The most he'll say are things like 'I'm not a republican and I'm not a royalist. I genuinely hold a neutral position. Rather, the work I've done around the image of the Queen is an exploration of national symbols and representation.'[7] Might it only be a matter of time before the letter from the Cabinet Office arrives on Locke's doormat? Or are his depictions just too discomfiting, or too wacky?

'Hew Locke's Depictions of Royalty' was previously published in a special issue of *International Review of African American Art*, issue 29.4, 'Black Atlantic Dialogues', March 2020.

Notes

1 https://www.telegraph.co.uk/culture/art/art-reviews/9303655/The-Queen-Art-and-Image-at-National-Portrait-Gallery-Seven-magazine-review.html (accessed September 21, 2019).

2 The defining scholarly work on Enwonwu is Sylvester Ogbechie's *Ben Enwonwu: The Making of an African Modernist* (Rochester Studies in African History and the Diaspora) (Rochester, NY: University of Rochester Press, 2008).

3 https://benenwonwufoundation.org/presenting-the-sculpture-of-hm-queen-elizabeth-ii-by-ben-enwonwu-mbe-on-the-occasion-of-the-visit-of-hrh-the-prince-of-wales/.

4 Sylvester Ogbechie, *Ben Enwonwu: The Making of an African Modernist*, Rochester, NY: University of Rochester Press, 2008: 132.

5 The Union flag would ordinarily never be flown at half-mast, to signify the passing of a royal, not even a king or a queen. Upon the death of a monarch, an heir immediately assumes the throne. 'The king is dead, long live the king!', or simply 'long live the king!' is a traditional proclamation made following the death of a monarch and the immediate ascension to the throne of a new monarch. Seemingly contradictory, the phrase is used to simultaneously announce the death of the previous monarch and assure the populace of continuity by saluting the new monarch. The flying of the Union flag at half-mast contradicts this message (not that Diana Princess of Wales was anywhere near to being, or having been, a ruling monarch).

6 'A Sargasso Sea-Hoard of Deciduous Things . . . : Hew Locke and Sarat Maharaj in conversation', *Hew Locke*, published on the occasion of the exhibition Hew Locke, the New Art Gallery, Walsall, 29 April–6 June, 2005, p.10.

7 The quote came from a feature on Locke in *HIGH LIFE* British Airways magazine. A reproduction of a work by Hew Locke (the Queen, depicted through drawings of the United Kingdom's national flowers) graced the cover of the in-flight magazine's August 2015 issue, which declared itself to be 'THE BRITISH ISSUE'. Locke had been commissioned to illustrate the cover and had produced one of his images of Her Majesty Queen Elizabeth II. Pages 10–11 of the magazine carried a feature on Locke, describing him as 'the celebrated contemporary artist [who has] created an image of the Queen from Britain's national flowers.'

SECTION FOUR

Black Artists in History

Chapter 31
Section Four Introduction

Time was, or at least, time might have been, when the writing or assembling of Black British art histories was a relatively uncomplicated, matter. Historically (and we are now perhaps, able to utilize of such an adverb) the curating or creating of Black British art histories were for the most part centred on correcting or addressing the systemic absences and disregarding of such artists. This making visible of marginalized, excluded, or not widely known histories was what historically characterized certain aspects of my writing. As important as this approach has been, when looking to parts of the international arena, as an art historian of African Diasporic art and visual culture, the opportunity arises to bring into play, in my research, a range of contrasting considerations. An examination of art in the Caribbean, and art histories within specific Caribbean countries, affords important opportunities to animate perspectives that exist in marked contrast to the writing of Black British art histories. 'Independence and Nation Building in Caribbean Art', a concise, new previously unpublished text, considers the ways in which certain artists' practices can be read as contributing to the independence era agendas of nation-building in a country such as Jamaica. 'Art and Society', Jonathan Greenland's interview with me for *Jamaica Journal*, Kingston, Jamaica, December 2006 was a chance to reflect on my then-recent curatorial undertaking, *Curator's Eye II – Identity & History: Personal and Social Narratives in Art in Jamaica*, National Gallery of Jamaica, Kingston, December 2005–March 2006. This section also contains another new, previously unpublished text, 'Black Artists and the Greater London Council'. Much of the research for it was undertaken for my PhD, *Black Visual Arts Activity in England 1981–1986: Press and Public Responses* (Goldsmiths College, University of London, 1998).

Chapter 32
Independence and Nation Building in Caribbean Art

The years spanning 1960 to 1975 encompass a fascinating era in the development of Caribbean art. Considered by many to be little more than a holiday destination, for those in the know the Caribbean remains one of the world's most interesting and complex regions. The countries of the Caribbean, at once united and divided by the great expanse of the Caribbean Sea, are home to a wide range of religions, cultures, nationalities, ethnicities, and peoples. While Spanish-speaking Cuba and French-speaking Haiti are often seen as the artistic giants of the region, equal stature can be afforded to the biggest English-speaking island of the Caribbean, Jamaica. Together with thousand-miles-away neighbours such as Trinidad and Tobago, Barbados, and Guyana, the English-speaking Caribbean has produced much of the most dynamic art to come out of the region during the 20th century.

The early to mid-1960s were heady days for the people of the Caribbean. Cuba, the giant of the Caribbean, had recently emerged from a violent, protracted revolution that culminated in 1959 with the establishment of a radically altered country, founded on socialist – and subsequently – communist ideals. Thereafter, the political and cultural complexion of the entire region was transformed. Nineteen sixty-two saw the independence of two of the Caribbean's largest English-speaking countries, Jamaica and Trinidad and Tobago. Barbados gained independence a few years later. During this time, Caribbean artists became preoccupied with many new questions. What would independence mean for the peoples of the region, including its artists, poets, novelists, and thinkers? What role(s) could such individuals play in contributing to the lives of the region's people? How could artists assist in the enterprise of nation building? Should the artist remain at arm's length from the new governments that were taking power across the Caribbean?

The early 1960s were busy years for the artists of the region. Not surprisingly, given the poignancy of independence/post-independence moments, artists had a hefty task in visualizing the changes their respective countries were undergoing. Independence granted countries the ability to demonstrate that they could move out of the shadows of their colonial masters, thereby proving to themselves and the world that countries such as Jamaica and Trinidad and Tobago could, metaphorically speaking, stand on their own two feet. Artists were a huge part of this effort, and Jamaican painter Karl Parboosingh's *Cement Company* of 1966 is a particularly significant example of such a message. With its deliberate focus on the cement works located near Kingston's airport rather than the luscious landscape of Jamaica, the painting exhibits pronounced associations with socialist realism. In this image of studious and determined industry, the cement works are presented as an affirming and reassuring site of production and manufacture, evocative of building projects and industrialization across the country and further afield. The painting depicts a massive industrial complex with the distinctive features of the landscape and terrain of Kingston and Port Royal in the background. Though a modest fishing vessel is portrayed on the sea that occupies much of the painting, an industrial cargo carrier dominates the smaller boat. Paintings like *Cement Company* celebrated independence and the anticipated economic strength it would bring for the country and its people. In *Jamaican Art: An Overview – With a Focus on Fifty Artists*, Petrine Archer-Straw and Kim Robinson summed up the determined mood of the times:

> Independence had been attained in 1962 and had brought with it an air of challenge which characterised the period: the mining of bauxite was becoming more and more profitable, while commercial activity and tourism were also growing; and the construction industry was thriving as never before in response to the growing needs of a developing economy and the growing aspirations of the people.[1]

Edna Manley, an English-born sculptor who moved to Jamaica in the early 20th century, was one of the first artists of the Caribbean region to visualize the agenda and task of nation building. Her sculptures of the 1920s and 1930s, particularly works such as *Negro Aroused*, were celebrated for the decisive ways in which they captured the mood of the people in their struggle for political change and progress. Manley's work continued in a similar vein in the decades following Jamaica's independence, while other artists set about the task of commemorating Black heroes and historical figures marginalized or pointedly obscured by a colonial government determined to assert European dominance, including in the cultural realm.

One cannot look critically or substantially at art in the Caribbean region without taking into account what artists in the Caribbean diaspora were concurrently concerning themselves with. In this regard, the Caribbean Artists Movement (CAM) was an important and influential cultural initiative, centred on the work, dialogues, and interconnectedness of a number of key Caribbean-born writers and artists of the 1960s and 1970s. CAM began in London in 1966, reflecting the extent to which London had become an important focal point for ambitious, creative people from the Caribbean and elsewhere in the world, as well as a destination for economic migrants in search of better lives for themselves and their families. At its core, CAM was a forum for the exchange of ideas relating to the role, and the work, of Caribbean-born writers, artists, scholars and activists.[2] Barbadian doctoral candidate Edward Kamau Brathwaite and Trinidadian publisher John La Rose formed CAM. Anne Walmsley observed, 'Brathwaite and La Rose each knew and admired the other's poetry. When they met they found each other to be nurturing a similar idea: an organisation of Caribbean writers and artists.'[3] Amongst the influential body of Caribbean writers, visual artists, poets, dramatists, and cultural/educational activists associated with CAM were Ronald Moody, Aubrey Williams, Errol Lloyd, and Andrew Salkey, as well as CAM's founders, Edward Kamau Brathwaite and John La Rose. CAM was a decidedly pan-Caribbean initiative, and its members sought to address questions that reflected the pressing concerns of the moment: How could the artists and writers of the region best establish themselves in the challenging environments of cities such as London? How could they contribute to the arts, culture, and literature of the country to which they had migrated? What should the concerns of the Caribbean artist be? In the light of seismic changes in the region, how could Caribbean history be understood, or reinterpreted? Looming large over these questions was perhaps the inevitable consideration of how best to characterize the specificities of Caribbean art and identity. Such were the concerns and questions that occupied and challenged those associated with the Caribbean Artists Movement.

By the mid-1970s, some Caribbean artists were beginning to locate themselves within the distinctly international context of Pan-Africanism, associating themselves with a loose assortment of political and cultural ideas that over time morphed into the notions of African diaspora so commonly held today. These artists were drawn to designations of racial identity as a means of framing or advancing their own practice. In 1977, Nigeria mounted an ambitious festival of arts, music, dance, literature, and culture called Festac '77. This was the second Black and African Festival of Arts and Culture, an extravaganza that brought together artists, writers, performers and others from the Black and African world in an African-centred program of events, performances, activities and exhibitions taking place, for the most part, in the former Nigerian capital of Lagos.

By way of London and elsewhere, a number of Caribbean artists were represented at Festac '77, including: Winston Branch from St Lucia; Armet Francis, Neil Kenlock, Ronald Moody and Ossie Murray, all born in Jamaica; and Donald Locke and Aubrey Williams, both born in Guyana. These artists exhibited alongside others from elsewhere in the Black world, such as Emmanuel Taiwo Jegede and Uzo Egonu, both from Nigeria itself (though living in London), and Sue Smock, an African American artist born in New Orleans, Louisiana. The artists represented many different types of art practices, from the demonstrations of abstraction that lay at the heart of the paintings of Branch and Williams, to the pronounced manifestations of African cultural identity in the work of Nigerian artists Egonu and Jegede, to the ecological and environmental concerns frequently manifested in Moody's work. These artists, with a comprehensive range of formal concerns, came together as practitioners of the Black, African and Pan-African worlds. Festac '77, in concert with other factors such as the increasing internationalism of reggae music and global reach of Rastafari did much to reorient Caribbean art towards an international, and particularly diasporic, arena.

'Independence and Nation Building in Caribbean Art' is a new previously unpublished text.

Notes

1 Petrine Archer-Straw and Kim Robinson, *Jamaican Art: An Overview – With a Focus on Fifty Artists*, Kingston, Jamaica: Kingston Publishers Limited, 1990: 57.

2 Anne Walmsley, a distinguished scholar of Caribbean art and supporter and friend of Aubrey Williams, was responsible for a comprehensive appraisal of CAM. *The Caribbean Artists Movement, 1966–1972: A Literary and Cultural History* (London: New Beacon Books, 1992). For the 1997 exhibition catalogue *Transforming the Crown*, Walmsley contributed the essay 'The Caribbean Artists Movement, 1966–1972: A Space and a Voice for Visual Practice.'

3 Anne Walmsley, 'The Caribbean Artists Movement, 1966–1972: A Space and a Voice for Visual Practice,' in *Transforming the Crown* (Caribbean Cultural Center: New York, 1997): 46.

Chapter 33
Black Artists and the Greater London Council

A little remembered episode in the emergence of Black British artists during the 1980s related to the activities of the Greater London Council (GLC), in seeking to utilize the practices of said Black artists. These GLC initiatives represented a major intervention, on a local governmental level into Black visual arts activity.

> The Ethnic Arts Sub-Committee of the GLC, for the last 4 years, has tried to respond to the burgeoning, profuse and multiple talents of London's black communities. We have tried to ensure that individual artists and groups working in many different fields were allowed and helped for the first time to display their talents and richness of experience to their fellow Londoners.[1]

By 1984, Black British artists (particularly those living within the capital) had achieved a previously unknown collective visibility, and galleries and art critics were taking some notice of them. This had been due to a number of factors. Chief amongst them, the flourishing activity and the quantity of self-initiated exhibitions that took place in the early 1980s. Secondly, exhibitions such as *Into the Open*, did much via the national press and other avenues to introduce the work of Black artists to wider audiences. *Into the Open* represented the first time a major publicly-funded gallery responded to a broad range of work by (primarily) younger Black artists. Similarly, the press coverage generated by that exhibition represented the first attempts by a national newspaper, the *Guardian*, to acknowledge this wide body of practitioners. Also by 1984, the London-wide local government body, the Greater London Council (GLC), was similarly taking some notice of Black artists.

The GLC had no established history of supporting Black visual arts activity. But in what transpired to be no more than a two-year period (1984–6) of the final GLC administration (under the leadership of Ken Livingstone) it became a key player in initiating and funding Black visual art activity within the capital. This support took a number of forms and this text assesses the GLC's initiatives as they related to Black artists.

The GLC, Strategic Patronage and Other Considerations

As a funding agency with resources to distribute, the GLC did not simply exist as, and more importantly, was not *perceived* as, a grant-giving body. The GLC managed to create the formidable impression that the very *existence* of Black artists had been made possible only through its benevolence, patronage and support. The GLC's erratic and muddled contributions rapidly assumed mythic, Herculean proportions, substantially detached from the realities of its modest and consistently problematic involvement with Black artists. (A significant proportion of this involvement took place in the final, frantic days of the terminated Livingstone administration.)

The myth that the GLC made massive and life-giving contributions to the development of Black (visual) arts activity was a resilient one and a number of commentators, clearly annoyed by it, have made caustic references to the GLC and its attendant mythology. These commentators, despite the exasperated nature of their comments, were nonetheless attempting to make important points that put the contributions of the GLC into a historical context. Errol Lloyd wrote that 'some people have mistakenly assumed that there was no black creativity before the advent of the GLC'.[2]

Several months before Lloyd made these comments, the editor of *Artrage* (which described itself as an 'Inter-cultural Arts magazine') passed a more cutting remark when he wrote an editorial under the title 'VULGAR ASSUMPTIONS' 'it has been rumoured that there was life – and black people making art – before the GLC'.[3] Lloyd and E. A. Markham (the *Artrage* editor responsible for the above comment) were both seeking to make the point that the contributions of the GLC towards the development of Black visual arts activity, whilst being acknowledged, should not be taken out of context, or blown out of proportion. Particularly as such contributions occurred over a relatively brief period in the middle of the 1980s. Despite Lloyd's anxieties, he was still minded to talk up the GLC's contributions. 'The GLC was instrumental, however, through its funding policies in liberating some of the dynamism within the black community by providing much needed resources'.[4]

The above paragraphs need to be put into a wider context. The 1980s heralded the arrival of a new breed of Labour Party local government politician. These people, epitomized by the GLC leader Ken Livingstone, regarded themselves as visionaries and prided themselves on their socialist credentials and convictions, and a certain propensity to activism. Livingstone was elected leader of the GLC following the Labour Party GLC victory of 8 May 1981. It was around this time that sections of the press began to refer to him as 'Red Ken'.[5] Livingstone regarded himself as an impeccable anti-racist, thereby ensuring (by virtue of his position as leader of the GLC) that Black people in London would at last be acknowledged and addressed in some manner. He 'signified the priority attached to the issue of "race" by assuming the chairpersonship of the newly created Ethnic Minorities Committee himself'.[6] By this time, the Parliamentary Labour Party had emphatically lost two consecutive elections to the Conservative Party, led by Margaret Thatcher. The Parliamentary Labour Party seemed no match for Thatcher – the 'Iron Lady' (one of the names a largely adoring 'Fleet Street' press dubbed her). Armed with sizeable Tory majorities and supported by a largely gushing mainstream media, Thatcher set about slaying anything and everything that she considered to be a socialist/trade union dragon. Dissent in the country at large seemed, at various times, to be widespread, and Thatcher provoked and indeed, seemed to thrive on an almost tactile hatred of her, her policies and her ministers. Even so, she contemptuously trampled the Parliamentary Labour Party, and revelled in the rampage that became known as 'Thatcherism'.

Within this context, some of the Labour-controlled city and town halls in major urban areas around the country became embattled bastions of the vestiges of particular strands of Labour Party socialism. The foremost and most notable example of this was the cash-rich GLC, the London-wide local government authority that coordinated the delivery of a range of rate-payer services over and above those provided by the Boroughs into which London was divided. The formidable impression existed that the GLC's coffers were full to bursting, and that it could dispense money, with largesse, on projects signifying London's 'ethnic' communities. As noted by John Carvel, the GLC's 'main financial problem was the exact opposite of the one faced by other councils. Persistently the GLC committees failed to spend the allocations for which they had budgeted. Hard as they tried, they just could not shift the money fast enough'.[7] The leaders of the GLC took the view that the grass-roots people of London could be acknowledged and that political (and specifically, electoral) support could be rewarded and/or encouraged by financial patronage of the electorate in the form of grants for community, cultural, sporting and recreational activity. Perhaps anticipating the strategy that would be adopted by New Labour when it came to power in 1997, Livingstone's GLC Labour believed that it could make over its own image, through governmental policies and the strategic dispersal of funds. Furthermore, for Livingstone's GLC, as mentioned earlier, such grants helped to disperse amounts of cash surpluses.

Politicians had always sought to influence their electorates with *bribes* or *rewards* and this strategy (clear, obvious and direct as it was) caused considerable consternation amongst those Conservative politicians in opposition at County

Hall (the seat of the GLC) and those in national government. According to John Carvel, through this system of strategic patronage 'The Tories began to worry that Labour had invented a piece of political machinery capable of delivering large block votes at election time'.[8] What was radically different about the strategy of the last GLC administration was that it made a concerted effort to patronize certain ethnic minority and political groups that traditionally and historically, had been ignored or discounted by local government and funding bodies. This was a new type of political activity that signalled a conscious, or different type of politicization of local government politics. According to some commentators, 'The curtain had opened on a four-year political drama that would change the face and image of local government forever.'[9] Likewise, an admirer of the GLC referred to this as 'new politics [that] managed to challenge and transcend many of the outmoded dogmas of traditional Labour politics'.[10] Groups perceived as representing the 'Black community' were targeted for funding, as were assorted groups rallying around banners of identity, expression and political belief that conspicuously deviated from what the ideology of Thatcherism took to be the 'norm'. This was not to say that Livingstone and company were simply and mischievously setting up Black people and others such as the unemployed and peace campaigners as anti-Thatcher shock troops, although there was an element of this in the GLC's strategies and agendas. This was made clear when on 'May 28 [1981], *London Labour briefing* published its victory issue under the headline LONDON'S OURS, in which Livingstone pledged to use County Hall as an open campaigning base to bring down the Thatcher government.'[11]

The impression existed that some of the GLC's funding was being allocated to groups and campaigns that were considered anathema (for reasons of sexual orientation, 'political' beliefs or racial identity) to Thatcher's Tories. For example, publicity campaigns by the Campaign for Nuclear Disarmament (CND) were supported by the GLC – the Tory government having committed itself to a vigorous programme of nuclear armament and nuclear power. In 1985 the GLC published TARGET LONDON, 'A Set of Photomontage Posters by Peter Kennard'. The introductory notes to the boxed set read

> What plans have the Government drawn up to protect Londoners in times of nuclear war? What do nurses, doctors and scientists think of these plans? How has the GLC worked towards peace?
>
> This poster exhibition designed for Londoners, attempts to answer these questions in an attractive and accessible format. Ideal for display in schools, youth clubs, community centres or as posters for the home.

One writer, John Roberts, has referred to the GLC's attitude towards Black artists as one of 'positive discrimination'. In a 1987 conversation with the artist

Sonia Boyce, he proposed the following question: 'Do you think the GLC's promotion of 'positive discrimination' was a hindrance or a help?'[12] In her reply, Boyce pointed out some of the difficulties that were inherent in the GLC's strategy of making a determined push to patronize (in a non-pejorative sense of the word) Black people and Black artists.

> It was a big hindrance, but it was also a big help. What the GLC did was give communities the resources to mobilise on a different scale. They made it seem possible that a local government could provide opportunities for black people. Unfortunately, the GLC's policy decisions really did confuse and blur the edges of what was tokenistic and what wasn't.[13]

The GLC's attitude towards 'groups' in the all-important 'community' was not just a localized, extraordinary intervention; it illustrated some seismic shifts in particular areas of politics and political activity in Britain. Much of this new political activity was anti-Thatcher and anti-Conservative and existed very much in opposition to what could be termed the 'status quo'. Yet much of this same political activity was not necessarily pro-Labour, or 'socialist', in any hitherto conventional sense. Traditionally, the Labour Party had drawn support from many 'working-class' people and their 'middle-class' sympathizers. Though the Labour Party claimed to be something of a 'broad church', in actuality it traditionally held the political, social and economic aspirations of the labouring (white) male to be of central importance. The idea being that what materially and socially advanced the white, working-class labouring/unemployed white male would inevitably, by extension, benefit his 'family' and his Black neighbours and workmates. From its earliest days, the Labour Party had held the aspirations and material well-being of the heterosexual white working-class male and 'his family' as being paramount. Decades came and went, world wars came and went, political events (such as the enfranchisement of women and the immigration of African-Caribbean and South Asian people) came and went, violent racial clashes involving immigrants and their offspring also came and went. The Labour Party courted (or paid lip service to) the votes of Black people, immigrant people and women but ultimately, it attended to the needs of none of these groups, choosing instead to maintain its established and traditional agenda. One commentator noted caustically that, as far as the Labour Party establishment of these various periods were concerned, 'Any attempt [by Labour Party activists/supporters] at drawing on the strength of those affected by discrimination was dismissed, ironically, as divisive and separatist.'[14]

By 1977, disillusionment with the established political parties was widespread. Unfortunately for James Callaghan, Labour prime minister at the time, it was the governing Labour Party that bore the brunt of this disillusionment:

> when faced with the most serious economic crisis since the Thirties, the party which had been elected to achieve an irreversible shift in wealth and power had acted instead to break strikes, impose wage controls, enter the EEC on ludicrously unfavourable terms, prune the welfare state, produce the sharpest fall in living standards in one year since the early 19th century and sit out a level of unemployment which no post-war Conservative government would have dared to permit. From Official Secrets to H Block, the Labour Cabinet had been conservative and cowardly. By the winter of '78 it had been deserted by even its most devoted ally, the TUC. Morale among the constituency rank and file was low and Michael Foot's annual list of legislative measures passed failed to convey any real sense of achievement. [Foot was at the time Leader of the House of Commons]. Among long-suffering working class voters general indifference was tempered by a sense of political loss that went beyond any particular setback or betrayal. The seemingly impersonal forces of inflation and unemployment had ripped the illusion of affluence apart and crushed whole communities.[15]

Concurrently, there was also disillusionment with many other aspects of existing cultural and political structures. Black youth had given forceful expression to their disillusionment and within white neighbourhoods and white suburbia, this was the age of 'punk' and the 'National Front'. The culture of 'punk' could be said to have been 'Premised on the now-fading affluence of the teenage consumer and the mass communications aspect of the leisure industries, the mechanisms of white youth culture provided the means to popularize oppositional ideas forged in the powerlessness of youth.'[16] Further to this, Paul Gilroy observed that 'political themes have begun to displace moral and generational conflict as the raw material for young people's cultural expression.'[17] Gilroy described a process 'which has been fuelled at each stage by youth's own perception of economic crisis and the consequent crisis of social relations' and suggests that 'It was in "punk" subculture that youth's marginality came face to face with these crises.'[18] During the 1970s, the National Front gave extra-parliamentary expression to anti-Black, anti-immigration sentiments. In the 1974 general election, it fielded ninety candidates and secured 113,844 votes. In local government elections of the same year 'the NF averaged nearly 10 per cent of the poll in several districts of London.'[19]

Though parliamentary politics continued in a 'business as usual' manner, beyond the Houses of Parliament, some important changes in socialist politics were taking place. It was clear to many that apart from the wide-ranging failures of the Labour Party, its central positioning of the heterosexual labouring/unemployed white male was, at best, insufficient, and at worst, discriminatory, backward and unable to deal with the complexities and disillusionment of the times. The United States, during the 1960s, had seen the development of what became known as 'identity politics', within which political agendas were defined and conducted on the basis of an individual's specificity (beyond what was taken as being heteronormative) and the needs/demands of particular *groups* of people. This in effect meant that the agendas of heterosexual white males, whether working class or middle class, could no longer be regarded as the *norm*, to which all other non-male, non-white people had to be subservient, or with which they had to make accommodation.

Three major movements propelled identity politics into a central position of importance. The first was the women's movement, the second was the Black Power Movement and the third was the campaign for homosexual equality. Activists representing these groups campaigned not just to be accepted and treated as equal citizens under the law, but also to have their identities respected and regarded as being important and valid. Britain developed its own versions of identity politics and it was these agendas that were incorporated into the governmental and funding strategies of town hall politicians in the 1980s, to be used and exploited, particularly by bodies such as the GLC. Kwesi Owusu welcomed these developments: 'The new politics was based on utilising the grossly underrated strength and power of specific constituencies of people and movements, including the elderly, youth, Black women, women, people with disabilities, and the peace and gay movements.'[20]

Another important factor that informed such local government strategies was that in the wake of the serious 1981 riots, 'inner-city' deprivation and disadvantage were cited and accepted by local and central government politicians as contributing to Black Britain's widespread alienation from mainstream society and resentment and hostility towards its most visible symbol – the police. Zig Layton-Henry, 'putting it bluntly', noted that 'Lord Scarman [appointed by the government to ascertain the cause of the 1981 riots] found that the riots were essentially an outburst of anger and resentment by young blacks against the police.'[21] As Paul Gilroy has commented, 'The Labour administrations elected in the metropolitan counties during the spring of 1981 were quick to institute a range of special agencies and programmes of work charged with the task of addressing the ethnic minority needs to which the burning and looting had given a supposedly inarticulate expression.'[22] Sums of money, some of them significant, were made available for a range of 'inner-city renewal' projects, aimed at improving the domestic and social fabric of Black people deemed to be disadvantaged. Carvel noted that 'By Christmas 1983, the GLC had funded more than 1,000 voluntary organizations and its annual grants budget was running at nearly £40 million a year.'[23] More detail regarding GLC funding was provided by Gilroy: 'In 1982–3, the first year in which the [Ethnic Minorities] committee had a budget for grants, over 300 applications were received for the annual budget of £850,000. The following year the committee's grants budget had risen to approximately £2.5 million.'[24] By 1984, according to the *Guardian*, GLC grants to 'ethnic minority organisations' amounted to £5 million.[25] Local government politicians had other *politically strategic* reasons for channelling funds to 'Black community' projects. The 1981 riots, as far as some politicians and others were concerned, 'represented the formation of an alienated or dissident urban underclass, [so] the growth of specialized anti-racist initiatives was a vehicle for reincorporation of these marginal elements into the rituals of the political system.'[26]

It was in this context, as well as the contexts outlined earlier in this chapter, that money for projects and other initiatives were made available by the GLC. On a borough-by-borough basis, such funding was also made available (although this depended on the political complexion of each town hall's administration). Within the wider context of this study, Islington Council, in North London, made the most significant and strategically important funding available when it allocated building, operating and programming costs, from 1983 onwards, to The Black-Art Gallery.[27]

As Gilroy has suggested (regarding the funding strategies of the GLC) 'The motives behind these developments were diverse.'[28] It is for this reason that the contributions and influence of Black councillors should also be acknowledged. *The Politics of Race in Britain* (Zig Layton-Henry, 1984) stated that, 'The involvement of Asians and West Indians in the Labour Party is most noticeable in the Greater London area, and sixty-seven Labour councillors of Asian or West Indian origin were elected to London borough councils in May 1982. Black Labour councillors did exceptionally well in Brent, where twelve were elected.'[29] These councillors and other Black political activists demanded space and resources for their own agendas. 'Pressure on the [GLC] from specialized community relations agencies coincided with the growth of black political activism inside the Labour Party.'[30] These were the days when agitation for a Black caucus or 'Black sections' first began to percolate. The voices behind this agitation 'issued warnings that the electoral allegiance of black populations in urban areas could no longer be taken for granted by Labour.'[31] These voices were seeking 'mutual political acknowledgement', suggesting that Black electoral votes might now come with a funding price tag.

This was the background to the arts funding strategies of the GLC. Though the Conservative central government initially made money available for urban renewal schemes, it had no time for (visual) arts activity, in and of itself, for its own sake, from any quarter. Such thinking was born out of the sentiment that 'art' was largely unimportant or irrelevant to 'ordinary' people. Karin Woodley, writing in the winter 1988 issue of *Artrage*, quoted a Conservative MP as typifying this anti-art position. Rubbishing the notion that arts activity was an important and intrinsic component of culture and cultural identity, Terry Dicks was quoted as saying 'We are told that the arts are part of our heritage . . . I do not believe that, and most ordinary people in Britain . . . laugh at the proposition that arts reflect our heritage.'[32]

This refusal to accept that public funding had a major role to play in developing and sustaining (visual) arts activity was a direct tenet of Thatcherism, which saw an urgent and consistent need to curb and restrain, wherever possible, public expenditure in a large number of areas. The 1979 Conservative election manifesto had stated, 'Any future government which sets out honestly to reduce inflation and taxation will have to make substantial economies, and there should be no doubt about our intention to do so.'[33] Concurrently, Thatcherism promoted the view that the 'market' could and should take care of everything. Within the context of widespread central government cuts and a reliance on financial 'markets', the dismissal of the importance, relevance and validity of (visual) arts activity was an inevitable consequence. So, in this respect, the attitude of central government sharply contrasted and conflicted with the attitude of the GLC, which regarded strategically allocated money for arts activity to be money well spent. 'Funding for the arts and cultural centres was increased, particularly outside the traditional "centres of excellence." By 1983 the GLC was investing over £7.5 million in the arts across London.'[34] Livingstone reiterated this contrasting approach to arts funding in an appraisal of the GLC's involvement with London's art activity, 'because the Tories had cut back the spending [on arts provision] we knew that had to be a bad thing, therefore we should have more of it.'[35]

The Thatcher period coincided closely with the most significant decade of Black visual arts activity in Britain to date. The unmistakable emergence of a politicized body of Black artists was overshadowed by this relatively new fiscal ideology that mesmerized and enthralled the 'Tory' press at both a national and local level. In turn, the Tory press were able to influence or reflect, to some degree, 'public opinion'. This fiscal ideology, as represented in the press, held that public money could either be used prudently or used foolishly. The labels of 'wise' spending or 'foolish' spending were of course loaded, subjective, largely artificial and frequently spurious constructs. Their purpose was to validate or invalidate certain lifestyles and political positions, and funding became an issue that demonized those recipients seen as being 'takers from', rather than 'givers to' the public purse and local government money.

There was, within the Tory press, frequently expressed opposition to the funding strategies of the GLC. It mattered little that the sums of money involved were, in comparison to other and overall budgets, minuscule and negligible. As John Carvel noted, 'In political terms the big area of difficulty was not the total amount of money spent, but the way in which a small, fraction of it was distributed by way of grants to voluntary organisations.'[36] 'Squandered money' stories were fabricated or distorted to suggest that significant sums of (white) tax-payers, and rate-payers' money were being 'wasted' on projects, grants and other initiatives that were designed to benefit or otherwise improve the lives and welfare of undeserving people deemed to be beyond 'normal' society, such as groups including Black/immigrant/refugee people, together with homosexuals of both genders. Thatcherism, as manifested in the press, very effectively suggested that money and resources taken from hard-working, tax/rate paying 'ordinary' people was being 'squandered' on 'minority' groups, whose agendas ranged from the trivial to the subversive and dangerous. Thatcherism saw itself as having a duty to limit, in whatever ways possible, this apparent 'abuse' of public money. For 'ordinary' and 'public' read 'white, heterosexual, Conservative/conservative and for 'minority' read 'Black', 'gay', 'lesbian', 'single-mother', 'refugee' and so on. As Carvel reported in his study of Livingstone,

> The one issue which the Tory opposition succeeded in getting across to the electorate was that the Livingstone administration was giving unprecedented financial support to women's groups, ethnic minority groups, gays and other campaigners against the white, male heterosexual order in society. Week by week stories appeared in the press ridiculing or condemning grants to bodies with exotic sounding titles.[37]

This aggressive denouncement by the Tory media was a reflection of the extent to which the agendas and activities of non-male or non-white or non-heterosexual people now formed some of the most formidable non-parliamentary or extra-parliamentary opposition to the Conservative Party. Commentators noted that 'It was the Labour-controlled Council's policies for tackling the denial of equal opportunities for women, and ethnic minority groups that most enraged the Tories across the water [from GLC County Hall], in Parliament.'[38] The main culprits for 'wasting' 'public' money were taken to be the Labour-controlled local authorities, epitomized by the GLC. Until its demise, the GLC was held by the Tory press and by Thatcher herself to be the principal squanderer of public money within the capital. The Tory newspapers, supported by the hostility of Thatcherites in national and local government, mounted a relentless barrage of anti-GLC criticism that created a climate in which the Council's abolition (by the Conservative government) became inevitable. Norman Tebbit, one of the ministers in Thatcher's cabinet, candidly confessed that the GLC and other metropolitan councils were 'Labour-dominated, high-spending and at odds with the government's view of the world.'[39]

Carvel indicated the extent to which GLC funding strategies also alarmed some within Livingstone's own party: 'Conservative criticism of GLC grants capitalised on popular prejudices against gays, lesbians and blacks. Since these prejudices appeared to be particularly strong among the white working class, this brought the GLC into disrepute in many bedrock Labour areas. The disaffection of Labour voters became a major reason for criticism of the GLC within the Labour Party, especially outside London in areas where 'traditional' socialist values had not had to come to terms with the demands of the women's movement and the increased aspirations of disadvantaged minorities.'[40]

Thatcherism held the view that the wisdom and necessity of 'minority' spending by local authorities should be questioned and criticized at all times. In this sense, much of the Tory press cast itself as the selfless champions and supreme defenders of the 'silent majority' – the masses of 'ordinary' people who found themselves marginalized in their own country by a bewildering array of special-interest minorities who were intent on siphoning off ever greater sums of money offered up by left-leaning councillors anxious to pamper everybody/anybody except the God-fearing, law-abiding, white, heterosexual, nuclear family, 'ordinary' citizen.

In what became a familiar spectacle, arts, social, community and political projects deemed to be peripheral were attacked and condemned as being a waste of public money, on the basis that curtailing such areas of expenditure was in the financial and political interests of 'ordinary' tax and rate payers. Apart from this 'economic' angle, the Tory media portrayed individual and collective 'minority' interests and agendas as being a menace to society that had to be identified as such. Thus, Black community groups and initiatives were frequently charged with anti-white racism, with abusing the hospitality and fairness of the Great British public, and with not fully comprehending the extent to which Britain saw itself as being a tolerant and fair multicultural society.[41]

An indication of the extent of the government's single-minded campaign to curtail this GLC funding was made clear in an article in the *Guardian* titled 'Squeeze on Ethnic Funding.' The article claimed that

> The Government plans to remove from elected local authorities the power to fund ethnic minority groups. This follows the revelation that the Greater London Council is spending some £5 million a year to fund minority organisations.
>
> Home office ministers believe that part of this money is going to 'loonie' or politically motivated groups and are determined to stop it.[42]

Thus far, this text may have given the impression that the GLC had itself taken on the role of a grant-awarding body, responding to the initiatives and budgets set before it. This however was not the case. Had it been so, the role of the GLC would essentially have been no different from that of the Greater London Arts Association (GLAA) or the Arts Council. Although this was not to say that GLAA or the Arts Council had, prior to the mid-1980s, taken much funding interest in Black arts activity. The GLC ran rings around these established funding agencies when it began to fund Black artists' work. As Owusu commented 'Within a mere four years it succeeded in doing what other funding agencies, including those with a specific responsibility for the arts, had failed to do in more than two decades.'[43] What made the intervention/contribution of the GLC so important and intriguing an aspect of mid 1980s Black visual arts activity in Britain was that it was GLC staff/employees who directly initiated and directed the projects in which Black visual artists were involved.

This (at least within the *modus operandi* of funding bodies) was an extraordinary and peculiar situation. Unwilling to simply respond to Black artists' initiatives or requests for money, the GLC took it upon itself to direct and initiate activity. It remained unclear as to why this should have been the case. The early years of the 1980s had witnessed the development of cultural activity that took many forms and occurred in many places. There was no shortage of individuals, groups and projects that were in urgent need of funding and were successfully engaged in creating and exhibiting visual arts products.

Rasheed Araeen: 'So Much for the GLC's Antiracist Policy!'

One of the key players in this regard was Rasheed Araeen, who had undertaken much work relating to Black artists in Britain. One of the exhibitions Araeen curated was 'The Essential Black Art'.[44] Araeen had first proposed the exhibition to the GLC in 1984, and sought funding from them several years before the exhibition eventually took place in 1988. Given the GLC's stated position and campaigns against racism, given its apparent political position of respecting identity politics and given that it had money available to support arts activity, Araeen was confident that the GLC Department for Recreation and the Arts would financially support his exhibition proposals and other initiatives.

The GLC were not sufficiently impressed with Araeen and his proposal. Or at least, not impressed enough to offer him grant aid. A press release issued by Araeen in March 1986 pointed to his frustration and undisguised bitterness at having his exhibition proposal rejected by those he contemptuously termed 'appointed black functionaries'. He also derided the GLC's supposed 'antiracist' policy, clearly (though unconvincingly) arguing that a body such as the GLC, with funds available, could and should demonstrate its antiracism by supporting his initiatives. The press release in question related to 'Third World Within', an exhibition hastily assembled by Araeen that took place at Brixton Art Gallery.[45] 'Third World Within' was apparently taking place as a last-minute substitute for the unrealized 'The Essential Black Art'. Wasting no time, Araeen began the press release by boldly stating 'We regret to announce that the original show ESSENTIAL BLACK ART scheduled to open to public on 31st March has now been cancelled due to lack of support and funding from the GLC.'[46]

Towards the end of the press release, Araeen added detail to this statement, as follows:

> An application for the funding of this exhibition as well as for a comprehensive catalogue was submitted to the GLC *two years* ago, and since then our application has been on a High Priority list. But, at the same time nothing was

> done by the GLC's appointed black functionaries (whose very job was to deal with such matters) to take it out from their cold storage. Only recently a report was prepared with recommendations (after we had lobbied some politicians) and up to last week we were being promised about the money. But, finally came the No. It is disturbing and shameful paradox that an institution (GLC) which has been loudly proclaiming its antiracism has in fact badly failed to support and fund important projects which are about the history of antiracist struggle within the arts . . . Instead it has wasted enormous amount (sic) of public money in support of amateurish/mediocre activities and cheap exotic entertainment (under the name of ethnic arts which in fact reinforce racial stereotypes). So much for GLC's antiracist policy![47]

The intemperate language of the press release reflected the undisguised contempt that Araeen had for the GLC. Not only because it would not fund his exhibition initiatives, but also because he saw their strategy towards Black artists as being part and parcel of the ongoing marginalization and other problems facing Black artists.

To speak of the 'GLC' as such might be misleading. It would be more accurate to reference the Ethnic Arts sub-committee, which in turn was an extension of the Department for Recreation and the Arts. The Ethnic Arts sub-committee had a number of officers and at one time or another took on staff to undertake specific functions or projects, but these officers and employees maintained a discreet presence. There also existed a Race Equality Unit, an Ethnic Minorities Unit, and an Ethnic Minorities Committee. But the relationship of these 'units' and 'committees' to each other and to the public was never clear. It may have been that all these 'committees', 'units' and 'departments' were all one and the same, or overlapped significantly, but again, no-one outside of the GLC knew.

The GLC initiated and funded several 'Ethnic Arts' conferences. One of these was *Black Artists White Institutions* held at Riverside Studios, Hammersmith, 4 November 1985. It had been one such GLC conference held 28 May 1982 that led to the setting up of the GLC Ethnic Arts subcommittee. Despite these conferences there were no mechanisms for direct dialogue between officers of the GLC and members of the public. Even Owusu, a gushing admirer of the GLC admitted that it had 'failed to develop . . . a democratic system of community representation on its committees.'[48] Paul Gilroy concurred, noting that, 'The GLC's attempts to develop popular anti-racism tended to lack the active participation of large numbers of black people.'[49]

It was the frustration of not being able to engage in tangible and meaningful dialogue with the GLC that led Araeen to contemptuously speak of self-referencing 'appointed black functionaries.' He claimed that 'The Essential Black Art' was not the only exhibition proposal with which the GLC were unimpressed. In the postscript to *The Other Story* catalogue, Araeen also claimed that he approached them over a two-year period from 1983 to 1985 with a proposal for what would eventually manifest as 'The Other Story' exhibition.[50] Araeen claimed that having had his proposal rejected by the Arts Council on several occasions, he 'then spent two years marching up and down the corridors of the socialist GLC, but without result.'[51] The tone of these comments revealed that Araeen's contempt for the GLC had not diminished in the three years since his 'Third World Within' press release. In the 'postscript' to *The Other Story* catalogue, Araeen added for good measure that, 'In fact my dealing with the GLC was one of the most humiliating experiences of my life.'[52] Comments such as this imply that between Araeen and the GLC there existed a permanent and prickly stand-off. This was not necessarily the case. A sufficient degree of dialogue existed between Araeen and the GLC for the latter to commission the former as part of its Black Visual Arts Forum to produce a research paper on the *History of Black Artists in Britain*. In a footnote to *The Other Story* catalogue 'postscript', Araeen conceded that 'I did receive some money from GLAA (the Greater London Arts Association) and the GLC in 1983 for preliminary research work.'[53] In addition to this, Araeen's self-published 1984 collection of essays and articles, *Making Myself Visible* contained a 'GLC funded' logo, though the extent or nature of the funding was not indicated in the publication.

It was difficult to identify a coherent and coordinated GLC strategy towards Black visual artists. Instead, there seemed to have been a number of initiatives, some of them haphazard, some of them seemingly less so. It seemed that one of the GLC's strategies towards Black artists was to threaten to withdraw its funding from galleries and arts centres that steadfastly maintained programming policies that discriminated against Black people and Black artists. Lubaina Himid claimed that this strategy was directly responsible for her curating the Black women artists' exhibition 'The Thin Black Line'. Himid wrote that 'The GLC had threatened to withdraw its considerable contribution to the ICA if something black did not appear in that [presumably 1985/6] financial year.'[54]

Under Livingstone, the GLC apparently made 'an early threat (later withdrawn) to suspend £550,000 of grants to the Royal Opera House, Covent Garden, and redistribute the money to grassroots organisations like community arts centres.'[55] Owusu concurred, regarding the existence of another, similar strategy. He claimed, in *The Struggle for Black Arts in Britain*, that

> A significant challenge was thrown out to mainstream cultural institutions such as those of the South Bank complex. They were asked to provide written statements of their Equal Opportunity and anti-racist politics (that last word is probably a typographical error and should probably have been policies), and plans for improvements in such areas as Black representation in management, employment and programming.[56]

Evidence of this is provided in a letter dated 8 October 1985, from the Director of Recreation and the Arts issued by the GLC itself, inviting attendance to a *Black Artists – White Institutions Conference.* The letter read

> The role of Mainstream Arts Institutions in the development of Black Arts is crucial and the Race Equality Unit has begun to develop a programme of monitoring and evaluating the Anti Racist and Equal Opportunity Policies of all Mainstream Arts Institutions funded by the GLC. The emphasis has been on persuading Mainstream Arts Institutions to develop and implement Anti Racist and Equal Opportunity Policies with regards to the employment, representation, programming and training of black artists.[57]

Kwesi Owusu – a Gushing Admirer

To find substantial and sympathetic references to the GLC's support of Black artists we need to reference Owusu, who dedicated a chapter of his 1986 book *The Struggle for Black Arts in Britain*, to discussing the GLC. He likened their belated support for Black Arts to a 'lame duck' that was 'suddenly . . . ready to fly.' Mindful of the criticism levelled at the GLC, Owusu felt compelled to defend the body when he wrote

> we believe that despite all the criticisms which can be made of it, it broke new ground in the funding and promotion of Black arts in London. Consequently, our assessment of the Council's achievements is underlined not so much by the heights it reached or the problems which it encountered, as by the depths from which it had to rise.[58]

Owusu summarized what he considered to be the achievements of the GLC as follows: 'Since the election of a Labour majority in the early Eighties, the impact of the GLC on Black Arts in London has . . . been noticeable and considerable. Within a mere four years it succeeded in doing what other funding agencies, including those with a specific responsibility for the arts, had failed to do in more than two decades.'[59]

Perhaps within the context of this text we ought not to be too accepting of Owusu's complimentary assessment of the GLC. He himself was from a performing arts background and it may well have been the case that (as he claimed) Black art forms such as theatre, carnival, film-making, poetry and music all benefited from GLC support. The same cannot be said about the GLC's attitude towards the capital's Black visual artists. A comparative assessment of the GLC's funding strategies towards the various Black arts forms lies beyond the scope of this text; but as far as the work of Black visual artists was concerned, it was GLC staff/employees who directly initiated and directed the projects in which Black visual artists were involved.

This was, on the face of it, a unique situation. (Though we would need, as suggested in the previous paragraph a comparative study to confirm or refute this.) Unwilling to simply *respond* to Black artists' initiatives or requests for money, the GLC took it upon itself to direct and initiate activity. It was difficult to identify a coherent and coordinated GLC strategy towards Black visual artists, although one thing was certain, they saw art not so much as creative expression with its own integrity and its own terms of reference; instead, they regarded art as something to prop up, illustrate or visually embellish other initiatives and projects. Other than this, the GLC saw art activity as illustrating, or being the artistic face of, its projects and its anti-racist campaigns. Visual artists were never respected for the individuality of their practice; instead, they were regarded as symbolic and politically representative components of some sort of anti-racist ethnic jigsaw. *The GLC Anti-Racist Murals*, involving a number of Black artists, were an example of this.

According to Chila Kumari Burman, there was only one occasion on which a Black woman artist received funding from the GLC 'as an individual.'[60] This Black woman artist (unnamed within Burman's text) was apparently 'funded for a year on the condition that she was attached to a community arts centre as a community artist. Plus, the stipulation was made that the work she produced should not reflect her desires as an individual but the interests of the Black community.'[61] Though within this text, Burman was casting this unnamed artist as a victim of sexism, she proceeded to make an important point that had a wider, non-gendered application. 'The GLC had ignored the importance to the Black community of the experience of individual Black women and had funded her on the basis of a historical notion of 'community' or 'ethnic community' arts.'[62]

This particular notion of 'community' – alluded to by Boyce earlier in this chapter and here by Burman was critical, as it lay at the heart of the GLC's attitude towards Black artists and the people around them. Here, a reference to militant Black Art advocates such as Larry Neal and Ron Karenga is of some consequence. Within the GLC's attitude and strategy towards Black artists can be seen conspicuous strands of what has come to be known as 'the burden of (racial) representation' – the view that Black artists cannot, without difficulty, be accorded the right or the privilege to create work free from externally enforced pressures, such as representing a wider social or political grouping of people. In its own extrapolated way, the Black Art/Black Power manifesto influenced the thinking of the GLC, demanding as it did, a disinclination to aesthetic individualism and promoting instead, an explicit interplay between the work of Black artists and the Black community.

Black artists have for years felt the pressure of this burden of representation. The artist Sutapa Biswas asked the question, 'Why do we always have to address themes of racism and migration [within our work as artists]?'[63] Paul Gilroy has referred to the burden of representation as 'the question of . . . the black artist in the public sphere as figures in public politics.'[64] Sabera Bham explained this burden as follows:

> The migrant/black practitioner is considered the voice for the black community as if she or he were its appropriately designated public 'representative'. This role has fallen upon the shoulders of Black artists, not so much out of individual choice, but as a consequence of 'structures of racism' that have historically marginalised their access to the means of cultural production. . . . When a black artist becomes visible, their work is burdened with a whole range of extra-artistic concerns, because, in their relatively isolated positions as one of the few black practitioners in any given field (*sic*). They are seen as representatives who speak on behalf of, and are thus accountable to their community.[65]

One of the major difficulties here was that, in part at least, what became known as 'the burden of representation' stemmed from the militant and exacting Black Art/Black Power manifesto, originally championed by Black American activists and subsequently copied so enthusiastically by a number of Black British artists.

It was an attempt to extricate Black artists from this burden of representation – a search and a plea for artistic freedom that one Black woman artist has alluded to.

> Black artists can do everything, allow everything to everybody. Let us think of ourselves as being able not just [to] have one line but many lines going out to every direction because we're people . . . Some abstract paintings are lovely for what paintings are. But if a Black person does it, they shouldn't be persecuted because they're not doing what is considered to be Black art . . . whatever way you present it, it's still a part of yourself.[66]

Standing firm against the onrushing tide of post-modernity and new debates that questioned the validity of fixed readings of 'identity' and 'experience', the GLC mounted a series of exhibitions under the no-nonsense banner of 'The Black Experience'.[67] These exhibitions projected particular social and political readings on the lives and experiences of Black people in London. In not one instance, as Kumari Burman reported, were Black artists, or was *a* Black artist, allowed the freedom to contextualize themselves and their work. It remained a significant irony that the only artist who appeared to have extracted some GLC funding to support his own initiative was Rasheed Araeen (a severe critic of the GLC), for his 1984 book, *Making Myself Visible* as referenced earlier. In her text,

'There Have Always Been Great Blackwomen Artists', Kumari Burman claimed that there had in fact been one Black male artist who had been funded by the GLC 'without any pre-conditions except that he produce a certain amount of work'[68], although the claim was not substantiated and no artist's name was mentioned. Within this text, Kumari Burman made a number of serious claims and allegations, though she was unwilling or unable to substantiate them. There was also the problem, within her text, of artists being quoted anonymously.

The GLC's attitude towards the visual arts was another example of how Black artists were pigeon-holed and bullied. The GLC took the view that 'art' had to be channelled and exposed through 'community arts' avenues, for fear of it being regarded as inaccessible or elitist, were it to emerge in such contexts as the modernist white cube. In this regard, the attitudes of the GLC were not dissimilar to some of the views about 'art' expressed by those who ran The Black-Art Gallery (the Organisation for Black Arts Advancement and Learning Activities (OBAALA)). Both OBAALA and the GLC distrusted 'art' for its own sake. Rather, they preferred to regard art as an expression of certain types of ethnic, cultural, racial or political identity. For OBAALA and the GLC, any art that fell beyond such readings, or any art that could not be shoe-horned into such readings, was to be marginalized and regarded as suspect.

It was clear that the GLC did not *trust* artists to make and exhibit work on their own terms. Even those who had developed incisive opinions on the politicization of the Black artist were given short thrift.[69] The GLC worry that 'art' should not appear to be 'elitist' or 'inaccessible' translated into them disregarding anything that would exist within a 'mainstream' art establishment context. Despite the existence within London of a large number of professional Black visual artists, the GLC failed, refused, or was unable to facilitate a single Black artist exhibition within an established London gallery.[70] In this sense it perpetuated the art establishment marginalization of the Black artist, by dictating that the only work by Black artists that it would support was work that was 'educational', 'illustrative' and 'communicative'. Many artists, many types of artists would view their work as 'educational', 'illustrative' or 'communicative'. But the GLC were interested only in certain constructions of the adjectives 'educational', 'illustrative' and 'communicative.' Such work had to exist beyond the supposedly elitist 'gallery' context and could only gain exposure through channels constructed and operated by GLC staff and those Araeen disparaged as 'black functionaries.'

Only venues regarded as 'community' galleries or 'community' centres could, as far as the GLC was concerned, be suitable for Black artists. Himid and Owusu have told us that the GLC put pressure on 'mainstream' galleries to include Black artists within their programmes, but (apart from a passing reference to 'integrated programming' in the letter dated 8 October 1985, from the Director of Recreation and the Arts issued by the GLC itself, inviting attendance to a *Black Artists – White Institutions* Conference, referenced earlier in this text) we know nothing of what the GLC would ideally like to have seen. Himid claimed 'The Thin Black Line' came about because of such pressures (on, in this instance, the ICA) though it is intriguing to consider the question of whether the GLC were happy with the spectacle of ten Black women artists crammed into a somewhat constrained and marginalized concourse space (the work of the eleventh artist, sculptor Veronica Ryan, appeared in a room elsewhere in the ICA).[71]

Returning briefly to the matter of Araeen's rejected exhibition proposals, it could reasonably be speculated that the GLC rejected the proposals not simply because it was unimpressed with them. The proposals might well have been rejected because the GLC worried that by seeking to locate Black artists' work, literally and metaphorically within the mainstream gallery environment, Araeen was orienting the exhibition away from 'ordinary' people and towards a more 'exclusive' gallery audience. The GLC unswervingly regarded the modernist, 'white cube' art gallery as an alienating entity with which it did not feel comfortable. Instead of seeking to encourage a greater number and range of people to develop reciprocal relationships with art galleries, the GLC circumvented or dismissed the potential of the 'art gallery' and embarked on projects which, as they saw it, would take art directly to 'the people', or into places where 'the people' already went. In effect, the GLC patronized Black artists and considered that it knew what was best for them and their work.

Owusu, in praising the GLC seemed to care or know nothing about the problematic nature of their 'support' for Black artists. This was evidenced by his references to an exhibition funded by the GLC and organized by them and a body known as the Caribbean Crafts Circle. The exhibition, 'New Horizons' took place at the beginning of 1985[72] at the Royal Festival Hall. Owusu referred to 'New Horizons' as a 'good example' of the GLC's contributions to the welfare of Black arts in London, but 'New Horizons' was a messy and problematic exhibition. There was a total of forty-four artists in the exhibition, their countries of birth ranging from Nigeria to Malaysia, Taiwan to India, Zimbabwe to Jamaica. Their practices ranged from pottery to photography, fashion design to jewellery, calligraphy to painting. Whilst not denying the validity and importance of each of these artists and each of their art forms, the bringing and lumping together of so many disparate practices was not good, as it served to 'hyper-ethnicize' the artists, banding them all together as 'Artists from outside of the European sphere.'[73] But this was not what they were – it was what the exhibition had made them. Each of these artists had either been born/brought up in Britain, or had made Britain (or more specifically London) their permanent or temporary home. Some of them, such as Keith Piper and Lubaina Himid produced work that had overt social or political narratives. Others, such as Brian Tai-Shen Wang, practiced a more traditional form of Chinese calligraphy. These artists had little or nothing in common except that they had been thrown together in the exhibition. Within the catalogue, no attempt was made to construct a curatorial thesis, except that these were 'artists . . . offering us the opportunity to appreciate the energy of ideas and forms which cross the boundary between "art" and "craft."'[74]

Whilst this sentiment could be applied to some of the artists in the exhibition, many more artists were pursuing and developing art practices that could be located in various other contexts. Documentary photography was one such context, fashion design another. Jewellery was another such context, as was kinetic sculpture. The work of other artists, such as Piper, could more easily be located in a 'Black Art/Black Power' context than as some sort of fusion between 'art' and 'craft.' That such a disjointed exhibition could be regarded by Owusu as a 'good example' of anything, puts much of his enthusiasm for the GLC into a sobering context. 'New Horizons' existed firmly within the vein of 'ethnic arts.' That is, an attitude towards 'non-European' artists that continually sought to ethnicize them and their practice, and confuse or interchange genuinely 'traditional' forms of art activity with practice that owed nothing, in any literal sense, to 'non-European' cultures.

The establishment of the term and the construct of 'ethnic arts' could be traced back to a report titled *The Arts Britain Ignores* written by Naseem Khan in 1976.[75] 'Ethnic Arts' tended to define and regard the arts and cultural expressions of Black (or more specifically, non-white) people in fixed terms. 'Culture' was regarded as a fixed self-referencing entity that the peoples of the world carried with them for all time, as part of a historic continuum. The mass of Black people in Britain had begun arriving there from elsewhere in the world during the period of the late 1940s to early 1960s; little more than a decade and a half before Khan's report. These people never really stopped being 'Indian' or 'West Indian' or 'Nigerian' or whatever, even though they became or already were *bona fide* British citizens and residents. Furthermore, the 1970s saw the widespread migration to Britain of 'East African Asians' – particularly those 50,000 expelled by Idi Amin from Uganda in 1972.[76] Within this historical context it was not surprising (it may even have been appropriate) for Khan to regard and discuss arts activity along self-referencing lines of ethnicity. But these were changing times, and at precisely the moment that Khan was undertaking her research, a new generation of Black British youngsters was finding its feet, and establishing its own parameters of Black British identity. When a vocal minority of these Black British youngsters immersed themselves in art practices, they called it 'Black Art' and imbued it with a multiplicity of functions that owed much (consciously or otherwise) to Pan-Africanism and Socialist Realism. Cultural Nationalism also had a place in their work, but 'ethnic arts' as the particular construct it was, was emphatically bypassed.

What the GLC did was to confuse (or fail/refuse to differentiate) between 'ethnic art' and 'Black art'. It located the latter within the former and applied the construction of the former to the workings of the latter. In the mid-1970s there may have been a need to identify and support 'ethnic art', but by the early 1980s there existed a new generation of artists who went *beyond* ethnic arts and attempts to ethnicize them appeared particularly clumsy and flat-footed.

Whilst the Black Art/Black Community position advocated by the likes of Keith Piper and Donald Rodney had been right for the time and had closely aligned with the cultural/political positions of young Black Britain in the riot-torn Britain of early 1980s, such cultural and political positions were not inflexible and over a period of time, changed circumstances and changed contexts required new strategies that jettisoned apparently rigid positions of representation. The priorities of and possibilities for Black artists had changed rapidly by the time the GLC took an active interest in these practitioners. Yet the GLC seemed unaware of or insensitive to the existence of new strategies and tended to locate Black artists, irrespective of the nature of their work, in the fixed cultural and political space of the early 1980s.

Araeen had long warned against attempts to ethnicize and marginalize the Black artist. He could have been talking about 'New Horizons' when, in 1978 he wrote (regarding the exhibition 'Afro-Caribbean Art', 'There will in fact be many such exhibitions, supported by the establishment, taking place under various ethnic titles during the coming years . . . which will attempt to *re-ethnicize* the black artist and thereby marginalize further his/her role in this society.'[77]

The GLC *Anti-Racist Mural Project*

On more than one occasion the GLC commissioned Black artists to produce sets of murals. Once, for an initiative known as the *Anti-Racist Mural Project* and once to decorate hoardings around the Roundhouse building in Camden Town, London.[78]

For the anti-racist mural project, through 'internal structures' it commissioned four teams of two artists: Shanti Panchal and Dushka Ahmad, Gavin Jantjes and Tam Joseph, Lubaina Himid and Simone Alexander, Keith Piper and Chila Burman. These artists were commissioned to produce preliminary sketches, finished proposals, and finally, to execute the murals at permanent or temporary sites around London. The murals were reported to have cost £10,000 each.[79] There is no evidence that the murals were requested, demanded or needed by any body or persons apart from the GLC itself. The artists themselves merely responded to the GLC's invitations (and willingly took the lucrative sums on offer). Furthermore, although the GLC professed to have embarked on extensive rounds of 'community consultation', there is significant evidence that 'community groups' and 'community' individuals, at at least two mural sites, voiced loud and concerted objections to the murals or specific aspects of them.[80]

In the Foreword to a brochure documenting the murals, the coordinator of the project, Sheila Seepersaud-Jones wrote that 'The GLC Arts and Recreation

Committee allocated funds for Black/Asian artists to paint murals on appropriate themes on strategically located buildings in London, particularly in those areas which have a historical connection with the black presence or have experienced racial conflict.'[81] In this sentence, the words 'appropriate' and 'strategically' sum up the GLC's attitude towards Black artists. Unable or unwilling to give Black artists the resources to continue to produce and exhibit work, the GLC instead, selected artists, told them what they could or could not paint and told them where to paint. The GLC itself established the project and set all the terms of reference. Whether the murals were wanted by the artists or the 'community' was never an issue. The GLC wanted the murals to demonstrate their 'London against Racism' campaign. Nothing else mattered. Within the parameters of this project, Black artists were being told that their value, worth or usefulness lay in them painting 'appropriate' community murals for 'appropriate' communities. It was an emphatic pigeon-holing and marginalizing of the artists, in which the artists themselves were implicated.

Ultimately, the GLC failed to make any lasting or positive contributions to the profile or the fortunes of Black artists as a collective body. A few Black artists, those who painted the murals mentioned in this chapter, each received several thousand pounds. The murals at the Roundhouse were, in time, flyposted over, their obliteration acting as a visual representation of the death of the Roundhouse 'Black Arts' project. The Piper/Kumari Burman and the Himid/Alexander murals, executed on hardboard panels, were never properly publicly exhibited. They have since either been destroyed or lost. The Jantjes/Joseph Brixton mural, though it survived in perfect condition for several years, was eventually painted over.

The GLC had had the potential to financially aid and facilitate the work of London's Black artists. It chose not to do so, attempting instead what could most favourably be described as a strategic policy of intervention, consistently linked to its anti-racism campaigns. This strategic policy of intervention prioritized the GLC's own political agenda and was primarily informed by the GLC's image of itself as a righteous anti-racist government that alone knew best how to provide for its citizens.

In this regard, it was different from, but not much better than the funding bodies like the GLAA and the Arts Council that had both, until the late 1980s, largely disregarded Black visual artists. But this is perhaps too uncharitable an assessment of the GLC. Because like the major institutions that initiated large-scale, all-inclusive exhibitions of Black artists' work, before, during and after the period of the GLC, the efforts of what was a governmental body symbolized, in its own problematic ways, a sort of 'acknowledgement' of Black artists.

The limitations of the GLC's involvement with Black artists mirror the limitations and failures of much of its involvement with Black people in London. This involvement had an inadequate base because the GLC's 'formal and institutionally-based politics of anti-racism which emerged . . . in the aftermath of the 1981 riots'[82] had 'tended to lack the active participation of large numbers of black people.'[83] Furthermore, it could be said that the needs, agendas and aspirations of Black people and Black artists had to follow one of the GLC's primary aims alluded to earlier in this chapter – that of reincorporating the perceived 'alienated or dissident [Black] urban underclass . . . into the rituals of the political system.'[84] Gilroy summarised this problem as follows: 'The task of advancing anti-racism [was] collapsed into the specific strategic priorities of the GLC, a model which regardless of its in-house effectiveness, is not universally applicable to anti-racist politics in non-institutional settings but which is none the less offered up as a general blueprint.'[85] Given the wide-ranging pessimism of this assessment of the GLC, it was inevitable that its critics would speculate about what might have happened if the GLC had had greater respect for the needs, agendas and aspirations (as well as the creative strengths) of Black people and Black artists. Paul Gilroy, for example, mused 'It is impossible not to wonder what might have happened if [Black Hip-Hop youth] culture had been given some place in the council's definitions of anti-racist activity.'[86]

'Black Artists and the Greater London Council' is a new, previously unpublished text. Much of the research for it was undertaken for my PhD, *Black Visual Arts Activity in England 1981–1986: Press and Public Responses* (Goldsmiths College, University of London, 1998).

Notes

1 Ken Little, 'Foreword' for the Arts Programme for the GLC Race Equality Unit season *The Black Experience*, January/February 1986, p. 2.

2 Errol Lloyd, 'An Historical Perspective' Introduction to the catalogue accompanying the exhibition *Caribbean Expressions in Britain*, Leicestershire Museum and Art Gallery, 16 August–28 September 1986, pp. 3–7 (p. 6).

3 E A Markham, *Artrage* Issue No. 11 Winter 1985, p. 1.

4 Errol Lloyd, 'An Historical Perspective', p. 6.

5 John Carvel, *Citizen Ken*, London: Chatto & Windus / The Hogarth Press 1984, p. 86, and Ken Livingstone, *If Voting Changed Anything, They'd Abolish It*, London: Fontana / Collins 1988, p. 146.

6 Paul Gilroy, *There Ain't No Black in the Union Jack*, London: Hutchinson, 1987, p. 137.

7 Carvel, *Citizen Ken*, p. 205.

8 Carvel, *Citizen Ken*, p. 208.

9 Nita Clarke and Phil Evans, *London for Beginners*, Writers and Readers Publishing Cooperative Society Ltd., 1985, p. 138.

10 Kwesi Owusu, *The Struggle for Black Arts in Britain*, Comedia Publishing Group 1986, p. 85.

11 Carvel, *Citizen Ken*, p. 86.

12 Sonia Boyce, in conversation with John Roberts, *Third Text* No. 1 Autumn 1987 pp. 55–64 (p. 59).

13 Boyce, in conversation with John Roberts, p. 59.

14 Owusu, *The Struggle for Black Arts in Britain*, p. 85.

15 David Widgery (ed.) *The Book of the Year*, Ink Links Ltd. 1980, p. 3.

16 Stuart Hall and Tony Jefferson (eds.) *Resistance through rituals: Youth subcultures in post-war Britain*, Hutchinson, 1976, quoted in Paul Gilroy, 'Steppin' out of Babylon – race, class and autonomy', in Centre for Contemporary Cultural Studies, *The Empire Strikes Back,* Hutchinson 1988, pp. 276–314 (p. 296).

17 Paul Gilroy, 'Steppin' out of Babylon – race, class and autonomy', p. 296.

18 Gilroy, 'Steppin' out of Babylon', p. 296.

19 Nigel Fielding, *The National Front* (International Library of Sociology), London, Boston and Henley: Routledge & Kegan Paul, 1981, quoted in Paul Gilroy*, There Ain't No Black in the Union Jack*, p. 118.

20 Owusu, *The Struggle for Black Arts in Britain*, p. 85.

21 Lord Scarman, *The Brixton Disorders, April 10–12, 1981*: Inquiry Report. Chmn. Lord Scarman, Stationery Office Books, 1981, p. 45, quoted in Zig Layton-Henry, *The Politics of Race in Britain*, London: George Allen & Unwin, 1984, p. 162.

22 Gilroy, *There Ain't No Black in the Union Jack*, p. 136.

23 Carvel, *Citizen Ken*, p. 208.

24 GLC (1985) Anti Racist Programme 1984: Review and Assessment, unpublished paper, quoted in Gilroy, *There Ain't No Black in the Union Jack*, pp. 137–138.

25 Carvel, *Citizen Ken*, p. 110.

26 Gilroy, *There Ain't No Black in the Union Jack*, p. 138.

27 The Black-Art Gallery eventually collapsed when Islington Council withdrew its funding on 31 December 1992. For a study of the gallery see 'The Rise and Fall of The Black-Art Gallery', in Eddie Chambers, *Black Artists in British Art: A History Since the 1950s*, London and New York: I B Tauris, 2014.

28 Gilroy, *There Ain't No Black in the Union Jack*, p. 138.

29 Zig Layton-Henry, *The Politics of Race in Britain*, London: George Allen & Unwin 1984, p. 173.

30 Gilroy, *There Ain't No Black in the Union Jack*, p. 138.

31 Gilroy, *There Ain't No Black in the Union Jack*, p. 138.

32 Karin Woodley, 'A Farewell to Arts' (a discussion of Tory funding policies and their relationship to the arts), *Artrage* Winter 1988, pp. 2–4.

33 Carvel, *Citizen Ken*, p. 110.

34 Nita Clarke and Phil Evans, *London for Beginners*, p. 148.

35 Ken Livingstone, 'The GLC's Arts Experience', *Art Monthly*, April 1986, pp. 2–3.

36 Carvel, *Citizen Ken,* p. 206.

37 Carvel, *Citizen Ken*, pp. 206–207.

38 Clarke and Evans, *London for Beginners*, p. 148.

39 Norman Tebbit, quoted in Ian Gilmour, *Dancing With Dogma: Britain Under Thatcherism*, London: Simon & Schuster, 1992, in turn, quoted in Will Hutton, *The State We're In*, London: Jonathan Cape, 1995, p. 37.

40 Carvel, *Citizen Ken*, p. 207.

41 For a study of this, and for references and examples, see Paul Gilroy, *There Ain't No Black in the Union Jack.*

42 John Torode, 'Squeeze on ethnic funding', *Guardian*, 7 March 1984, p. 28.

43 Owusu, *The Struggle for Black Arts in Britain*, p. 104.

44 *The Essential Black Art*, Rasheed Araeen, Zarina Bhimji, Sutapa Biswas, Sonia Boyce, Eddie Chambers, Allan deSouza, Mona Hatoum, Gavin Jantjes and Keith Piper, Chisenhale Gallery, London, 5 February to 5 March 1988 and touring.

45 *Third World Within: An exhibition of the work of AfroAsian Artists in Britain*, organized by Rasheed Araeen, Rasheed Araeen, Saleem Arif, David A Bailey, Sutapa Biswas, Avtarjeet Dhanjal, Uzo Egonu, Mona Hatoum, Merdelle J-Irving, Gavin Jantjes, Houria Niati, Keith Piper, and Kumiko Shimizu. Brixton Art Gallery. 31 March to 22 April 1986.

46 Press release for *Third World Within*, issued 15 March 1986.

47 Press release for *Third World Within*.

48 Owusu, *The Struggle for Black Arts in Britain*, p. 86.

49 Gilroy, *There Ain't No Black in the Union Jack*, p. 150.

50 *The Other Story: Afro-Asian artists in post war* Britain, curated by Rasheed Araeen for the Hayward Gallery, 29 November 1989 to 4 February 1990.

51 Rasheed Araeen, 'Postscript', *The Other Story* catalogue, South Bank Centre 1989, p. 105.

52 Araeen, 'Postscript', p. 105.

53 Araeen, 'Postscript', p. 106. Possibly, Araeen was referring to a research paper he authored for the GLC's *Black Visual Arts Forum*, titled *History of Black Artists in Britain* (though the Forum was said to have come into existence in January 1985).

54 Lubaina Himid, 'Mapping: A Decade of Black Women Artists 1980-1990', in *Passion: Discourses on Blackwomen's Creativity*, Urban Fox Press, 1990, pp. 63–72 (p. 65).

55 Carvel, *Citizen Ken*, p. 86.

56 Owusu, *The Struggle for Black Arts in Britain*, p. 89.

57 Document in the possession of this researcher.

58 Owusu, *The Struggle for Black Arts in Britain*, p. 26.

59 Owusu, *The Struggle for Black Arts in Britain*, p. 104.

60 Chila Kumari Burman, 'There Have Always Been Great Black Women Artists', in *Charting the Journey: Writings by Black and Third World Women*, London: Sheba Publications, 1988, p. 296.

61 Kumari Burman, 'There Have Always Been Great Black Women Artists', p. 297.

62 Kumari Burman, 'There Have Always Been Great Black Women Artists', p. 297.

63 Quoted in Pratibha Parmar (director) *The Colour of Britain*, Hauer Rawlence Productions, for the Arts Council of England and Channel Four Television 1994, quoted in Sabera Bham, 'Crossing the Boundaries of Difference: Black Women

Artists in Britain' BA Hons., Cultural and Media Studies dissertation, Newport School of Art and Design, 1996 (p. 12).

64 Paul Gilroy, 'Nothing But Sweat inside my Hand: Diaspora Aesthetics and Black Arts in Britain', contained in ICA document *Black Film British Cinema*, ICA Pub. 1988 pp. 44–46 (p. 44).

65 Sabera Bham, 'Crossing the Boundaries of Difference: Black Women Artists in Britain', p. 13. For an additional discussion of 'the burden of representation', see Kobena Mercer, 'Black Art and the Burden of Representation', *Third Text*, issue 10 Spring 1990, pp. 61–78.

66 Quoted in Kumari Burman, 'There Have Always Been Great Black Women Artists'.

67 The GLC Race Equality Unit presented *The Black Experience* – 'A London-wide Black arts programme reflecting historical and contemporary Black experiences through a variety of art forms.' *The Black Experience* ran from February to March 1986 and included exhibitions, photography, visual arts and film.

68 Kumari Burman, 'There Have Always Been Great Black Women Artists', p. 297.

69 I have earlier in this text mentioned the way in which Rasheed Araeen felt 'humiliated' by GLC rejections of his exhibition proposals.

70 The sole exception being the pressure Himid reported the GLC as bringing to bear on the ICA, leading to *The Thin Black Line*.

71 Particularly whilst a solo exhibition by a white male artist appeared in the main gallery spaces of the ICA, concurrent with the showing of *The Thin Black Line*.

72 *New Horizons,* GLC Royal Festival Hall, 18 January to 5 February 1985.

73 Introduction to *New Horizons* catalogue, GLC Royal Festival Hall 1985, p. 5.

74 Introduction to *New Horizons* catalogue, GLC Royal Festival Hall 1985, p. 5.

75 This report had been commissioned by the Arts Council of Great Britain, Calouste Gulbenkian Foundation and the Community Relations Council, and was published in May 1976.

76 See entry on AMIN Idi, *c.* 1925 – Uganda Military ruler (later president) (1971–9) *Dictionary of African Historical Biography*, University of California Press, 1989, p.259.

77 Rasheed Araeen, 'Afro-Caribbean Art', *Black Phoenix,* No 2 Summer 1978 pp. 30–31.

78 The Roundhouse was one of the GLC's ill-fated initiatives towards the Black arts. They had intended to fund and support the establishment of a 'centre of excellence' for all aspects of Black arts activity. Before the GLC was abolished, it attempted to rush through major funding for the exhibition (figures of £7 million have been quoted), but was prevented from doing so. In any event, the Roundhouse project was bedevilled with internal strife, personality clashes, allegations of gross mismanagement and embezzlement, internecine warfare and political intrigue. A fuller assessment of the Roundhouse project falls beyond the scope of this research. Apart from murals painted by Tam Joseph, Chila Burman, Lubaina Himid and Shanti Panchal, the only involvement that Black visual artists had with the project was when the building opened for less than two weeks – *Twelve Days at The Roundhouse* – from 19–31 March 1986. An exhibition was held in the building as part of this. No documentation relating to this exhibition exists.

79 The figure of £10,000 was quoted by Anwar Tambe in the *Southall Gazette*, Friday 14 June 1985. The front-page article was titled 'Race mural is "waste of cash"'.

80 Evidence of objections to the murals is available from several sources. The *Southall Gazette* (Friday 14 June 1985), offering a front-page editorial on the mural plans of Keith Piper and Chila Burman, wrote 'Spending £10,000 of ratepayers' money on this mural is a disgrace. Paintings of this kind are meaningless to the majority of people in Southall.' In an interview in *Artrage* magazine (Winter 1985 issue 11 pp. 15–17) between Chila Kumari Burman and Errol Lloyd, Kumari Burman went into detail about other vociferous objections to plans for the mural. The coordinator of the mural project, Sheila Seepersaud-Jones, in the Foreword to a brochure documenting the project, made a number of references to objectors and objections to two of the proposed murals. Brochure titled *GLC anti-racist mural project 1985*. Published by the GLC 1985, unpaginated.

81 Sheila Seepersaud-Jones, Foreword to brochure *GLC anti-racist mural project 1985*. Published by the GLC 1985, unpaginated.

82 Gilroy, *There Ain't No Black in the Union Jack*, p. 115.

83 Gilroy, *There Ain't No Black in the Union Jack*, p. 150.

84 Gilroy, *There Ain't No Black in the Union Jack*, p. 138.

85 Gilroy, *There Ain't No Black in the Union Jack*, pp. 144–145.

86 Gilroy, *There Ain't No Black in the Union Jack*, p. 151.

Chapter 34
'Art and Society': Jonathan Greenland Interview with Eddie Chambers

How would you describe the theme of the *Curators Eye II* exhibition for a layperson?
The exhibition explored the many ways in which Jamaican artists engage with and interpret Jamaica's history and their place within it. Of course, some viewers might be of the opinion that the theme of the exhibition applied to some artists more than others. But it was very important to me that it wasn't overly didactic. I hoped to keep the message of the work open. Two good examples are Shosana Fagan and Tricia Gordon-Johnston. I see them as artists whose work has no single, explicit 'meaning' or 'idea', rather, their work is particularly open-ended in its readings. With Tricia's work that was displayed in *Curator's Eye II*, its redness was strongly symbolic, to me at least, of blood, and that can evoke the violent history of Jamaica. Or maybe it is menstruation. In many ways the overwhelming redness could refer to either a womb or a wound. Now, with Shosana, I see her as disrupting our comfortable notions of domesticity. She had these sheets strung out across the gallery like laundry, but they were blackened, defaced and torn. Sheets remind me of bed and healing, and rest, love and sleep.

And privacy . . .
Yes, but she drove a coach and horses through all that! There was almost a suggestion of violence tied up in the work. The sheets looked abused or burnt.

Do you think it was a feminist work?
I think the feminist leanings were very strong. The sheets were covered in text but the text was not legible, and evoked the sense of voices not being heard,

experiences not being acknowledged. There was – again, at least to me – great violence in the work; it also makes me think of victims of violence.

Then there were Keisha Castello's works: these hybrid creatures were displayed in cases all along the wall. I see them as a metaphor for Caribbean hybridity in visual form. Maybe they are a play on the motto 'Out of Many, One People' as the pieces comprise so many different elements and forms. And although the artist had just recently made the work, they looked like they were dug up like that!

Do you think you were projecting this theme onto the different works? There are many artists around the world working in similar forms and they are not necessarily reflecting the Jamaican experience.

Maybe I was. But this is the job of the curator: to interpret. Like an art historian. Mine is not the only and absolute interpretation of the work. In fact, I dislike the idea of the art historian as being something like a dispassionate librarian or authority. For one thing, it causes all sorts of problems when curators are considered to be the arbiters of truth. It has a false implication of objectivity which I don't think the term 'art history' necessarily carries. As a curator I want, first and foremost, for viewers to know that what I'm presenting is my opinion and should not be seen as carrying any sort of factual objectivity.

I respect this statement of openness and vulnerability very much. How can curators foster and encourage this sense of discourse and differing opinions?

I think that in general, it's difficult for many people of influence in the art world to accept the notion of divergent opinions having equal intellectual or curatorial value, because the dominant culture within art history and the art gallery is to privilege the idea of the 'expert' or the 'learned authority'. It is of course correct that if someone has spent many years learning about a particular aspect of art history, then their opinion must count for something. But it is in my view wrong to suggest or imply that other opinions have an inherently lesser credibility. I believe that we should allow for multiple art histories, as well as multiple curatorial perspectives. But I don't think that the art world is necessarily comfortable with that type of openness or vulnerability. I think the problem is even more acute in environments in which positions of influence or professional opportunities are relatively few. In answer to your question, I would say that those in positions of influence need to actively be cognisant of the curatorial aspirations of others and to respect the idea that curatorial and art historical plurality is a good thing.

What other links did you see between the works in *Curator's Eye II*?

There were many cross-references: one strong visual link was that iconic image of the slave ship. You saw it repeated in many different ways in Charles Campbell's work and Christopher Clare's and also K. Khalfani Ra's.

How did the work of those particular artists relate to your theme?

It's clear from looking at the titles of the work in the exhibition by K. Khalfani Ra that he's keen, anxious even, to intervene into Jamaica's history and pass highly opinionated, perhaps even highly contentious, commentary on that history. First and foremost, I see his very distinctive use of nails as a powerful, yet surprisingly open-ended symbolism: nails as a symbol of suffering and pain and violence on the one hand; nails as a symbol of creativity, construction, production on the other hand. The nails in his work in *Curator's Eye II* remind me in particular of enslaved people, packed into the holds and decks of slave ships. This is profound work by an artist clearly committed to engaging with history for the good of himself, and others living at the present time.

Charles Campbell's work was also evocative of the slave trade. This artist manages to turn something particularly traumatic, murderous and brutal into art works that are almost beautiful. His very beautiful, very moving, very simple paintings of migratory flocks of birds in flight are amongst my favourite works by Campbell in this exhibition. Migration (or multiple processes of migration) lies at the heart of African diaspora sensibilities and this artist captures that sense of importance incredibly well.

And you used some older work by Christopher Clare.

I saw a reproduction of a painting by Christopher Clare some years ago. It was a re-presentation of the iconic image of the slave ship, crammed with its human cargo, like so many sardines in a tin. I was immediately struck by Clare's painting. It had an almost haunting beauty, despite the horror of what was being depicted. Christopher Clare was one of the first Jamaican artists that I wanted to see when I began my research into this exhibition earlier this year. I was delighted when the opportunity presented itself to include in *Curator's Eye II* one of his 'slave ship' paintings. This one, a sombre yet majestic work in four sections, again re-presented the slave ship. This time, the wretched inhabitants of the slave ship were transformed into a dignified shoal of humanity: liberated souls swimming with purpose and grace. The piece speaks of the seas as a merciful receiver of tormented people, choosing the taking of their own lives by drowning over the relentless horrors of the slave ship.

Whenever I walked past Khepera Hatshepwa's installation I felt this intense, silent, brooding energy.

Khepera's work was clearly – to me at least – about the need for and the importance of building sustainable African-Caribbean family units: units that are in turn nurtured and sustained by a supportive community. The work speaks of family units, and individuals within these families needing to be acknowledged and supported and kept safe from harm. With so many people living broken, fractious and dysfunctional lives, progressive economic, political, social and cultural agendas need to be accompanied by healing processes that seek to bring an almost medicinal good to black people. Khepera's work spoke to me about these ideas.

How did you choose the pieces by Omari Ra?

I love oversized, cinematic images and I especially liked the blackness of the portraits. Even in Jamaica, an overwhelmingly black country, this stood out. In these portraits the people were wearing hats and one of them was holding what might be a rifle. I asked the artist if it was a reference to cowboys and he said 'Maybe.' Omari Ra's not didactic. He never says, 'This is what the work is about.' I think these images of his are, in their own ways, quite confrontational. I am particularly intrigued by what the black image means in Jamaica, because in the USA and the UK it comes with a great deal of baggage. If you see the black image in advertising or art, you seldom have the option of reading it in a race-neutral way. We tend to read it in a very different way to an image of a white person. Generally, I am very interested in the ways in which the black image might be read, here in Jamaica. Might the black image be read in ways that are race-specific? Or race-neutral? Or both, perhaps? I see Omari Ra's work as confronting and visualising ideas of blackness. These are ideas that some people might find uncomfortable.

I find Ebony Patterson similarly confrontational. She had these large images of naked black women in the exhibition. They definitely evoke nakedness rather than nudity. In many ways they are the antithesis of the conventional woman as depicted in advertising, the media, etcetera. Ebony's work in some ways might amount to a declaration of identity that flies in the face of proscribed and choking notions of femininity. The bodies in Ebony's work are deviant, naked, raw, and unvarnished, and we simply cannot ignore these monumental, imposing bodies.

I could be wrong, of course, but it seems to me that to be black in Jamaica is not – in and of itself – entirely seen as beautiful or respectable. The image that Jamaica projects, the celebration of the 'browning', Jamaica's colour-coding (as I would call it), all these things imply that hybridity makes beautiful. This in turn implies that what is perceived as being 'undiluted' African is in some ways less 'beautiful'. It seems to me that there is great beauty in the figures in Ebony's work. Not a conventional notion of beauty and perhaps not a mainstream Jamaican notion of beauty, but beauty nonetheless.

How did Chris Irons fit into the theme?

I saw the two dogs as a metaphor of the JLP [Jamaica Labour Party] and PNP [People's National Party]: One body with two heads. For such a relatively young country, one thing that continually dismays me is the two-party system in Jamaica. They became entrenched so rapidly. I listen to the radio, read the newspapers, and the hegemony of the JLP and PNP is never, ever questioned. In a democracy the people deserve more than a choice between Tweedle-dee and Tweedle-dum.

In the USA and UK, it is the same, of course. You can either vote Republican or Democrat, Conservative or Labour, but the political tribalism is not such a problem. In Jamaica it is a problem and has caused the shedding of so much blood. I see the Chris Irons piece as symbolising a dysfunctional system at war with itself, with ordinary people, poor people as the victims of this constant political warfare.

What about the work of Andrae Green?

The strange thing is I've always found when I'm in Jamaica that Cuba and Haiti might as well be somewhere near Australia, even though they are near neighbours. Jamaica is isolated insofar as English being its dominant language. It is surrounded by Cuba, Mexico, and Haiti and yet there are varying language barriers, with Spanish and French/Creole being the dominant languages of these other countries, respectively. To what extent do language barriers create cultural barriers? Andrae's work is all about Haiti. The painting in the exhibition explores a dialogue between a man in Jamaica and what is happening in a neighbouring country. I like this work because it extends the pan-Caribbean dialogue.

Is this why you chose the work of Remond Mangoensemito?

Remond is from Suriname but he studied at Edna Manley College. His painting is of a huge red rooster and I have always found the rooster very evocative of Caribbean culture. It makes me think of vodou, ritual sacrifice and mythology.

One thing that struck a lot of people about this exhibition was how young many of the artists are.

Yes, many of them are young. But it was never intended to be like this; that is, I didn't have a policy of picking younger artists. I picked them because they were new artists to me. I'd not seen their work before. But some are not new or emerging: Carol Crichton is a good example. Her work fits perfectly into the theme of the exhibition and her concerns resonate with those of the other artists: her focus on geography – physical, historical and psychological; her exploration of land, *The Land,* as she sees it. So, the answer is a lot are young, but I didn't exclude anybody on the basis of age.

Some of Carol's work was as close as it comes to the more mainstream interest in Jamaican landscape painting. Did you consider this tradition to be of importance to the theme of the show?

Yes, because questions about 'land' and 'landscape' are in my view at the heart of cultural and national identity. Access to land is obviously a highly political (or highly politicised) issue, especially in a country such as Jamaica. And ideas of 'landscape' are eternally fascinating because landscape is always such a constructed commodity. I think Carol's work subtly unpicks and reconfigures a sense of the Jamaican landscape.

Oneika Russell is a very interesting young artist who explores different materials and technologies.

Yes, one of her works in the exhibition was a series of pieces that explored Manet's painting *Olympia*. This is a very famous French painting of a young, naked prostitute lying on a bed. But Oneika took a long look at the black servant woman in the painting who is almost always ignored by many people. Even art historians have ignored the black woman in writing about *Olympia*. She is mainly mentioned as being some kind of compositional colour balance to the white prostitute! There is hardly ever any mention of her and her own personhood. Oneika gave full life and sustenance to this woman and explored all aspects of her appearance. So in a general sense Oneika explored the role of the black woman and her invisibility. I think there is a link with Ebony Patterson in that sense. They both seem to give a platform and a voice to black women.

Was there also a link with Oya Tyehimba?

Oya's work in the exhibition related to a specific moment in Australian aboriginal history: the clearing of Tasmania of its native people. This reference to Tasmania reached far beyond the black diaspora; it exists as a symbol of white persecution; it exists as a symbol of resistance and defiance. What fascinates me is that the artist reaches into history and pulls this woman out of time and gives her a modern-day resonance.

Can you tell us why you chose the Zawdie Reece painting?

Well, Zawdie is something of a mystery to me. In fact, I never actually met him! But the work is a strong exploration of self. I find the concept of the 'self-portrait' to be fascinating. And given the history of Jamaica it has added poignancy. To confront one's physical nature is a powerful thing, but in the Jamaican context you are confronting so many things, not just weight or gender, but also slavery. What different factors have gone into creating your physical being: Africa, the Middle Passage, a plantation owner, a sailor, a member of the British army who was stationed here. It is never really addressed but it is always there, and in a way that the sugar-coated gloss of 'Out of Many, One People' does not really address. To confront one's self is always a profound act in Jamaica.

From what you have said, many of the works in the show were very serious and strongly evoked the painful history of Jamaica, as well as the present; do you feel that it lacked some of the humour and playfulness of the way Jamaican artists deal with their lives?

Absolutely not. I can't see how anyone can suggest that the show might have lacked humour or playfulness. We only have to look at the work of artists such as Keisha Costello and Oneika Russell to see an abundance of humour. Elements of Carol Crichton's work also resonate with subtle but distinct humour. Of course, if people insisted on seeing the exhibition as a grim and cheerless selection, that's their choice. But I certainly didn't see the exhibition in those sorts of terms. I saw it as being, in parts, very consistent with the humour and playfulness of the way Jamaican artists deal with their lives and their environment.

What parallels, if any, do you see between the contemporary art scene and contemporary society in Jamaica?
I'm not sure that we can speak of genuine parallels between the contemporary art scene and contemporary society in Jamaica. I think elements of contemporary society in Jamaica are in some ways deeply dysfunctional, as are, in my view, elements of society in countries such as the UK and the USA and elsewhere in the world. At the same time of course, Jamaica is a confident and robust country, very much part of the modern and contemporary world. But its art scene pretty much functions in a sort of parallel universe, so evidence of significant interplay between 'visual art' and 'society' is hard to convincingly pin down. However, in curating this exhibition I was keen to explore some of the ways in which artists in Jamaica offered unflinching or candid commentary on Jamaican society and history.

Carolyn Cooper [guest speaker at the opening] took issue with your statement that it was impossible to talk of Jamaican art, in the sense of it being a national school, and this reminded me of something Stuart Hall has said: that the moment when everything can be defined in terms of territorially bounded Jamaica is finished because globalisation has finished it. Is that something you would agree with?
I think that's a very interesting idea. In response to Carolyn's insistence that there ought indeed to be something particularly or peculiarly 'Jamaican' about the Jamaican art scene, the question then has to be, 'What might those things be?' For the life of me I can't identify or even locate them. Non-Jamaicans (if I can use that term – that is, people born elsewhere in the world, but who have migrated to Jamaica) have had a commanding influence on the notion of 'Jamaican art.' Jamaican literature, music or dance on the other hand, always strike me as resonating with pronounced 'indigeneity', or very strong African or Caribbean influences. In areas of such as literature, music or dance, it's not difficult, in my view, to identify specific strands of Jamaicanness. But I think the world of the visual arts is an altogether different prospect.

What would you say about the state of contemporary art in Jamaica?
I'd say that generally, the state of contemporary art in Jamaica is healthy. And I think that opportunities such as 'Curator's Eye' are good because they offer the possibility of different perspectives and different artists having a profile. In undertaking my research last summer, I constantly came across artists expressing the sentiment,

the impression, that the Jamaican art scene is dominated by a limited and privileged number of practitioners. This may or may not actually be true, but it's a formidable impression. In theory, exhibitions such as *Curator's Eye II* offer the prospect of a wider or a different selection of artists to have their work seen.

How did this exhibition fit in with your interests as an art historian and a curator generally?

The exhibition fitted in very well. In my ongoing curatorial work, I'm keen to work with artists I feel have not had, or are not getting, the exposure they deserve. I deliberately sought to bring this principle to *Curator's Eye II*. It is, of course, for others to judge the degree to which I may have achieved this.

How easy was it for you as a British-based curator to curate an exhibition in Jamaica?

I think that any experienced curator with some knowledge of art in Jamaica would, whilst respecting the challenges, be up to the task. I think one of the biggest challenges I faced was seeking out the work of artists whose names and practice were, by and large, unfamiliar to me. I'd made a number of trips to Jamaica over the years, plus of course I'd read the art books and seen some of the catalogues. But I think for the casual observer, getting beyond the familiar names of Jamaica's art scene can be quite a challenge. In this regard, being able to catch the Edna Manley College [of the Visual and Performing Arts] painting degree show was a great help. That's where I came across artists such as Shosana Fagan and Tricia Gordon-Johnston, whose work was new to me. Whilst I have enormous respect for all those artists who have established names and reputations for themselves in Jamaica, I wanted to curate something new, something different, at least in terms of my own grasp of art in Jamaica. That lead me to a distinctly younger group of practitioners, though it did of course also lead me to Carol Crichton. Jamaica can be a challenging environment, though that possibly applies to residents and visitors alike. Having a familiarity with how things are in Jamaica was a great help to me in working on the exhibition. If my very first visit to the island had been to work on *Curator's Eye II*, I think I'd have had greater challenges.

Did you face any significant cultural challenges?

Having been to Jamaica a number of times before, including several periods of teaching at Edna Manley College, I pretty much knew what to expect in Jamaica. Between 1993 and 2002 I made seven visits, so I really don't think I faced any unexpected cultural challenges, as you've termed them. I think by its nature the art world can be a very peculiar sort of thing. That goes for elsewhere in the world as much as it goes for Jamaica. Understanding and navigating such peculiarities will, in my view, always be the main challenge facing a visiting curator.

Who or what has been your greatest influence?

I'm not sure that I have a 'greatest' influence, but as a student, some twenty-five years ago, I was profoundly influenced by the work of an artist and writer named Rasheed Araeen. In his own way, he gave me a blueprint for how an artist could make strategic interventions, how an artist could be an activist, and how an artist could challenge accepted notions of art history. He was an enormous influence on me.

Do you have any advice for aspiring Caribbean curators?

I think opportunities for aspiring Caribbean curators are few and far between. Realistically, it's not possible for an independent curator to sustain his or her practice (let alone, a reasonable level of income) working only in a Caribbean country. My advice would be to seek curatorial training and gallery experience outside of the region. That will put aspiring curators in a commanding position to make interventions back in their respective countries.

'Art and Society', Jonathan Greenland interview with Eddie Chambers, was first published in *Jamaica Journal*, Kingston, Jamaica, Vol. 30, Nos. 1–2, December 2006: 30–37. It is reproduced here with the kind permission of the Institute of Jamaica.

SECTION FIVE

Criticize

Chapter 35
Section Five Introduction

'I'm fed up, 'cause all you wanna do is criticize.' So sang Alexander O'Neal on 'Criticize' a celebrated track from *Hearsay*, his era-defining, hugely popular album of 1987. While the section features several pieces of art criticism, it takes its name from the longest text in the section, 'Criticize: Press Responses to *Black Art an' done* and *The Pan-Afrikan Connection* exhibitions.' These exhibitions were organized in the early 1980s by a small group of Black art students and young artists, all of whom had West Midlands connections. Mainstream reviews of Black artists' exhibitions, taking place across the span of several decades, not infrequently (though perhaps inadvertently) revealed pathologies of race that often made such reviews difficult reading. My PhD, awarded by Goldsmiths College, University of London, in 1998 had looked at *Black Visual Arts Activity in England 1981–1986: Press and Public Responses*, and had sought to reflect on said pathologies, where they revealed themselves in exhibition reviews, a number of which were decidedly clumsy in their use of language. Though the doctoral project drew a line under itself in 1986[1], the reviews attracted by *The Other Story*, in 1989, are a veritable treasure trove of reading race through art criticism. O'Neal may have been exasperatedly singing about the antics of someone within his social circle, a potential or an ex-lover perhaps, criticizing his friends, his ideals, his lifestyle, but as grateful as artists can be for press attention, they have also, on occasion, found themselves 'fed up' with certain art criticism. This section contains the last of six new texts, 'Criticize.' As with my text on Black artists and the Greater London Council, in the previous section, much of the research for 'Criticize' was undertaken for my PhD.

Notes

1 I argued in my doctoral project that 1986 marked the beginning of the end of a brief period of attention to Black artists from a small number of mainstream galleries. *From Two Worlds*, the Whitechapel Art Gallery's eclectic bringing together of a number of artists, using assorted criteria of profile and ethnicity, signalled that Black artists' Warhol-esque fifteen minutes of fame were about to be up.

Chapter 36

Contemporary Art or Contemporary African Art?: The Inevitable Death of the Latter

Over the course of the last century – from its beginning through to its end – we witnessed what I would call the inevitable death of contemporary African art. Africa had extensive contact with much of the world for centuries before the arrival of the European powers, but these few notes will attempt to argue that the internationalisation of much of the African continent has created and resulted in a situation in which the very notion of contemporary African art must, I believe, be called into question.

At the beginning of the 20th century, African art was straightforward enough. What I mean of course is that constructed ideas of what constituted African art were simple, linear and easily understood. Popularly regarded (within the culture of European/white imperialism) as the Dark Continent, Africa was a largely self-referencing and geographically self-contained entity. Beyond those captured during the centuries of the Atlantic and the Arab slave trades, relatively few African people travelled or ventured beyond the boundaries of the continent. It was all so simple. African people lived in Africa and African art was stuff made, up to the beginning of the last century, in the sub-Saharan part of the continent by black-skinned makers whose personal identities were not a primary factor in making the objects. The objects in turn were produced for a variety of rituals and practices that the West has traditionally regarded as not much more than superstitious mumbo-jumbo.

In the days of yore, writings about what I would here describe as 'ye olde worlde African art' was the preserve of older white men. I make mention of 'old school' African art in an attempt to distinguish that entity from its precocious relative (so-called 'contemporary' African art) which is the subject of this article. The last time we [in the UK] saw a spirited defence of this antiquated approach to African art was 1995's *Africa: Art of a Continent* presented by the Royal Academy. The exhibition was a culturally neat and tidy summary of Europe's classic construction of African art. Historical, anonymous, masks, carvings, bronze casts. Primarily sculptural forms that centred on spirituality, ritual and the cycle of live and death. Those deemed to be experts or authorities on Africa art from way back when were as clearly and as formidably identifiable as the art itself. The self-proclaimed experts were the ethnographers, the anthropologists, the collectors, the museum curators and the academics. To a man, they tended to be, er, men. As in white, older and alternately pompous or paternalistic towards their subject matter. Hence we had a situation in which the acknowledged experts in the field of African art were not even African and not even Black.

Though these experts still tend not to be African or Black, over the course of the past twenty or thirty years, assorted writers and researchers have, with varying degrees of success, made attempts to chart the development of a modern and contemporary African art that struggles to gravitate away from constraining and antiquated notions of African art. In this regard, a pioneering study was Ulli Beier's *Contemporary Art in Africa* published in 1968. A few years later, in 1973 came Marshall W. Hunt's *African Art: The Years Since 1920*. We can think of Kojo Fosu's *20th Century Art of Africa* published in Nigeria in 1986. We can also think of the exhibition catalogues *Africa Now* and *Africa Explores* (both 1991) and the Whitechapel (London) Art Gallery's *Seven Stories About Modern Art in Africa* – that particular exhibition being one of the centrepieces (alongside the previously mentioned *Africa: Art of a Continent* presented by the Royal Academy) of the UK's *africa* (*sic*) *95* programme. And there are more recent efforts such as André Magnin and Jaques Soulillou's *Contemporary Art of Africa* (1996). There are of course a number of other publications that could be mentioned.

What these assorted publications point to is the concerted attempt (as mentioned earlier) to chart the development of a contemporary African art that struggles for modernity and even postmodernity. But these books also indicate an equally concerted attempt to wrestle authority on African art away from old white men; an attempt to pluralise not only the language employed to discuss and describe African art, but also to pluralise the pool of aforementioned experts and authorities. Kojo Fosu ensured a place in history for himself by being one of the first African scholars to author a definitive work on the contemporary art of Africa. Individually and collectively, the authors of the other studies I've mentioned, such as André Magnin and Jaques Soulillou, have challenged the stranglehold that old white duffers such as William Fagg had on the subject of African art. In this endeavour, the likes of Beier, Fosu and Magnin have latterly been joined by Sidney Littlefield Kasfir.

A new book, written by Littlefield Kasfir attempts to go several stages further than earlier studies on contemporary African art. It does so by weaving a range of narratives that work to both identify and unravel the complexities of the contemporary 'African' artist and their practice. Littlefield Kasfir embarked on a wide-ranging and critical appraisal of preceding studies such as the ones I've mentioned, as well as 'drawing liberally upon them as sources'.

In her introduction, she states that 'What this book describes are the major transformations that occurred within African artistic practice as a result of the colonial incursion, with an emphasis on the period beginning in the 1950s with the transition from late colonialism to political statehood'. We can glean some notion of the complexities of the arguments and debates that Littlefield Kasfir orders within her book by looking at the sub-headings within her introduction: *Contemporary or modern? The modern and the colonial, The postcolonial and the postmodern* and finally *The new art map of the continent*. In the words of the preface, 'each chapter attempts to deal with a major issue surrounding the history of contemporary African art since the 1950s'.

But in attempting to construct and describe a broader artistic geography, Littlefield Kasfir, perhaps unwittingly, irreversibly unravels the entire edifice of 'contemporary African art'. What becomes apparent in reading this book is that contemporary African art has none of the clear-cut terms of reference that throughout much of the last century were used to describe 'ye olde worlde African art.' As problematic as old school terms of reference for African art might be, there are (for those of us intent on describing ourselves as African) nevertheless many things which are comforting and reassuring within exhibitions such as 'Africa: Art of a Continent'. But in looking critically at books such as this by Littlefield Kasfir, those of us looking for reference points of culture, history and identity to sustain our own senses of being African can find little or nothing with which we can be meaningfully sustained. Let me explain. Few of the artists described in this book are constrained by geographical borders. So if African art in its contemporary framing is not located by geography, how then is it possible for us to call it by its popular name of contemporary African art? What the likes of Littlefield Kasfir and Magnin make clear is that many practitioners calling themselves African artists (or being happy to be identified as such) live outside of the continent. Can one be an African artist and live outside of the continent? Contemporary African art has become an assortment of international commodities, no less than many of the artists discussed in this book – who live and work in countries/continents other than the ones in which they were born.

In what senses can we refer to contemporary African art? Certainly not on the basis of skin-colour. To use skin-colour as any definitive criterion would mean to exclude those white artists from South Africa. It's certainly true that very few other white/European artists born/living/working within the African continent would particularly wish to be described as 'African artists'. But I'm not sure that the same could be said of white artists from South Africa. After all, part of the historical and political intransigence of white South Africa has been its determination to be seen as having an indigenous and indelible presence within the southern part of the continent. Within her book, Littlefield Kasfir includes and discusses white South African artists such as William Kentridge, so if we insist on suggesting that African art can only be made by black-skinned Africans, then we are showing the middle finger to white South Africa and the William Kentridges of that country.

Again, in what senses can we refer to contemporary African art? Certainly not on the basis of country of birth. Littlefield Kasfir's discussions include artists who have long since ceased to live and work permanently within any African country (choosing instead to live/work in Western Europe or the United States). One of the principal enigmas of this unravelling is the means by which time and again Littlefield Kasfir is able to designate London-born Yinka Shonibare as a 'Yoruba artist', whilst simultaneously ignoring in their entirety those such as London-based (East) Africa-born Asian artists such as Shaheen Merali (Tanzania) and Zarina Bhimji (Uganda). The existence of Africa-born Asian artists such as Merali is a golden opportunity for staid and restrictive notions – 'traditional' 'modern' and 'postmodern' – of African art to be turned on their heads. Yet the African origins of certain 'Asian' artists are deemed insufficient by the likes of Littlefield Kasfir to draw them into the sphere of African art.

Within these contexts it becomes almost a nonsense to speak of contemporary African art as any sort of recognisable entity – however fluid and complex such an entity may be. On reading this book the inescapable conclusion is that there is no such thing as contemporary African art – only contemporary artists with an assortment of links to the continent – some strong, some tenuous. Put simply, many African artists are too well-travelled for the entire edifice of contemporary African art to be prescribed in any way whatsoever – being that by geography or ultimately slippery notions of African identity. And if we can accept that notions of African art cannot be prescribed or imposed, then we may as well accept that the concept of African art is too vague, slippery or elusive to have any real meaning. Can one be African, not having been born within the continent? Can one be African simply because one happens to live within the continent? Can national or continental identity be passed on irrespective of where one lives or is born?

Littlefield Kasfir never faces up to the contradictions in her construction of contemporary African art. Nor does she face up to the difficulties of these types of questions. Even so, hers is a useful book, in which she shows herself unwilling to shirk at least a few vexatious questions. For example, she convincingly summarises the curious position of Black South African artists within their own country; a country which 'positions [them] there in ways that are reminiscent of African-American, Native American and Hispanic artists in the United States – enclaved groups defined primarily by race or ethnicity in relation to art world institutions which are still overwhelmingly white.' And speaking of South Africa's white artists, critics, curators and academics, Littlefield Kasfir writes that 'they cannot choose to ignore the conditions of their privilege.' Unless I'm very much mistaken, this is precisely what they have done. It would have been good if Littlefield Kasfir had taken this motley crew to task.

We need to resist the idea that there is such a thing as contemporary African art. Otherwise we give tacit approval to backward notions that locate identity and culture as fixed, permanent and inflexible entities. As I suggested earlier, in reading this book the inescapable conclusion is that there is no such thing as contemporary African art – only contemporary artists with an assortment of links to the continent. So-called African artists themselves need to work out if clinging to the banner of African art is anything more than a flimsy means by which their work can be exhibited, collected or written about by people who insist on seeing identity, culture and the world in fixed, self-referencing, linear terms.

'Contemporary Art or Contemporary African Art?: The Inevitable Death of the Latter' was first published in *Crossroads: Africa in the Twilight – essays on African art and the African situation*, published by the Pan-African Circle of Artists/ National Gallery of Art, Nigeria, 2000.

Chapter 37

Richard Hylton, *The Nature of the Beast: Cultural Diversity and the Visual Arts Sector: A Study of Policies, Initiatives and Attitudes 1976–2006*, Afterword

Reading *The Nature of the Beast* is indeed a dispiriting experience. With pronounced attention to detail, Richard Hylton has produced an invaluable, engaging and highly readable history that walks us through three decades of muddled institutional thinking about cultural diversity and the initiatives such thinking has spawned. What becomes clear, with each paragraph, with each chapter, of this study is that each 'new' initiative has, over the years, failed to learn from the mistakes and failures of those that had preceded it. It's as if, for the Arts Council, when it comes to 'ethnic' art, 'ethnic minority' art, 'minority ethnic' art, 'culturally diverse' arts et cetera et cetera., each new initiative is created in year zero. Hylton's focused, yet dispassionate and disinterested (as in unbiased by personal interest or advantage; not influenced by selfish motives) study tells an engrossing tale of muddle, duplicity, incompetence, opportunism and fudge. And as Hylton himself suggests, one possibly unforeseen consequence of his thoroughness is that it gives initiatives such as decibel and all of its weird and wonderful predecessors, a sense of coherence and strategy that in reality is wholly absent.

London has always had the highest concentration of Black artists in the country. Simultaneously, however, it's always been (with sporadic and problematic exception) the city in which Black artists have had the most derisory profile. In thirty years, no amount of institutional tinkering has changed that. There can be no greater evidence of the wholesale failure of 'diversity' initiatives within the visual arts than this. Unfortunately, it can then be expected, as Hylton predicts, that the establishment of the inIVA/Autograph Rivington Place venture will work to solidify (rather than challenge) Black artists' exclusion from London's principal galleries.

Hylton's study points out to us, or reminds us, of the severe limits of half-hearted institutional efforts to diversify the art world. The high point, thus far, in the collective fortunes of Britain's Black artists seems to have been the relatively intense level of activity generated in the 1980s. Yet, the bulk of this activity took place outside of any of the Arts Council's numerous initiatives on cultural diversity. In this instance, we can be sure that bottom up has been way more effective than top down.

In 2006, the whole sorry and miserable history that Hylton outlines must surely, for the honest reader, consign 'cultural diversity' in the visual arts to the dustbin. Substantial, stand-alone exhibitions of individual Black artists' work are now more of a rarity than they have been for many a year. This, as Hylton points out, is the lasting legacy of a funding system that is unable or unwilling to effectively deal with discriminatory practices within the institutions it funds. It chooses, instead, to set up largely ineffectual parallel structures that are fixated on the notion of 'cultural difference'. In addition, as Hylton has pointed out, the collapse of a significant number of Arts Council-sponsored/funded capital projects, plus the shaky financial and artistic health of many, many others should give us cause to doubt the effectiveness, viability and wisdom of 'cultural diversity' initiatives championed and peddled by this dictatorial funding body.

Thus far, would-be students of the recent history of Black artists in Britain have only had access to modest or inadequate publications. It may not have been his intention, but Hylton has, inadvertently perhaps, produced the most authoritative modern history of Black artists' activity in Britain. In this regard, we have much to thank him for.

Ironically, given that it is central government that has mostly been responsible for imposing its ideas of multiculturalism and cultural diversity, we may yet be approaching a time when this same government is responsible for the compulsory dismantling of these same agendas. Very recently, the government seems to have set its face against 'multiculturalism'. Having previously been happy to promote and impose its own assorted forms of it, ministers have now, apparently, judged that the time is right (for reasons of political expediency and as a sop to the mob) to attack 'multiculturalism' and to call for its reining in. It will be fascinating, over the course of the coming years, to see if this mood change will signal the end the Arts Council's piecemeal obsession with cultural diversity.

Afterword by Eddie Chambers for Richard Hylton's book, *The Nature of the Beast: Cultural Diversity and the Visual Arts Sector: A Study of Policies, Initiatives and Attitudes 1976–2006*, Institute of Contemporary Interdisciplinary Arts, Bath, 2007: 166–7.

Chapter 38
Black is a Color: (A History of African American Art): Book Review

Black is a Color claims to be 'both a historical study and a critical analysis [that] paints a picture of an America marked by its slave past, in which African American contemporary artists have been able to build a remarkable and engaged body of work to challenge the cultural and political consequences of racial discrimination'. Recently issued by the French publisher Dis Voir this book takes its place alongside a fairly crowded bookshelf of introductory texts on the history of African American art. Beginning with James Porter's pioneering study *Modern Negro Art*, first published in 1943 and reprinted several times since, through to the recent Thames & Hudson 'World of Art' offering, *Black Art: A Cultural History*, first published in 1997, reissued in 2002 and written by Richard J Powell, the student of African American art has no shortage of historical overviews to choose from. It is in many ways a brave scholar who seeks to bring something new and original to the study of the discipline, in terms of broad introductions.

And yet Elvan Zabunyan, the author of this book, does indeed manage to write something fresh, something different. Rather than attempting a plodding, chronological assessment, Zabunyan offers a livelier, more animated interpretation of what she sees as some of the key characteristics and tensions of African American visual art practice of the 20th century. It is clear that she seeks to set her study apart from more generalised survey texts when she writes 'Other general studies published at the end of the 1970s and in the 1980s offered an exhaustive interpretation of African American art in a descriptive manner. But none of them analysed the transformation of Black practices parallel to those of White practices during the thirty years (1970–2000) when, with no distinction in color, artists participated in a true revolution of visual forms.' Zabunyan uses as her vehicle, questions and matters centring on perceived, received and projected identities. So the ways in which African Americans have been treated within the cultural and the political arena take their place, within this book, alongside debates about how black artists in the US have fashioned a range of practices that are reflective of their history, identity and status.

Whilst African American artists have a history that spans several centuries, it was arguably the 20th century that saw the production of some of their most dynamic work. Similarly, it was the 20th century that witnessed, and gave rise to some of the most considered debates about what it meant to be an African American and an African American artist. To this end, *Black Is a Color* very much focuses on African American artistic developments over much of the past eighty years or so, but Zabunyan is at all times keen not to decontextualize the African American artist. So rather than producing yet another study that looks at their practice in isolation, she consistently relates the work of these artists to both the racism and indifference of wider society, as well as to artistic and intellectual developments within American and international art practice. Zabunyan has strong words to say about the treatment of African American artists by the general body of art historians and academics. She flatly declares 'The non-existence of Black art in the general history of American art is linked to the peripheral position of minorities' artistic practices in western culture.'

The book begins with a series of interlinked discussions about the two monumental events that bookend African American artistic and cultural practice during the course of the 20th century, and how black America moved from the first of these seismic events to the other. 'From the Harlem Renaissance to the Civil Rights Movement: the transformation from Negro to Black' introduces us to (or reminds us of) the principal characters, movements and ideas that lead to the creation of such a large body of fascinating art practice. So Zabunyan begins with a discussion of Alain Locke, who in 1925 edited *The New Negro*, the publication that rapidly came to symbolise the Harlem Renaissance. We go on to read about the Harmon Foundation, WEB Du Bois, Zora Neale Hurston, Langston Hughes and the other characters whose work defined the cultural aspirations of a nation within a nation. As the century progresses Zabunyan discusses the importance of Romare Bearden and his attempts to create and champion aesthetics and cultural sensibilities that addressed the mid to late 20th-century African American condition.

Zabunyan's subsequent chapter, 'A Black Consciousness' offers a very useful overview of various attempts, within America and beyond, to fashion cultural responses that had ideas of black resistance at their core. To this end, she provides very useful summaries of Négritude and the Black Art(s) Movement. These summaries involve tackling different questions about the contradictions that lie at the heart of much African American cultural positioning. If racial identity is an accident of birth, what place then for race-based cultural manifestos? Should black artists fashion their art and cultural practice in response to, or reaction against, racism and white supremacy? And what place for those black artists who are determined not to let racial matters unduly influence (in their view) their practice? Zabunyan takes us through the cultural and political fortunes of black America, in its 20th-century quest to tackle, navigate and respond to these questions.

Rather than offering a dispassionate chronology of the major African American artists of the 20th century, Zabunyan chooses instead to look at the specifics of a handful of artists that she feels have a particular relevance to debates about identity and the ways in which they have taken to task American cultural hegemony. So we read detailed, involved overviews of the practice of artists such as David Hammons, Adrian Piper, Carrie Mae Weems and Renée Green. These chapters are particularly useful as they provide a much-needed supplement to the reductive ways in which these artists' work is often discussed by contemporary art critics. Artists such as Piper and Hammons distinguished themselves by consistently stepping outside the boundaries of accepted art practice. Yet in doing so, they have it seems rarely been discussed as anything other than, or more than, late 20th-century African American artists. Within the space available (or the space she gives herself) Zabunyan attempts to put the work of these artists into wider contexts, as well as discussing its relationship to the dominant racial, cultural and political hegemony.

The book's biggest flaws relate to the translation from its original French, into English. Much of the translating is poor, leading to many paragraphs being difficult to read and digest. Page after page of *Black Is a Color* is afflicted by this translating, leading to numerous sentences that either make little or no sense, or require some additional translating by the reader. For example, in the preface the writer thanks Adrian Piper 'the first artist I met in 1993'. Elsewhere, we read, '[David] Hammons was aware of his identity from very early on'. The book's unreadable sentences include the concluding sentiment that 'To build a history of African American visual arts is to allow the possibility to think the aesthetic and political reality off a culture where effective fragmentation is not always a dispersion but also a consideration.' And there's plenty more where that came from.

Despite these flaws, *Black Is a Color* is for the most part a welcome addition to our knowledge of African American artists and the sophistication of our understanding of their practice. Its approach sets a standard that other art historians would do well to take note of, and to learn from.

This review of Elvan Zabunyan, *Black is a Color: (A History of African American Art)*, published by Dis Voir, 2005, was first published in *Art Monthly,* London, Number 294, March 2006: 36–37.

Chapter 39

Black My Story, (Museum De Paviljoens, Netherlands, 2003): Book Review

Black My Story has been published as an accompanying volume to an exhibition of the same name that recently took place at the Museum De Paviljoens, Almere in the Netherlands. The exhibition featured the work of five artists with not much in common, save for the relatively unremarkable fact that they were all born in countries other than the ones in which they currently live and work. Jimmy Durham, Remy Jungerman, Samson Kambalu, Shirana Shahbazi and Chikako Watanabe were brought together by the apparently eclectic whim of the exhibition's curator, Macha Roesink.

The book comprises potted histories and biographical sketches of each of the artists, embellished with illustrations of their work and family-album type photographs. The book's press release states that the five authors, Cecilia Fajardo Hill, Bert Steevensz, Steve Chimombo, Tirdad Zolghadr and Nov Amenororiu respectively 'portray their engaging and personal visions on the life and work of the artists'. These contributions are book-ended by an introductory essay by Christopher Joon-Hai Lee and a postscript by Roesink. Lee summarises the exhibition as 'a momentary cultural site, global in content but also local, even individual, in meaning. It halts globalisation as not a homogenizing process, but as a process of deterritorialisation – where individuals move and re-imagine themselves and in the process further diversify how one sees and understands the world. Such imagery practices are particularly significant in a global political climate where stereotypes tend to carry more social value and meaning than individuality.' Earlier, Lee had spoken of the exhibition as having a need to 'emphasise the personal over the conventional, the individual perspective over that of the stereotype'.

This is alarming stuff. Not because these ideas are new or challenging, but because these ideas have been knocking about for God knows how many years. The international-mega exhibition has for many years privileged those artists who have a compulsive habit of flying hither and yon at the drop of a hat. To the point of being mundane, the language of deterritorialisation and of individuals simultaneously embodying multiple identities has long since become staple curatorial fodder. We might even suggest that in the current cultural/artistic climate, if an artist cannot demonstrate some hither and yon credentials or impulses, then he or she had better get used to being ignored by curators mesmerised by ultimately fatuous talk of deterritorialisation. Save for the ethnographic/anthropological exhibition, those artists who are unable/unwilling to traverse the globe are rendered significantly less visible and less attractive to the curator's wandering eye.

None of the artists in *Black My Story* are symbolic of the raggedy arsed refugee fleeing persecution or the 'economic migrant' seeking a better life. Instead, (at a time when most people in the West would still equate going abroad with going on holiday) the exhibition privileges those artists who are ascribed some sort of specialness due to the fact that they no longer live in the countries they were born in and can apparently travel the globe at will. But that in itself hardly makes someone remarkable or unusual or deserving of attention as an artist or as a person. Given the phenomenal patterns of migration that the world has seen in the 20th century, there can scarcely be a country that has not witnessed nor played host to multiple types of migration. I wonder if the likes of Lee and Roesink have only just caught up with this?

Lee's introductory notes make significant mention of the September 11 attacks. But such references – irrespective of what they actually amount to – have long since become wearisome, specious and, in many instances, even comical. *Private Eye* regularly runs a column featuring the best/worst of these references. My recent favourite was the straight-faced claim by the communications director of a chain of cheap American eateries that 'the emotional and economic turmoil of 9/11 has prompted people to reconnect with friends and family through casual dining'. With September 11 being up for grabs by all and sundry, the wisest amongst us would do well to avoid referencing it at all – especially in the mock-worthy tones that Lee uses.

For the most part though, *Black My Story* is a worthwhile project if for no other reason than it allows us the opportunity to visit (or revisit) the practice of a number of very interesting artists. I was gratified to learn a little of the history of contemporary art in Malawi, that sliver of a country towards southern Africa. Chimombo's profile on Kambalu made fascinating reading. For example, a couple of years ago the artist made a celebrated piece of work called *Holy Balls* – 'fifteen soccer balls covered completely with pages torn from the Christian Bible. With this balls [*sic*] one could "exercise in order to exorcise"'. The biographical sketches on these artists are however, for the most part, supplied by writers with similar profiles and instincts. Only Amenororiu seems not to have been seduced by a frequent flyer programme.

Towards the end of her postscript, Roesink poses multiple questions, each one relating to the perceived identity/label of each of the artists. For example: 'Your father is Dutch and your mother is from Suriname or the other way around – how would you define yourself? What if you were born in Tehran but grew up in Germany since the age of ten and pursued your whole art education in Switzerland?' If you are serious about eschewing limiting and inadequate labels of national identity, one would presumably call oneself a world citizen, a citizen of the global community, or some such thing. The notion of the stateless world citizen (as in, the individual rejecting spurious and inappropriate labels of national identity) is not new. Important ideologies such as anarchism and Pan-Africanism were in a variety of ways committed to the process of redefining one's identity by refusing to accept the notion of national borders and boundaries. Marcus Garvey once declared the whole world to be his province. Roesink should know stuff like that. Furthermore, one wonders what planet she has been living on if she has only just woken up to the 20th century's remarkable patterns of migration and to the idea that an art exhibition such as hers can research 'the complexity of art, a person, nationality, religion or race and favour(s) multitude instead of a world based on dichotomy'.

The question that all this generates is this: what validity if any can be attached to work by artists for whom international travel and mobility define their very existence and ideology within the art arena? When reading the publication, the supplementary abiding question that *Black My Story* poses is, are the people linked with it being clever or too clever for their own good? The title *Black My Story* is credited to Kambalu, for a street work he undertook in Amsterdam in 2000. No mention is made anywhere of the much earlier use of the term by Ziggy Marley, for a song that he co-wrote with his brother Stephen for the 1989 Ziggy Marley and the Melody Makers record, *One Bright Day*. On the jacket of the book, the title of the publication is written twice, forming a cross, which in turn is replicated many times over to form a patterned motif. Symbolic of Malcolm, the X is of course the 'blackest' letter in the alphabet. And the book itself was launched on August 17, that (as the birthday of Marcus Garvey) being one of the blackest days of the year. Perhaps I'm reading too much into the packaging and launch date of the publication, but this is quite possibly, inevitable, as many people have fought for the right for black to be more than a (skin) colour and to mean something other than that which is bad or negative. For something to be called *Black My Story*, it's a bit rich for no-one linked to the project to at least mention in passing the efforts of these people and some of the ways in which these efforts have fed into or, indeed, contrasted with the notion of deterritorialism and of individuals simultaneously embodying multiple identities.

This review of *Black My Story*, (Museum De Paviljoens, Netherlands, 2003), was previously published titled 'MULTIPLE IDENTITIES Deterritorialism' in the 'Polemic' section of *Art Monthly*, London, Number 272, December 2003–January 2004: 41–42.

Chapter 40
Criticize: Press Responses to *Black Art an' done* and *The Pan-Afrikan Connection* Exhibitions

When the exhibition *Black Art an' done* took place at Wolverhampton Art Gallery in the spring of 1981, it happened to coincide, with uncanny prescience, with the era-defining riots that took place in Brixton that same month. There was perhaps a fortuitous symmetry between the posturing and much of the work of the five young Black males in the exhibition, and the cataclysmic events that took place in that district of South London that had, ever since the mid-twentieth century, come to be synonymous with the presence in Britain of Caribbean migrants and their children. The exhibition secured a relatively substantial amount of press coverage from a range of print media – local newspapers, through to a review in the national press (the *Guardian*). A range of weekly print media – such as *Caribbean Times*, *West Indian World*, *Jamaican Weekly Gleaner*, and the *Weekly Journal* – helped to define and sustain Caribbean immigrant communities. Several of these newspapers reviewed early exhibitions by these young Black artists when they took place in venues in London in 1982 and 1983, thereby adding another important dimension to Black Art's exposure and reception.

Traditionally, British press reviews of Black artists' exhibitions were themselves something of a rarity, as were of course the exhibitions themselves. Even so, press coverage of exhibitions such as *Black Art an' done* and *The Pan-Afrikan Connection* represented the most dramatic of shifts. Whereas, a 1978 review[1] of an exhibition of work by Jamaican-born painter Errol Lloyd was critiqued in reference to the European artists Henri Matisse, Salvador Dali and Paul Gauguin, by contrast, *Black Art an' done* was linked by several reviewers to such concerns and references as 'race relations', 'unemployment' and 'South Africa.' This was a dramatic new development, wholly in keeping with, and reflective of, Black Art itself.

Black Art an' done was reviewed for the *Guardian* by its then northern art critic, Irene McManus. She began by claiming that, 'their art is really just a collection of political posters – some good, some bad, some indifferent . . . It is all a bit impassioned and youthful and crude. And the written messages embellishing almost every picture are a bit oppressive.'[2] She proceeded to concede, 'What the hell – they need to be there.'[3] McManus established a relationship between sentiments in the exhibition's catalogue and the fractious manifestation around the West Midlands of what were, at the time, referred to as 'race relations'. 'But the way race relations are shaping up in cities like Coventry, you can't help feeling that these young West Indians are right to demand that Black art has to be "a tool to assist us in our struggle for liberation".'[4] Perhaps because so many of the artists were from Wolverhampton, and linked into sophisticated networks of education, church, and community, or perhaps because the exhibition struck such a chord with alienated constituencies, McManus made reference to the exhibition 'attracting an army of people who've never set foot in an art gallery before.' She likewise praised Wolverhampton Art Gallery itself, awarding it 'Full marks . . . for giving [the artists] a venue.'[5] McManus singled out for particular praise the 'furious' work of Keith Piper, and she referenced works by him of unbounded art historical significance, within the history of Black British artists' practice. Piper was the first British artist to resurrect the eighteenth-century plan of a slave ship. Like a number of Black-British artists would subsequently do, Piper found himself drawn to the infamous lithograph of a slave ship, the Brookes of Liverpool. The origins of these lithographs of slave ships and their contents date back to the abolitionist movements of the late eighteenth and early nineteenth centuries. The abolitionists had seized on this simple but effective graphic device as a means of driving home the horrors that had to be endured by captured Africans during the Middle Passage; the nightmarish journey by sea that took enslaved Africans from their homelands to slavery and death in the 'New World'.

However, these powerful lithographs would in time take on a significance that went way beyond the propaganda value of their day. The passage of time did little or nothing to diminish the memory of slavery on the collective and individual psyche of New World Africans and their descendants, in what we now commonly refer to as the African Diaspora. Indeed, a century and a half after the phased abolition of slavery by the British parliament, Keith Piper pointed to the ways in which plans of laden slave ships were, in early 1980s Britain, starting to become iconic shorthand graphic signifiers for the miserable, wretched legacy of slavery and the myriad ways in which that legacy spawned a thousand black liberation struggles. The use of the slave ship motif by Piper encapsulated and denoted much in the way of black history, particularly as lived by himself and the peoples to whom he extended empathy. The signifiers of enslavement, exploitation, bondage, torture and death were very much present in his use of the slave ship image. Furthermore, the redemptive expressions of survival, perseverance and the struggle for humanity were not far from any reading of the slave ship's plan.

Perhaps because Piper had opted to use the plan of the slave ship as a discrete visual, that reeled viewers in, McManus described this visualizing of torture, inhumanity and death as being a 'rather fetching motif.' As with much of the press coverage Black artists would receive from this early 1980s moment onwards, there was to be a troubling use of pronouns in McManus' review. It was clear that such reviewers' use of *you* – as a second person singular or plural – had in mind readers of a similar demographic, educational background, and cultural leaning (with its corresponding lack of awareness of what might now be called diaspora aesthetics). Such pathologies were revealed in her references to Piper's use of the slave ship image. The ignorance of the plan of a slave ship that McManus freely declared was reinforced by her concluding that the image's origins presumably lay with slavers rather than its correct origins with the abolitionist movement. 'A few of Piper's pieces come with a recurrent, rather fetching motif – a tiny diagram presumably from a slaver's manual of the 18th century, showing a slave ship crammed stem to stern exactly like a sardine tin. You only work out what it is when you get right up close and really look into it, then it jolts you nastily.' In the mid-1970s Burning Spear's seminal 'Slavery Days' had located the remembering of the days of slavery and its horrors at the heart of consciousness. In a multiplicity of ways, radical and bold young artists such as Piper and Donald Rodney likewise reflected Burning Spear's insistent and emotive question, 'Do you remember the days of slavery?'[6]

Mention has previously been made of the extent to which there was, within such exhibitions, an abundance of exigent social and political messages, thereby declaring educating and consciousness raising as important functions of Black art. McManus confessed, 'I hadn't realised Britain was still the main overseas backer of apartheid till I looked at – read – one of Keith Piper's furious pictures'[7], further declaring 'I could have done with more of this subtle, jarring imagery.'[8] There was an important and telling nomenclatural aspect to McManus' review. Though all of the artists were born or raised in Britain, in keeping with the times, she described them as being 'West Indian.' The artists were British by birth, upbringing and citizenship, and individually and collectively, theirs was as British an experience as anyone else's, although a Britishness with radically different terms of reference.

Terry Grimley, writing in the *Birmingham Post*, began his review by stating that 'an' done' was 'an untranslatable piece of West Indian patois with a meaning somewhere between "that's that" and "so there".'[9] Echoing the *Guardian* review, he described the work as being 'raw and in some cases downright crude.'[10] Noting that it was unusual for a group of twenty-year-olds to be given a major exhibition slot in a municipal gallery (or noting that it was unusual to see the work of Black artists in a gallery setting), Grimley wrote 'the decision to show it seems to have been justified by the interest it has generated.'[11] Stuart Hall had, with great eloquence, described the racial urgencies of the times and the resulting strategies of these 'Black Art' practitioners as having 'produced a polemical and politicized art: a highly graphic, iconographic art of line and montage, cut-out and collage, image and slogan; the "message" often appearing too pressing, too immediate, too literal, to brook formal delay and, instead, breaking insistently into "writing".'[12] Picking up on this extensive use of image and text in 'Black Art an' done', both McManus and Grimley describe the work in the exhibition as 'posters', thereby seeking to emphasize the importance of the message in these artists' work.

Black Art an' done took place in the early summer of 1981. The major urban disturbances in the St Paul's area of Bristol had taken place a year earlier. About six weeks before the exhibition opened, sustained and extensive rioting had erupted in Brixton. Grimley alluded to these street battles when he wrote that 'these drawings and collages reflect much of the bitterness and frustration of young people of West Indian descent that has found more violent expression in Bristol and Brixton.'[13] Grimley described the work of several of the artists as 'powerfully designed, but . . . its unrelieved stridency depressing. The image of the clenched fist smashing glass is open to various interpretations, not all of them constructive.'[14] Piper's work was singled out for particular praise, although it was also said that, 'His work lacks nothing in anger.'[15] Anger and angry were, respectively, the noun and the adjective often reached for by reviewers of these early exhibitions, although Shakka Dedi was one artist in particular who had sought to call out the use of such descriptives.[16] The word 'anger' was aired further when Wolverhampton's local evening paper, the *Express & Star*, headlined an item about the exhibition *Black Anger in Art* (claiming that it was 'designed to show the sense of alienation, anger and frustration that led to the riots in Bristol and Brixton').[17] Quoting from the press release the article alluded to the group's Black Power/Black Art manifesto: 'The five artists all share the same preoccupation with the culture and civil rights of black people in this country and abroad.'[18] Subsequently, the same paper printed another item about the exhibition. Again, the artists were described as being 'West Indian', and again, the paper made reference to the exhibition's title, stating that 'an' done' was 'Jamaican for finished or the end.'[19] It was said of the exhibit that, 'It shouts angrily about unemployment, racism and South Africa.'[20] These subjects were indeed amongst those concerns exercising the new generation of Black youngsters, doing much to frame their collective sense of self.

A year or so later, with a slightly different grouping, the artists undertook their first exhibition in London, at Covent Garden's Africa Centre, an Africa-oriented educational and cultural facility. The press response for the exhibition, titled *The Pan-Afrikan Connection* reflected something of the extent to which the 'Black

Art' manifesto that was central to it struck a responsive and understanding chord with some of the capital's art reviewers, a number of whom were themselves Black, and who wrote or otherwise worked for Black radio programmes, newspapers and magazines.

Though the noun 'spunk' tended to exist, in a British context, as vulgar slang for semen, Sarah Kent, writing in *Time Out* magazine was perhaps using the word as it more commonly existed in a US context, (informally meaning courage and determination) when she described the exhibition as being 'full of anger and spunk.'[21] By the late 1970s a range of factors pointed to the emergence and ensuing hegemony of a new term to describe Black people – the catch-all term 'ethnic minority'. It might perhaps be more accurate to suggest that Black people – those of African-Caribbean background were *amongst* those to whom the term was liberally applied. Ernest Krausz's *Ethnic Minorities in Britain*, published in 1971, pointed to the ways in which this new term (supplanting as it often did terms such as 'coloured') had the intention and effect of corralling Black Britons and others away from more general notions and identities as British and towards a somewhat lumpen and subaltern category, fixed and constraining in equal measure. Notwithstanding the inherent effect of the term 'ethnic minority' to render – those so designated – as peripheral, Krausz's book was presented, not surprisingly perhaps, in decidedly upbeat terms.

> In all the literature on race relations in Britain, scarcely any attempt has hitherto been made to compare the situation of coloured immigrants with that of other minorities. Yet, such a comparison is essential if a total sociological understanding of Britain's minorities is to be attained.
>
> In this book, Dr Krausz brings together historical, statistical and sociological material on the Jews and the Irish, the Poles and other European groups, as well as the coloured minorities. He surveys their cultural backgrounds and motivations for migration, their demographic structure, their employment and housing situations and native British reactions towards them.
>
> Startling similarities emerge between most minorities, alongside pronounced differences. Prejudice against minorities, for example, seems constant, however widely their socio-economic advancement in Britain may vary.[22]

Though Krausz's study was presented as 'a hope-inspiring contribution towards a full understanding of the workings of human society in what has so far proved one of its most unhappy aspects', it nevertheless contained much that pointed to the problematic pathologies with which immigrants were associated. Alongside what appeared to be benign sentiments about the 'West Indians', were others that were altogether more troubling. It was in this regard that the sentences, 'There are a number of factors which suggest that West Indians have been strongly Anglicized even before their arrival in this country. English, spoken with a particular dialect, is the mother tongue of most of them; they are familiar with English place-names and customs and with *the* English sport – cricket; most of them are Christian; and their educational system follows that of England,'[23] appeared alongside a sentence such as 'Most of them are drawn from the semi-rural colonial proletariat and the background of slavery has left a distinctive mark on their way of life, as for instance in regard to family organization.'[24]

The emergence and ensuing hegemony of 'ethnic minority' as a term to describe Black people was resisted by many young Black people themselves, who preferred instead the term Afro-Caribbean, reflective perhaps of the popularity in the US of the term Afro-American. 'Ethnic minority' brought with it, for Black artists, an imposed designation of their practice under the again, catch-all term, of 'ethnic arts'.[25] It was in part a conspicuous circumventing of the 'ethnic arts' category that singled out young artists such as Johnson, Piper, Rodney, and Smith, as being different types of artists. Reviewing *The Pan-Afrikan Connection*, the art critic of *City Limits*[26] wrote that this exhibition 'Escaped imposing categories of "ethnic art"'[27] and, like other reviewers had done, quoted the line from our press release that read 'Black Art must respond to the realities of local, national, and international Black communities.'[28]

The *City Limits* review printed a photograph of one of the most successful pieces of work in the exhibition, *13 Killed*, a mixed media work about the Deptford fire of the previous year in which thirteen young Black people lost their lives under highly suspicious circumstances.[29] As if to acknowledge the potency and continued relevance of the piece, *City Limits* accompanied the photograph of the artwork with the words, in parentheses, 'A year and a half after the Deptford fire, parents of those killed recently, won leave to appeal against the coroner's open verdict.' This particular reviewer went on to favourably compare the exhibition to another (though much larger) exhibition of students' work. 'Like *New Contemporaries* (ICA) this is an exhibition organized by art students. But instead of hopefully submitting a piece to be accepted into an atmosphere of vague pluralism, these artists have constructed a show with a powerful identity and purpose.'[30] A visitor to the exhibition compared *The Pan-Afrikan Connection* to *New Contemporaries*, though he or she opted for brisker language than Nigel Pollitt, the *City Limits* reviewer: 'STUFF THE YOUNG CONTEMPORARIES AT ICA. THIS IS THE ONE. KEEP AT IT. VERY GOOD.'[31] Such sentiments were an affirmation of several of the artists' opinions that the typical art student embodied a certain self-indulgence and as a direct consequence, was socially and politically peripheral. Here, in Central London, was an emphatic rebuttal of the established art school ethos, in which real world references to a tragic fire, coroner's verdicts, appeals, and the passage of time could be placed alongside a reproduction of an art work which had terms of reference that contradicted its creation within an art school studio. Concluding his review, Pollitt noted that it was 'exceptional to see an exhibition like this in the London galleries.'[32]

Such art, such an exhibition, was wholly in keeping with the dramatic times. Instead of hearing 'of wars and rumours of wars' as predicted in Matthew 24.6 (King James Version), the people of Britain had heard of riots and rumours of riots.[33] The cataclysmic riots of 1980 and 1981 were a constant reference point for *The Pan-Afrikan Connection's* reviewers and audiences alike. The *Jamaican Weekly Gleaner*[34] carried a review of *The Pan-Afrikan Connection*, titled "'Black Art" Message Praised', which began with references to the exhibition being opened by Darcus Howe, who was at the time, editor of *Race Today* magazine and, along with Linton Kwesi Johnson and others was a member of the Race Today Collective. In recalling Howe's comments, the *Gleaner* noted, 'However, the exhibition was not only praised for its creativity, but for its message – a message which Mr Howe protested, black people have been saying everywhere.'[35] Like other reviewers had done, the *Gleaner* article quoted the group's trademark assertion. 'They believe that Black Art (which is what they call their work) must respond to the realities of the local, national and international Black communities.'[36] This was the first such exhibition to include the work of Black women artists, one of whom was Claudette Johnson. Her reported quote within the *Gleaner* article was 'I have tried to displace the stereotype of black women. The paintings attempt to express the myriad aspects of oppression, racism and sexism that have shaped black women. My work deals with specific events but without responses [such as]; anger, frustration, fear and depression.'[37] Thus, within Johnson's quote could be identified the development referred to by Stuart Hall – 'a second set of impulses, less overtly political, though no less "engaged" with wider issues: concerned with exploring the experience of, and resistance to, racism, but in a more subjective idiom.'[38] Perhaps employing the journalistic strategy of ending such a feature on an optimistic, upbeat and celebratory note, this article ended with a quote from Keith Piper, 'At the end of the day, Keith Piper . . . summed up the future of black artists in Britain. He said "Black Art has a future as long as black people have".'[39]

At the time of *The Pan-Afrikan Connection* there existed a Black cultural magazine called *Frontline*. The magazine, which cast itself as an independent and radical magazine, with Pan-Africanist sensibilities, printed a review of the exhibition that developed some of the themes touched on by the *Gleaner* article. Conspicuously eschewing use of the word anger, the review, written by Yvonne Neverson successfully drew out three thrusts that lay behind the creation of the work, and the framing of the exhibition. Neverson began her article, 'The Africa Centre has recently presented an exhibition of contemporary art by five young black artists. Paintings, silk-screen prints, sculpture, drawings and photographs combined to make visually powerful statements about black people's historical and contemporary experiences in America, Afrika and Britain.'[40] Neverson was the first writer to note the title of the exhibition and the thinking that lay behind it – the aspiration to connect with Pan-Afrikan peoples, noting 'The title . . . was a conscious choice made to recognise three things:

the historical dispersion of black people throughout history

the racial injustices experienced by black people throughout the world

[the need] to create and develop black culture.'[41]

During the late 1970s, early 1980s and beyond, the perceived and accepted progressive thinking amongst *conscious* Black people was that culture was a near-tactile entity that had to be reclaimed, nurtured and sustained. Culture was not considered to be something that Black people had, irrespective of where and who they were. Nor was it accepted that 'culture' could, or did, rightly and reasonably consist of innumerable elements and influences, some of them discernibly 'African', 'Caribbean', or 'Black', but many of them, less so or by no means so. The ways in which migration and life in 'the West' impacted upon Black people's 'culture' were denied, viewed as suspect, or regarded as undermining Black people's true African selves. Contemporary reggae music resonated with references to the righteousness of a distinct *Afrocentric* existence, both culturally and mentally. Those who were sufficiently 'conscious' should 'know themselves' and orient themselves towards the motherland of Africa and the existence of African diasporic peoples across the globe, hence the perceived need 'to create and develop black culture.'[42] This, at a time when reggae singer Ijahman Levi implored, 'Culture-less Israel, please know yourself,'[43] and reggae group Black Uhuru declared, 'my culture is growing stronger and I hope I never surrender.'[44]

The *City Limits*' reviewer had positively contrasted the proactive stance of the art students with the somewhat passive undertaking of submitting work for hoped-for consideration – 'Like *New Contemporaries* (ICA) this is an exhibition organised by art students. But instead of hopefully submitting a piece to be accepted into an atmosphere of vague pluralism, these artists have constructed a show with a powerful identity and purpose.'[45] Neverson too drew specific attention to this strategy, but located it within the context of that which the art students, for the most part, claimed to be rejecting. 'All five artists are at art colleges and have consciously rejected the European ideological model of "art for art's sake" favoured by art institutions. They have chosen to utilize their learned methods, techniques and skills to express their political commitment to the black struggle.'[46] Within the work on show, Neverson alluded to the elements that influenced the formative identity of 1970s young Black Britain. Consciousness was the watchword, and Neverson looked on approvingly: 'Institutions are attacked (red/yellow/green colours streaming down the face of a smiling Queen); heroes praised (portraits of Martin Luther King and Bob Marley); victims honoured (portraits of the 13 teenagers killed in a fire in Deptford).'[47]

Neverson then went on to reference the multiple historical strands in which the work could be located. She saw *The Pan-Afrikan Connection* as representing a continuum of 'voices exposing the black experience' – voices that were first raised by those she referred to as having been exiled from the Caribbean.

> This artistic/political consciousness has its immediate roots in the black political movements in the USA, Caribbean, Afrika and Britain throughout the sixties and seventies. Such growing awareness recognised, acknowledged and articulated the historical legacies of slavery, colonialism, racism and oppression – the sum total of the presence, experience and perspective of black people throughout the world.
>
> In Britain, the voices exposing the black experience were initially those of exiles from the Caribbean.[48]

Perhaps referring to the wider presence of Caribbean migrants, or perhaps referring to the work of the Caribbean Artists Movement, a pioneering association of Caribbean-born poets, writers, artists and intellectuals formed in London in the mid-1960s,[49] Neverson continued,

> The source of their creative inspiration was the Caribbean as they remembered it. This was the colourful background to their sense of isolation and displacement experienced in Britain. Concurrent with this was the development of radical politics influenced by similar movements in the USA. Liberation struggles in Afrika highlighted the extent of militancy to which black people committed themselves in order to achieve freedom.'[50]

Neverson was perhaps the only reviewer to comment, with noted empathy on the issue of identity as it related to these artists. Whilst reviewers were generally wont to describe these artists as 'West Indian', Neverson looked deeper and noted the 'Britishness' of these artists – a 'Britishness' that set them apart from an older generation of Caribbean-born painters. 'These young artists are not exiles. They were born here and draw their inspiration not from the sun and warmth of the Caribbean, but from the grey, cold stillness of this political, economic and social climate.'[51]

Although *City Limits* had printed a photograph of one of the works in the exhibition, Neverson was the first reviewer to talk to any degree about the work itself. Her written description of one of the pieces in *The Pan-Afrikan Connection*, *Black British*, served as a very adequate summation of the actual work itself.

> 'BLACK BRITISH' shows a black arm extended in a handshake with a Union Jack arm. At the point of their contact, Rasta colours are placed. At the same point of intersection, a white, jagged diagonal line moves along the black arm, slicing the small red star on the wrist. The white diagonal meets a black jagged edge which cuts vertically down the black arm. Above and below this, is the question Black British?[52]

Like Pollitt, the *City Limits*' reviewer, Neverson also singled out the work of the moment, Piper's *13 Killed* piece. The suspicious death of thirteen young Black people, less than a year and a half earlier, was like an open wound, a running sore on the body of Black Britain, and was very much uppermost in the consciousness of many people. Describing *13 Killed* as 'Also political but using another set of imagery', she wrote that this work 'attacks the state by paying homage to the victims of the Deptford fire'. On a horizontal plane of scorched wallpaper are thirteen postcards with photographs of each child. Next to each portrait is the demand:

> Send this one back to the People
> Brother Owen survived 15 years with us
> 15 years in Babylon
> During his 16th year Babylon
> Snuffed him out
> Send this one back to the People
> and let them demand an answer![53]

Neverson's concluding sentiments encapsulated the dominant strands that comprised Black British cultural identity of the period. 'The artists see their role as visual underliners of the experience of black people. By using symbols, events, trends, music and politics which are relevant and significant to black people, their work already has a strong basis from which it can grow and strengthen as they continue.'[54]

Rasheed Araeen, who had already written about the work of Black artists,[55] visited *The Pan-Afrikan Connection* during its showing. Impressed with what he saw, he proceeded to write a major article that drew heavily on the exhibition. His text 'Paint it Black' appeared in *City Limits*.[56] It was a heady, potent piece of writing in which Araeen remonstrated against what he saw as the racist conditions that made the work of *The Pan-Afrikan Connection* artists necessary and almost inevitable. He also called on the art world and the people of Britain to take a serious, considered and respectful look at what these five (and other) Black artists had to say. Pointing to the mood of the times and the urgency with which these artists and others were pursuant of explicitly socially coded cultural expression, 'Paint it Black' was introduced as follows: 'Politics and art, like politics and sport, is an unpopular mix in this country. The implication is that artists have their minds on higher things than jobs, housing, self-respect. Black artists in Britain think it's time for a change . . .'[57]

Like Neverson's, Araeen's article was written from an informed and empathetic position. Araeen's piece was largely unedited and faithful to the original text, which a couple of years later appeared as 'ART FOR UHURU: Some reflections on the recent emergence of black consciousness in art' in Araeen's book *Making*

Myself Visible. The comments book for *The Pan-Afrikan Connection* had emerged as an important vehicle through which visitors could voice their opinions. Mention was made, earlier in this text of one visitor's declared preference for the exhibition over and above *New Contemporaries*, on show at the ICA, just a relatively short walk away from the Africa Centre. Araeen began his piece with quotes from the 'unusually animated' visitors' book.[58] He was keen to stress the art school context within which most of the artists worked, though whilst Neverson judged that the exhibition reflected a rejection of art for art's sake, Araeen perceived a particular tension. 'These artists are still in art school. How can they achieve the sense of 'some bodiness' in an educational context dominated by European artists? The stamp is there. The *visual* quality is no different from what one would see in diploma shows. But there is a difference that separates them significantly from the rest.'[59] He subsequently continued, 'Behind what may appear to be art school exercises, mixed with political slogans, there is evidence of a subtlety with which it attempts to turn the whole prevailing notion of art upside down.'[60]

Whilst identifying a number of aspects of the exhibition's Black Art manifesto, Araeen also attempted to simultaneously locate the artists' relationship with both the art world and the wider society. Paraphrasing the influential art critic, John Berger, Araeen wrote,

> John Berger once wrote about the difficulty of being a good artist in a post-war period, when the humanist values of Europe lay shattered in the rubble of its ruined cities. But the devastation did not stop. It continued somewhere else. And the difficulty of being a *good* artist is still there, and more so if you are a black person (i.e. Afro/Asian) living in a white society such as Britain. You not only encounter what goes on every day in a racist society, but your role as an artist is also proscribed and limited.[61]

In the early 1980s, the private gallery sector bore little resemblance to its subsequent manifestation. From the late 1980s onwards, Cork Street was no longer the only part of London synonymous with the presence of private galleries. Such business initiatives were established in no end of 'transitioning' districts at all points of the compass beyond the immediate centre of London. When Araeen penned his 'Paint it Black' text, the epicentre of London's private gallery sector was located in Bond Street/Cork Street, and Araeen saw no prospect of these artists making it onto the rosters of the streets' august galleries. 'These artists know very well that they will never be accepted as blue-eyed boys of the Bond Street gallery circuit.'[62] Araeen argued that the validity of the work lay in the view that it reflected the hostilities of the wider society. 'Can we really forget what we encounter in our daily lives, and then try to make art that has no relation to our own experience? How can we be insensitive to a social environment such as Dominic Dawes points out?'[63]

In this text, Araeen did much to demonstrate and create the tangible and respect-demanding notion of a 'Black' art history, or an art history that rightly included Black artists. He believed that the studying of both the historical and the contemporary practice of Black artists should rank and did rank alongside any other aspect of art history. One of the most important aspects of 'Paint It Black' was the way in which Araeen disparaged conventional, dominant, though in many respects wholly spurious academic notions within the discipline of art history, of distance, objectivity and impartiality. He did this by placing himself, his affinities and his own agenda at the centre of his text. Mention was made, earlier in this text, of a troubling use by reviewers of pronouns such as 'we'. Araeen however, had delivered a text that vigorously challenged such use, and his use of this particular pronoun was markedly different: 'Can we really forget what we encounter in our daily lives?' and 'What we see in Britain now is the increasing development of a neo-colonial situation.'[64]

But Araeen's was a fluid use of 'we' – that sometimes referred to dominant patterns of thought, and at other times to reflect a body of people whose awareness existed as a consequence of their subaltern status. His 'Paint It Black' article continued, 'we are still trapped in the myth of the artist who transcends all hostile social conditions to produce masterpieces, without the sense of belonging to a continuity of history or without a history being sympathetic to one's role as a producer of ideas.'[65] In summing up his article, Araeen wrote,

> The seriousness with which these artists take their role deserves our utmost admiration. There is an acute sense of purpose generally lacking in the art world. It is significant that they are not worried about individual styles – although each one shows a distinct personality in the work. They use all kinds of material . . . in a genuine spirit of experimentation, exploration and reflection. The present result may be crude and rough, and even hybrid, but that is not important at the moment. What is really significant is the presence of tremendous energy, the sense of full commitment and definite direction which, it is hoped, will develop into a more significant visual articulation.'[66]

Among Araeen's concluding sentiments were, 'The work may be loud and noisy. But then, it is partly deliberate: the attempt is to express anger and frustration.

The work of these young black artists represents not only an authentic black voice, but it is a voice of humanity that refuses to be brutalized and insensitized.' Furthermore, in his opinion, 'No masterpieces are being offered here, since conditions to make masterpieces do not exist. What is being expressed is more important and urgent. It is a critical consciousness, if not conscience, of our time. And we ought to pay serious attention to it.'[67]

The depth of the analysis in these articles indicated the extent to which these artists were considered to be developing a new way of making art that took as its starting point the realities of Black identity within a British context. Although Neverson played up the Pan-Africanist nature of much of the work, whilst Araeen played it down, there was no doubting the degree to which the exhibition's reviewers heralded the arrival of a new type of Black artist for a new moment.

'Criticize: Press Responses to *Black Art an' done* and *The Pan-Afrikan Connection Exhibitions*' is a new, previously unpublished text. Much of the research for it was undertaken for my PhD, *Black Visual Arts Activity in England 1981–1986: Press and Public Responses* (Goldsmiths College, University of London, 1998).

Notes

1 Una Howe, review of an exhibition of Errol Lloyd's paintings held at the Jamaican High Commission, 19 May–9 June 1978, *Race Today* July/August 1978 p.119.

2 Irene McManus, 'Black Art an' Done' (sic). The *Guardian* 17 June 1981 p.10.

3 McManus, 'Black Art an' Done', p.10.

4 McManus, 'Black Art an' Done', p.10.

5 McManus, 'Black Art an' Done', p.10.

6 'Slavery Days', Burning Spear, from the album *Marcus Garvey*, Island Records, 1976.

7 McManus, 'Black Art an' Done', p.10.

8 McManus, 'Black Art an' Done', p.10.

9 Terry Grimley, 'Black Art', Birmingham 1981: 4.

10 Grimley, 'Black Art', p.4.

11 Grimley, 'Black Art', p.4.

12 Stuart Hall, 'Black Diaspora Artists in Britain: Three "Moments" in Post-war History', *History Workshop Journal* Issue 61, Spring 2006: 17.

13 Grimley, 'Black Art', p.4.

14 Grimley, 'Black Art', p.4.

15 Grimley, 'Black Art', p.4.

16 With the word 'angry' being by far the most frequently used descriptive to appear in mainstream press articles about exhibitions such as *Black Art an' done*, pretty much the only comment that took issue with this came from the artist, poet and cultural activist Shakka Dedi. Writing in 1984, the then Director of The Black-Art Gallery observed that, 'in many cases the realities being dealt with by artists . . . [are] often misinterpreted by white/European viewers who see the work as being "angry" and "aggressive", when in reality there is little or no anger expressed – but simply the visually stunning and dynamic presentation of hard, cold facts.' Shakka Dedi, 'Black Art in Britain Today', *Arts Review* 9 November 1984: 557.

17 Anon, 'Black anger in art', *Express & Star*, Wolverhampton, 5 June 1981: 14.

18 Anon, 'Black anger in art', p.14.

19 Anon, 'Black anger in art', p.14.

20 Anon, 'Black anger in art', p.14.

21 Sarah Kent, 'Students Shows' (about *The Pan-Afrikan Connection,* Eddie Chambers, Dominic Dawes, Claudette Johnson, Wenda Leslie and Keith Piper. Africa Centre 4 May–4 June 1982) *Time Out,* 21–27 May 1982 p.81.

22 Ernest Krausz, *Ethnic Minorities in Britain*, MacGibbon & Kee, London, 1971, flyleaf.

23 Krausz, *Ethnic Minorities in Britain*, p.15.

24 Krausz, *Ethnic Minorities in Britain*, p.15.

25 For an examination of the rise of the term 'ethnic arts' as a constraining but seemingly inescapable term to describe the various practices of *non-white* artists, see Richard Hylton, *The Nature of the Beast: Cultural Diversity and the Visual Arts Sector – A Study of Policies, Initiatives and Attitudes 1976–2006*, published by the Institute of Contemporary Interdisciplinary Arts, University of Bath, 2007.

26 Founded in 1981, *City Limits* magazine was a London arts listing magazine that during its existence rivalled *Time Out* magazine. Presenting itself as a more politically progressive magazine than its rival, *City Limits* ceased publication in 1993. During its existence, it proved itself to be a dependable listings source for Black artists' exhibitions in the capital.

27 Nigel Pollitt, 'Exhibitions', *City Limits*, 28 May–3 June 1982. pp. 62–63.

28 Pollitt, 'Exhibitions', pp.62–63.

29 For a discussion of the tragedy, see *The New Cross Massacre Story: Interviews with John La Rose*, published by the Alliance of the Black Parents Movement, Black Youth Movement and the Race Today Collective, 1984; 'The Deptford Fire, Accident or Arson?', *Unsolved* 42 (1984): 829–48.

30 Pollitt, 'Exhibitions', pp.62–63.

31 Comments book, *The Pan-Afrikan Connection,* Eddie Chambers, Dominic Dawes, Claudette Johnson, Wenda Leslie and Keith Piper. Africa Centre, 4 May–4 June 1982.

32 Pollitt, 'Exhibitions', pp.62–63.

33 Described as filmic commentary on 'Radical resistance in the postwar British Caribbean community, from the 1948 Nationality Act to the 1958 Brixton riots' *Riots and Rumours of Riots* (1981 34 mins) was a film made by director Imruh Caesar. The British Film Institute charaterizes the film as 'Inspired by the 1981 "race riots", director Caesar Imruh (sic) explores the origins of radical Black consciousness in 1980s Britain by charting the experience of the preceding generation. Part essayistic meditation and part oral history, the film layers audio-visual archive material with recorded testimony. The resulting timeline begins with post-WWII migration following Caribbean contributions to the war effort and ends with reflections on the 1958 Brixton riots sparked by racism.' https://player.bfi.org.uk/rentals/film/watch-riots-and-rumours-of-riots-1981-online accessed 20 May 2018.

34 Anon, *Jamaican Weekly Gleaner* '"Black Art" message praised', (reporting on *The Pan-Afrikan Connection,* Eddie Chambers, Dominic Dawes, Claudette Johnson, Wenda Leslie and Keith Piper. Africa Centre, 4 May–4 June 1982) June 2 1982, p.5.

35 Anon, *Jamaican Weekly Gleaner* '"Black Art" message praised', p.5.

36 Anon, *Jamaican Weekly Gleaner* '"Black Art" message praised', p.5.

37 Anon, *Jamaican Weekly Gleaner* '"Black Art" message praised', p.5.

38 Hall, 'Black Diaspora Artists in Britain: Three "Moments" in Post-war History', pp.17–18.

39 Anon, *Jamaican Weekly Gleaner* '"Black Art" message praised', p.5.

40 Yvonne Neverson, 'Review of *The Pan-Afrikan Connection*' exhibition at The Africa Centre, 1982. *Frontline* magazine August–October 1982 p.122.

41 Neverson, 'Review of *The Pan-Afrikan Connection*', p.122.

42 Neverson, 'Review of *The Pan-Afrikan Connection*', p.122.

43 'Africa', from album *Africa*, Ijahman Levi, Jahmani label, 1985.

44 Black Uhuru, 'Leaving to Zion', from the album *Showcase*, Taxi label, 1979.

45 Pollitt, 'Exhibitions', pp.62–63.

46 Neverson, 'Review of *The Pan-Afrikan Connection*', p.122.

47 Neverson, 'Review of *The Pan-Afrikan Connection*', p.122.

48 Neverson, 'Review of *The Pan-Afrikan Connection*', p.122.

49 For a study of the Caribbean Artists Movement, see Anne Walmsley, *The Caribbean Artists Movement 1966–1972: A Literary & Cultural History*, London: New Beacon Books, 1992.

50 Neverson, 'Review of *The Pan-Afrikan Connection*', p.122.

51 Neverson, 'Review of *The Pan-Afrikan Connection*', p.122.

52 Neverson, 'Review of *The Pan-Afrikan Connection*', p.122.

53 Neverson, 'Review of *The Pan-Afrikan Connection*', p.122.

54 Neverson, 'Review of *The Pan-Afrikan Connection*', p.122.

55 With Mahmood Jamal, Araeen had edited and produced three copies of *Black Phoenix: a Journal of Contemporary Art & Culture in the Third World,* No. 1, Winter 1978; No. 2, Summer 1978; No. 3, Spring 1979. The forerunner of *Third Text*, each issue of *Black Phoenix* contained articles on the work of Black artists, most notably perhaps, Araeen's review of 'Afro-Caribbean Art', *Black Phoenix* No. 2 Summer 1978: 30–31.

56 Rasheed Araeen, 'Paint it Black', *City Limits* No. 45 August 13–19 1982.

57 Araeen, 'Paint it Black', pp. 46–47.

58 Araeen, 'Paint it Black', pp. 46–47.

59 Araeen, 'Paint it Black', pp. 46–47.

60 Araeen, 'Paint it Black', pp. 46–47.

61 Araeen, 'Paint it Black', pp. 46–47.

62 Araeen, 'Paint it Black', pp. 46–47.

63 Araeen, 'Paint it Black', pp. 46–47. In the unpaginated catalogue for *Black Art an' done*, Dominic Dawes had written 'In our towns and cities, on your subway walls etc. and just as much in our minds, there is racial abuse: WOGS GO HOME. N.F. RULES. BLACK BASTARDS. ETC. but who made us the so-called "bastards"?'

64 Araeen, 'Paint it Black', pp. 46–47.

65 Araeen, 'Paint it Black', pp. 46–47.

66 Araeen, 'Paint it Black', pp. 46–47.

67 Araeen, 'Paint it Black', pp. 46–47.

SECTION SIX

Outernational

Chapter 41
Section Six Introduction

The locution 'outernational' was one of a number of expressions that emerged from the fascinating Jamaican-esque, oftentimes music-associated, tendency to not only take familiar words and turn these words on their heads, or turn them inside out, but to simultaneously inflect the new versions of these words with enhanced meanings. The gravitation of the *outernational* is so much more expressive than the international, which by comparison seems and sounds lame and inward-looking. No-one can ever identify the authors of such linguistics, though the rapid ways in which they, sometimes momentarily, become a common lingua franca is a testament to the originality and novelty of such new words. Collectively, these words contribute to a dynamic lexicon of language that enhances the meanings and understandings of no end of words. *Understand* became *overstand*, or *ovastan'*. After all, to overstand something is surely to gain a sort of mastery over the thing in question. Oppression becomes downpression, the easily imagined downward trajectory inherent in the new word effortlessly emphasizing the subaltern space occupied by those who were downpressed. Similarly, when affection exists between two people, they ought really to be said to appreci-love (rather than appreci-hate) each other. Such were the playful, yet nuanced and dynamic ways in which words within the dominant language were flipped, turned on their heads, or turned inside out. The *outernational*, with its orientation towards the heavens or spaces far across the sea, is so much more evocative and dare I say, correct, than *international*. The section's two texts reflect on visual art undertakings in the outernational arena – the Āsìkò pop-up art school project developed by the Lagos-based curator Bisi Silva (who sadly passed away in 2019), and a text commenting on the impact and reach of art from Jamaica, when travelling to and emerging in a space such as the Royal West of England Academy, which in 2016 hosted *Jamaican Pulse: Art and Politics from Jamaica and the Diaspora*.

Chapter 42
Àsìkò Goes Outernational

We have grown accustomed to the centre of gravity of African art, in many of its manifestations, being located outside, or beyond, the continent itself. The shifting of the centre of gravity arguably began with the plundering of African art, in previous centuries, in incidents of pillage such as Britain's Punitive Expedition towards the end of the 19th century, that saw the hugely important West African centre of art and culture, Benin, plundered and prized objects (which became known as the 'Benin bronzes') summarily auctioned, dispersed and making their way into European museums and private collections. Such unvarnished theft and reappropriation has ensured that by as early as the mid-20th century, historical, traditional or religious African art became something associated with western academics, collections and auction houses, perhaps even more so than its association with the continent itself.

Fast forward a number of decades and the emergence of contemporary African art has a centre of gravity not unlike that of its older antecedents. Rather than looking at cities across the continent as settled destinations for, and homes of, contemporary African art, pretty much all of the world's most powerful and financially resourced curators, collectors, museum directors and gallerists are more minded to see African cities as points from which art can be collected and placed in seemingly more deserving or better homes in Europe or the US. Consequently, the real business of buying, selling, exhibiting (and the related practices of teaching African art) frequently takes place thousands of miles away from the continent itself. These are of course fiendishly complicated matters, not least because so many artists from different countries and cities across Africa are now located in cities across Europe and North America. Successful contemporary African artists are now as likely – or, more likely – to live and work in cities such as London, Brussels, Paris or New York, rather than cities such as Kinshasa, Lagos, Nairobi or Dakar. Furthermore, most of the best spaces in which contemporary African artists get to show are located beyond, rather than within, the continent of Africa itself. We can now perhaps speak of contemporary African art as having a global presence, but this should not diminish our understanding of the ways in which Africa itself is arguably disadvantaged and almost marginalized in these narratives.

Beginning perhaps with figures such as Léopold Sédar Senghor and Alioune Diop, visionary voices have sought to create spaces, forums and environments in which African arts had platforms every bit as important as any other, right there on the continent itself. From spectacular events such as the first World Festival of Negro Arts (*1er Festival Mondial des Arts Nègres,* aka FESMAN) and Nigeria's Festac'77, through to more recent undertakings such as the 1990s biennales in Johannesburg and the ongoing Dak'Art', in Dakar, Senegal and the Cairo Biennale, concerted attempts have been, and are being, made to give Africa's audiences as much chance of seeing art by Africa's artists, as say, audiences in Paris, New York or London.

Enter the astonishing work of the Àsìkò programme of international workshops, which sees artists, writers and curators from countries across the continent in dialogue with each other, and in dialogue with a number of their counterparts working in the US and several countries across Europe. By bringing these groups of practitioners and professionals into an intense period of dialogue, debate and exchange with each other, and, equally as importantly, locating the venues for such engagement and interaction within African cities such as Accra and Dakar, Bisi Silva and her colleagues are able to undertake and achieve a number of

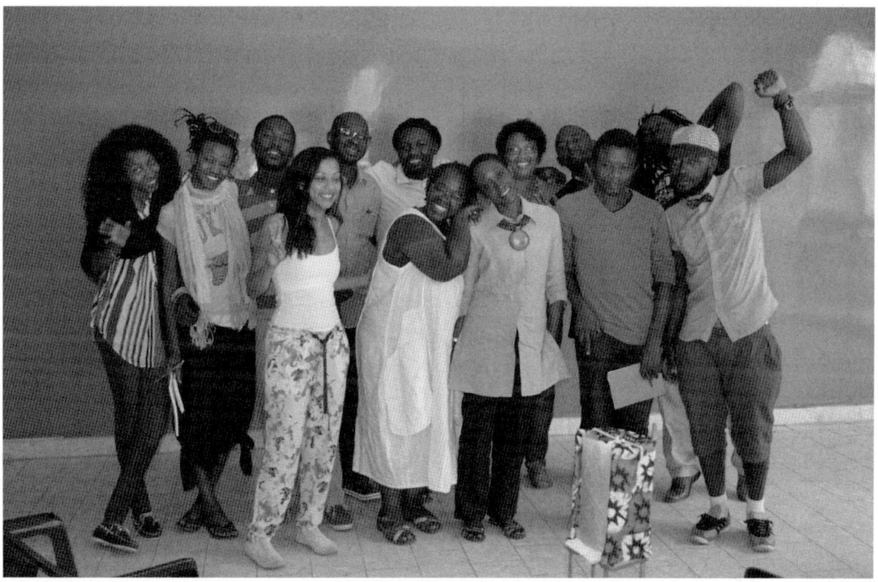

Figure 42.1 Bisi Silva (centre) with Àsìkò participants, Piscine Olympique Nationale, Dakar, Senegal, 2014. Left to right: Taiye Idahorm, Kitso Lynn Lelliott, Kwasi Ohene-Ayeh, Dana Whabira, Lassana Igo Diarra, Cliford Zulu, Bisi Silva, N'Goné Fall, Rosana Paulino, Serubiri Moses, Eza Komla, Rafiy Smith Okefolahan, and Tito Valery. Photo: © Erin Rice.

important and wonderful things. In the first instance, the Àsìkò workshops demonstrate the extent to which inter, or intra continental African travel is, or quite rightly ought to be, as important for the continent's artists as travel to destinations outside of the continent. What differences or commonalities can individual practitioners tease out when they are exposed to each other's practices? And for those seeking to contribute to Àsìkò by joining the workshops from cities in Europe or the US, what professional experiences can be shared in ways that are mutually beneficial and encouraging?

Though contemporary African artists have grown accustomed to making cogent, dynamic and fascinating contributions to curatorial landscapes across the world, such platforms are seldom without their complications. What the Àsìkò workshops do is create intellectually and creatively stimulating spaces which seek to be free from the range of problematic pathologies that can so easily come to the fore when an African artist – almost irrespective of the nature of his or her work – is exhibited in Europe or the US or Japan, for example. Not only do the workshops create environments in which contributors can speak freely and candidly, they can do so knowing that they have created for themselves nurturing and mutually respectful environments.

There is, critically importantly, a sense of intellectual rigour and questioning that pervades and characterizes the Àsìkò workshops. Institutions of learning across the continent should of course be homes to such critical thinking, but far too often, those living and working within Africa find themselves needing to get such stimulation from sources outside of the continent. This of course points to the earlier references about the ways in which centres of learning and debate about contemporary African art are, as much as the art itself, located in Europe and the US. Àsìkò workshops represent a fabulous and much-needed opportunity for a consistently high level of questioning, debate, and critical thinking about art and visual culture to take place in centres such as Lagos, Accra, and Dakar.

With funding for the arts in many African countries being next to none existent, and with a frequently small and sometimes marginalised infrastructure of galleries, there is a chronic and ever-present need for spaces in which the continent's artists can share ideas and can expose their work to each other in an environment of mutual respect and vigorous enquiry. Àsìkò provides such platforms, and it is of critical importance that the workshops grow from strength to strength, becoming an ever more familiar and much-needed presence on the continent.

'Àsìkò Goes Outernational' was previously published in *Àsìkò: On the Future of Artistic and Curatorial Pedagogies in Africa*, Centre for Contemporary Art, Lagos, 2017.

Chapter 43
Jamaican Art Goes Outernational

Together with broader exhibitions of Caribbean art, exhibitions of art from Jamaica such as *Jamaican Pulse: Art and Politics from Jamaica and the Diaspora* are a relative rarity in England, taking place, on average, since the mid-1990s, much less than once a decade.

The first exhibition of Jamaican art to be shown in this country took place within a year of the Caribbean island's independence, granted in 1962. Titled *Face of Jamaica*, the exhibition toured Germany and the UK in 1963 and 1964. Another significant contribution to the showing of work from the Caribbean in this country, was the opening, in the early 1960s, of the Commonwealth Institute in London. Over the course of the next decades, the Commonwealth Institute became an important venue for the showing of work by artists from the wider Caribbean, and Jamaica itself. One such important early exhibition was *Caribbean Artists in England.*[1] The exhibiting artists included a number of practitioners from Jamaica: Karl Craig, Errol Lloyd, Ronald Moody, Vernon Tong, and Ricardo Wilkins (later known as Kofi Kayiga). Exhibitions such as this continued in a variety of iterations for a number of years, and for the most part they were organized by the artists themselves. The next major undertakings were shows organized in conjunction with the Caribbean Focus festival of 1986, the centrepiece of which was *Caribbean Art Now*, which billed itself as 'Europe's first exhibition of contemporary Caribbean art'.[2]

Notable exhibitions since have included Petrine Archer Straw's *New World Imagery: Contemporary Jamaica Art* in 1995 and *Back to Black: Art, Cinema and the Racial Imaginary* (2005), an exhibition for which she was one of the curatorial team, held at Whitechapel Art Gallery, London, as part of the Africa 05 festival. Although exhibitions such as *New World Imagery: Contemporary Jamaica Art* and *Back to Black* tended to operate in an uncomfortable space between an art world ill at ease dealing with Black artists, particularly Black British ones, and an art world anxious and determined to declare a certain internationalism, they were, even so, exhibitions that gave gallery audiences a sense of the vibrancy and originality of Jamaican art. There have of course been an equivalent number of these exhibitions held in the US and Canada, one of the first of which was *Jamaican Art Since the Thirties*, held at Spelman College, Atlanta University Center, in 1969. In this respect, a particularly fascinating undertaking was Veerle Poupeye's *Contemporary Jamaican Art, Circa 1962 / Circa 2012*, held at the Art Gallery of Mississauga, Ontario, in 2012. This overview of Jamaican art was very much part of international celebrations for the country's fifty years of independence.

Whilst the above initiatives decisively point to the ways in which the broader African diaspora mutated to create its compelling Caribbean dimension, *Jamaican Pulse: Art and Politics from Jamaica and the Diaspora* differs from the above exhibitions in one critical and fascinating respect. That is, the way in which it offers us a reliable glimpse into the routes taken in the creation of the Jamaican diaspora itself. In this sense, with its inclusion of artists from English cities such as Birmingham and London, and US cities such as Lexington, Kentucky and Newark, New Jersey, and with both of the exhibition's curators having longstanding links to Bristol, *Jamaican Pulse* can be easily understood in terms of the 'rhizomatic'[3], Jamaica itself being very much like the stem of a plant that sends out roots and shoots as it spreads.

A number of artists in *Jamaican Pulse* from the Jamaican diaspora engage with Jamaica in particularly fascinating ways, while others have a relationship

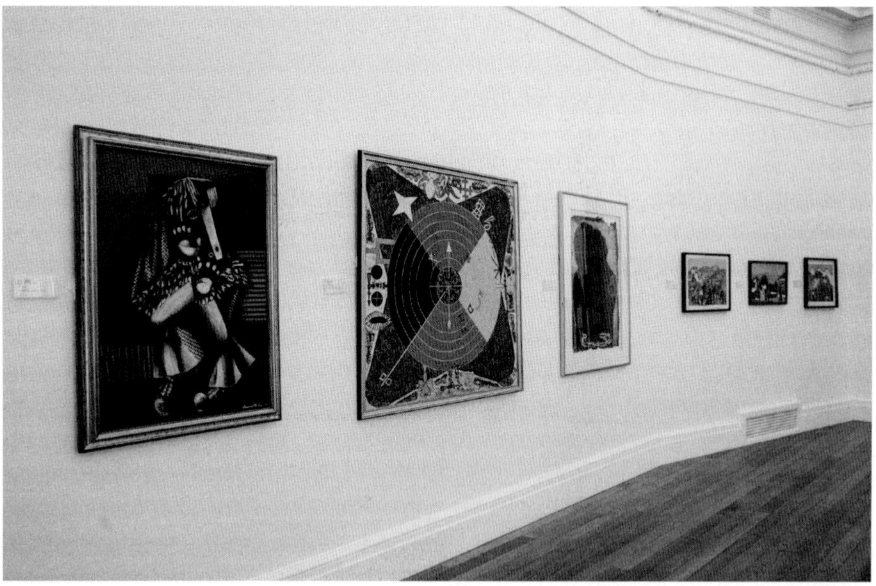

Figure 43.1 Installation view, *Jamaican Pulse: Art and Politics from Jamaica and the Diaspora*, Royal West of England Academy, Bristol, 25 June – 11 September 2016 © Royal West of England Academy, Bristol.

with the country primarily through being the children of Jamaican immigrants. The assorted contributions of Hurvin Anderson, Barka, Graeme Mortimer Evelyn, Gerard Hanson, NT and Barbara Walker make the British dimensions of the exhibition particularly engaging. Though figurative elements tend to characterise the work that has been selected from these artists, beyond that, their work is extraordinarily broad in its enquiries and medium, which has long since been a characteristic of Jamaican art.

With Jamaica being just about one hour's flying time from Miami, many US-based artists of the Jamaican diaspora are well able to maintain a presence and a visibility on the island. The same presence and visibility cannot, in any genuine sense, be said of British artists of Jamaican heritage, who, in the Jamaican art scene, are pretty much conspicuous by their absence. We can at least though, within *Jamaican Pulse: Art and Politics from Jamaica and the Diaspora,* see artists from Jamaica exhibited alongside artists of Jamaican descent.

'Jamaican Art Goes Outernational' was first published as a text for the exhibition catalogue *Jamaican Pulse: Art and Politics from Jamaica and the Diaspora,* Royal West of England Academy, Bristol, 25 June–11 September 2016.

Notes

1 Commonwealth Institute Art Gallery, Kensington High Street, London, 22 January–14 February 1971. The exhibition featured some 17 practitioners, showing fabrics, paintings, sculpture and ceramics.

2 Commonwealth Institute Art Gallery, Kensington High Street, London, 17 June–4 August 1986. Jamaican artists were amongst the Caribbean practitioners represented in such exhibitions.

3 Rhizomatic learning is a way of thinking about learning based on ideas described by Gilles Deleuze and Félix Guattari in their 1980 book, *A Thousand Plateaus*. A rhizome, sometimes called a creeping rootstalk, is a stem of a plant that sends out roots and shoots as it spreads.

Index